D0216351

Biological, Psychological, and Environmental Factors in Delinquency and Mental Disorder

Recent Titles in
Bibliographies and Indexes in Sociology

Cubans in the United States: A Bibliography for Research in the Social
and Behavioral Sciences, 1960-1983
Compiled by Lyn MacCorkle

Demography of Racial and Ethnic Minorities in the United States: An
Annotated Bibliography with a Review Essay
By Jamshid A. Momeni

Sociology of Poverty in the United States: An Annotated Bibliography
Compiled by H. Paul Chalfant

Biological, Psychological, and Environmental Factors in Delinquency and Mental Disorder

AN INTERDISCIPLINARY BIBLIOGRAPHY

Compiled by

DEBORAH W. DENNO

and

RUTH M. SCHWARZ NOV 2 1 1987

Foreword by
Marvin E. Wolfgang

Prepared under the auspices of the Center for Studies in Criminology and Criminal Law, University of Pennsylvania

Bibliographies and Indexes in Sociology, Number 4

GP

Greenwood Press
Westport, Connecticut • London. England

Library of Congress Cataloging in Publication Data

Denno, Deborah W.
  Biological, psychological, and environmental factors
in delinquency and mental disorder.

  (Bibliographies and indexes in sociology,
ISSN 0742-6895 ; no. 4)
  "Prepared under the auspices of the Center for Studies
in Criminology and Criminal Law, University of
Pennsylvania."
  Includes index.
  1. Criminal psychology—Bibliography. 2. Deviant
behavior—Bibliography. 3. Mentally handicapped and
crime—Bibliography. 4. Environmental psychology—
Bibliography. 5. Sociobiology—Bibliography.
I. Schwarz, Ruth M. II. University of Pennsylvania.
Center for Studies in Criminology and Law. III. Title.
IV. Series.
Z5703.4.P8D46 1985   [HV6080]   016.3642   85-5620
ISBN 0-313-24939-3 (lib. bdg. : alk. paper)

Copyright © 1985 by the Center for Studies in Criminology and Criminal Law,
University of Pennsylvania

All rights reserved. No portion of this book may be
reproduced, by any process or technique, without the
express written consent of the publisher.

Library of Congress Catalog Card Number: 85-5620
ISBN: 0-313-24939-3
ISSN: 0742-6895

First published in 1985

Greenwood Press
A division of Congressional Information Service, Inc.
88 Post Road West, Westport, Connecticut 06881

Printed in the United States of America

10 9 8 7 6 5 4 3 2 1

CONTENTS

FOREWORD

A comprehensive bibliography on any topic is a valuable asset. A bibliography that is interdisciplinary is an important contribution to each represented discipline and to the elevation of scholars' perspectives. If, in addition, a bibliography has a cross-indexing as intricate and complete as <u>Biological, Psychological, and Environmental Factors in Delinquency and Mental Disorder</u>, it is a landmark publication.

With all of this intricacy, this bibliography has a startling, sterling quality: it is amazingly easy to use. The consumer can range from topic to discipline to source and volume, number and pages with superb speed and clarity. I have been involved in bibliographies and indexing for many years, but I am most appreciative of this bibliography because it is one of the most thorough I have yet witnessed.

I have observed the care and meticulous concern these editors have had for this project over several years. I applaud their work, for I am impressed with the detail and the thoroughness of this enterprise.

I commend this bibliography to all scholars and practitioners who have any interest in these disciplines of biology, psychology, sociology, social psychology, neurology. Here is the most careful selection of the best available evidence, selected by highly informed editors of the literature.

Marvin E. Wolfgang
Philadelphia, Pennsylvania
April 1985

ACKNOWLEDGMENTS

This volume was supported in part by a grant from the Center for the Study of Crime Correlates and Criminal Behavior of the National Institute of Justice (81-IJ-CX-0086-S1). The grant was awarded to the Center for Studies in Criminology and Criminal Law at the Wharton School, the University of Pennsylvania, for the project entitled, "A Longitudinal Study of Biosocial Factors Related to Delinquency and Crime." Points of view in this volume are those of the authors and do not necessarily represent the views of the U.S. Department of Justice.

The authors wish to express their gratitude to Marvin E. Wolfgang, Director of the Center for Studies in Criminology and Criminal Law, for his intellectual inspiration and support that made possible the completion of this volume. Professor Wolfgang's extensive background in interdisciplinary research and criminological indexing greatly enriched our knowledge of worthwhile directions to pursue in the content and organization of this work.

Thanks also to Dr. Helen Erskine, the present grant monitor, and Winifred Reed, the former grant monitor, for their interest in and encouragement of the Biosocial Project.

We are indebted to Steven Aurand, statistical applications analyst at the Center for Studies in Criminology and Criminal Law, for his invaluable suggestions, skills, computer programming, and assistance throughout the course of the work on this volume.

We extend our appreciation to Selma Pastor, librarian at the Center for Studies in Criminology and Criminal Law, for her excellent work on the copyediting and appearance of the manuscript and for her attention to detail.

The efforts of other members of the staff of the Center for Studies in Criminology and Criminal Law merit recognition: the organizational acumen of Erica Ginsburg, the administrative capabilities of Rhoda Piltch, and the typing skills of Esther Lafair all greatly expedited the completion of this project.

Mary R. Sive, acquisitions editor at Greenwood Press, provided apt suggestions on the format and organization of this volume, for which we are thankful.

Finally, we owe a debt of gratitude to the many graduate students, research assistants, and other employees of the Center for Studies in Criminology and Criminal Law who so diligently contributed to this project: Fazal Ahmed, Etannibi Alemika, Soraya Amanullah, Ting-Shih Chia, David Fialkoff, Vera Huang, Mark Keintz, James Lystad, Emmanuel Olowu, Neal Roden, and Kara Rubenstein.

INTRODUCTION

During the past decade, there has been a large increase in the number of interdisciplinary fields and in the number of scholars in established fields whose research needs require that they cross disciplinary boundaries. A recent study of
library records at Virginia Polytechnic Institute, for example, showed extensive
interdisciplinary reading by the ten thousand faculty members and students sur-
veyed. More than half of the physics books and most of the psychology books were
borrowed by faculty members from outside those departments. The study concluded
that "library systems that divide collections among specialized branches . . . may
narrow the vision and research of their users" (Magarrell, 1984).

The bibliography and index presented in this volume were created by the Center for Studies in Criminology and Criminal Law at the University of Pennsylvania
in response to the rapidly growing need for interdisciplinary research materials
dealing with the intersection of the biological and social sciences (see Dietz,
1978; Rappeport, 1975; and Wolfgang, Figlio, and Thornberry, 1975). This volume
is designed specifically for researchers interested in biological, medical, sociological, and psychological factors associated with crime and mental disorder.
Three general subject areas are covered: 1) biological, psychological, and environmental influences on child development, 2) biological, physiological, and
medical factors associated with brain functions and central nervous system disorders, and 3) biological, psychological, and sociological factors related to
mental disorder and crime. Thus, criminologists, corrections administrators,
sociologists, psychologists, psychiatrists, pediatricians, lawyers, and others
should find the materials in this volume useful.

The manuscript has three major sections. The first is a Bibliography with
over two thousand entries selected from a variety of sources. Each entry, identified by a number, is followed by a series of topic codes specifying the primary
subject matter of that entry. The second section (Appendix) presents a hierarchical listing of the subject headings used to classify the contents of the bibliographic entries. Each heading is listed with its assigned topic code. The third
section is the Index, which links subject headings in the Hierarchical Listing to
entries in the Bibliography. The headings, arranged alphabetically, are followed
by a list of numbers identifying those entries in the Bibliography that pertain to
the subject heading.

By referring to the Index, users of this volume can obtain a list of resource
materials relevant to a given subject area. Alternatively, by consulting the Bibliography, users can determine the subject matter of a particular entry.

BIBLIOGRAPHY

The Bibliography contains 2,207 references that were collected in conjunction
with an ongoing research project at the Center for Studies in Criminology and
Criminal Law. This project involves the examination of biological and environmental factors associated with crime and violence in a sample of over nine thousand
subjects. The mothers of these subjects were participants in the Philadelphia
Collaborative Perinatal Project (CPP) at Pennsylvania Hospital between 1959 and
1966. Pennsylvania Hospital was one of twelve medical centers selected by the
National Institute of Neurological Diseases and Stroke for a nationwide study of
medical, biological, psychological, and environmental influences in the first
seven years of childhood. Supplemental school and police records were collected
by the Criminology Center to provide educational achievement and offense information about the subjects throughout their juvenile and young adult years (see
Denno, 1982 for a more detailed description).

Entries in the Bibliography were drawn from a wide range of disciplines. The three major sources were: 1) publications dealing with the CPP data, 2) major social science and medical abstracts, and 3) bibliographies and abstracts obtained from an online literature search carried out by the National Criminal Justice Reference Service (NCJRS) of the National Institute of Justice.

Online literature searches were conducted in four databases: 1) the Medical Literature Analysis and Retrieval System (MEDLARS), 2) Psychological Abstracts, 3) Sociological Abstracts, and 4) the Social Science Citation Index. These searches cover the time period ranging from January 1966 through June 1984. Key references published prior to 1966 are included in the Bibliography because they provide important background information in certain subject areas.

The four databases were also searched manually for the years 1979 to 1981 to test the reliability of the online literature searches. The concordance between the computerized and manual searches was high, suggesting that the online searches were able to identify the vast majority of relevant references.

Two broad topic areas, incorporating relevant subtopics, were searched in MEDLARS:

1) Sociopathy. The subheadings searched included "social behavior disorders" (e.g., minimal brain dysfunction), "antisocial personality," "criminal psychology," "crime," "social problems," and "criminology."

2) Birth Trauma. The subheadings searched included "social behavior disorders," "antisocial personality," "pregnancy complications," "labor complications," "perinatal complications," and "birth defects."

In Psychological Abstracts, Sociological Abstracts, and the Social Science Citation Index, the topics searched included "antisocial personality," "crime," "criminals," "criminology," "physical disorders," and "psychological disorders."

Pertinent references were also selected from the extensive bibliographic materials and online databases compiled by NCJRS. Searches were conducted using the same topic headings and time periods examined in the medical and social science databases.

Bibliographic entries in this volume are arranged alphabetically by author or by document title if no author is mentioned. Each entry is identified by a five-digit number. The topic codes listed after each entry indicate the subject matter of the reference. The subject headings corresponding to each topic code can be found in the Hierarchical Listing.

The following citation is an example of a bibliographic entry:

02400   Andrew, J.M. The classic Wechsler P-V sign and violent crime. Crime and/et Justice, 1978, 6(4), 246-248. Topic codes: BL04D,BL70D,CC371, CC81Y,CE,SF11,SQ11,TB96D.

The entry number is 02400, and the article is assigned eight different topic codes. The first code (BL04D) indicates that the article concerns the relationship between age and crime whereas the second and seventh codes (BL70D and SQ11) specify that sex differences in crime are also examined. The article focuses on the crime categories of "Juvenile Delinquency" (CC371), "Violent Offenders and Violence" (CC81Y), and "Crime Seriousness" (CE). The impact of the environment on crime is also discussed (SF11). The article examines the difference between the Performance and Verbal subtests of the Wechsler Intelligence Scale in relation to criminal behavior (TB96D). Thus, topic codes indicate the specific variables discussed in a reference, the particular kinds of samples or behaviors studied, as well as the tests or specific measures used.

APPENDIX: HIERARCHICAL LISTING

The Appendix (Hierarchical Listing) contains subject headings and subheadings drawn from a broad range of disciplines. These headings are organized under eight major topic areas: 1) "Biological Factors," 2) "Criminology and Criminological Factors," 3) "Diseases, Injuries, and Symptoms," 4) "Behavioral and Mental Disorders," 5) "Named Groups and Study Methods," 6) "Behavior, Behavioral Mechanisms, and Psychological Processes," 7) "Sociological Factors," and 8) "Tests and Measures."

In each of the eight topic areas, subject headings and their corresponding subheadings are arranged at five different indentation levels. An increasing level of indentation represents an increasing level of specificity of a subject area.

Four standard subheadings appear under most of the major headings. These subheadings are: 1) "and Behavioral and Mental Disorders," 2) "Antisocial Personality," 3) "and Crime," and 4) "and Later Outcome." Subheadings usually begin with the word "and" or fall below other subheadings beginning with "and."

Each subject heading in the Hierarchical Listing has a corresponding "topic code" consisting of letters and numbers that specify a particular indentation level. The eight major topic headings constituting the first level are each represented by a single letter: "B" designates "Biological Factors," "C" designates "Criminology and Criminological Factors," etc. Subheadings at the second indentation level are identified by one of the eight major subject heading letters, plus an additional letter. Subheadings at the third level are designated by two letters and a two-digit number. Subheadings at the fourth level are represented by two letters, a two-digit number, and an additional letter. Subheadings at the fifth level are identified by two letters, a two-digit number, and two additional letters. Some of the subheadings under the third major subject category, "Diseases, Injuries, and Symptoms," are arranged as follows:

D	Diseases, Injuries, and Symptoms
DA	Exposure to Toxic Substances
DA04	Alcohol Drinking and Alcoholism
DA04B	and Behavioral and Mental Disorders, Other
DA04BB	Antisocial Personality
DA04D	and Crime
DA15	Drug Abuse
DA15B	and Antisocial Personality
DA15D	and Crime

Thus, the Hierarchical Listing shows the relations among subject headings. The listing can also direct users to research topics in areas they might not otherwise consider.

Subject headings in the Hierarchical Listing were devised after a detailed reading of the majority of the references in the Bibliography, and after an examination of the major indexes, manuals, and dictionaries in relevant fields. Headings that were chosen met at least two of the following five criteria: 1) selected for study in the CPP, 2) referred to in the project's police, court, and school records, 3) referred to frequently in the bibliographic references, 4) frequently found to be associated with delinquency or crime, or 5) named by other indexes and references.

The headings, format, and organization of the Hierarchical Listing were derived from a variety of sources including: 1) other bibliographies, 2) CPP manuals and publications, 3) the Criminology Center's police, court, and school record information, 4) numerous indexes on medicine, law, and the social sciences, and 5) pertinent manuals, textbooks, and dictionaries [1]. However, the principal model for the Hierarchical Listing was the National Library of Medicine's (NLM's) List of Medical Subject Headings, which orders hierarchically those subject headings printed in NLM's Index Medicus, as well as other headings used to categorize the Index Medicus headings.

INDEX

The Index presents an alphabetical listing of the major subject headings used to classify the bibliographic entries. The subject headings and related subheadings are each followed by a series of five-digit numbers that specify the references in the Bibliography pertaining to the given topic area. In this way, the Index provides a link between entries in the Hierarchical Listing and entries in the Bibliography.

The following listing illustrates the organization of the Index:

> Psychotherapy
>   See:
>   Behavior Modification and Mental
>   Health Services
> Psychotic Disorders (MU) 04400,08400,
>   20630,22100,32980,37150,48250,48700,
>   59820,61900,62330,64550,66130,66160,
>   67200,71600,72660,74000,87250,89340,
>   89360,92320,99145,99365,99885.
>   and Crime (MU11) 06000,28550,28590,
>   29250,41990,44430,44460,44600,
>   45050,45330,45500,46030,46530,
>   46560,47200,51900,52000,52300,
>   52770,53235,53900,62780,66950,
>   69225,84520,88400,98150,98745,
>   98750,98843,99055,99153,99240,
>   99590,99915.
>   See also:
>   Schizophrenia

For information on "Psychotherapy," a user would turn to the Index heading "Behavior Modification and Mental Health Services." The heading "Psychotic Disorders," with topic code "MU," is followed by twenty-five entry numbers indicating those references in the Bibliography dealing with that general topic. The more specific heading, "Psychotic Disorders and Crime" ("MU11"), is followed by entry numbers for thirty-five bibliographic references. Further information on "Psychotic Disorders" can be found under the subject heading "Schizophrenia."

Bibliographic entries were classified using the most specific topic codes possible. If a reference dealt with the subject "Psychotic Disorders and Crime" ("MU11"), it would not also be given the topic code for the more general subject, "Psychotic Disorders" ("MU"), unless it also contained a lengthy discussion of psychotic disorders per se. Thus, in order to locate all references pertaining to "Psychotic Disorders," a user would have to search under two headings: the heading for "Psychotic Disorders" ("MU") and the subheading for "Psychotic Disorders and Crime" ("MU11").

All medical, psychological, and sociological tests are located in a separate section of the Index under the heading "Tests and Measures." This section has two parts. In the first part, tests are grouped by generic headings, such as "Psychological Tests" and "Achievement Tests." In the second part, the names of individual tests are listed, such as "Wechsler Intelligence Scale for Children (WISC)." Three other headings followed by many subheadings are: 1) "Criminality," 2) "Juvenile Delinquency," and 3) "Violent Offenders and Violence."

The Index contains three kinds of cross-references: 1) "See," 2) "See also," and 3) "See under." "See" is used following terms that are not subject headings in the Index, and it refers users to appropriate headings in the Index. "See also" directs users to other headings that may be of interest: for example, "Brain. See also: Electroencephalography." "See under" is used to guide the reader to subheadings located under major headings in the Index: for example, "Bayley Scales. See under: Tests and Measures."

Bibliographic entries are classified according to standardized definitions derived from manuals, dictionaries, and other sources. The topical classification of a given reference does not reflect the exact terminology used by particular authors, but rather the basic concepts they discuss. For example, a reference using the term "prematurity" would be classified under the heading "Prematurity" only if the term refers to a gestation period of less than thirty-seven weeks. If the term instead refers to a birth weight of less than 1,500 grams, the article would be classified under the heading "Birth Weight, Low."

Two methods are used in the classification of bibliographic references: 1) the standard methods followed by current periodical indexes for references presenting new information or data (see Borko and Bernier, 1978; Collison, 1959; Jonker, 1964), and 2) an alternate method for references that include literature reviews or no new information. Standard periodical classification is based on the new information, theories, or discoveries presented in the bibliographic references. In some cases, novel data from graphs and charts are classified even if they are not discussed directly by an author. In turn, many bibliographic references are literature reviews or include large review sections containing no new information or theories. Classification of these reviews focuses on what information is most significant and what the author discusses at length. In general, bibliographic entries in this volume are classified in greater detail than in larger indexes, such as Index Medicus.

This volume was prepared to aid individuals engaged in interdisciplinary research on delinquency and mental disorder. Special efforts were made to address those problems frequently encountered by interdisciplinary researchers: for example, the differences across disciplines in study methods, publications, research orientation, reference materials, and the use of terminology. It is intended that this volume will facilitate links among many different disciplines and thus encourage comprehensive and creative approaches to research, planning, and policy development.

NOTE

1. Indexes consulted for subject headings in the biological and social sciences include: Index Medicus, the Psychological Abstracts Thesaurus, Psychological Abstracts, Sociological Abstracts, the Science Citation Index, the Social Science Citation Index, and the Criminology Index (Wolfgang, Figlio, and Thornberry, 1975). The sources of subject headings in the areas of crime, aggression, and violence include: Use of Criminology Literature (Wright, 1974), Criminological Bibliographies (Davis, 1978), and Criminology and the Administration of Criminal Justice: A Bibliography (Radzinowicz and Hood, 1976). However, the principal sources were the Criminology Index (Wolfgang, Figlio, and Thornberry, 1975) and Crime and Delinquency Abstracts. The interdisciplinary indexes which were used include: the International Bibliography of the Forensic Sciences (Eckert, 1980), and the American Journal of Law and Medicine (Pies, Norris, and Anderson, 1976).

The most frequently consulted manuals and dictionaries were the Diagnostic and Statistical Manual III (DSM III) of the American Psychiatric Association (1980) and Stedman's Medical Dictionary (1976). Additional dictionaries used to develop the structure of the hierarchical listing are: A Dictionary of Sociology (Mitchell, 1968), A Modern Dictionary of Sociology (Theodorson and Theodorson, 1969), A Dictionary of General Psychology: Basic Terminology and Key Concepts (Heidenrich, 1968), Dictionary of Behavioral Science (Wolman, 1973), A Psychiatric Glossary (American Psychiatric Association, 1980), and Psychiatric Dictionary (Campbell, 1981).

REFERENCES

American Psychiatric Association. Diagnostic and Statistical Manual of Mental Disorders (3rd ed.). Washington, D.C.: American Psychiatric Association, 1980.

American Psychiatric Association. A Psychiatric Dictionary (5th ed.). New York: Oxford University Press, 1981.

Borko, H., and Bernier, C.L. Indexing Concepts and Methods. New York: Academic Press, 1978.

Campbell, R.J. Psychiatric Dictionary (5th ed.). New York: Academic Press, 1981.

Collison, R.L. Indexes and Indexing. London: Ernest Benn, Ltd., 1959.

Davis, B.L. (ed.). Criminological Bibliographies: Uniform Citations to Bibliographies, Indexes and Review Articles of the Literature of Crime Study in the United States. Westport, Conn.: Greenwood Press, 1978.

Denno, D. Sex differences in cognition and crime: Early developmental, biological, and sociological correlates. Unpublished doctoral dissertation, University of Pennsylvania, 1982.

Dietz, P.E. Medical criminology notes #3: Access to medical literature in medical criminology. Bulletin of the American Academy of Psychiatry and the Law, 1978, 6(1), 110–117.

Eckert, W.G. (ed.). The international bibliography of the forensic sciences: 1980. Inform [International Reference Organization in Forensic Medicine and Sciences, Wichita, Kan.], 1980.

Heidenreich, C.A. A Dictionary of General Psychology: Basic Terminology and Key Concepts. Dubuque, Iowa: Kendall/Hunt, 1968.

Jonker, F. Indexing Theory, Indexing Methods and Search Devices. New York: Scarecrow Press, Inc., 1964.

Magarrell, J. Notes on . . . libraries. Chronicle of Higher Education, 1984, 28(4), 3.

Mitchell, G.D. (ed.). A Dictionary of Sociology. Chicago: Aldine Publishing Co., 1968.

Pies, H.E., Norris, J.A., and Anderson, P.J. Topical index to selected medicolegal information. American Journal of Law and Medicine, 1976, 2, 177–212.

Radzinowicz, L., and Hood, R. Criminology and the Administration of Criminal Justice: A Bibliography. London: Mansell, 1976.

Rappeport, J.R. A functional information retrieval system for forensic psychiatrists: One man's system. Bulletin of the American Academy of Psychiatry and the Law, 1975, 2, 216–219.

Stedman's Medical Dictionary (23rd ed.). Baltimore: The Williams & Wilkins Co., Publishing Company, 1968.

Theodorson, G.A., and Theodorson, A.G. A Modern Dictionary of Sociology. New York: Thomas E. Crowell Co., 1969.

Wolfgang, M.E., Figlio, R.M., and Thornberry, T.P. Criminology Index: Research and Theory in Criminology in the United States, 1945–1972 (Vols. I and II). New York: Elsevier, 1975.

Wolman, B.B. (ed.). Dictionary of Behavioral Science. New York: Van Nostrand Reinhold Company, 1973.

Wright, Martin (ed.). Use of Criminology Literature. Hamden, Conn.: Archon Books, 1974.

Biological, Psychological, and Environmental Factors in Delinquency and Mental Disorder

BIBLIOGRAPHY

00100　Abrams, B.F., Schultz, S.R., Margen, S., and Ogar, D.A. Perspectives in
clinical research: A review of research controversies surrounding the
Feingold diet. Family and Community Health, February 1979, 1(4), 93-113.
Topic Codes: BD52,BD52B,BD52D,CC11D,DA,DD00,M,MG30,NA07B,NA07DD,PE,PG,
SR01.

00200　Ackerman, P.T., Dykman, R.A., and Peters, J.E. Hierarchical factor pat-
terns on the WISC as related to areas of learning deficit. Perceptual and
Motor Skills, 1976, 42, 583-615. Topic Codes: BL11,BN04,DT44,MG,MH,ML,
MM,MS04,NA07B,NA07I,PC,PE10,PG,PI,PN,PP,PS,SC18,SC70,TA04,TA52,TA80,TB09B,
TB95B,TB98B.

00300　Adams, R. Review of Ecologic-Biochemical Approaches to Treatment of Delinquents and Criminals, edited by L.J. Hippchen. Journal of Criminal Justice, 1979, 7, 269-273. Topic Codes: BD11,BD52D,CG,CV52D,SF11.

00400　Adams, T.C. Some MMPI differences between first and multiple admissions
within a state prison population. Journal of Clinical Psychology, July
1976, 32(3), 555-558. Topic Codes: BL04,CC11P,CC11U,MG11,NL48,PM,TB15B,
TB61B,TB98D.

00500　Adams, V. Studies relate physical causes to delinquency. New York Times,
June 26, 1979, C1-C3. Topic Codes: CC37B,CC37F,CC37K,CC37L,CC81D,CT57BB,
CT57BD,DD10D,DK07D,DK18SD,DT52D,SI57GD,TB35D.

00525　Adamska, H. Family environment and peer group behavior. Polish Psychological Bulletin, 1981, 12(4), 219-223. Topic Codes: CC37,DT44,MG,NA07B,
NH,SI,SJ07,SW.

00550　Agarwal, H.C., Mohan, D., and Mukerji, D.P. Eneuresis: An etiological
and therapeutic review. Indian Journal of Medical Sciences, October 1967,
21(10), 668-675. Topic Codes: BL04D,CC37A,CC37B,CC37W,CV06,DK,MG18,MQ,
MX07,NE37,NH59,NL,PE10,PG,SH59,SI57,SR04,TA57.

00600　Ahmed, F. Blood pressure, skeletal maturation and deviant behavior: A
literature review. Unpublished manuscript, University of Pennsylvania,
1981. Topic Codes: BE,BL08BD,BL67,DD28,N,SF26,SJ22,SN,TA80.

00650　Ahn, H. Electroencephalographic evoked potential comparisons of normal
children and children with different modes of underachievement [doctoral
dissertation, University of Iowa, 1977]. Dissertation Abstracts International, January 1978, 38(7), 3453B. Topic Codes: BK11B,BL18,BN44,NA07,
NA07I,PE10,PE64,PG,PP,TA55.

00700　Ahn, H., Brown, D., John, E.R., Kaye, H., Prichep, L., and Trepetin, M.
Developmental equations for the electroencephalogram. Science, December
1980, 210(12), 1255-1258. Topic Codes: BK11B,BL11,NA,NA07I,P,PG,TA52,
TA55,TB35.

00800　Aiken, T.W., Stumphauzer, J.S., and Veloz, E.V. Behavioral analyses of
non-delinquent brothers in a high juvenile crime community. Behavioral
Disorders, August 1977, 2(4), 212-222. Topic Codes: CC37K,CC37L,MX,PE68,
PY,SF11,SI57P,SR,SU.

00900   Aird, R.B., Venturini, A.M., and Spielman, P.M. Antecedents of temporal lobe epilepsy. Archives of Neurology, January 1967, 16, 67-73. Topic Codes: BL11,BP47,DD08K,DK07,DK09,DK18S,DP,DT04E,DT67,MG,MG18,NA07D,NA07I, PG,TB35.

00910   Albert, J.M., Elie, R., Cooper, S.F., Clermont, A., and Langlois, Y. Efficacy of SCH-12679 in the management of aggressive mental retardates. Current Therapeutic Research, June 1977, 21(6), 786-795. Topic Codes: BB07,DD,DD00,DD02,DD02B,DK46,DK46B,M,MC,MF,MO,MO07,PE,PE10.

00930   Albert, M.I. Short-term memory and aphasia. Brain and Language, January 1976, 3(1), 28-33. Topic Codes: BN70,DT13,DT46,DT71,MH,MN,MY,NL,PE70,PT, PM,PQ,TA55.

00950   Albert, M.I., Silverberg, R., Reches, A., and Berman, M. Cerebral dominance for consciousness. Archives of Neurology, June 1976, 33(6), 453-454. Topic Codes: BK11B,DK09,NL.

00960   Alford, R., and Alford, K.F. Sex differences in asymmetry in the facial expression of emotion. Neuropsychologia, 1981, 19(4), 605-608. Topic Codes: BL67D,BN44,NA,P,PO,SQ,T.

00970   Allen, H.E. Bio-social correlates of two types of antisocial sociopaths [doctoral dissertation, Ohio State University, 1969]. Dissertation Abstracts International, August 1970, 31(2), 841A. Topic Codes: BL25, BL25BB,BL25D,C,DT44,DT44BB,DT44D,ME,ME07,NE59,PP07B,TA02B,TA03.

00990   Allen, L.S. An examination of academic and behavioral characteristics of boys and girls who have been identified as learning disabled [doctoral dissertation, University of Northern Colorado, 1975]. Dissertation Abstracts International, May 1976, 36(11), 7281A-7282A. Topic Codes: BL11, DT44B,MG,MM07,NA07B,PE10,PG,PP07,TA74,TA80.

00995   Allen M., and Wellman, M.M. Hand position during writing, cerebral laterality and reading age and sex differences. Neuropsychologia, 1980, 18, 33-40. Topic Codes: BK11B,BL70,BN44,NA07B,NA07I,PE,PE10,PE64,PG,PN,PO, TA04,TA59D,TA80.

01000   Allen, M.G., Cohen, S., Pollin, W., and Greenspan, S.I. Affective illness in veteran twins: A diagnostic review. American Journal of Psychiatry, November 1974, 131(11), 1234-1239. Topic Codes: BI07,BL04B,BP02,DD00, DD02B,MB,MF,NA44,NH74B,NJ,PE,SF07,SH74B,SR01,TA02,TA80.

01100   Allen, M.J. The role of vision in learning disorders. Journal of Learning Disabilities, August/September 1977, 10(7), 411-415. Topic Codes: BL31,DD81,DT44,MM,NA31F,PK,PP,TB35.

01150   Allen, R.P., Safer, D., and Covi, L. Effects of psychostimulants on aggression. Journal of Nervous and Mental Disease, February 1975, 160(2-1), 138-145. Topic Codes: BD07,BL04,BL11,BN04B,CC37A,CC37B,CC37C,CC37K, CC37P,CQ37,CQ59,CV15,DD00,DD02B,MF,MG11,MK,NA07,NA07B,NA07D,NA07I,NL48B, PC,PE04,PE10,PE68B,PG,TA02,TA74,TB.

01200   Allison, T.S., and Allison, S.L. Time-out from reinforcement: Effect on sibling aggression. The Psychological Record, 1971, 21, 81-86. Topic Codes: CV06,MC,NA07B,PE04,PE10,SR03.

01300   Allsop, J.F., and Feldman, M.P. Personality and antisocial behavior in schoolboys: An item analysis of questionnaire measures. British Journal of Criminology, October 1976, 16(4), 337-351. Topic Codes: BL04,BL18, CC37C,CC37J,CC37W,CL,ME07,MG11B,MQ11,PA,PE08D,PE64D,SC70D,SR04B,TA59, TB37D.

01400   Alpert, M., and Martz, M.J. Cognitive views of schizophrenia in light of recent studies of brain asymmetry. In C. Shagass, S. Gershon, and A.J. Friedhoff (eds.), Psychopathology and Brain Dysfunction. New York: Raven Press, 1977. Topic Codes: BL25B,BN44B,DK07B,DK18SB,DT13B,MH07,PI07,PO07, TB35B.

01500   Altemus, L.A., and Ferguson, A.D. Comparative incidence of birth defects
in Negro and white children. _Pediatrics_, 1965, 36(1), 56-61. Topic
Codes: BB,BL67,DD02,SN,SW.

01600   Altus, W.D. Birth order and its sequelae. _Science_, January 7, 1966, 151,
44-49. Topic Codes: BL70,PE64,PM,PT,SC18,SC70,SI57,SJ07,SJ07B,SJ22,SQ,
TB61,TB68.

01700   Altus, W.D. Birth order and scholastic aptitude. _Journal of Consulting
Psychology_, 1965, 29(3), 202-205. Topic Codes: BL70,PE64,SC18,SC70,SJ07,
SJ22,SQ,TA59D.

01800   Ambrose, G.C. Are conduct disorders in children caused by too much emotional pressure? _Lancet_, April 1, 1978, 8066, 703-704. Topic Codes:
MG11,SI57.

01900   Amiel-Tison, C. A method for neurological evaluation within the first
year of life: Experience with full-term newborn infants with brain injury. _CIBA Foundation Symposium_, 1978, 59, 107-137. Topic Codes: BL07B,
DD08K,DF06B,DF34,DK,DP11,DP44,NA33B,NA33I,NA44,NJ,TA52M,TB02.

02000   Anastasi, A. Intelligence and family size. _Psychological Bulletin_, 1956,
53, 187-209. Topic Codes: BI,NH74,PE64,PM,SC70,SF,SF26,SH74,SJ07,SJ22,
SW,TB78.

02100   Anchor, K.N., Sandler, H.M., and Cherones, J.H. Maladaptive antisocial
aggressive behavior and outlets for intimacy. _Journal of Clinical Psy-
chology_, October 1977, 33(4), 947-949. Topic Codes: CC11P,CC81D,CC81S,
CT57,MC11,MEO7,MX,PE04D,PE08D,PE68,PT11,SR,SR03B,SR04B,TAO2,TA59.

02140   Anderson, C.M. Minimal brain damage. _Mental Hygiene_, Spring 1972, 56(2),
62-66. Topic Codes: BD52,BL70B,BPO2B,BP52,CV52,DF60B,DK48B,DP11B,DT42B,
MG48B,MLO2,PE44B,PNO7,PY,SFO7,SI57P,SQO7,SU.

02150   Anderson, C.M. _Society Pays: The High Costs of Minimal Brain Damage in
America_. New York: Walker & Co., 1972. Topic Codes: BD52,BL70B,BPO2B,
BP52,CV52,DF60B,DK48B,DP11B,DT42B,MG48B,MLO2,PE44B,PNO7,PY,SFO7,SI57P,
SQO7,SU.

02180   Anderson, D.R. Prevalence of behavioral and emotional disturbance and
specific problem types in a sample of disadvantaged preschool-aged children. _Journal of Clinical Child Psychology_, Summer 1983, 12(2), 130-136.
Topic Codes: MG,NAO7D,SWO7.

02200   Anderson, R.E. Where's Dad?: Paternal deprivation and delinquency.
Archives of General Psychiatry, June 1968, 18, 641-649. Topic Codes:
BLO4D,BL67D,CC37L,CC37Z,CT59,SF26DD,SI46D,SI48D,SI59D,SJ09D,SN11,SW11.

02250   Andolina, R.M. A neuropsychological assessment of hyperactivity: The effects of a sugar elimination diet on attention span and behavior dysfunction [doctoral dissertation, United States International University,
1981]. _Dissertation Abstracts International_, May 1982, 42(11), 4566B.
Topic Codes: BD52B,MG,MG30.

02300   Andrew, J.M. Are left-handers less violent? _Journal of Youth and Ado-
lescence_, 1980, 9(11), 1-9. Topic Codes: BL48D,BL70,BL70D,BN44,BN44D,
CC37F,CC37R,CC81,CC81R,CC81Y,CE,CQ81,CT81,DKO7D,DK18D,DK48D,DTO6,DT15,
DT48D,MGO4,MG48D,MLO4,ML15,MT48D,NE81,PE48D,PO,PO11,PR11,SF11,SQ,SQ11,
TB40D,TB96D.

02400   Andrew, J.M. The classic Wechsler P-V sign and violent crime. _Crime
and/et Justice_, 1978, 6(4), 246-248. Topic Codes: BLO4D,BL70D,CC371,
CC81Y,CE,SF11,SQ11,TB96D.

02450   Andrew, J.M. Delinquency: Correlating variables. _Journal of Clinical
Child Psychology_, 1981, 10, 136-140. Topic Codes: BA,BD52,CC11A,CC11C,
CC11D,CC11G,CC11I,CC11L,CC11M,CC11N,CC11P,CC11T,CC24,CC37B,CC37G,CC37H,
CC37I,CC37J,CC37K,CC37M,CC37N,CC37P,CC37Q,CC37U,CC37Z,CV13,DDO3,MAO7,MA11,

MC,MF11,MG02B,MG02D,MG11,MI,MK,MM,MV11,MX07,MX11,NA07B,NA07D,NA07ID,NH59D,
NH70,PE10,PE30D,PE64,PE68D,PG11,PP,SB,SF,SH59B,SH59D,SH59J,SJ07B,SJ07D,
SJ22B,SJ22D,SR01,SR02,SR03B,SS,SW07,SW11,SW56.

02500   Andrew, J.M. Delinquency: Intellectual imbalance? Criminal Justice and
Behavior, March 1977, 4(1), 99–104. Topic Codes: CC371,TB96D.

02600   Andrew, J.M. Delinquency, sex, and family variables. Social Biology,
1976, 23(2), 168–171. Topic Codes: BL67D,BL70D,SF11,SJ09D,SJ22D,SN11,
SQ11.

02700   Andrew, J.M. Delinquency, the Wechsler P>V sign, and the I-level system.
Journal of Clinical Psychology, 1974, 30(3), 331–335. Topic Codes: MQ11,
NL48D,TB91C,TB96D.

02800   Andrew, J.M. Delinquents and the Tapping Test. Journal of Clinical Psychology, July 1977, 33(3), 225–231. Topic Codes: BL04,BL11C,BL70,CC371,
DK48D,MG48D,NA07ID,PG11,PM,SF,SQ,TB40D,TB93,TB95.

02900   Andrew, J.M. Immaturity, delinquency, and the Wechsler P>V sign. Journal
of Abnormal Child Psychology, 1974, 2(3), 245–251. Topic Codes: BL04D,
CC37A,CC371,TB91C,TB96D.

03000   Andrew, J.M. Laterality on the Tapping Test among legal offenders. Journal of Clinical Child Psychology, Summer 1978, 7(2), 149–150. Topic
Codes: BN44,BN44D,PO,PO11,TB40D.

03100   Andrew, J.M. Neuropsychological testing and assessment among drug-using
delinquents. Drug Abuse and Alcoholism Review, Summer 1979, 1–10. Topic
Codes: CC37F,CC37I,DA15D,DK07,MI07,NC80,PE15D,TA59D,TB46.

03200   Andrew, J.M. Parietal laterality and violence. International Journal of
Neuroscience, 1980, 11, 1–7. Topic Codes: BA,BK11B,BN44BB,BN44D,CC37A,
CC37B,CC37F,CC37G,CC37R,CE81,CG11C,CJ,CQ37,CQ59,NA07B,NA07I,NE37,NL48D,
PE10,PO07,PO11,SQ,TA74.

03250   Andrew, J.M. Reading and cerebral dysfunction among juvenile delinquents.
Criminal Justice and Behavior, June 1981, 8(2), 131–144. Topic Codes:
BN44D,CC37H,CC37I,CC37J,CC37R,DT15B,ML15B,PO11,TA03,TA55,TB40D,TB98D.

03400   Andrew, J.M. Verbal I.Q. and the I-level classification system for delinquents. Criminal Justice and Behavior, June 1980, 7(2), 193–202. Topic Codes: BL04D,BL11C,BL67D,BL70D,CC24B,CC37A,CC37G,CC37H,CC37Q,CC37Y,
CC371,CE81,CQ37,MQ11,NA07ID,NE37,NE59,NL48B,NL48D,PG11,PM11,PY11,SI57PB,
SN11,SQ11,SU11,TB91C,TB93D,TB95D,TB96D.

03500   Andrew, J.M. Violence among delinquents by family intactness and size.
Social Biology, Fall 1978, 25, 243–250. Topic Codes: BL67D,BL70D,CC81A,
CC81N,CC81V,CE,CY,SF11,SJ09D,SJ22D,SN11,SQ11.

03600   Andrew, J.M. Violence and poor reading. Criminology, November 1979,
17(3), 361–365. Topic Codes: BI11,BL11C,BL70D,CC37G,CC37H,CC37J,CC37L,
CC37N,CC37Q,CC37Y,CC37Z,CC371,CC81J,CC81Q,CC81U,CC81V,CC81W,CC81Y,CE81,
CT81,CY,ML03,MM11,NA07B,NA07DF,NE37,NL48D,PA11,PE10,PE44,PE44D,PE64,PE64D,
PG11,PN11,PP11,SC70D,SN11,SQ11,SW11,TA04,TB93D,TB95D,TB96D,TB98D.

03650   Andrew, J.M. Violence and the Tapping Test. Crime and/et Justice, 1977,
5, 225–231. Topic Codes: BL48D,BL70D,BN44D,CC37L,CC37R,CC37Y,CC81Y,CE,
CY,DT48D,MT48D,PE48D,PO11,PR11,SQ11,TB40D,TB96D.

03700   Andrew, J.M. Violent crime indices among community-retained delinquents.
Criminal Justice and Behavior, 1974, 1(2), 123–130. Topic Codes: BL67D,
BL70D,CC81,CC81Y,CE,CY,SF11,SN11,SQ11.

03800   Andrew, J.M. Why can't delinquents read? Perceptual and Motor Skills,
1978, 47, 640. Topic Codes: BL67D,BL70D,DT15B,ML15B,PM11,SN11,SQ11,
TB93D,TB95D,TB96D,TB98D.

03900   Andrew, J.M., and Bentley, M.R.   The quick minute: Delinquents, drugs, and time. Criminal Justice and Behavior, June 1976, 3(2), 179-186. Topic Codes: BL04D,BL67D,DA04D,DA15D,DK07D,DT59D,MD11,MI07,MR11,PE06D,PE15D, PS11,SF11,SN11.

04000   Andrew, J.M., and Bentley, M.R.   Quick tests of organicity among drug-using delinquents. Criminal Justice and Behavior, March 1978, 5(1), 75-92. Topic Codes: BL48D,CC37F,CC37I,CC37L,CC37R,CC37Y,CC37I,DD26D, DT48D,MT48D,PE48D,PR11,TB40D,TB66D,TB78D,TB87C,TB93B,TB95D.

04010   Andy, O.J., and Velamati, S.   Limbic system seizures and aggressive behavior (super-kindling effects). Pavlovian Journal of Biological Science, October-December 1978, 13(4), 251-264. Topic Codes: BK11BL,CV15B,DK07, DK09,DK18,MC,MT,SR03,TA52,TA80.

04015   Angrist, B., and Gershon, S.   Clinical effects of amphetamine and L-Dopa on sexuality and aggression. Comprehensive Psychiatry, November-December 1976, 17(6), 715-722. Topic Codes: BK11B,CV15B,DD00,MC,MI,MK,MU70,MV07, PE04,PE15,PE66B,TA02,TA59.

04020   Annett, M.   The binomial distribution of right, mixed and left handedness. Quarterly Journal of Experimental Psychology, 1967, 19, 327-333. Topic Codes: BI,BN44,NL,PO,TA55.

04030   Annett, M.   A classification of hand preference by association analysis. British Journal of Psychology, 1970, 61, 303-321. Topic Codes: BK11B, BN44,NC80,PO,TA,TB49.

04040   Annett, M.   The distribution of manual asymmetry. British Journal of Psychology, 1972, 63, 343-348. Topic Codes: BI,BK11B,BL70,BN44,ML,NH,NH59P, NL48,PO,SB,SF,SH59,SH59J,SH59R,SI48,TB49B.

04050   Annett, M.   Hand preference and the laterality of cerebral speech. Cortex, 1975, 11, 305-328. Topic Codes: BK11B,PO,TA80,TB49B.

04070   Annett, M.   Handedness in families. Annals of Human Genetics, 1973, 37, 93-105. Topic Codes: BN44,NH,PO.

04075   Annett, M.   Handedness in the children of two left-handed parents. British Journal of Psychology, 1974, 65, 129-131. Topic Codes: BB48,BI, BK11B,BL11,BL48,BN44,DD02K,MT48,NA07I,NH,PE10,PG,PO,SB,SC,SD11,SH11,TB49.

04080   Annett, M.   Laterality of childhood hemiplegia and the growth of speech and intelligence. Cortex, 1973, 9, 4-33. Topic Codes: BK11B,BL11,BL48B, BL70B,BN44B,BN68,BN70,BP02B,BP44,DD00,DD02B,DD02KB,DD08K,DD26B,DF34,DK07, DK18B,DK46B,DP44,DT06,DT42B,DT44B,DT48B,DT67,DT71,MG,MH07,ML,ML02,ML04, MM07,MO07,MT,NA07B,NA07D,NA07I,NA31A,NA31C,NH65,NH70,PA,PE10,PE48B,PE68B, PG,PI07,PO07,PO33,PP07,PR07,SI,SR01,TA02,TA52,TA55,TA59D,TA80,TB49B,TB78B, TB95B,TB96B.

04090   Annett, M.   A model of the inheritance of handedness and cerebral dominance. Nature, 1964, 204, 59-60. Topic Codes: BA,BK11B,BN44D,CC11M, DT06,N,PO11,SI,SU.

04100   Annett, M., and Ockwell, A.   Birth order, birth stress and handedness. Cortex, 1980, 16, 181-188. Topic Codes: BL70,BN44,DP60,PO,SJ07,SQ.

04200   Annett, M., and Turner, A.   Laterality and the growth of intellectual abilities. British Journal of Educational Psychology, 1974, 44, 37-46. Topic Codes: BL04,BL70,BN44,MG,NA07B,NA07D,PE10,PO,SQ,TA04,TB33G,TB95.

04280   Anolik, S.A.   Family influences upon delinquency: Biosocial and psychosocial perspectives. Adolescence, Fall 1983, 18(71), 489-498. Topic Codes: BA,CC11K,CC11M,SF11,SI57D,SS09.

04300   Anolik, S.A.   Personality, family, educational, and criminological characteristics of bright delinquents. Psychological Reports, 1979, 44, 727-734. Topic Codes: CC37B,CC37J,CC37L,CC37Q,CC37W,CC37I,TB78D,TB93D,TB95D.

04310   Apgar, V. A proposal for a new method of evaluation of the newborn infant. Current Researches in Anesthesia and Analgesia, July-August 1953, 32(4), 260-267. Topic Codes: BL06,BL07B,BL22,BL29,BL33,BL59,BP02,BP44, BP61,DF06B,DF48,DP11,DP44,DP48,NA31F,NA31R,SJ07,TA52K,TA52M.

04330   Apgar, V., Holaday, D.A., James, L.S., Weisbrot, I.M., and Berrien, C. Evaluation of the newborn infant - second report. Journal of the American Medical Association, December 13, 1958, 168(15), 1985-1988. Topic Codes: BB,BD,BE,BL07B,BL22,BP02,BP04,BP22,BP44,DF06B,DF34,DF48,DP11,DP44,DP48, NA31C,NA31F,NA31R,NA33B,NA33F,NA33I,PE34,TA52K,TA80.

04350   Arajarvi, T.K.M., Repo, I., and Torma, S. On specific reading and writing difficulties of pre-adolescents. Psychiatrica Fennica, 1974, 231-236. Topic Codes: DT15,DT42,MG,ML,ML15,NA07D,PE44,PN.

04400   Armentrout, J.A. Parental child-rearing attitudes and preadolescents' problem behaviors. Journal of Consulting and Clinical Psychology, 1971, 37(2), 278-285. Topic Codes: BL04,BL70,MG,MG11,MQ,MU,NA07D,NH59E,PE64B, SC70B,SH59F,SI57,SQ,TA02,TA59.

04500   Arnold, J.E., Levine, A.G., and Patterson, G.R. Changes in sibling behavior following family intervention. Journal of Consulting and Clinical Psychology, 1975, 43(5), 683-688. Topic Codes: CV06,MG11B,NH65B,SI57, TA02.

04530   Arnold, J.E. Minimal brain dysfunction: A hydraulic parfait model. Diseases of the Nervous System, April 1976, 37(4), 171-173. Topic Codes: BD52B,BI,BK11B,BL11,DA44MB,DK48B,MG48B,NA07B,NA07I,PE10,PE64B,PE68,PG, SI07.

04560   Arnold, J.E., and Smeltzer, D.J. Behavior checklist factor analysis for children and adolescents. Archives of General Psychiatry, June 1974, 30(6), 799-804. Topic Codes: BL11,BN04B,BN68,CC37A,CC37B,CC37K,CC37S, CC37Z,DD,DK48B,DT44,DT69,MF,MG11,MG18,MG21,MG30B,MG48B,MK,MM,MP,MV,NA07B, NA07DB,NA07DF,NA07I,PA,PC,PE10,PE22,PE52,PE64B,PE68B,PG,PP07,SC70B,SF07, SI,SR01,SW,TA02,TA80.

04590   Aronfreed, J. Discussion: Developmental gains in moral judgment. American Journal of Mental Deficiency, 1974, 79(2), 113-154. Topic Codes: BL04,DT13B,MH07,NA07D,PI07,PY,SU.

04620   Ashem, B., and Janes, M.D. Deleterious effects of chronic undernutrition on cognitive abilities. Journal of Child Psychology and Psychiatry and Allied Disciplines, January 1978, 19(1), 23-31. Topic Codes: BD52B,BL11, DD00,DD02,NA07B,NA07I,NL07,PE10,PG,PI,PP07,SC70,SF,TA02,TA80,TB40.

04640   Atkins, J.W. Delinquency as a function of self-esteem [doctoral dissertation, University of Oregon, 1973]. Dissertation Abstracts International, March 1974, 34(9), 4650B. Topic Codes: CC37W,CC37Z,CC37I,NA07B,PT74B, TA03,TA59.

04646   August, G.J., and Stewart, M.A. Familial subtypes of childhood hyperactivity. Journal of Nervous and Mental Disease, June 1983, 171(6), 362-368. Topic Codes: MG,MG30,NH59B,NH59E.

04647   August, G.J., and Stewart, M.A. Is there a syndrome of pure hyperactivity? British Journal of Psychiatry, March 1982, 140, 305-311. Topic Codes: MG,MG30,TB95B.

04648   August, G.J., Stewart, M.A., and Holmes, C.S. A four-year follow-up of hyperactive boys with and without conduct disorder. British Journal of Psychiatry, August 1983, 143, 192-198. Topic Codes: MG,MG11,MG30.

04650   Aurand, S.K. Review of the major tests of intellectual functioning in the Collaborative Perinatal Project. Unpublished manuscript, University of Pennsylvania, 1978. Topic Codes: NA07I,NA33F,PM,TA59D,TB05,TB09,TB44, TB68,TB78,TB95,TB98.

04670   Austin, R.L. Race, father-absence, and female delinquency. Criminology, 1978, 15(4), 487-504. Topic Codes: CC24,CC37M,CC37Y,CC37Z,CG11P,CQ22, CQ37,NE22,NE37,NH59F,NH59GI,NL22D,NL48D,SH59JL,SH59RL,SI22D,SI48D,SI59D, SJ09D,SN11,SQ11,TA03.

04700   Aydin, O., and Markova, I. Attribution tendencies of popular and unpopu-lar children. British Journal of Social and Clinical Psychology, 1979, 18, 291-298. Topic Codes: BL04,BL70,MX,NA07B,PE10,PE68,PT,SQ,SR,TA59.

04750   Bachman, J.G. Delinquent behavior linked to educational attainment and post-high school experiences. Unpublished manuscript, Survey Research Center, Institute for Social Research, University of Michigan, 1978. Topic Codes: CC37I,CC37J,CC37Z,NA44,NJ,SC18D.

04800   Bach-y-Rita, G., Lion, J.R., Climent, C.E., and Ervin, F.R. Episodic dys-control: A study of 130 violent patients. American Journal of Psychia-try, May 11, 1971, 127(11), 1473-1478. Topic Codes: CC81B,CC81C,CC81H, CC81I,CC81K,CC81M,CC81N,CC81O,CC81R,CC81S,CV06C,DK48,MG48,TB09D,TB72B, TB93D.

04900   Bach-y-Rita, G., and Veno, A. Habitual violence: A profile of 62 men. American Journal of Psychiatry, September 1974, 131(9), 1015-1017. Topic Codes: CC81D,CC81F,CC81S.

05000   Bacola, E., Behrle, F.C., De Schweinitz, L., Miller, H.C., and Mira, M. Perinatal and environmental factors in late neurogenic sequelae. American Journal of Diseases of Children, October 1966, 112, 359-374. Topic Codes: BL07B,BL07BB,BL11,BL27,BL70,BP26,DF06B,DF06BB,DF67B,DK,DK46,DP11,DP60, DT08E,MO,NA07I,NA33I,NH59PF,NL48,PG,PM,SH59RF,SQ,TA52M,TB25,TB78,TB89, TB95.

05050   Bailey, R.H. Violence and Aggression (Book 1). New York: Time-Life Books, 1976. Topic Codes: CC81,CQ81,CT81,MC,NE81,PE04,SR03.

05100   Baizerman, M., Sheehan, C., Ellison, D.L., and Schlesinger, E.R. A cri-tique of the research literature concerning pregnant adolescents, 1960-1970. Journal of Youth and Adolescence, 1974, 3(1), 61-75. Topic Codes: BP,BP46.

05200   Bakan, P., Dibb, G., and Reed, P. Handedness and birth stress. Neuropsy-chologia, 1973, 11, 363-366. Topic Codes: BN44,DP,DT04E,NH,PO,SH.

05300   Baker, A.H., Kostin, I.W., Mishara, B.L., and Parker, L. Delinquency and stimulation seeking: Re-analysis of Petrie's study of kinesthetic after-effects. Perceptual and Motor Skills, 1974, 39, 400-402. Topic Codes: BL70,CC37H,SQ.

05400   Baker, D. Chromosome errors and antisocial behavior. Critical Reviews in Clinical Laboratory Sciences, January 1972, 3(1), 41-101. Topic Codes: BB70B,BI07,DD02ND,DT04ED.

05430   Baker, D., Telfer, M., Richardson, C.E., and Clark, G.R. Chromosome er-rors in men with antisocial behavior: Comparison of selected men with Klinefelter's syndrome and XYY chromosome pattern. Journal of the Ameri-can Medical Association, November 1970, 214(5), 869-878. Topic Codes: BA,BB07,BB11,BB70D,BL05,CC11D,CC11E,CC11M,CC11U,CC37N,ME,NE59,NL,TA52.

05460   Baker, H.J., and Stoller, R.J. Sexual psychopathology in the hypogonadal male. Archives of General Psychiatry, 1968, 18, 631-634. Topic Codes: BB70B,BL70,MV,SQ07.

05470   Baker, I., Hughes, J., Street, E., and Sweetnam, P. Behavior problems in children followed from 5 to 81/2-9 years of age and their relation to ed-ucational attainment. Child Care, Health and Development, November 1983, 9(6), 339-348. Topic Codes: MG,PE64B.

05480   Baker, L., Cantwell, D.P., and Mattison, R.E. Behavior problems in chil-dren with pure speech disorders and in children with combined speech and language disorders. <u>Journal of Abnormal Child Psychology</u>, June 1980, 8 (2), 245-256. Topic Codes: BL11,BN70,DT42,DT71,MG,ML,MY,NA07D,PE44,PE70, PN.

05500   Baldwin, J. Social area analysis and studies of delinquency. <u>Social Science Research</u>, 1974, 3, 151-168. Topic Codes: CC37,CC37L,CC67,CG,CQ37, CQ67,NE37,NE67,SF11,SF26DD,SW11.

05600   Balkan, S., and Berger, R.J. The changing nature of female delinquency. <u>Sociological Abstracts</u>, 1979, 27(supplement 94), abstract S10920. Topic Codes: BL70D,CC37,CC67,CC81,CQ37,CQ67,CQ81,CT59,CT81,NE22,NE37,NE67,NE81, SQ11.

05630   Balow, I.M. Lateral dominance characteristics and reading achievement in first grade. <u>Journal of Psychology</u>, 1963, 55, 323-328. Topic Codes: BN44H,NA07,PO33,TA04.

05660   Balow, I.M., and Balow, B. Lateral dominance and reading achievement in the second grade. <u>American Educational Journal</u>, 1964, 1, 139-143. Topic Codes: BK11,BN44,DT42,ML,NA07I,PE44,PE64,PG,PN,PO,SC70.

05690   Barack, L.I., and Widom, C.S. Eysenck's theory of criminality applied to women awaiting trial. <u>British Journal of Psychiatry</u>, November 1978, 133, 452-456. Topic Codes: CC11P,CC11U.CC24,CQ22,NE22,TB38B.

05700   Barclay, A., and Carolan, P. A comparative study of the Wechsler Intelligence Scale for Children and the Stanford-Binet Intelligence Scale, form L-M. <u>Journal of Consulting Psychology</u>, 1966, 30(6), 563. Topic Codes: BL04,BL67,SN,TB78,TB95.

05800   Barnes, J., and O'Gorman, N. Anthropometrical features of delinquent boys. <u>Journal of the Irish Medical Association</u>, January 27, 1978, 71(1), 15-18. Topic Codes: BE30,CC37E,CC37G,CC37L,CC37X.

05900   Barnes, J., and O'Gorman, N. Some medical and social features of delinquent boys. <u>Journal of the Irish Medical Association</u>, January 27, 1978, 71(1), 19-22. Topic Codes: CC37B,CC37K,CC37L,CC37O,CC37P,CC37I,CV30D, DD81D,MG18D,NH67,SJ22D,SL11,SW,TB95D.

05930   Barr, G.D., Allen, C.M., and Shinefield, H.R. Height and weight of 7500 children of three skin colors. <u>American Journal of Diseases of Children</u>, December 1972, 124, 866-872. Topic Codes: BE,BI,BL06,BL11,BL67,BL70,DD, NA07,NA07I,NL48,PG,SN,SQ,TA80.

05950   Barroso Aguirre, J.Z. Etiology of infantile psychoses. <u>Neurologia, Neurocirugia, Psiquiatria</u>, 1975, 16(3), 161-166 (in Spanish). Topic Codes: BI07,BL04B,BL31,BL52DB,BP02,BP59,DF34,DP11B,DP46,MG04,NA31C,NA31D, NH59,NL,PE32,PE34,PL,SH59,SR01.

05970   Bartak, L., and Rutter, M. Causes of infantile autism: Some considerations from recent research. <u>Journal of Autism and Childhood Schizophrenia</u>, 1971, 1(1), 20-32. Topic Codes: BP02B,DP11B,MG04.

06000   Bartol, C.R. <u>Criminal Behavior: A Psychosocial Approach</u>. Englewood Cliffs: Prentice-Hall, 1980. Topic Codes: BA,BB70B,BK04BB,BK04D,BK11B, CC11C,CC11H,CC11O,CC11P,CC24,CC37K,CC37Q,CC81,CJ,CQ22,CQ37,CT57F,CT68, CV06,CV13,CV15,MB11,MC,MD07B,MD11,MS02,MS04B,MU11,MU70B,MV,PG11,PT11,SA11, SF11,SI,SS09,SU11,SW07B,SW11.

06030   Bassett, J.E., Gayton, W.F., Blanchard, E.B., and Ozmon, K.L. Birth order and perceptual motor performance. <u>Perceptual and Motor Skills</u>, December 1977, 45(3, part 2), 1076-1078. Topic Codes: BL48,BP07,DT59,MR,MT48,NL, PE48,PR,PS,SJ05,SJ07,TA59D.

06060   Bastiaans, J., and Van der Ploeg, H.M. Control and regulation of aggression. <u>Psychotherapy and Psychosomatics</u>, 1978, 29(1-4), 40-48. Topic Codes: CG11P,SR03.

06090   Bateman, B.D. Educational implications of minimal brain dysfunction.
        Reading Teacher, April 1974, 27(7), 662-668. Topic Codes: BK11B,BL11,
        DD00,DD02,DK48B,DT44,MG48,MH,MM,PE10,PE64,PG,PI,PP,SC70.

06100   Bates, J.E., Bentler, P.M., and Thompson, S.K. Measurement of deviant
        gender development in boys. Child Development, 1973, 44, 591-598. Topic
        Codes: BL04,BL11,MG,NA07D,NA07I,PG,TA57.

06200   Bauer, G.E. and Clark, J.A. Personality deviancy and prison incarcera-
        tion. Journal of Clinical Psychology, April 1976, 32(2), 279-283. Topic
        Codes: CC11C,CC11U,CC67B,MS02,TB61B.

06230   Baughman, E.E., and Dahlstrom, W.G. Negro and White Children: A Psycho-
        logical Study in the Rural South. New York: Academic Press, 1968. Topic
        Codes: NA07B,NA07I,NL,PA,PE10,PG,PM,SB,SC18,SC59,SC70,SF26,SH59,SI57,SJ,
        SN,SS,SW16,SW18,SW33,SW56,TA04,TA57,TA74,TB61,TB78,TB95.

06260   Bayley, N. Behavioral correlates of mental growth: Birth to thirty-six
        years. American Psychologist, 1968, 23(1), 1-17. Topic Codes: BL31,
        BL52,BL70,DD,NA44H,PE10,PE32,PG,PK,PM70,PN,PT74,SB,SQ,SU,TA52K,TA59D,TB05,
        TB93,TB95.

06300   Bayley, N. Consistency and variability in the growth of intelligence from
        birth to eighteen years. Journal of Genetic Psychology, 1949, 75, 165-
        196. Topic Codes: BL04,BL11,NA07I,PG,PM,TA59D,TB42,TB78,TB95.

06350   Bayley, N., and Schaefer, E.S. Correlations of maternal and child behav-
        iors with the development of mental abilities: Data from the Berkeley
        Growth Study. Monographs of the Society for Research in Child Develop-
        ment, 1964, 29(6, serial no. 97). Topic Codes: BI,BL11,BL31,BL48,BL70,
        BN04,DT13,MH,NA07B,NA07ID,NA31F,NA44F,NH11,NH59PF,NJ,PE10,PE32,PG,PI,PK,
        PM,PY,SH59RF,SI48,SQ,SW,TA04,TA52K,TA55,TA59D,TA80,TB78.

06370   Beaumont, Y.G., and Dimond, S.Y. Interhemispheric transfer of figural
        information in right- and low-right-handed subjects. Acta Psychologica,
        1975, 39, 97-104. Topic Codes. BK11B,BN44,DT59,NA,NL,PO,PS,TA55,TB81.

06400   Beck, S.J., and Ollendick, T.H. Personal space, sex of experimenter, and
        locus of control in normal and delinquent adolescents. Psychological Re-
        ports, 1976, 38, 383-387. Topic Codes: CC37W,PM,SW.

06500   Becker, G. Visual acuity, birth order, achievement versus affiliation,
        and other Edwards Personal Preference Schedule scores. Journal of Psycho-
        somatic Research, 1965, 9, 277-283. Topic Codes: DD81,PT,SJ07,TA59.

06600   Beckwith, L. Relationships between infants' social behavior and their
        mothers' behavior. Child Development, 1972, 43, 397-411. Topic Codes:
        BL70,MX,NA31D,NH04,PE32,PE68,SH04,SI48,SQ,SR,SW,TB25.

06700   Bee, H.L., Van Egeren, L.F., Streissguth, A.P., Nyman, B.A., and Leckie,
        M.S. Social class differences in maternal teaching strategies and speech
        patterns. Developmental Psychology, 1969, 1, 726-734. Topic Codes:
        BL11,DT13,MH,NA07I,NL48,PG,PI,SI48,SW.

06800   Begun, J.H. The sociopathic or psychopathic personality. International
        Journal of Social Psychology, Spring 1976, 22(1), 25-46. Topic Codes:
        CG,CV06C,CV13D,MS04,MS04B,NH59PJ,SH59RJ.

06880   Behrman, R.E. Differences in WISC Verbal-Performance categories and read-
        ing achievement among black, urban school children [doctoral dissertation,
        Northern Illinois University, 1980]. Dissertation Abstracts Internation-
        al, October 1981, 42(4), 1541A. Topic Codes: BL11,BL70,NL07,PE64,PM,TB95.

06900   Behrman, R.E., Babson, G.S., and Lessel, R. Fetal and neonatal mortality
        in white middle class infants. American Journal of Diseases of Children,
        June 1971, 121, 486-489. Topic Codes: BL06,BL27,BP26,DF34,DF48,DP48,
        NA33B.

07000   Beintema, D.J. A Neurological Study of Newborn Infants. London: Spas-
         tics International Medical Publications, 1968. Topic Codes: BD30,BL06,
         BL33,BL48,BL70,BP,BP04,BP44,BP46,BP47,BP53,BP57,BP61,DF34,DP,DP22H,DP44,
         DP58,DP60,DP81,DT08,DT48,MT48,MX,NA33,NA33B,NA33D,NA33F,NA33I,PE34,PE48,
         PE68,PL,PR,SQ,SR,TA52M,TB02.

07030   Beiser, M. A psychiatric follow-up study of "normal" adults. American
         Journal of Psychiatry, May 1971, 127(11), 1464-1472. Topic Codes: BL70,
         DD00,DD02B,MF,NA,NL48B,PA,PE,SQ,TA02,TA59.

07050   Beitchman, J., Bell, K., and Simeon, S. Types of disorders and demo-
         graphic variables in a Canadian child psychiatry population. Canadian
         Psychiatric Association Journal, March 1978, 23(2), 91-96. Topic Codes:
         NA07,PE,SA07,SQ07,SW07.

07200   Bell, R.Q. A reinterpretation of the "direction of effects in studies of
         socialization." Psychological Review, March 1968, 75(2), 81-95. Topic
         Codes: BI,BL11,BL70,CC37L,MG30,NA07I,NH74,PG,PY,SH74,SI57,SI57P,SQ,SU.

07230   Bellak, L. A possible subgroup of the schizophrenic syndrome and implica-
         tions for treatment. American Journal of Psychotherapy, April 1976, 30
         (2), 194-205. Topic Codes: BD07,BI,BK11B,BN,DD00,DD02B,DK07B,DK48B,MF,
         MG02,MG30B,MG48B,MU70,PA,PE,S.

07250   Belmont, L., and Birch, H.G. Lateral dominance, lateral awareness and
         reading disability. Child Development, 1965, 36, 57-71. Topic Codes:
         BK11B,BL11,BN44,BN68,DT44,MM,NA07B,NA07I,PE64,PG,PO,PP,TA04,TB93,TB95.

07300   Belmont, L., and Marolla, F.A. Birth order, family size and intelligence.
         Science, 1973, 182, 1096-1101. Topic Codes: PM,SJ07,SJ22.

07350   Benbow, C.P., and Stanley, J.C. Sex differences in mathematical ability:
         Fact or artifact? Science, 1980, 210(12), 1262-1264. Topic Codes: BI,
         BL70,DT44,MM,NA,PE64,PM70,SB,SQ,SU,TA04,TA80.

07400   Bender, L. Children and adolescents who have killed. American Journal
         of Psychiatry, December 1959, 116, 510-513. Topic Codes: CC37B,CC37E,
         CC37I,CC37K,CC37L,DT15,MG,MG02,MG02D,MG11B,ML15,NA07D,NA07DB,NH65.

07450   Bender, L. Psychopathic personality or schizophrenia in adolescence.
         Biological Psychiatry, 1971, 3(3), 197-204. Topic Codes: CC37B,DP,MG,
         MG02B,MG02D,MG04GB,MS04,MU70,NA07D,NH65B,PM,SF07,SJ09B,SW07.

07455   Benezech, M., and Bourgeois, M. Medico-psycho-social syndrome of poly-
         gonosomies (XXX, XXY, XYY syndromes). Encephale, 1976, 2(4), 305-315.
         Topic Codes: BB07,BB11,BB70B,BE07,BE11,BI07B,BI11,BK11,CC11E,CC11F,CC11M,
         CC11O,CC11T,DD02KD,DD02ND,DK07D,DK18,DK48,ME,N,PE08,TA52,TA55,TB35.

07460   Benezech, M., Bourgeois, M., and Noel, B. XYY men: Psychiatric and
         criminologic aspects. Annales Medico-Psychologiques, October 1974, 2(3),
         365-394. Topic Codes: BB70B,BB70D,CC11M,DD02ND,DD02NF.

07465   Benjamins, J.K. Learning disabilities among adolescents: An annotated
         literature review (1962-1973). Catalog of Selected Documents in Psychol-
         ogy, February 1977, 7, 17. Topic Codes: DT13,DT15,DT44,MH,ML15,MM,NA,
         NL,PI,PM,PP,SC70,TA04,TA55,TA59D,TA80.

07470   Benson, R.C., Shubeck, F., Deutschberger, J., Weiss, W., and Berendes, H.
         Fetal heart rate as a predictor of fetal distress. Obstetrics and Gyne-
         cology, August 1968, 32, 259-266. Topic Codes: BB,BE,BL06,BL07B,BL22,
         BL29,BP22F,BP44,DF06B,DP44,NA31C,NA33F,NC44,NL48,PE32,PE34,PK,PL,TA52K,
         TA52M,TA80,TB02.

07500   Benton, A.L. Minimal brain dysfunction from a neuropsychological point of
         view. New York Academy of Sciences - Annals, 1973, 205(29), 29-37. Topic
         Codes: BL48B,DK07B,DK46,DK48,DT06,DT48B,MG,MG11,MG30,MG48,ML04,MO,MT48B,
         NA07D,PE48B,PM,PR07,TB02,TB95B.

07530   Berendes, H.W. Birth asphyxia and neurologic deficit: Report from the
         NINDB Collaborative Perinatal Study. In L.S. James, R.E. Myers, and G.E.
         Gaull (eds.), Brain Damage in the Fetus and Newborn from Hypoxia or
         Asphyxia. Report of the 57th Ross Conference on Pediatric Research.
         Columbus: Ross Laboratories, 1967. Topic Codes: BP02,DF34,DK,DT04E,
         NA33B,NC44.

07540   Berendes, H.W. Fetal distress: Its significance in neurological and men-
         tal impairment of childhood. Perinatal Factors Affecting Human Develop-
         ment. Proceedings of the special session held during the eighth meeting
         of the PAHO (Pan American Health Organization) Advisory Committee on Medi-
         cal Research, 1969, scientific publication no. 185, 228-238. Topic Codes:
         BL04B,BL07BB,BL22,BL27KL,BL52DB,BP02B,BP22F,BP26GD,BP44,BP47,BP53,BP59,
         DD02B,DD08K,DF06BB,DF34,DF70B,DK07B,DK09B,DK46,DP11B,DP44,DP46,DT13B,
         DT44B,DT52B,MH07,MM07,MO07,NA44D,NC70,NJ06,NL48,PI,PK,PM,PP07,SW07,TA55,
         TA59D,TB78,TB95.

07560   Berendes, H.W. Neurological sequelae of perinatal complications. Pro-
         ceedings of the Thirteenth International Congress of Pediatrics, 1972, 3,
         631-637. Topic Codes: DK,DP11.

07570   Berendes, H.W. Obstetrical complications and mental deficiency. Pro-
         ceedings of the International Copenhagen Congress on the Scientific Study
         of Mental Retardation, 1964, 306-316. Topic Codes: BL04B,BL07BB,BL22,
         BL27KL,BL52DB,BP02B,BP22F,BP26GD,BP44,BP47,BP53,BP59,DD02B,DD08K,DF06BB,
         DF34,DF70B,DK07B,DK09B,DK46,DP11B,DP44,DP46,DT13B,DT44B,DT52B,MH07,MM07,
         MO07,NA44D,NC70,NJ06,NL48,PI,PK,PM,PP07,SW07,TA55,TA59D,TB78,TB95.

07600   Berg, N.L. Self-concept of neurotic and sociopathic criminal offenders.
         Psychological Reports, 1974, 34, 622. Topic Codes: CC11C,CC11P,CC11U,
         MQ11,MS04B,PT11,TB61B.

07700   Berger, E., and Berger-Margulies, J. Frequency of minor nervous dysfunc-
         tion in school children. Journal of Neurology, 1978, 219, 205-212. Topic
         Codes: BL48,DK48,DT44B,DT48,DT52,MG30,MG48,MM07,MT48,PE48,PE64B,PP07,PR,
         SC70B,SW07.

07750   Bergman, R.E. The Sociopath: Selections in Anti-Social Behavior. Jeri-
         cho, New York: Exposition Press, 1968. Topic Codes: MS04B.

07800   Bergstrom, K., and Bille, B. Computed tomography of the brain in children
         with minimal brain damage: A preliminary study of 46 children. Neuro-
         padiatrie, 1978, 9(4), 378-384. Topic Codes: BL70,DK07,DK48,DT52,MG48,
         SQ,TB96.

07900   Berkowitz, L. Some determinants of impulsive aggression: Role of media-
         ted associations with reinforcements for aggression. Psychological Re-
         view, March 1974, 81(2), 165-176. Topic Codes: CT57F,CX,MC11,MK11,NE79,
         PE04D,PE30D,SF11,SR03B.

08000   Berkowitz, L., and Frodi, A. Stimulus characteristics that can enhance or
         decrease aggression: Associations with prior positive or negative rein-
         forcements for aggression. Aggressive Behavior, 1977, 3, 1-15. Topic
         Codes: MC11,MK,PE04D,PE30,PT74,SI57J,SR03B.

08030   Berkson, G. Abnormal stereotyped motor acts. Proceedings of the Ameri-
         can Psychopathological Association, 1967, 55, 76-94. Topic Codes: BL48,
         BL48B,DT48,DT48B,MT48,MT48B,PE48,PE48B,PR,PRO7.

08100   Berman, A., and Siegal, A.W. Adaptive and learning skills in juvenile de-
         linquents: A neuropsychological analysis. Journal of Learning Disabili-
         ties, 1976, 9(9), 583-590. Topic Codes: CC37B,CC37F,CC37H,CC37S,CC37I,
         MG11B,TB46B,TB87C,TB93D,TB96D.

08150   Berndt, T.J. The effect of reciprocity in aggressive and prosocial inter-
         actions on moral judgment and causal attributions [doctoral dissertation,
         University of Minnesota, 1975]. Dissertation Abstracts International,
         July 1976, 37(1), 517B-518B. Topic Codes: NA07B,PE04,PE10,PE68,SR,TA.

08200   Bernstein, J.E., Page, J.G., and Janicki, R.S. Some characteristics of
         children with minimal brain dysfunction. In C.K. Conners (ed.), Clinical
         Use of Stimulant Drugs in Children. Amsterdam: Excerpta Medica, 1974.
         Topic Codes: BE,BL04,BL06,BL07,BL11,BL31,BN44,BP04,BP07B,BP47,BP89,DF,
         DF06,DK48,DK48B,DP,DP81,DT04E,DT42,MG,MG30,MG48,MG48B,ML,NA07D,NA07I,
         NA31C,NA31F,NH59GG,NH59PJ,NH65,NH65B,NL48,PE44,PG,PK,PN,PO,SH59JJ,SH59RJ,
         SJ05B,SJ07.

08300   Bernstein, R., and Corsini, R.J. Wechsler-Bellevue patterns of female de-
         linquents. Journal of Clinical Psychology, 1953, 9, 176-179. Topic
         Codes: BL04,CC371,MS04B,NL22,PM,TB93D,TB96BB,TB96D.

08400   Beumont, P.J.V. The endocrinology of psychiatry. In K. Granville-
         Grossman (ed.), Recent Advances in Clinical Psychiatry (no. 3). New
         York: Churchill Livingstone, 1979. Topic Codes: BD07,BD70,BK,BK11B,
         BL70B,BN04,BP02B,CV15B,DD15,DK07B,MB,MQ,MU,MU70,PC,SQ07.

08450   Bierer, J. Can psychopathic behavior be changed? International Journal
         of Social Psychiatry, 1977, 23(4), 291-303. Topic Codes: CC11C,CV06C,
         DD02D,ME,MS04,NL,PE08.

08500   Biles, D. Birth order and delinquency. Australian Psychologist, Novem-
         ber 1971, 6(3), 189-193. Topic Codes: CC37L,SJ22D.

08600   Billak, R.J. An analysis of the effects of various lengths of incarcera-
         tion on various types of offenders as measured by anxiety, hypomania, and
         criminality scales [doctoral dissertation, Kent State University, 1976].
         Dissertation Abstracts International, June 1977, 37(12, part 1), 7538A-
         7539A. Topic Codes: CC11C,CC11P,CC11U,CV13D,MG11.

08700   Billingslea, F.Y. The Bender Gestalt: A review and a perspective. Psy-
         chological Bulletin, 1963, 60(3), 233-251. Topic Codes: DK07,PM,PT,
         TB09,TB09B,TB09K.

08730   Bilmes, M. The delinquent's escape from conscience. American Journal of
         Psychotherapy, October 1965, 19(4), 633-640. Topic Codes: CC37B,CC37H,
         CC37M,CQ37,DT13D,DT59D,MH11,MQ11,MX11,NE37,NH59F,PE10,PI07,PS11,SH59H,
         SR02.

08750   Bingley, T. Mental symptoms in temporal lobe epilepsy and temporal lobe
         gliomas with special reference to laterality of lesion and the relation-
         ship between handedness and brainedness. Acta Psychiatrica et Neurologi-
         ca, 1958, 33, supplement 120. Topic Codes: BN44B,DK07B,DK18SB,PO07.

08800   Birch, H. (ed.). Brain Damage in Children: The Biological and Social
         Aspects. New York: The Williams & Wilkins Co., 1964. Topic Codes:
         BK11B,BL11,DD26BB,DD26D,DK07BB,DK07D,MG02B,NA07D,NA07I,PE10,PG,SF,SH,TA80.

08900   Birch, H., Thomas, A., and Chess, S. Behavioral development in brain-
         damaged children. Archives of General Psychiatry, December 1964, 11, 596-
         603. Topic Codes: BL11,BL48,DK07,DT13,DT42,DT48,MG,MG30,MH,MK,ML,MT48,
         NA07D,NA07I,NA44D,NJ06,PE30,PE44,PE48,PG,PI,PN,PR,PT74,SI57,TB02,TB42,
         TB78,TB95.

09000   Birdsall, N. An economic approach to birth-order effects (Economic Growth
         Center, discussion paper 313). Unpublished manuscript, Yale University,
         May 1979. Topic Codes: BL04,BL11,NA07I,NH59PF,PG,SC18,SH59RF,SI48,SJ07,
         SJ22,SW.

09100   Birkett, P. Measures of laterality and theories of hemispheric processes.
         Neuropsychologia, 1977, 15, 693-696. Topic Codes: BN44,PO,TB81.

09200   Birns, B. The emergence and socialization of sex differences in the ear-
         liest years. Merrill-Palmer Quarterly of Behavior and Development, 1976,
         22(3), 229-254. Topic Codes: BD,BI,BL70,DT13,MC,MH,NA07B,NA31D,NA33D,
         NC44,PE04,PE10,PE32,PE34,PI,PT,PY,SF,SI22,SI57,SI57P,SQ,SR03,SU.

09230   Birns, B., and Golden, M. Prediction of intellectual performance at 3 years from infant tests and personality measures. <u>Merrill-Palmer Quarter-</u><u>ly of Behavior and Development</u>, 1972, 18(1), 53-58. Topic Codes: BL31, BL48,MH,ML,MM,NA31D,NA31F,NA44,PK,TB25,TB78.

09250   Bischof, N. A systems approach toward the functional connections of at-tachment and fear. <u>Child Development</u>, December 1975, 46(4), 801-817. Topic Codes: BL11,BN04,MM,PA,PE10,PG,PI,PK,PL,PP,SF,SH,SI46B,SI48B,SI57P, SR,SU.

09300   Bishop, D.V.M. Comment on "Registered Criminality in Families with Chil-dren at High Risk for Schizophrenia." <u>Journal of Abnormal Psychology</u>, 1976, 85(2), 240-242. Topic Codes: CC37M,MU70B,NH59GD,NH59PD,NH67, SH59JD,SH59RD,SI59.

09350   Bishop, E.H., Israel, S.L., and Briscoe, C.C. Obstetric influences on the premature infant's first year of development: A report from the Collabo-rative Study of Cerebral Palsy. <u>Obstetrics and Gynecology</u>, November 1965, 26, 628-635. Topic Codes: BB48B,BB48D,BD07,BE07,BL07BB,BP02B,BP44,BP46, BP53,BP57,DD02,DD08K,DF06BB,DF34,DF48,DF60BB,DP11B,DP44,DP46,DP81,MG,NC44, NL48B,PG,PK,PL,TA02,TA52K,TA52M,TA80.

09370   Black, F.W. Cognitive, academic, and behavioral findings in children with suspected and documented neurological dysfunction. <u>Journal of Learning</u> <u>Disabilities</u>, March 1976, 9(3), 182-187. Topic Codes: BB07,BK11B,BL11, DD00,DD02B,DK07B,DK11B,DK18B,DK48B,MG48B,MH07,MM07,NA07DD,NL48B,PG,PI,PM, PP07,TA02,TA04,TA55,TA59D,TB35B,TB95B,TB98B.

09400   Black, F.W. WISC verbal-performance discrepancies as indicators of neuro-logical dysfunction in pediatric patients. <u>Journal of Clinical Psychol-</u><u>ogy</u>, 1974, 30, 165-167. Topic Codes: BL04,BL48B,DP11B,DT48B,DT59B,MG30, MR07,MT48B,PE48B,PM,PR07,PS07,TB35B,TB95B,TB96B,TB98.

09500   Black, W.A.M., and Hornblow, A.R. Intelligence and criminality. <u>Austra-</u><u>lian and New Zealand Journal of Criminology</u>, 1973, 6, 83-92. Topic Codes: BL67,BL67D,CC37Q,CC371,CT57F,DK46D,MG11,MO11,MS04B,PM11,SC18D,SF11,SN, SN11,TB72B,TB78D,TB93D,TB96B,TB96BB,TB96D.

09600   Blackburn, R. Aggression and the EEG: A quantitative analysis. <u>Journal</u> <u>of Abnormal Psychology</u>, 1975, 84(4), 358-365. Topic Codes: BL04,BN04D, MC11,MS02,MV11,PC11,PE04D,PM,SR03B,TB35D,TB93D.

09700   Blackburn, R. Cortical and autonomic arousal in primary and secondary psychopaths. <u>Psychophysiology</u>, 1979, 16(2), 143-150. Topic Codes: BK04BB,BL08BD,BL25BB,BN04BB,DD28D,MS04B,MX11,PC07B,PE68D,SR02,TA02B,TA04, TA59,TB35BB,TB61B.

09800   Blackburn, R. An empirical classification of psychopathic personality. <u>British Journal of Psychiatry</u>, 1975, 127, 456-460. Topic Codes: MC11, MK11,MS04B,PE04D,PE30D,SR03B,TB61B,TB93D.

09850   Blain, D. Avoidance-learning deficits in criminal offenders [doctoral dissertation, McGill University (Canada), 1973]. <u>Dissertation Abstracts</u> <u>International</u>, July 1974, 35(1), 494B-495B. (Copies available from the National Library of Canada at Ottawa.) Topic Codes: BN04D,CC11C,CC11D, CC81,CE,CV06C,CV13,CV15D,DT44BB,DT44D,MM07B,MM11,NE59,NE81,NL,PP07B,TA59D, TA80,TB.

09870   Blair, D. Medicolegal implications of the terms "psychopath," "psycho-pathic personality" and "psychopathic disorder" (part 2). <u>Medicine, Sci-</u><u>ence and the Law</u>, April 1975, 15(2), 110-123. Topic Codes: M,MF,SF07B, SL.

09900   Blake, A., Stewart, A., and Turcan, D. Parents of babies of very low birth weight: Long term follow-up. <u>CIBA Foundation Symposium</u>, 1975, 33, 271-288. Topic Codes: BL07BB,DF06BB,NA44D,NH59P,NJ06,SH59R,SI48,SI57, TA04,TA59,TB09K,TB78,TB95.

09910   Blanchard, J.B., and Mannarino, F. Academic, perceptual, and visual levels of detained juveniles. In L.J. Hippchen (ed.), Ecologic-Biochemical Approaches to Treatment of Delinquents and Criminals. New York: Van Nostrand Reinhold Company, 1978, 341-351. Topic Codes: CC371,DD81D, DT59D,MR11,NE37,PS11,TA80,TB98D.

09930   Bleicher, S.J. Hypoglycemia. In M. Ellenberg and H. Rifkin (eds.), Diabetes Mellitus: Theory and Practice. New York: McGraw-Hill, 1970, 958-989. Topic Codes: BD30D,BD30HB,BD52B,BK04B,BK11,BL04,BL07B,BL27KL, BL33,BL52D,BP52,DD15,DD30B,DF06B,DF34,DK09B,NA33A,PL,TA52,TA52M.

09960   Bleuler, M. The offspring of schizophrenics. Schizophrenia Bulletin, Spring 1974, 8, 93-107. Topic Codes: BB07,BI07B,BL11,BL70BB,DD00B,ME,MF, MG02,MH,MS04,NH04,NH59B,NH59E,NH59F,NH59GB,NH59GG,NH59PB,NH59PH,NH63B, NH65B,NH70B,NL22B,PA,PE08,SH04BB,SH59D,SH59F,SH59JB,SH59R,SH59RB,SH70B, SI07,SJ09B.

09990   Block, W.M. Cerebral dysfunctions: An attempt at clarification. Behavioral Neuropsychiatry, 1974-1975, 6, 3-5. Topic Codes: BK11B,BL52D,DD26, DK07,DK09,DT13,MH,PI,PM.

09995   Bloom, B.S. Stability and Change in Human Characteristics. New York: John Wiley & Sons, Inc., 1964. Topic Codes: BD52B,BD70K,BE30C,BI,BL04, BL05,BL06,BL11,BL70B,DT13,DT44,DT59,MC,MH,MM,MR,MS,NA07I,NA44H,NH70,NH74, NJ12,NL,PE04,PE64,PE68B,PG,PI,PM,PP,PS,PT,SC70,SF07,SH70,SH74,SQ,SR03,SW, TA04,TA59D,TA80,TB55.

10000   Bloom, R., and Entin, A.D. Intellectual functioning and psychopathology: A canonical analysis of WAIS and MMPI relationships. Journal of Clinical Psychology, October 1975, 31(4), 697-698. Topic Codes: NL48,PM07,TB61, TB93.

10100   Blum, R.H. Toward a developmental approach in criminology: Clues from drug studies. Unpublished manuscript, n.p., n.d. Topic Codes: BL04B, BL11C,CC11H,CC37I,CC67,CG,CQ67,CT57,CT59,DA04D,DA15D,DD00,MD11,MG02B,MI07, NA07ID,NA44P,NE67,NH65B,NH67,NJ23,PE06D,PE15D,PE64B,PG11,SC70B,SF07,SI57B, SW.

10130   Blythe, P. Minimal brain dysfunction and the treatment of psychoneuroses. Journal of Psychosomatic Research, 1978, 22(4), 247-255. Topic Codes: BK11B,BL11,CC11F,DD02B,DD02D,DK07B,DK07D,DK48B,DK48D,DT44B,DT44D,DT48B, DT48D,DT52B,DT52D,DT59,MF11,MG02B,MG48B,MG48D,MM07,MM11,MT48B,MT48D,PE10, PE48B,PE48D,PG11,PP,TB35B,TB35D.

10190   Bobbitt, R.G. An interaction of anxiety and aggressive habit strength on aggressive behaviors [doctoral dissertation, Florida State University, 1974]. Dissertation Abstracts International, February 1975, 35(8), 4159B-4160B. Topic Codes: BL08BD,BL25B,BL25D,CC11U,NE59,TA80,TB.

10200   Bock, R.D., and Kolakowski, D. Further evidence of sex-linked major-gene influence on human spatial visualizing ability. American Journal of Human Genetics, 1973, 25, 1-14. Topic Codes: BD,BI,BL11,BL70,BN44,DT13,DT46, MH,MN,NA07I,NH59,PG,PI,PM,PO,PQ,SF,SH59,SQ,SW,TA59D,TB15,TB68.

10230   Boelkins, R.C., and Heiser, J.F. Biological bases of aggression. In D.N. Daniels, M.F. Gilula, and F.M. Ochberg (eds.), Violence and the Struggle for Existence. Boston: Little, Brown, 1970, 15-52. Topic Codes: BD70B, BK11B,CC81,MC,PE04,SF26D,SR03.

10300   Bogen, J.E. The other side of the brain: I. Dysgraphia and dyscopia following cerebral commissurotomy. Bulletin of the Los Angeles Neurological Societies, April 1969, 34(2), 73-105. Topic Codes: BK11B,BL04, BL52D,BN44B,DD00,DD02B,DD26B,DF60BB,DK07B,DK18B,DT42,DT48,DT67,DT71,ML02, ML04,N,PE44B,PE48B,PO07,PRO7,TA02,TA52,TA55,TA59,TA80,TB49.

10450   Bogen, J.E. Some questions, assumptions and problems involved in associating dyssocial behavior with disorders of cerebral function. In W.L. Smith and A. Kling (eds.), Issues in Brain/Behavior Control. New York: Spectrum, 1976. Topic Codes: DK07D,ME,MX,PE08,PE68,SR04.

10500   Bogen, J.E., and Bogen, G.M. The other side of the brain: III. The cor-
        pus callosum and creativity. Bulletin of the Los Angeles Neurological
        Societies, October 1969, 34(4), 191-220. Topic Codes: BK11B,BL52DB,
        BN44B,DD02B,DD26B,DK07B,MH07,MT48,PE44B,PE48B,PE70D,PI07,P007,TA02,TA52,
        TA55,TA80.

10600   Bogen, J.E., Dezure, R., Tenhouten, W.D., and Marsh, J.F. The other side
        of the brain: IV. The A/P ratio. Bulletin of the Los Angeles Neurologi-
        cal Societies, April 1972, 37(2), 49-61. Topic Codes: BK11B,BL52DB,
        BN44B,DD02B,DD26B,MH07,MT48B,PE44B,PE48B,PE70D,PI07,P007,TA02,TA52,TA55,
        TA80.

10650   Boggs, T.R., Hardy, J.B., and Frazier, T.M. Correlation of neonatal serum
        total bilirubin concentrations and developmental status at age eight
        months. Journal of Pediatrics, October 1967, 71, 553-560. Topic Codes:
        BD30BA,BL33,BL48,DD00,DD02B,DF34,NC44,PK,PL,PR,TA02,TA52K,TA52M,TA80,TB05.

10660   Bohannan, P. Patterns of homicide among tribal societies in Africa. In
        M.E. Wolfgang (ed.), Studies in Homicide. New York: Harper & Row, 1967,
        211-237. Topic Codes: CC81,CT57F,NL07D,SN11,SQ11.

10670   Bohman, M. Some genetic aspects of alcoholism and criminality: A popula-
        tion of adoptees. Irish General Psychiatry, March 1978, 35(3), 269-276.
        Topic Codes: BI07,BI11,CC11H,CC11M,DA04D,MD11,PE06D.

10680   Bohman, M., Cloninger, C.R., Sigvardsson S., and von Knorring, A.L. Pre-
        disposition to petty criminality in Swedish adoptees: I. Genetic and
        environmental heterogeneity. Archives of General Psychiatry, November
        1982, 39(11), 1233-1241. Topic Codes: BI11,CC11H,CC11M,CT59,DA04D,MD11,
        NH04D,NH59D,NH59F,PE06D,SH04D,SH59D,SH59H.

10700   Boklage, C.E. The sinistral blastocyst: An embryologic perspective on
        the development of brain-function asymmetries. In J. Herman (ed.), The
        Neuropsychology of Left-Handedness. New York: Academic Press, 1980.
        Topic Codes: BI07,BL22,BN44,BN44B,BP22F,MB,MU70,NH04,NH65,NH74B,PO,P007,
        SH04,SH74B.

10800   Boll, T.J. Psychological differentiation of patients with schizophrenia
        versus lateralized cerebrovascular, neoplastic, or traumatic brain damage.
        Journal of Abnormal Psychology, 1974, 83(4), 456-458. Topic Codes: BL04,
        DK07B,MU70,NH74B,PM,SH74B,TA80,TB87.

10830   Bolman, W.M. Aggression and violence in children. Current Problems in
        Pediatrics, July 1974, 4(9), 1-32. Topic Codes: CC81F,NA07B,PG11,SH11,
        SI11,SI57.

10890   Bolton, F.G., Reich, J.W., and Gutierrez, S.E. Delinquency patterns in
        maltreated children and siblings. Victimology, Summer 1977, 2(2), 349-
        357. Topic Codes: CC37B,CC37M,CQ37,CT57BD,CX,DD10D,NE37,NE79,NH59F,
        NH59GD,NH59GI,NH70D,PE68D,SH11,SH59JD,SH59JL,SH59RL,SH70D,SI22D,SI48D,
        SI57GD.

10900   Boone, S.L. Language, cognition, and social factors in the regulation of
        aggressive behavior: A study of black, Puerto Rican, and white children
        [doctoral dissertation, Rutgers University - The State University of New
        Jersey, 1975]. Dissertation Abstracts International, January 1976, 36(7),
        4338A. Topic Codes: BL04,BL11,BL70,MC,MV,MX,NA07B,NA07I,PE04,PE10,PE66,
        PE68,PG,SQ,SR,SR03,SR69,TA59.

11000   Boone, S.L., and Montare, A. Test of the language-aggression hypothesis.
        Psychological Reports, 1976, 39, 851-857. Topic Codes: BL67,DT13,DT42,
        MC,MH,ML,NA07B,PE04,PE10,PE44,PE64,PI,PN,SC70,SN,SR03,SW,TA04,TB95.

11100   Booner, B.E. Aggression in children: Developmental and functional as-
        pects [doctoral dissertation, Boston University School of Education,
        1976]. Dissertation Abstracts International, September 1976, 37(3),
        1463A-1464A. Topic Codes: BL04,BL67,DT42,MC,ML,NA07B,PE04,PE10,PE44,PN,
        SN,SR03,SW,TA04,TB95.

11150   Borgaonkar, D.S., and Shah, S.A. The XYY chromosome male or syndrome.
         Progress in Medical Genetics, 1974, 10, 135-222. Topic Codes: BB70D,BE,
         CQ59,CV13DA,DD02NF,NE59.

11200   Borgstedt, A.D., and Rosen, M.G. Medication during labor correlated with
         behavior and EEG of the newborn. American Journal of Diseases of Chil-
         dren, 1968, 115, 21-24. Topic Codes: BN04,BP04,DK09,NA33D,NA33I,NL48,PC,
         PE34,TA52M,TB02,TB35.

11300   Borkovec, T.D. Autonomic reactivity to sensory stimulation in psycho-
         pathic, neurotic, and normal juvenile delinquents. Journal of Consulting
         and Clinical Psychology, 1970, 35(2), 217-222. Topic Codes: BL25BB,
         BN04BB,CC37B,CC37T,CC371,MC11,MG,MK11,MS04B,NA07D,PC07B,PE04D,PE30D,SR03B,
         TA04.

11400   Borriello, J.F. Patients with acting-out character disorders. American
         Journal of Psychotherapy, January 1973, 27(1), 4-14. Topic Codes: CC11C,
         CV06C,MS04B.

11450   Bouma, H., Legein, C.P., and Van Rens, A.L. Visual recognition by dys-
         lexic children: Further exploration of letter, word and number recogni-
         tion in 4 weak and 4 normal readers. IPO Annual Progress Report, 1975,
         no. 10, 72-78. Topic Codes: DD81,DT15,MG,ML15,NA07D,TA02,TA59D.

11500   Bower, T.G.R. The visual world of infants. Scientific American, December
         1966, 215(6), 80-92. Topic Codes: DD81,NA31D,PE32.

11600   Bowker, L.H. The incidence of female crime and delinquency: A comparison
         of official and self-report statistics. International Journal of Women's
         Studies, 1978, 1(3), 178-192. Topic Codes: BL70,BL70D,CC11,CC24,CC37,
         CC67,CC81V,CG,CG11P,CQ11,CQ22,CQ37,CQ67,CT57F,CT59,NE11,NE22,NE37,NE67,
         NL22,SQ,SQ11.

11700   Bowker, L.H. Menstruation and female criminality: A new look at the
         data. Paper presented at the annual meeting of the American Society of
         Criminology, Dallas, November 1978. Topic Codes: BL70D,CC11D,CC11S,CC24,
         CQ22,MC,NE22,PE04,PT74B,SQ11,SR03.

11750   Bowlby, J. Effects on behavior of disruption of an affectional bond.
         Eugenics Society Symposium, 1968, 4, 94-108. Topic Codes: MF,PE.

11800   Boyatzis, R.E. Alcohol and interpersonal aggression. Advances in Experi-
         mental Medicine and Biology, 1977, 85B, 345-375. Topic Codes: BD11,
         BD70B,BK11,BL48D,BL70D,BN04D,CC11H,CC81B,CX,DA04D,DT48D,MC,MC11,MD11,
         MT48D,MX11,NE79,PC11,PE04,PE04D,PE06D,PE48D,PE68D,PR11,PY11,SF11,SI57PB,
         SQ11,SR02,SR03,SR03B,SU11,SW,TA59.

11850   Boyle, A.M., and Whitlock, F.A. Genetics, drug dependence and schizophre-
         nia. Australian and New Zealand Journal of Psychiatry, June 1976, 10(2),
         169-171. Topic Codes: BI07,DA15,MI,MU70,PE15.

11900   Brackbill, Y. Long term effects of obstetrical anesthesia on infant auto-
         nomic function. Developmental Psychobiology, 1977, 10(6), 529-535. Topic
         Codes: BK04,BP04,NA31R,NC44,TA04,TA52K.

12000   Brackbill, Y., and Broman, S.H. Obstetrical medication and development
         in the first year of life. Unpublished manuscript, n.p., January 15,
         1979. Topic Codes: BD30,BD30B,BL06,BL31,BL48,BL70,BP02,BP04,BP44,BP53,
         DK09,DT48,MT48,NA31F,NA31R,NC44,PE48,PK,PR,SQ,SW,TA52K,TB02,TB05.

12100   Brackbill, Y., Kane, J., Manniello, R.L., and Abramson, D. Obstetric pre-
         medication and infant outcome. American Journal of Obstetrics and Gyne-
         cology, 1974, 118, 377-384. Topic Codes: BP02,BP04,DP11B,NA33D,NA33I,
         PE34,TA52M,TB02.

12150   Bradford, J.M., and McLean, D. Sexual offenders, violence, and testoster-
         one: A clinical study. Canadian Journal of Psychiatry, June 1984, 29
         (4), 335-343. Topic Codes: BD70B,CC81B,CC81E,CT68,DA04D,MD11,PE06D.

12200   Bradley, C. Characteristics and management of children with behavioral
         problems associated with brain damage. Pediatric Clinics of North Ameri-
         ca, 1957, 4, 1049-1060. Topic Codes: CV06,CV15B,DK07B,DK07D,DK48B,MG,
         MG30,MG48B,MK,NA07D,PE30.

12270   Bradley, R.H., Caldwell, B.M., and Elardo, R. Home environment, social
         status, and mental test performance. Journal of Educational Psychology,
         1977, 69(6), 697-701. Topic Codes: NA07,NL,SF,SH59RF,SI57J,TB78.

12300   Bradley, R.W. Birth order and school-related behavior. Psychological
         Bulletin, 1968, 70(1), 45-51. Topic Codes: BL70,MC,NA07B,PE04,PE10,
         PE64,PM,PT,SC18,SC70,SJ07,SQ,SR03.

12400   Bradshaw, J.L., and Taylor, M.J. A word-naming deficit in nonfamilial
         sinistrals? Laterality effects of vocal responses to tactistoscopically
         presented letter strings. Neuropsychologia, 1979, 17, 21-32. Topic
         Codes: BL70,BN44,BP,DD81,DP,DT42,ML,NH,PE44,PN,PO,SH,SQ,TB81.

12440   Braine, M.D.S., Heimer, C.B., Wortis, H., and Freedman, A.M. Factors as-
         sociated with impairment in the early development of prematures. In P.H.
         Mussen, J.J. Conger, and J. Kagan (eds.), Readings in Child Development
         and Personality (2nd ed.). New York: Harper & Row, 1970. Topic Codes:
         BL31,DF34,DF60B,NA31F,NA33B,PK.

12450   Branch, C., Milner, B., and Rasmussen, T. Intracarotid sodium amytal for
         the lateralization of cerebral speech dominance. Journal of Neurosurgery,
         1964, 21, 399-465. Topic Codes BK11B,BL11,BL31,BL33,BN44B,DD,DK07,DK18,
         NA,NL,PO07,TA02,TA52,TA55,TA59D,TA80.

12500   Brand, M.M., and Bignami, A. The effects of chronic hypoxia on the neo-
         natal and infantile brain. Brain, 1969, 92, 233-254. Topic Codes: BD30,
         BD30B,BL07,DF06,DF48,DF60,DF67,DK07,DK09,DP48,DT04,NA31R,NA33I,TA52K,
         TA52M.

12550   Brane, M.S. Three paths to schizophrenia: A systematic comparison of
         childhood, poor premorbid, and good premorbid onsets [doctoral disserta-
         tion, Wayne State University, 1975]. Dissertation Abstracts Interna-
         tional, May 1976, 36(11), 5780B. Topic Codes: BI07,BL11,BL31,BN68,BN70,
         BP02B,BP44,BP53,DD00,DD02B,DF34,DP11B,DP44,MG02B,MU70,MW,MY,NL48B,PE10,PG,
         PK,PL,TA02,TA59.

12600   Brazelton, T.B. Psychophysiologic reactions in the neonate: II. Effect
         of maternal medication on the neonate and his behavior. Journal of Pedi-
         atrics, April 1961, 58(4), 513-518. Topic Codes: BP04,NA33D,NA33I,PE34,
         TA52M.

12700   Breland, H.M. Birth order, family size and intelligence. Science, 1974,
         184, 114. Topic Codes: DT42,ML,PE44,PM,PN,SJ07,SJ22,TB72.

12730   Brickman, A.S., McManus, M., Grapentine, W.L., and Alessi, N. Neuropsy-
         chological assessment of seriously delinquent adolescents. Journal of the
         American Academy of Child Psychiatry, July 1984, 23(4), 453-457. Topic
         Codes: CC37B,CC37T,CC371,NA31D,TA03,TA55.

12750   Briggs, G.G., and Nebes, R.D. Patterns of hand preference in a student
         population. Cortex, 1975, 11, 230-238. Topic Codes: BK11B,BL70,BN44,NA,
         NL48,PO,TA55,TA80,TB49.

12790   Brittain, R.P. The sadistic murderer. Medicine, Science and the Law,
         October 1970, 10(4), 198-207. Topic Codes: CC11C,CC11E,CC11G,CC11L,
         CC11N,CC11P,CC11S,CC67B,CC81D,CC81F,CC81N,CC81Q,CC81S,CC81V,CE,CG11CC,
         CG11T,CQ11,CQ59,CQ67,CQ81,CT68,CT81,CV13DA,CZ07,DD02B,DD02D,MC11,MS02,
         MV07,MV11,MX07,MX11,NE59,NE67,NE81,SI07,SI11,SI48B,SI48D,SQ11,SR03B,SR69B,
         SR69D,SU,SY,TA59,TA70.

12800   Broadbent, D.E. Attention and the perception of speech. Scientific Amer-
         ican, April 1962, 206(4), 143-151. Topic Codes: BK11B,DT59,MR,PS,TB02.

12900   Broder, P.K., Dunivant, N., Smith, E.C., and Sutton, L.P. Further observations on the link between learning disabilities and juvenile delinquency. Unpublished manuscript, National Center for State Courts, Williams-
burg, Virginia, July 1980. Topic Codes: BL04,CC37,CC37H,CC67,CG11P,CQ37,
CQ67,CV13D,NE37,NE67,PE64D,SC70D,SW,SW16,TA03,TB09D,TB95D.

13000   Broman, S.H., Kolata, G.B., and Brackbill, Y. Obstetrical medication
study. Science, August 1979, 205, 446-448. Topic Codes: BL31,BP04,
NA31F,NC44,NC59G,PK.

13050   Broman, S.H., Nichols, P.L., and Kennedy, W.A. Precursors of low I.Q. in
young children. Proceedings of the 80th Annual Convention of the American
Psychological Association, 1972, 7, 77-78. Topic Codes: BE30C,BL33,BL48,
BL67,BL70,DK46,DT48,MO,MT48,NA31R,NA33F,NA44B,NC22,NH59PF,NJ03,PE48,PL,PM,
PR,SH59RF,SN,SQ,TA52K,TB05,TB78.

13100   Broman, S.H., Nichols, P.L., and Kennedy, W.A. Preschool I.Q.: Prenatal
and Early Developmental Correlates. Hillsdale, New Jersey: Lawrence
Erlbaum Associates, 1975. Topic Codes: BD30BA,BE30C,BIO7,BK11B,BL05,
BL06,BL07B,BL08B,BL22,BL27,BL31,BL33,BL59,BP02,BP22F,BP26,BP44,BP46,BP47,
BP48,BP53,BP61,BP63,BP70,BP89,DF06B,DF34,DF48,DF67B,DP11,DP22,DP44,DP46,
DP48,DT08E,NA31F,NA33F,NC44,NC59G,PK,PL,PM,PR,SH59JB,SH59RA,SH59RF,SH59RH,
SL,SN,SW,TA52M,TA80,TB02,TB05,TB78.

13150   Broverman, D.M., Klaiber, E.L., Kobayashi, Y., and Vogel, W. Roles of
activation and inhibition in sex differences in cognitive abilities. Psychological Review, 1968, 75, 23-50. Topic Codes: BD70,BI,BK11B,BL11,
BL48,BL52D,BL70,BNO4,DT42,DT44,DT48,DT59,ML,MM,MR,NL,PC,PE44,PE48,PP,PR,
PS,PY,SB,TA80,TB40,TB93,TB95.

13190   Brown, C.R. The use of benzodiazepines in prison populations. Journal of
Clinical Psychiatry, March 1978, 39(3), 219-222. Topic Codes: CC11H,CE,
CG11,CQ59,CV15B,CV15D,DA15D,DD01,MC11,MIO7,NE59,PE15D,SF,SR02,SR03B,SS09,
TA03,TA80.

13200   Brown, C.W.M. Sex chromosome aneuploidy in man and its frequency, with
special reference to mental subnormality and criminal behavior. International Review of Experimental Pathology, 1969, 7, 31-97. Topic Codes:
BB70B,BB70D,CC11D,CC11M,CC11N,CE,CQ59,DD02B,DD02D,DD02ND,DD02NF,MO,NE59,
SQ07,SQ11.

13250   Brown, G., Chadwick, O., Shaffer, D., Rutter, M., and Traub, M. A pro-
spective study of children with head injuries: III. Psychiatric sequelae.
Psychological Medicine, February 1981, 11(1), 63-78. Topic Codes: DD26B,
DK07B,MG.

13300   Brown, J.V., Bakeman, R., Snyder, P.A., Fredrickson, W.T., Morgan, S.T.,
and Hepler, R. Interactions of black inner-city mothers with their newborn infants. Child Development, 1975, 46, 677-686. Topic Codes: BL06,
BL27,BL70,BP04,BP26,BP44,BP53,BP57,NA33D,NA33I,NL07,PE34,SI48,SQ,TA52M.

13400   Brown, R.T., and Quay, L.C. Reflection impulsivity in normal and behavior disordered children. Journal of Abnormal Child Psychology, 1977, 5
(4), 457-462. Topic Codes: BL04,BL04B,DT13B,MG11,MH07,MK,PE30,PI07,PM,
TA02,TA59.

13600   Brown, W.A., Manning, T., and Grodin, J. The relationship of antenatal
and perinatal psychologic variables to the use of drugs in labor. Psychosomatic Medicine, March-April 1972, 34(2), 119-127. Topic Codes: BP04,
BP44,DP,TB74,TB86,TB93.

13605   Brown, W.K. Black female gangs in Philadelphia. International Journal
of Offender Therapy and Comparative Criminology, 1979, 21(3), 221-228.
Topic Codes: BL70,CC24,CC37L,CC81V,CQ22,CQ37B,NE22,NE37D,NL07,NL22,
SF26DD,SQ,SW11.

13610   Bryan, M.M. California Achievement Tests. In O.K. Buros (ed.), The

Eighth Mental Measurements Yearbook (vol. I). Highland Park, New Jersey: Gryphon Press, 1978, 35-37. Topic Codes: TB21.

13620   Bryant, E.T. The relationship of learning disabilities, neuropsychological deficits, and violent criminal behavior in an inmate population [doctoral dissertation, California School of Professional Psychology, 1981]. Dissertation Abstracts International, November 1982, 43(5), 1607B. Topic Codes: CC11I,CC11O,CC81G,CC81Y,CQ59,DT44D,TA03,TA55.

13622   Bryant, E.T., Scott, M.L., Golden, C.J., and Tori, C.D. Neuropsychological deficits, learning disability, and violent behavior. Journal of Consulting and Clinical Psychology, April 1984, 52(2), 323-324. Topic Codes: CC81D,CC81G,CC81R,TA03,TA55.

13630   Bryden, M.P. Evidence for sex-related differences in cerebral organization. In M.A. Wittig and A.C. Petersen (eds.), Sex-Related Differences in Cognitive Functioning: Developmental Issues. New York: Academic Press, 1979, 121-143. Topic Codes: BK11B,BL70,BN44,MH,PI,PO,SQ.

13650   Bryden, M.P. Perceptual asymmetry in vision: Relation to handedness, eyedness, and speech lateralization. Cortex, 1973, 9, 419-435. Topic Codes: BK11B,BN44,DT59,MR,NA,NL,PO,PS,TA55,TB81.

13700   Buchsbaum, M., and Wender, P. Average evoked responses in normal and minimally brain dysfunctioned children treated with amphetamine. Archives of General Psychiatry, December 1973, 29, 764-770. Topic Codes: CV15B, DK48,MG48,TB35B.

13800   Buchtel, H.A., Rizzolatti, G., Anzola, G.P., and Bertoloni, G. Right hemispheric superiority in discrimination of brief acoustic duration. Neuropsychologia, 1978, 16, 643-647. Topic Codes: BN44,DT13,MH,PI,PO.

13900   Budoff, M., and Purseglove, E.M. Forms L and LM of the Stanford-Binet compared for an institutionalized adolescent mentally retarded population. In L. Terman and M. Merrill (eds.), Measuring Intelligence. Boston: Houghton-Mifflin, 1937. Topic Codes: TB78B.

14030   Buffery, A.W.H. Sex differences in the development of hemispheric asymmetry of function in the human brain. Brain Research, 1971, 31, 364-365 (Ebbs Abstracts). Topic Codes: BL70,MH,NA07I,PG,PI,SQ,TB81.

14050   Buikhuisen, W. Neuropsychological component of the Israeli Project. Unpublished manuscript, Kriminologies Institute, University of Leiden, Leiden, The Netherlands, 1979. Topic Codes: BK11B,BL11,CC11C,DK07D,DK48D, MG48D.

14100   Burgess, P.K. Eysenck's theory of criminality: A test of some objections to disconfirmatory evidence. British Journal of Social and Clinical Psychology, 1972, 11, 248-256. Topic Codes: BN04D,MG11,MQ11,MS04B,MX11, PC11,PE68D,PT11,SR02,TA03,TA59,TB38.

14150   Burke, A.W. Determinants of delinquency in female West Indian migrants. International Journal of Social Psychiatry, Spring 1982, 28(1), 28-34. Topic Codes: CC24,CC24B,CC37B,CC37K,CC37M,SF26D,SI46D,SI59D,SJ09D.

14200   Burnes, K. Patterns of WISC scores for children of two socioeconomic classes and races. Child Development, 1970, 41, 493-499. Topic Codes: BL04,BL67,NA07B,PE10,PM,SN,SW,TB95.

14250   Burstein, B., Bank, L., and Jarvik, L.F. Sex differences in cognitive functioning: Evidence, determinants, implications. Human Development, 1980, 23, 289-313. Topic Codes: BB70B,BD70K,BI07,BN44,NL,PG,PI,PN,PO,PP, PY,SB,SF,SU,TA04,TA55,TA57,TA59,TA80,TB78,TB81,TB93,TB95.

14300   Bush, M. The relationship between impaired selective attention and severity of psychopathology in acute psychiatric patients. British Journal of Medical Psychology, 1977, 50, 251-265. Topic Codes: BL70,DT13B,DT59B, MH07,MR07,MU70,PI07,PM,PS07,SQ,TA02,TA59D,TB33,TB61,TB93.

14400   Buss, A., Booker, A., and Buss, E. Firing a weapon and aggression. Journal of Personality and Social Psychology, 1972, 22(3), 296-302. Topic
Codes: CZ07,MC,PE04,SR03,SY11.

14500   Buss, A.H., and Durkee, A. An inventory for assessing different kinds of
hostility. Journal of Consulting Psychology, 1957, 21(4), 343-349. Topic
Codes: MC,MS,N,PE04,PE08,PT,PT74,TA02B,TA80,TB19.

14600   Butler, N.R., and Goldstein, H. Smoking in pregnancy and subsequent child
development. British Medical Journal, 1973, 4, 573-575. Topic Codes:
BL11,BP70,NA07I,NA44F,NJ09,PG,TA04,TA59D.

14700   Cadoret, R.J. Psychopathology in adopted-away offspring of biologic parents with antisocial behavior. Archives of General Psychiatry, February
1978, 35, 176-184. Topic Codes: BI07,BL70,ME,MS04,NH04B,NH59B,NH59E,
PE08,SF07,SH04B,SH59B,SH59F,SQ,SR04,SW,TA59.

14740   Cadoret, R.J., Cunningham, L., Loftus, R., and Edwards, J. Studies of
adoptees from psychiatrically disturbed biologic parents: II. Tempera-
ment, hyperactive, antisocial, and developmental variables. Journal of
Pediatrics, August 1975, 87(2), 301-306. Topic Codes: CC37BB,CC37G,
CC37S,DK48D,ME07,MG18D,MG30D,MP11,MS04B,NA07DF,NH04D,NH59B,PE08D,PE22,
PE52D,PE68D,PG11,PT74B,SH04D,SH59H,SR04B.

14750   Cadoret, R.J., Cunningham, L., Loftus, R., and Edwards, J. Studies of
adoptees from psychiatrically disturbed biological parents: III. Medical
symptoms and illnesses in childhood and adolescence. American Journal of
Psychiatry, November 1976, 133(11), 1316-1318. Topic Codes: CC37P,DD01,
NH04D,NH59B,SH04D,SH59B,SI57D,SL11,SQ07.

14800   Caldwell, B.M., and Drachman, R.H. Comparability of three methods of assessing the developmental level of young infants. Pediatrics, July 1964,
34(1), 51-57. Topic Codes: BL04,BL31,BL67,BL70,NA31F,PK,SN,SQ,TB25.

14850   Calegari, P. Methodological note on sequential researches in adolescence.
Archivio di Psicologia Neurologia e Psichiatria, July-September 1975, 36
(3), 353-362 (in Italian). Topic Codes: BL04,NA44S,NJ27,NL,PG.

14900   Calhoun, G., Connley, S., and Bolton, J.A. Comparison of delinquents and
nondelinquents in ethnicity, ordinal position, and self-perception. Journal of Clinical Psychology, January 1984, 40(1), 323-328. Topic Codes:
BL67D,BP07D,CC37H,CC37M,CC37W,CC37Y,SJ05D,SJ07D.

15000   California Commission on Crime Control and Violence Prevention. Birthing/
infant bonding. Unpublished manuscript, Sacramento, California, November
1980. Topic Codes: BL11C,BL22,BL31,BP,BP02B,BP02D,BP04,BP22F,BP44,CC81,
CQ81,CT57B,CT81,DD10,DF,DF60B,DP11B,NA07ID,NA31C,NA31F,NA33D,NA33I,NE81,
PE34,PG11,PK,SI22,SI46,SI48,SI57G,TA52M,TB02.

15100   California Commission on Crime Control and Violence Prevention. Birthing/
infant bonding: Public hearing; partial transcript. Unpublished manuscript, San Francisco, California, September 27, 1980. Topic Codes:
BL31,BP,BP02D,BP04,BP44,CC81,CQ81,CT57B,CT81,DD08K,DD10,DF60B,DK09,DP,
DP11,NA31F,NA44D,NE81,NJ06,PK,SF11,SI48D,SI57G,TB02.

15110   California Commission on Crime Control and Violence Prevention. California Commission on Crime Control and Violence Prevention annual report to
the California legislature, 1980. Unpublished manuscript, Sacramento,
California, 1981. Topic Codes: BA,CC81,CC81E,CC81L,CQ81,CT81,NE81,SF11,
SW11.

15150   California Legislature. Assembly Bill No. 23: An Act to Add Title 9
(Commencing with Section 14100) to Part 4 of the Penal Code, Relating to
Causes of Violence and Crime, 1979-80 regular session, 1979. Topic Codes:
BD30H,BD52D,BK11BL,BL11C,BL31,BP02D,BP44,CC81,CC81D,CC81F,CC81L,CC81R,
CQ81,CT81,CV06C,CV52D,DA04D,DA15D,DD01,DD30D,MD11,MG,MI07,NA07D,NA07ID,
NA31F,NE81,PE06D,PE15D,PG,PK,PT11,PV11,SF11,SI48D,SO11.

15300   Cameron, J.R. Parental treatment, children's temperament, and the risk of childhood behavioral problems: 1. Relationships between parental characteristics and changes in children's temperament over time. American Journal of Orthopsychiatry, October 1977, 47(4), 568-576. Topic Codes: BL11, BL31,BL70,MG,NA07D,NA07I,NA31F,NA44D,NJ06,PG,PK,PT74,SQ.

15350   Cameron, J.R. Parental treatment, children's temperament, and the risk of childhood behavioral problems: 2. Initial temperament, parental attitudes, and the incidence and form of behavioral problems. American Journal of Orthopsychiatry, January 1978, 48(1), 140-147. Topic Codes: BL11, BL31,BL70,MG,NA07D,NA07I,NA31F,NA44D,NJ06,PG,PK,PT74,SI57B,SQ.

15370   Camp, B.W. Verbal mediation in young aggressive boys. Journal of Abnormal Psychology, April 1977, 86(2), 145-153. Topic Codes: DT42B,MC,MG, ML02,NA07D,PE04,PE44B,PE64B,PN07,SC70B,SR03,SW07,TA02,TA59D,TA74,TB40B, TB53,TB95B,TB98B.

15400   Camp, B.W. WISC performance in acting-out and delinquent children with and without EEG abnormality. Journal of Consulting Psychology, 1966, 30(4), 350-353. Topic Codes: BL70,CC37B,CC37F,CC371,SQ,TB35B,TB95D, TB96D.

15500   Camp, B.W., Van Doorninck, W.J., Zimet, S.G., and Dahlem, N.W. Verbal attitudes in young aggressive boys. Journal of Educational Psychology, 1977, 69(2), 129-135. Topic Codes: BL04,BL11C,CC37B,CC371,DT13D,DT44D, MC11,MG11B,MH11,MM11,NA07ID,PE04D,PE64B,PG11,PI11,PP11,SC70B,SR03B,SW, TB53,TB95D,TB96D,TB98D.

15600   Campagna, A.F., and Harter, S. Moral judgment in sociopathic and normal children. Journal of Personality and Social Psychology, 1975, 31(2), 199-205. Topic Codes: BL11,DT13B,ME,MG11,MH07,MS04,NA07I,PE08,PG,PI07, PY,SI57P,SR04,SU,TB95B,TB96BB.

15700   Campbell, P.B. The definition and prevalence of learning disabilities. Paper presented at the ACLD Annual Conference, Kansas City, Missouri, March 3, 1978. Topic Codes: CC37H,CC37J,CC37L,DT44D,MM11,PP11,TA02,TA03, TA04,TA59D,TB09B,TB09K,TB95B,TB96B.

15850   Campbell, S.B., Breaux, A.M., Ewing, L.J., and Szumowski, E.K. A one-year follow-up study of parent-referred hyperactive preschool children. Journal of the American Academy of Child Psychiatry, May 1984, 23(3), 243-249. Topic Codes: MG,MG30,NA07D,NH59E,SH59F.

15900   Campbell, S.B., Schleifer, M., and Weiss, G. Continuities in maternal reports and child behavior over time in hyperactive and comparison groups. Journal of Abnormal Child Psychology, 1978, 6(1), 33-45. Topic Codes: DP11B,MG,MG30,NA07D,NA31D,NA44D,NJ06,PE32,PE64B,SC70B,TA57,TA74,TB78B.

16000   Campbell, S.B., and Steinert, Y. Comparisons of rating scales of child psychopathology in clinic and non-clinic samples. Journal of Consulting and Clinical Psychology, 1978, 46(2), 358-359. Topic Codes: MG,NA07D, PE64B,SC70B,TA57,TA74.

16100   Campion, E., and Tucker, G. A note on twin studies, schizophrenia and neurological impairment. Archives of General Psychiatry, October 1973, 29, 460-463. Topic Codes: BI07,BL22,BP22F,DD08K,DF48,DK09B,DP11B,DP48, DT04EB,DT52B,MU70,NA31R,NH59PB,NH59PJ,NH74B,SH59RB,SH59RJ,SH74B,TA52K.

16150   Canada Standing Senate Committee on Health, Welfare and Sciences. Child at Risk. Hull, Canada: Canadian Government Publishing Center Supply and Services, 1980. Topic Codes: BP02D,BP04,BP48,BP52,BP70,CC81T,CT57BD, DD10D,DF60BD,DP44,SI57D,SI57GD.

16160   Canter, R.J. Family correlates of male and female delinquency. Criminology, August 1982, 20(2), 149-167. Topic Codes: BL70D,CC37,CC37M,CQ37,NH, SH,SI,SI11.

16200   Cantwell, D.P. Genetic factors in the hyperkinetic syndrome. Journal of

the American Academy of Child Psychiatry, Spring 1976, 15(2), 214-223.
Topic Codes: BIO7,DK48,MG30,MG48,NH04B,NH59B,NH59E,NH65B,NH74B,SHO4B,
SH59B,SH59F,SH74B.

16300   Cantwell, D.P. Hyperactivity and antisocial behavior. Journal of the
American Academy of Child Psychiatry, 1978, 17(2), 252-262. Topic Codes:
BN04D,CC11C,CC11G,CC37B,DA04B,MD07,ME07,MG30B,MG30D,MQ,MS04,NH59B,NH59E,
NH65B,PC11,PE06B,PE08D,PE64B,SC70B,SH59B,SH59F,SR04B.

16400   Caplan, P.J. Erikson's concept of inner space: A data-based reevalua-
tion. American Journal of Orthopsychiatry, January 1979, 49(1), 100-108.
Topic Codes: BL70,DT13,MH,MV,NA07B,PF10,PF66,PT,PY,ST57P,SQ,SR69,SU.

16500   Capstick, N., and Seldrup, J. A study in the relationship between abnormalities occurring at the time of birth and the subsequent development of
obsessional symptoms. Acta Psychiatrica Scandinavica, 1977, 56, 427-431.
Topic Codes: DD08K,DK07B,DK48B,DP11B,MG48B,MQ,SI46B.

16600   Capute, A.J., Niedermeyer, E.F.L., and Richardson, F. The electroencephalogram in children with minimal cerebral dysfunction. Pediatrics, June
1968, 41(6), 1104-1114. Topic Codes: DK18,DK48B,DT52B,MG,MG48B,NA07D,
TB25B,TB35B,TB78B.

16700   Carroll, J.C. The intergenerational transmission of family violence: The
long-term effects of aggressive behavior. Aggressive Behavior, 1977, 3,
289-299. Topic Codes: CC81F,CC81L,CC81N,CC81V,CT57BD,DD10D,SI57D,SI57GD,
SI57J,TB66B.

16710   Carter, D. Comparison of manifest behaviors of urban children and adolescents classified as emotionally disturbed and socially maladjusted [doc-
toral dissertation, Rutgers University - The State University of New
Jersey, 1982]. Dissertation Abstracts International, April 1983, 43(10),
3284A. Topic Codes: MG,MX,SF26B.

16720   Carter, T.D. Torque and its relationship to academic achievement and behavioral problems in children as perceived by parents and teachers [doc-
toral dissertation, New Mexico State University, 1982]. Dissertation Abstracts International, December 1983, 44(6), 1729A. Topic Codes: BN44B,
MG,NA07D,TA02,TA57,TA74.

16725   Carter, T.D., and DeBlassie, R.R. Torque, academic achievement and behavioral problems in early adolescents. Journal of Early Adolescence, Spring
1984, 4(1), 83-91. Topic Codes: BN44,BN44B,DK,DK07B,MG,NA07B,PE64,PE64B,
PO,POO7,SC70,SC70B,TA02,TA55.

16740   Cascio, A., and Opice, B. Psychopathological considerations regarding so-
called antisocial behavior in epileptics. Lavoro Neuropsichiatrico, Janu-
ary-June 1974, 54(1-3), 269-277 (in Italian). Topic Codes: DK18D,ME,
PE08,SR04.

16800   Casey, P., and Rohn, R.D. Minimal brain dysfunction in suicidal adolescents. Journal of Pediatrics, December 1977, 91(6), 1029-1030. Topic
Codes: DK48,MG,MG48,MZ,NA07D,TB09B.

16820   Cashion, B.G. Female-headed families: Effects on children and clinical
implications. Journal of Marital and Family Therapy, April 1982, 8(2),
77-85. Topic Codes: BL11,CC37M,MG,NH59P,NH59PL,PE64,SJ09D.

16850   Caster, D.U. Locus of control, depression and sociopathy in chronic alcoholics. Biological Psychology Bulletin, December 1975, 4(3-4), 161-169.
Topic Codes: BD07,CC11C,CC11H,CC11P,DA04D,MD11,MS04B,NE11,PE06D,PT74B.

16860   Caster, D.U., and Parsons, O.A. Relationship of depression, sociopathy,
and locus of control to treatment outcome in alcoholics. Journal of Consulting and Clinical Psychology, October 1977, 45(5), 751-756. Topic
Codes: CC11C,CC11H,CC11P,CC11U,CC67B,CV06C,DA04B,MB,MD07,MS02,MS04,NE67,
PE06B,PT11,TA02.

16870   Centofanti, C.C. Selected somatosensory and cognitive test performances
as a function of age and education in normal and neurologically abnormal
adults [doctoral dissertation, University of Michigan, 1975]. <u>Disserta-
tion Abstracts International</u>, December 1975, 36(6), 3027B. Topic Codes:
BL04,DT13,MH,NA,SC.

16900   Cernkovich, S.A., and Giordano, P.C. A comparative analysis of male and
female delinquency. <u>Sociological Quarterly</u>, Winter 1979, 20, 131-145.
Topic Codes: BL70,CC37,CC37Y,CC67,CG11P,CQ37,CQ67,CT57,CT59,NE37,NE67,SQ.

17000   Cernkovich, S.A., and Giordano, P.C. Criminology: Delinquency, opportu-
nity and gender. <u>Journal of Criminal Law and Criminology</u>, 1979, 70(2),
145-151. Topic Codes: BL70,CC37L,CC37Y,CC37Z,SQ.

17100   Chafkin, S.H., and Cooney, T.E., Jr. Recommendation for grant/DAP action
on "Additional Allocation for Exploration of the Significance of Health
and Nutrition in Socially Troublesome Juvenile Behavior." Unpublished
manuscript, Ford Foundation, April 16, 1979. Topic Codes: BA,BD52D,BK,
BL11C,BL52DB,BL52DD,BP02B,CC37B,CC37F,CC37G,CC37K,CC37M,CC37P,CC37R,CC37T,
CC37U,CC37V,CC37X,CC37Z,CV52D,DD00,DD01,DD08KC,DD26B,DD26D,DK07D,DK09D,
DK11,DK18,DP11B,DP11D,DP22,DT44,MN,NA07B,PE10,PE44,PE64,PG,PP.

17130   Chaiklin, H., Chesley, F.D., and Litsinger, W.C. Delinquency and health
status. <u>Health and Social Work</u>, August 1977, 2(3), 24-37. Topic Codes:
BL08BD,CC37D,CC37P,CC37Z,CT57,DD01,DD28D,DD81D,DT30,MG18D,SL11,TA52.

17140   Chamberlain, G., and Banks, J. Assessment of the Apgar score. <u>Lancet</u>,
November 23, 1974, 7891, 1225-1228. Topic Codes: BL29,BL33,BP02,DF34,
DF48,DP48,NA33B,NA33I,PE34,PL,TA52M,TB02.

17150   Chamberlin, R.W. Management of preschool behavior problems. <u>Pediatric
Clinics of North America</u>, February 1974, 21(1), 33-47. Topic Codes:
BN68,CV06C,DT69,MB11,MG11,MG21,ML02,MW,MX07,MY,NA07B,NH59E,PA,PE10,PE22,
PE44B,PE68B,PE70,PN07,PT74,SH59JB,SH59RB,SI22B,SI48B,SI57B,TA02,TA57,
TA80.

17170   Chambers, N.A. Some relationships between cognitive development, role-
taking activity and level of moral development [doctoral dissertation,
George Peabody College for Teachers, 1975). <u>Dissertation Abstracts Inter-
national</u>, February 1976, 36(8), 4222B-4223B. Topic Codes: BL11,DT13,MH,
NL07,PG,PI,TA59,TA80.

17200   Chandler, M.J. Egocentrism and antisocial behavior: The assessment and
training of social perspective-taking skills. <u>Developmental Psychology</u>,
1973, 9(3), 326-332. Topic Codes: BL04BB,CC37G,CC371,CG11P,CV06C,ME07,
MG11,MX11,NL48,PE08D,PE68D,PY11,SI57PB,SR02,SR04B,SU11,TA03,TA59.

17300   Chardos, S.P. An investigation of the longitudinal predictive validity of
WISC IQ, sex, race, and SES in predicting high school GPA [doctoral dissertation, University of Georgia, 1975]. <u>Dissertation Abstracts Interna-
tional</u>, June 1976, 36(12), 6352B. Topic Codes: BL67,BL70,PE64,PM,SC70,
SN,SQ,SW,TB95.

17380   Chazan, M. Disadvantage, behaviour problems and reading difficulties.
<u>AEP Journal</u>, Winter 1982, 5(10), 3-6. Topic Codes: DT15,DT44B,MG,SW07.

17400   Chazan, M., and Jackson, S. Behavior problems in the infant school:
Changes over two years. <u>Journal of Child Psychology and Psychiatry and
Allied Disciplines</u>, 1974, 15, 33-46. Topic Codes: BL70,MC,MG,NA07B,
NA07D,NA44N,NJ20,PE04,PE10,PE64B,SC70B,SF26B,SQ,SR03,SW07,TA02,TA59,TA74.

17500   Chen, E. Twins reared apart: A living lab. <u>New York Times Magazine</u>,
December 9, 1979, 112-123. Topic Codes: BI,DT13,DT30,MH,NH74,PI,SF,SH74.

17570   Chesno, F.A., and Kilmann, P.R. Effects of stimulation intensity on sociopathic avoidance learning. <u>Journal of Abnormal Psychology</u>, April 1975,
84(2), 144-150. Topic Codes: BN04D,CC11C,CC11P,CC11U,CQ59,CV06C,CV13DA,

DT44D,MF11,MM11,MS04B,MX11,NE59,PC11,PE01,PE68D,PP11,PT74B,SR02,TA02B,
TB15B.

17600   Chess, S. Genesis of behavior disorders. In J.G. Howells (ed.), Modern
Perspectives in International Child Psychiatry (vol. 3). Edinburgh:
Oliver and Boyd, 1969. Topic Codes: BL11,DK07B,DK46B,MG,MO07,NA07D,
NA07I,NA31A,NA44D,NJ06,PG,PT74,TA57.

17700   Chess, S., and Hassibi, M. Behavior deviations in mentally retarded
children. Journal of the American Academy of Child Psychiatry, 1970, 9,
282-297. Topic Codes: BL04,BL11,BL48B,DK07B,DK46B,DT42B,DT48B,DT52B,MG,
ML02,MO07,MT48B,NA07D,NA07I,PE44B,PE48B,PG,PNO7,PRO7,TB78B.

17800   Chess, S., and Korn, S. Temperament and behavior disorders in mentally
retarded children. Archives of General Psychiatry, August 1970, 23, 122-
130. Topic Codes: DK46B,MG,MO07,NA07D,NA44D,NJ06,PT74,TB78B.

17900   Chess, S., Thomas, A., and Birch, H.G. Behavior problems revisited:
Findings of an anterospective study. Journal of the American Academy of
Child Psychiatry, 1967, 6, 321-331. Topic Codes: BL31,MG,NA07D,NA31A,
NA31F,NA44D,NJ06,PE64B,PK,PT74,PY,SC70B,SF07,SI57B,SI57P,SU.

18000   Chess, S., Thomas, A., and Birch, H.G. Distortions in developmental re-
porting made by parents of behaviorally disturbed children. Journal of
the American Academy of Child Psychiatry, 1966, 5, 226-234. Topic Codes:
BL11,MG,NA07D,NA07I,NA44D,NJ06,PG,TA57.

18100   Chess, S., Thomas, A., Rutter, M., and Birch, H.G. Interaction of temperament and environment in the production of behavioral disturbances in
children. American Journal of Psychiatry, August 1963, 120, 142-148.
Topic Codes: MG,NA07D,NA44D,NJ06,PT74,SF07,SI57B.

18200   Chi, J.G., Dooling, E.C., and Gilles, F.H. Left-right asymmetries of the
temporal speech areas of the human fetus. Archives of Neurology, June
1977, 34, 346-348. Topic Codes: BK11B,BN44,BP22,PO.

18300   Chilton, R.J., and Markle, G.E. Family disruption, delinquent conduct and
the effect of sub-classification. American Sociological Review, 1972, 37,
93-99. Topic Codes: BL70D,CC37L,CC37Y,CC37Z,CE,CG11P,NH59F,SF26D,SH59H,
SJ09,SQ11,SW11,SW33.

18400   Chipman, S.S., Lilienfeld, A.M., Greenberg, B.G., and Donnelly, J.F.
(eds.). Research Methodology and Needs in Perinatal Studies. Springfield: Charles C. Thomas, 1966. Topic Codes: BP,CG.

18500   Christiansen, K.O. Crime in a Danish twin population. Acta Geneticae
Medicae et Gemellologiae, 1970, 19, 323-326. Topic Codes: BL70,NH74D,
SF26D,SH74D,SQ.

18520   Christiansen, K.O. Threshold of tolerance in various population groups
illustrated by results from the Danish Criminologic Twin Study. In A.V.S.
de Reuck and R. Porter (eds.), The Mentally Abnormal Offender. Boston:
Little, Brown, 1968. Topic Codes: BI11,CC11M,CC37N,NH74D,PT11,SH74D.

18750   Chung, C.S., and Myrianthopoulos, N.C. Factors affecting risks of congenital malformations: I. Epidemiologic analysis; II. Effect of maternal
diabetes. Birth Defects, Original Article Series, The National Foundation for the March of Dimes, 1975, 11(10), 1-38. Topic Codes: BB,BL67,
BL70,BP02,BP46,BP47,BP70,DD02,DF48,DK09,DP,DP11,DP48,NA31,NH59,NH59P,SH59,
SH59R,SN,SQ.

18760   Chung, C.S., and Myrianthopoulos, N.C. Racial and prenatal factors in major congenital malformations. American Journal of Human Genetics, January 1968, 20, 44-60. Topic Codes: BL67,BP02,BP04,BP46,BP47,BP89,DF34,
DF48,DP11,NC44,PK,PL,TA52M,TA80,TB.

18780   Churchill, J.A., Berendes, H.W., and Nemore, J. Neuropsychological deficits in children of diabetic mothers. American Journal of Obstetrics and

Gynecology, September 1969, 105, 257-268. Topic Codes: BP02B,BP53,DF34, DP11,NA31A,NA31F,PK,PL,PM,TA52,TA52K,TA52M,TA55,TA59,TA80,TB05,TB78.

18790   Churchill, J.A., Willerman, L., Grisell, J., and Ayers, M.A. Effect of head position at birth on WISC verbal and performance IQ. Psychological Reports, October 1968, 23, 495-498. Topic Codes: BP02,BP44,DP44,NA31F, PG,PK,PM,TA52M,TB95,TB96.

18800   Cicirelli, V.G. Sibling constellation, creativity, IQ and academic achievement. Child Development, 1967, 38, 481-490. Topic Codes: BL70, BP07,NA07B,NH,PE10,PE64,PM,PT,SC70,SH,SJ05,SJ07,SJ22,SQ,TA04,TA59,TA59D, TB68.

18900   Cienek, R.P., and Cienek, Y.T. The possible continuum: Learning disabil-ities to delinquency. Paper presented at the annual meeting of the Amer-ican Society of Criminology, San Francisco, November 5, 1980. Topic Codes: CC37B,CC37H,CC37J,DT44B,DT44D,MG30D,MM07,MM11,PE64D,PP07,PP11, SC70D.

19000   Cieutat, V.J., and Flick, G.L. Examiner differences among Stanford-Binet items. Psychological Reports, 1967, 21, 613-622. Topic Codes: BL70, NC22,NC80,NL07,PM,SQ,TB78.

19060   Clancy, H.G. Integrating the environment in therapy. Man-Environment Systems, September 1976, 6(5), 305-312. Topic Codes: CV06,SF.

19070   Clarizio, H.F., and McCoy, G.F. Behavior Disorders in Children (2nd ed.). New York: Thomas Y. Crowell, 1976. Topic Codes: CC37B,CC37J, CC37M,CC37Z,DD00,MB,MC,ME,MF,MG02B,MG11,MX07,NA07D,NH59,NL,PE,PE10,PE64B, PE68B,PG,PY,SC70B,SF07,SH04B,SI07,SR01,SU.

19200   Clark, G.R., Telfer, M.A., Baker, D., and Rosen, M. Sex chromosomes, crime, and psychosis. American Journal of Psychiatry, May 1970, 126(11), 1659-1663. Topic Codes: BB70D,BE11,BL67,DD02NF,SN,TB61B.

19300   Clark, K.B. Color, class, personality, and juvenile delinquency. Jour-nal of Negro Education, 1959, 28, 240-251. Topic Codes: BL70,CC37A, CC37W,CC37Y,CC37Z,CT57,CT59,CX,NE79,SQ.

19350   Clark, M., Shapiro, D., Hager, M., Huck, J., and Abramson, P. The curse of hyperactivity. Newsweek, June 23, 1980, 59-62. Topic Codes: BD07, BD52B,CV15B,CV52B,DK48,DT44B,MG30,MG48,MK,MM07,NH04B,NH65B,PE30,PP07, SH04B.

19355   Clarke-Stewart, K.A. Interactions between mothers and their young chil-dren: Characteristics and consequences. Monographs of the Society for Research in Child Development, 1973, 8(6-7, serial no. 153). Topic Codes: BL11,BL31,BL67,BL70,NA07I,NA31D,NA31F,PE32,PG,PK,SF,SI48,SN,SQ,SS,SU,SW, TA80,TB02.

19360   Clemente, C.D., and Lindsley, D.B. (eds.). Brain Function: Aggression and Defense: Neural Mechanisms and Social Patterns (vol. 5). Berkeley, California: University of California Press, 1967. Topic Codes: BB11, BD11,BD30HD,BI11,BK04D,BK11B,BL04D,BL08BD,BL48D,BL52DD,BL67D,BL70D,BN04D, CC11A,CC11B,CC11C,CC11D,CC11F,CC11H,CC11I,CC11K,CC11M,CC11N,CC11O,CC11P, CC11T,CC81B,CC81C,CC81E,CC81G,CC81I,CC81M,CC810,CC81Q,CC81R,CC81S,CG11, CQ11,CQ81,DD02D,DK07D,DK09D,DK18SD,DT13D,DT42D,DT44D,DT48D,DT67B,MB11, MC11,MF11,MH11,ML03,MM11,MT48D,MV11,MX11,NA,NE,NL,PA11,PE01,PE04D,PE48D, PE66D,PE68D,PI11,PP11,PR11,PT74B,PY11,SQ11,SR03B,SU11,TA03.

19370   Clements, S.D. Minimal Brain Dysfunction in Children: Terminology and Identification; Phase One of a Three-Phase Project (NINDS monograph no. 3, U.S. Public Health Service Publication no. 1415). Washington, D.C.: U.S. Government Printing Office, 1966. Topic Codes: BL04B,BL52DB,CC37S, DD02B,DK48B,DT13B,DT44B,DT52B,MG30B,MG48B,MH07,MK,MM07,NA07D,PE10,PE30, PE64B,PE68B,PI07,PM07,PP07,SC70B,SR01,TA02,TA55,TA59D.

19380   Clift, J.L. The effects of prenatal stress upon children's academic achievement [doctoral dissertation, McNeese State University, 1973]. Dissertation Abstracts International, December 1973, 34(6), 2964B. Topic Codes: BL11,BP02,DP11,NA07I,PE10,PE64,PG,PM,TA59,TA80.

19500   Climent, C.E., and Ervin, F.R. Historical data in the evaluation of violent subjects. Archives of General Psychiatry, November 1972, 27, 621-624. Topic Codes: BL04,CC81B,CC81C,CC81D,CC81F,CC81H,CC81M,CC81N,CC81O, CC81V,CT57,CT57BD,CT57F,DD10D,DK07D,DT30,MGO2D,MZ,NL48,PV11,SC18D,SI57GD, SO11,SW.

19600   Climent, C.E., Ervin, F.R., Rollins, A., Plutchik, R., and Batinelli, C.J. Epidemiological studies of female prisoners: IV. Homosexual behavior. Journal of Nervous and Mental Disease, 1977, 164(1), 25-29. Topic Codes: CC11,CC11H,CC11P,CC24,CQ11,CQ22,CT57,CT59,MZ,NE11,NE22,SF11.

19700   Climent, C.E., Plutchik, R., Ervin, F.R., and Rollins, A. Epidemiological studies of female prisoners: III. Parental loss, depression and violence. Acta Psychiatrica Scandinavia, 1977, 55, 261-268. Topic Codes: CC11,CC11C,CC11L,CC24,CC81,CC81N,CQ11,CQ22,CQ81,CT81,MZ,NE11,NE22,NE81, NH59F,SH59H,SI46D,SI59D,TB61B.

19800   Climent, C.E., Raynes, A., Rollins, A., and Plutchik, R. Epidemiological studies of female prisoners: II. Biological, psychological, and social correlates of drugs and addiction. International Journal of the Addictions, 1974, 9(2), 345-350. Topic Codes: CC11,CC11C,CC11F,CC11H,CC11U, CC24,CQ11,CQ22,DA15D,MI07,NE11,NE22,PE15D,SF11,TB61B.

19900   Climent, C.E., Rollins, A., Ervin, F.R., and Plutchik, R. Epidemiological studies of women prisoners: I. Medical and psychiatric variables related to violent behavior. American Journal of Psychiatry, September 1973, 130(9), 982-990. Topic Codes: BL67,BL67D,CC11,CC11C,CC24,CC81C,CC81D, CC81H,CC81I,CC81K,CC81N,CC81O,CQ11,CQ22,DD01,DT30,MQ11,NE11,NE22,NH59F, SF11,SH59H,SI46D,SI59D,SJ09,SN,SN11,TB21D,TB61B,TB93B,TB93D.

20000   Cloninger, C.R. The antisocial personality. Hospital Practice, August 1978, 13(8), 97-106. Topic Codes: BI11,BL70,BL70D,CC11C,CC37P,DD00B, MGO2D,MS04B,NHO4D,NH59D,NH59F,NH59GD,NH59GI,NH63B,NH74D,SF11,SHO4D,SH59D, SH59H,SH59JD,SH59JL,SH74D,SI57BB,SJO9B,SQ,SQ11,SWO7B.

20100   Cloninger, C.R., Christiansen, K.O., Reich, T., and Gottesman, I.I. Implications of sex differences in the prevalences of antisocial personality, alcoholism, and criminality for familial transmission. Archives of General Psychiatry, August 1978, 35, 941-951. Topic Codes: BI07,BI11,BL70, BL70B,BL70BB,BL70D,CC11L,CC11S,DA04,MD,MS04B,NHO4D,NH63B,NH65B,NH74D,PE06, SF11,SHO4D,SH74D,SQ,SQ07,SQ07B,SQ11.

20200   Cloninger, C.R., and Guze, S.B. Psychiatric disorders and criminal recidivism. Archives of General Psychiatry, August 1973, 29, 266-269. Topic Codes: CC11,CC11A,CC11C,CC11G,CC11H,CC11L,CC24,CC67,CC67B,CG11P, CQ11,CQ22,CQ67,NE11,NE22,NE67,NH59B,NH59F,SC18D,SH59B,SH59H,SJO9.

20300   Cloninger, C.R., and Guze, S.B. Psychiatric illnesses in families of female criminals: A study of 288 first-degree relatives. British Journal of Psychiatry, 1973, 122(571), 697-703. Topic Codes: BL67,BL70,CC11, CC11C,CC11L,CC24,CQ11,CQ22,NE11,NE22,NH67B,NH67BB,SN,SQ.

20400   Cloninger, C.R., Reich, T., and Guze, S.B. Genetic-environmental interactions and antisocial behavior. In R.D. Hare and D. Schalling (eds.), Psychopathic Behaviour: Approaches to Research. New York: John Wiley & Sons, Inc., 1978. Topic Codes: BI11,BL70,DA04,MD,ME07,MS04B,NHO4D,NH63B, NH65B,NH67D,NH74D,PE06,PEO8D,SF11,SHO4D,SH74D,SQ,SRO4B.

20500   Cloninger, C.R., Reich, T., and Guze, S.B. The multifactorial model of disease transmission: II. Sex differences in the familial transmission of sociopathy. British Journal of Psychiatry, 1975, 127, 11-22. Topic Codes: BI07B,BL67,BL67BB,BL70BB,CC11C,MS04B,NH59E,NH63B,SFO7B,SH59F, SJO9B,SN,SNO7B,SQO7B.

20510   Cloninger, C.R., Sigvardsson, S., Bohman, M., and von Knorring, A.L. Predisposition to petty criminality in Swedish adoptees: II. Cross-fostering analysis of gene-environment interaction. _Archives of General Psychiatry_, November 1982, 39(11), 1242-1247. Topic Codes: BI11,BL59,BL67D, CC11H,CC11M,CC11T,CT59,DA04D,MD11,NH04D,NH59D,PE06D,SF11,SH04D,SH59D, SH59H,SW11.

20550   Cochrane, N. Assessing the aggressive components of personality: 1. Problems. _British Journal of Medical Psychology_, March 1975, 48(1), 9-14. Topic Codes: MC,PE04,SR03,TA59,TA80.

20560   Cochrane, N., and Neilson, M. Depressive illness: The role of aggression further considered. _Psychological Medicine_, May 1977, 7(2), 283-288. Topic Codes: MC,N,PE04,PE68,SR03,TA02,TA59,TA80.

20575   Cohen, C.I. Crime among mental patients: A critical analysis. _Psychiatric Quarterly_, Summer 1980, 52(2), 100-107. Topic Codes: CC11C.

20580   Cohen, D.J. Minimal brain dysfunction: Diagnosis and therapy. _Current Psychiatric Therapies_, 1977, 17, 57-70. Topic Codes: BK11B,BL11,DK07B, DK48,DK48B,DT13B,DT42B,DT44B,DT48B,DT52B,MG11,MG48B,MH07,ML02,MM07,MT48B, PE10,PE44B,PE48B,PE68B,PG,PI07,PN07,PP07,PR07,SC70B,SF07,SH59,SI57,SR01, TA02,TA52,TA55,TA74,TA80.

20600   Cohen, D.J., Caparulo, B.K., Gold, J.R., Waldo, M.C., Shaywitz, B.A., Ruttenberg, B.A., and Rimland, B. Agreement in diagnosis: Clinical assessment and behavior rating scales for pervasively disturbed children. _Journal of the American Academy of Child Psychiatry_, 1978, 17(4), 589-603. Topic Codes: DK07B,DK46,DT06,MG,MG04,ML04,MO,NA07D,TA02,TA57,TA59.

20630   Cohen, D.J., Caparulo, B.K., Shaywitz, B.A., and Bowers, M.B. Dopamine and serotonin metabolism in neuropsychiatrically disturbed children. _Archives of General Psychiatry_, May 1977, 34(5), 545-550. Topic Codes: BD30,BL11,DD02B,DT42B,MB,MF,MG04GB,MH,ML,MT,MU,MY,NA07B,NA07DD,NA07I,NL, PE10,PE44B,PE48B,PE64B,PE68B,PE70,PI07,PN07,PP07,PR07,SQ07,SR01,TA02, TA52K,TA52M,TA55,TA80.

20700   Cohen, G. Components of the laterality effect in letter recognition: Asymmetries in iconic storage. _Quarterly Journal of Experimental Psychology_, 1976, 28, 105-114. Topic Codes: BN44,DT13,MH,PI,PO,TB81.

20800   Cohen, G., and Martin, M. Hemisphere differences in an auditory Stroop test. _Perception and Psychophysics_, 1975, 17(1), 79-83. Topic Codes: BN44,DT42,DT59,ML,MR,PE44,PN,PO,PS.

20900   Cohen, M.D. Aggressive and inhibited behavior in reaction to provocation: An experimental investigation of Hewitt and Jenkins' rejection-aggression, repression-inhibition hypotheses [doctoral dissertation, Temple University, 1976]. _Dissertation Abstracts International_, June 1976, 36(12), 6374B. Topic Codes: MC,MV,PE04,PE66,SI57,SR03,SR69,TA59.

21000   Cohen, M.L., Garofalo, R., Boucher, R., and Seghorn, T. The psychology of rapists. _Seminars in Psychiatry_, August 1971, 3(3), 307-327. Topic Codes: CC11C,CC11G,CC11L,CC11P,CC81D,CC81F,CT57,CT68,CV06C,CV13D,MC11, PE04D,SR03B.

21100   Cohen, N.J., and Douglas, V.I. Characteristics of the orienting response in hyperactive and normal children. _Psychophysiology_, March 1972, 9(2), 238-245. Topic Codes: BL25B,BN04B,MG30,PC07,PM.

21140   Coid, J. Alcoholism and violence. _Drug and Alcohol Dependence_, February 1982, 9(1), 1-13. Topic Codes: CC11H,CC37I,CC81B,CC81D,CC81S,DA04D,MD11, MS02,PE06D.

21150   Coil, J.D., and Pennington, B.F. Children's perceptions of deviance and disorder. _Child Development_, June 1976, 47(2), 407-413. Topic Codes: BL04,BL11,BL70,MM,MX,NA07B,NA07I,NL48,PE10,PE68,PG,PY,SB,SC,SQ,TA80,TB.

21200   Colbourn, C.J. Can laterality be measured? _Neuropsychologia_, 1978, 16, 283–289. Topic Codes: BN44,PO,TB81.

21280   Cole, D.D. The relationship of adjustment and delinquent behavior with school grade, socioeconomic status, category of adjudication, race, and sex [doctoral dissertation, Oklahoma State University, 1981] . _Dissertation Abstracts International_, July 1982, 43(1), 291B. Topic Codes: BL67D,BL70D,CC37,CC37A,CC37J,CC37P,CC37Y,CC37Z,CG11CC,DD01,PA,PE64D,SW11.

21300   Cole, M., and Bruner, J.S. Cultural differences and inferences about psychological processes. _American Psychologist_, 1971, 26, 867–876. Topic Codes: BL67,DT13,DT42,ML,PE44,PI,PM,PN,SF,SN,TA59D.

21400   Coleman, J., Wolkind, S., and Ashley, L. Symptoms of behavior disturbance and adjustment to school. _Journal of Child Psychology and Psychiatry and Allied Disciplines_, 1977, 18, 201–209. Topic Codes: BL70,MG,NA07D,NA44, NH59P,NJ,PE64B,SC70B,SH59R,SQ,TA57,TA74.

21500   Coleman, L.S. Perspectives on the medical research of violence. _American Journal of Orthopsychiatry_, October 1974, 44(5), 675–687. Topic Codes: BB70D,CC81,CC81C,CC81I,CC81K,CC81M,CQ81,CT81,CV06C,CY,DD02NF,DK18B,DK18SD, DT10B,MT04B,NE81.

21550   Coleman, R.I., and Deutsch, G.P. Lateral dominance and right-left discrimination: A comparison of normal and retarded readers. _Perceptual and Motor Skills_, 1964, 19, 43–50. Topic Codes: BL,BN44H,DT44,MM,NA07B, NA07I,NL07,PE10,PG,PO33,PP,SW,TA80,TB12,TB95.

21580   Colligan, R.C. Psychometric deficits related to perinatal stress. _Journal of Learning Disabilities_, 1974, 7, 154–160. Topic Codes: BL11,BL31, BL33,BL70,BP02,BP44,BP46,BP47,BP53,BP63,DK48,DP11,DP44,DP46,MG48,NA07B, NA07I,NA44,NC80,NL48,PE10,PE32,PE34,PG,PK,PL,SQ,TA04,TA52K,TA52M,TA59, TA80,TB02,TB05,TB09,TB78,TB84,TB95,TB96.

21590   Collins, C.S. The comprehension of sentences describing temporal and spatial order by children with normal and deviant language development [doctoral dissertation, University of Illinois at Urbana-Champaign, 1974]. _Dissertation Abstracts International_, June 1975, 35(12, part 1), 6174B– 6175B. Topic Codes: BL11,DT42,ML,NA07B,NA07ID,NL48,PE10,PE44,PG,PN,TA80, TB.

21595   Colpaert, F.C. The ventromedial hypothalamus and the control of avoidance behavior and aggression: Fear hypothesis versus response-suppression theory of limbic system function. _Behavioral Biology_, September 1975, 15(1), 27–44. Topic Codes: BD07,BK11B,DD,DK07B,MC,MM,PE,PP07B.

21600   Commey, J.O.O., and Fitzhardinge, P.M. Handicap in the preterm small-for-gestational-age infant. _Journal of Pediatrics_, May 1979, 94(5), 779–789. Topic Codes: BB,BE30,BL05,BL07B,BL27K,BL31,BL70,BP02,BP26G,DD02,DF,DF06B, DF60B,DF70,DP11,DP22P,NA31C,NA31F,NA31R,NA44B,NJ03,NL48,PK,SQ,SW,TA52K, TB05.

21800   Committee on Drugs. Effect of medication during labor and delivery on infant outcome. _Pediatrics_, September 1978, 62(3), 402–403. Topic Codes: BP02,BP04,NA33D,NA33I,PE34,TA52M.

21950   Conner, R.L., and Levine, S. Hormonal influences on aggressive behavior. In S. Garattini and E.B. Sigg (eds.), _Aggressive Behavior_. New York: John Wiley & Sons, Inc., 1969. Topic Codes: BD11,BD70B,MC,PE04,SR03.

22000   Conners, C.K. Psychological assessment of children with minimal brain dysfunction. _New York Academy of Sciences – Annals_, 1973, 205, 283–302. Topic Codes: BL04,BL18B,BL48B,CV15B,DK07B,DK48B,DT44B,DT48B,MG,MG48B,MK, MM07,MT48B,NA07D,PE30,PE48B,PM07,PP07,PR07,SW,TA02,TA59D,TB09B,TB09K, TB33G,TB37B,TB46,TB57,TB66B,TB95B,TB96B,TB98B.

22100   Conners, C.K. Symptom patterns in hyperkinetic, neurotic and normal children. _Child Development_, 1970, 41, 667–682. Topic Codes: BL04,

BL04B,BL67,BL70,BN68,CC37B,DT69,MG,MG11,MG18,MG30,MQ,MU,MW,NA07D,PM,SN,SQ,
SW07,TA57,TB95.

22200   Conners, C.K. Treatment of young delinquent boys with diphenylhydantoin
         sodium and methyphenidate. _Archives of General Psychiatry_, February 1971,
         24, 156-160. Topic Codes: CC37B,CC371,CV15D,MC11,MK11,PE04D,PE30D,PE64D,
         SC70D,SR03B,TA02,TA03,TA59,TA74,TB66B,TB66D.

22300   Connor, J.M., Schackman, M., and Serbin, L.A. Sex-related differences in
         response to practice on a visual-spacial test and generalization to a re-
         lated test. _Child Development_, 1978, 49, 24-29. Topic Codes: BI,BL70,
         DT59,MR,NA07B,PE10,PM,PS,SF,SQ,TA59D.

22360   Conrad, P. The discovery of hyperkinesis: Notes on the medicalization of
         deviant behavior. _Social Problems_, October 1975, 23(1), 12-21. Topic
         Codes: BL11,DD00,DK48,MG30B,MG48,PE10.

22380   Cook, J.B. The assessment of spinal cord damage and factors influencing
         rehabilitation and survival. In D. Williams (ed.), _Modern Trends in_
         Neurology, vol. 4. New York: Appleton-Century-Crofts, 1967. Topic
         Codes: DD02,DK09,PR,SL,SW.

22500   Cook, T.H., and Solway, K.S. WISC subtest patterns of delinquent male re-
         tardates. _Psychological Reports_, August 1974, 35(1, part 1), 22. Topic
         Codes: BL67,CC37,CC37B,CC371,CC67,CQ37,CQ67,DK46D,MO11,NE37,NE67,SN,
         TB95B,TB95D.

22600   Cooney, T.E., Jr. Biological factors in socially troublesome juvenile
         behavior. Memorandum, Ford Foundation, Division of National Affairs,
         April 18, 1979. Topic Codes: BD30HB,BD52B,BD52D,BL67,CC37B,CC37C,CC37E,
         CC37F,CC37H,CC37K,CC37L,CC37O,CC37P,CC37S,CC37U,CC37X,CC37Y,CC37Z,CC81M,
         CT57,CT57BD,CT57F,CV52B,CV52D,DD00,DD10D,DD30B,DK07B,DP11B,DT44D,MG02D,
         MG11,MM11,MU70B,PP11,SI57GD,SN.

22700   Cooper, B., and Gath, D. Psychiatric illness, maladjustment and juvenile
         delinquency: An ecological study in a London bureau. _Psychological Medi-_
         cine, 1977, 7, 465-474. Topic Codes: BL70,CC37B,CC37L,CC37Z,MG,NA07D,
         SF07,SF26B,SF26D,SQ,SW07.

22800   Cooper, S.F., Leach, C., Storer, D., and Tonge, W.L. The children of psy-
         chiatric patients: Clinical findings. _British Journal of Psychiatry_,
         1977, 131, 514-522. Topic Codes: BL70,CV06,MG,MG11,NA07D,NH59B,NH59E,
         SH59B,SH59F,SQ.

22900   Copas, J.B., and Whiteley, J.S. Predicting success in the treatment of
         psychopaths. _British Journal of Psychiatry_, 1976, 129, 388-392. Topic
         Codes: CV06C,MG11,MS04B.

23000   Copeland, A.D. Psychologic management of the "acting out" adolescent.
         Clinical Pediatrics, April 1979, 18(4), 199-202. Topic Codes: CV06,MG,
         MK,NA07D,PE30.

23100   Copeland, A.D. Violent black gangs: Psycho- and sociodynamics. _Ado-_
         lescent Psychiatry, 1974, 3, 340-353. Topic Codes: CC37B,CC37G,CC37L,
         CC81L,CQ37B,NE37D,NL07D,SF26DD.

23150   Coplan, S. _Profile of the Juvenile Arsonist_. Seattle, Washington: Uni-
         versity of Washington, Center for the Assessment of Delinquent Behavior
         and Its Prevention, 1979. Topic Codes: CC37,CQ37,CT59B,NE37.

23200   Corballis, M.C. Is left-handedness genetically determined? In J. Herron
         (ed.), _Neuropsychology of Left Handedness_. New York: Academic Press,
         1980. Topic Codes: BI,BN44,DT42,ML,NH,NH59B,NH74,PE44,PN,PO,SF,SH,SH59B,
         SH74.

23300   Corballis, M.C., and Morgan, M.J. On the biological basis of human later-
         ality: I. Evidence for a maturational left-right gradient. _Behavioral_

and Brain Sciences, 1978, 2, 261-269. Topic Codes: BI,BL11,BL31,BL52D, BN44,DT13,DT42,MH,ML,NA07I,NA31F,PE44,PG,PI,PK,PN,PO.

23400   Coren, S., and Porac, C. Birth factors and laterality: Effects of birth order, parental age, and birth stress on four indices of lateral prefer- ence. Behavior Genetics, 1980, 10(2), 123-138. Topic Codes: BN44,BP46, DP11,DP22,DP44,PO,SF,SJ07.

23500   Corotto, L.V. The relation of performance to verbal IQ in acting out ju- veniles. Journal of Psychological Studies, 1961, 12(4), 162-166. Topic Codes: CC37B,CC371,MG11B,TB95D,TB96BB,TB96D.

23700   Cortes, J.B., and Gatti, F.M. Delinquency and Crime: A Biopsychosocial Approach - Empirical, Theoretical, and Practical Aspects of Criminal Be- havior. New York: Seminar Press, 1972. Topic Codes: BA,BE11,BL70D, CC11C,CC11D,CC11M,CC37B,CC37C,CC37K,CC37M,CC37N,CC37W,CG11P,DD,NH59D,NH74, NH74B,NH74D,NL48,PT11,PY11,SF11,SH59D,SH74B,SH74D,SI22D,SI48D,SI57D,SI57J, SI57PB,SI59D,SQ11,SU11,TB23B.

23800   Courville, C.B. Birth and Brain Damage. Pasadena: M.F. Courville, 1971. Topic Codes: BK11B,BL06,BL07B,BL22,BL27KL,BP02,BP04,BP22F,BP26GD,BP44, BP46,BP47,BP53,BP59,BP63,DD08K,DF06B,DF34,DF60B,DF70B,DP11,DP22,DP44,DP46, DT04E,NA33B,NL,PL,TA52M.

23820   Coutu, R.G. Rewarding academic performance versus rewarding on-task be- havior: An analysis of the effects on the disruptive behavior and academ- ic performance of learning disabled children [doctoral dissertation, Bos- ton College, 1982]. Dissertation Abstracts International, April 1983, 43 (10), 3266A. Topic Codes: DT44,PE64.

23900   Cowett, R.M., and Stern, L. Maternal thyroid status and the incidence of respiratory distress syndrome: Evaluation of a proposed relationship. Pediatrics, April 1975, 55(4), 497-499. Topic Codes: BL06,BP47,DF67.

24000   Craft, M. The natural history of psychopathic disorder. British Journal of Psychiatry, 1969, 115, 39-44. Topic Codes: BL04BB,CC11C,CC37B,CC67B, CT57,CT59,CV06C,MS04B.

24030   Craig, T.J. An epidemiologic study of problems associated with violence among psychiatric in-patients. American Journal of Psychiatry, October 1982, 139(10), 1262-1266. Topic Codes: CC81D,CC81R,CT57,DA04D,DK07D, MD11,MU70B,PE06D.

24100   Critchley, E.M.R. Reading retardation, dyslexia and delinquency. British Journal of Psychiatry, 1968, 114, 1537-1547. Topic Codes: BL04,BN44, BN44B,CC37B,CC37G,CC37H,CC37J,CC37L,CC37R,DT15,MG18D,ML15,NH59D,NH59F, PE64D,PO,PO07,SC70D,SH59D,SH59H,SJ09D,TA03,TA04,TA52,TB78D,TB95D.

24200   Cronbach, L.J. Essentials of Psychological Testing (3rd ed.). New York: Harper & Row, 1970. Topic Codes: BL67,BL70,CC37,MM,PM,PP,PR,SC59,SC70, SD,SF,SW,TA04,TA80,TB02,TB09,TB23,TB25,TB33G,TB38,TB51,TB53,TB61,TB66, TB68,TB74,TB78B,TB78D,TB86,TB93,TB95,TB96.

24230   Crook, W.G. Can what a child eats make him dull, stupid, or hyperactive? Journal of Learning Disabilities, May 1980, 13(5), 281-286. Topic Codes: BD52B,CV52B,DT44,MG,MG30,MM,NA07D,PP.

24300   Cross, H., and Tracy, J. Personality factors in delinquent boys: Differ- ences between blacks and whites. Journal of Research in Crime and Delin- quency, 1971, 8, 10-22. Topic Codes: BL04D,CC37A,CC37L,CC37Q,CC37W, CC37Y,CC37Z,CC371,MK11,PE30D,PT11,PY11,SI57PB,SU11,TA03,TA59,TB91C.

24400   Crowe, R.R. The adopted offspring of women criminal offenders. Archives of General Psychiatry, November 1972, 27, 95-103. Topic Codes: BI11, BL11C,BL70D,CC11,CC11D,CC11M,CG11CC,NE59,NH04D,NH67D,SH04D,SH59D.

24450   Crowe, R.R. Adoption studies in psychiatry. Biological Psychiatry, June 1975, 10(3), 353-371. Topic Codes: BI07B,BL11,CC11,CC11M,DD00B,DD02B,

MD07B,ME,MF,MG30BB,MU70,NH04BA,NH59B,NH65B,P,SH04B,SH59B,SH59D,TA02,TA59,
TA80.

24500   Crowe, R.R. An adoption study of antisocial personality. Archives of
General Psychiatry, December 1974, 31(6), 785-791. Topic Codes: BI07B,
CC11C,CC11L,CC11M,MS04B,NH04BA,NH04D,SF07B,SH04BB,SH04D,SI59,SW07B,TB61B.

24600   Crowe, R.R. An adoptive study of psychopathy: Preliminary results from
arrest records and psychiatric hospital records. Proceedings of the Amer-
ican Psychopathological Association, 1975, 63, 95-103. Topic Codes:
BI07B,CC11C,CC11L,CC11M,CC37B,CC37L,CC37N,MS04B,NH04BA,NH04D,NH59B,NH59D,
NH59E,NH59F,NH59PD,NH59PJ,NH59PL,SF07B,SH04BB,SH04D,SH59B,SH59D,SH59F,
SH59H,SH59RD,SH59RJ,SH59RL,SI46D,SJ09D,SW07B.

24700   Crowther, P. Psychological aspects of motherhood. Child Welfare, July
1975, 365-375. Topic Codes: BL31,DP,NA31D,NA31F,NC44,NC59G,NH59P,PA,
PE32,PK,PT,SH59R,SI46,SI46B,SI57B.

24800   Crump, E.P., Horton, C.P., Masuoka, J., and Ryan, D. Growth and development: I. Relation of birth weight in Negro infants to sex, maternal age,
parity, prenatal care, and socioeconomic status. Journal of Pediatrics,
December 1957, 51, 678-697. Topic Codes: BL06,BL27,BL67,BL70,BP,BP26,
BP46,BP57,BP59,DF60,NL07,SN,SQ,SW.

24900   Crump, E.P., Payton, E., and Horton, C.P. Growth and development: IV.
Relationship between prenatal maternal nutrition and socioeconomic index,
weight of mother, and birth weight of infant. American Journal of Obstetrics and Gynecology, March 1959, 77, 562-572. Topic Codes: BL06,BL70,BP,
BP02,BP52,NH59PF,NH59PP,NL07,SH59RF,SH59RP,SJ22,SQ,SW.

25000   Cullen, F.T., Golden, K.M., and Cullen, J.B. Sex and delinquency. Crim-
inology, November 1979, 17(3), 301-310. Topic Codes: BL70D,CC37,CC37W,
CC81V,CQ37,CT59,CT70,DA15D,MC11,MI07,NE37,PE04D,PE15D,PT11,SQ11,SQ70D,
SR03B.

25100   Cumming, S.T., and Carson, R.L. Maternal personality and the externaliz-
ing-internalizing symptom dimension in neurotic children. Proceedings of
the 75th Annual Convention of the American Psychological Association,
1967, 2, 181-182. Topic Codes: BL04B,BL70,MG,NA07D,NH59P,NH59PJ,SH59R,
SH59RJ,SQ,TA59.

25200   Cunningham, M.A., Pillai, V., and Rogers, W.J.B. Haloperidol in the
treatment of children with severe behavior disorders. British Journal of
Psychiatry, 1968, 114, 845-854. Topic Codes: BL04,CV15B,DT44B,MC,MG11,
MG30,MM07,PE04,PE64B,PM,PP07,SC70B,SR03,TA59,TA59D.

25300   Curman, H., and Nylander, I. A ten-year prospective followup study of
2268 cases at the child guidance clinics in Stockholm. Acta Paediatrica
Scandinavica, 1976, supplement 260, 1-71. Topic Codes: BL11,CV,MG02,
MG11,MG18,MG21,NJ,PE10,PG,SF07,SH59,SI57B,TA59,TA80,TB21,TB74.

25330   Curtis, J.H. Understanding the chronic youth offender: A "social dyslexia" model. Journal of Humanics, 1981, 9(2), 64-71. Topic Codes:
CC37,CC67,CQ37,CQ67,NE37,NE67,PY11,SI57PB,SU11.

25400   Cushner, I.M., and Mellits, E.D. The relationship between fetal outcome
and the gestational age and birth weight of the fetus. Johns Hopkins
Medical Journal, May 1971, 128, 252-260. Topic Codes: BL07B,BL27,BL67,
BP26,DF06B,DF48,DK,DP48,NA31R,NC44,SN,TA52K.

25500   Cuthbert, T.M. A portfolio of murders. British Journal of Psychiatry,
1970, 116, 1-10. Topic Codes: BL70D,CC11C,CC11H,CC37B,CC37L,CC81B,CC81D,
CC81K,CC81L,CC81M,CC81V,CT57F,CV13D,DT02B,MK11,MN04B,MS04B,PE30D,SQ11.

25600   Czudner, G., and Rourke, B.P. Age differences in visual reaction time of
"brain-damaged" and normal children under regular and irregular prepara-
tory interval conditions. Journal of Experimental Child Psychology, 1972,

13, 516-526. Topic Codes: BL04,BL11,DD08K,DD26,DF34,DK07,DT04E,NA07I,
NA33B,PG,TA52,TA55,TA80.

25700   D'Agostino, C.A. Performance of psychopathic and nonpsychopathic delin-
quent girls on the Kahn Test of Symbol Arrangement. Perceptual and Motor
Skills, 1976, 43, 1020-1022. Topic Codes: CC37,CC37I,CQ37,MG,MS04B,
NA07D,NE37,NL22,TA02B,TA59,TB61B.

25760   Dalby, J.T., Schneider, R.D., and Arboleda-Florez, J. Learning disorders
in offenders. International Journal of Offender Therapy and Comparative
Criminology, 1982, 26(2), 145-151. Topic Codes: CC37B,CC37H,DT44D,MG30D,
MM11,PP11.

25800   Dallas, J. Patient follow-up in a long-term study. Johns Hopkins Medical
Journal, May 1971, 128, 244. Topic Codes: BL06,DK,NC70,NC80,NH59P,
NH59PH,SH59RF,SH59RH,SW,TB95.

25900   Dalton, K. Ante-natal progesterone and intelligence. British Journal of
Psychiatry, 1968, 114, 1377-1382. Topic Codes: BD70,BL06,BL31,BP02,BP04,
BP46,BP53,DP60,NA31F,PE64,PK,PM,SC70.

25920   Dalton, K. Cyclical criminal acts in premenstrual syndrome. Lancet,
November 1980, 8203, 1070-1071. Topic Codes: BD11,BD70B,CC11D,CC24,
CQ22.

25950   Dalton, K. Menstruation and crime. British Medical Journal, 1961, 2,
1752-1753. Topic Codes: BA,CC24,CQ22,NE22,NE59,NL.

26000   Dalton, K. Prenatal progesterone and educational attainments. British
Journal of Psychiatry, 1976, 129, 438-442. Topic Codes: BD70,BP02,BP04,
DP60,PE64,SC18,SC70.

26100   Daly, R.F. Mental illness and patterns of behavior in 10 XYY males.
Journal of Nervous and Mental Disease, 1969, 149(4), 318-326. Topic
Codes: BB70B,BB70D,CC11C,CC11G,CT57,CT59,DD02ND,DD02NF,DK09B,TB61B,TB74B,
TB93D.

26200   Damon, A. Secular trend in height and weight within old American families
at Harvard, 1870-1965. American Journal of Physical Anthropology, July-
December 1968, 29, 45-50. Topic Codes: BE,NH,SH,SJ07,SW56.

26220   Daniel, A.E., Parraga, H., Beeks, E.C., and Belsky, D. Psychiatric diag-
nosis and pattern of drug abuse among violent adolescent criminals.
American Journal of Forensic Psychiatry, 1983, 4(1), 5-20. Topic Codes:
CC37B,CC37I,CC37T,CC371,DA15D,TB95D,TB98D.

26260   Darby, J.K. Neuropathologic aspects of psychosis in children. Journal
of Autism and Childhood Schizophrenia, December 1976, 6(4), 339-352.
Topic Codes: BB07,BK04B,BK11B,BN,DD00B,DK07BB,DK09B,DK11B,DK18B,DK46,
NA07,NA31A.

26300   Darlington, R.B. Preschool programs and later school competence of chil-
dren from low-income families. Science, April 11, 1980, 208, 202-204.
Topic Codes: NA44P,NH59PF,NJ23,NL48,PE64,SC59,SC70,SH59RF,SW,TA04,TB78,
TB95.

26400   D'Atri, D.A. Psychophysiological responses to crowding in prisons. Un-
published manuscript, Yale University School of Medicine, March 1978.
Topic Codes: BL08BD,BL59,BL67,CC11,CC11D,CC11P,CQ11,CV13D,DD28D,MG11,
NA44,NE11,NJ,PT11,SF07,SF11,SN,TA03,TA59.

26500   David, K.H. Cross-cultural uses of the Porteus Maze. Journal of Social
Psychology, 1974, 92, 11-18. Topic Codes: PM,TB66.

26600   David, O., Clark, J., and Voeller, K. Lead and hyperactivity. Lancet,
October 28, 1972, 7783, 900-903. Topic Codes: DA44MB,DK48,MG30,MG48,
NL48,TA02,TA52,TA57,TA74.

26700   Davids, A., and Falkof, B.B. Juvenile delinquents then and now: Compari-
         son of findings from 1959 and 1974. Journal of Abnormal Psychology, 1975,
         84(2), 161-164. Topic Codes: BL04D,BL67,BL70,CC37H,CC37K,CC37L,CC37W,
         DT13D,MH11,PI11,SF11,SN,SQ.

26750   Davids, A., and Holden, R.H. Consistency of maternal attitudes and per-
         sonality from pregnancy to eight months following childbirth. Develop-
         mental Psychology, May 1970, 2, 364-366. Topic Codes: BP,NA44,NC44,
         NC59G,NH59P,NJ,SH59R,SI48,TA59.

26800   Davies, J.G.V., and Maliphant, R. Refractory behavior in school and
         avoidance learning. Journal of Child Psychology and Psychiatry and Allied
         Disciplines, 1974, 15, 23-31. Topic Codes: BK04B,DT44B,MG11,MM07,PA,
         PP07,SI57J.

26900   Davis, H.M. Psychometric prediction of institutional adjustment: A
         validation study. British Journal of Social and Clinical Psychology,
         1974, 13, 269-276. Topic Codes: CC11C,CC11P,CC11U,CV06C,MC11,MX11,PA11,
         PE04D,PE68D,PT11,SR02,SR03B,TB19B,TB61B,TB66D.

27000   Davis, J.C., and Cropley, A.J. Psychological factors in juvenile delin-
         quency. Canadian Journal of Behavioral Science, 1976, 8(1), 68-77. Topic
         Codes: BL67,CC37G,CC37Q,CC37W,DT13D,MG11,MH11,MX11,PE68D,PI11,SN,SR02,
         TA03,TA59,TA59D.

27100   De Bault, L.E., Johnston, E., and Loeffelholz, P. Incidence of XYY and
         XXY individuals in a security hospital population. Diseases of the Ner-
         vous System, September 1972, 33(9), 590-592. Topic Codes: BB70B,BB70D,
         CC11C,CC11D,CC11I,CT59,DD02ND,DD02NF.

27150   Dee, H.L. Auditory symmetry and strength of manual preference. Cortex,
         1971, 7, 236-245. Topic Codes: BK11B,BN44,NL,PO,TA52,TB49.

27170   De Filippis, N.A. Application of a set of class-defining roles for the
         hyperkinetic reaction of childhood and the unsocialized aggressive reac-
         tion of childhood [doctoral dissertation, University of Iowa, 1976].
         Dissertation Abstracts International, June 1977, 37(12, part 1), 6320B.
         Topic Codes: BB07,BD,BL11,DD00,DD02B,DK48,MF,MG02B,MG48B,NA07B,PE10,PG,
         SR01,TA02,TA57,TA80.

27200   De Fries, J.C., Ashton, G.C., Johnson, R.C., Kuse, A.R., McClearn, G.E.,
         Mi, M.P., Rashad, M.N., Vandenberg, S.G., and Wilson, J.R. Parent-
         offspring resemblance for specific cognitive abilities in two ethnic
         groups. Nature, May 1976, 261, 131-133. Topic Codes: BI,DT13,MH,NH59B,
         PI,SH59B,TA59D,TB68,TB72.

27250   De Fries, J.C., and Plomin, R. Behavioral genetics. Annual Review of
         Psychology, 1978, 29, 473-515. Topic Codes: BI07,BL11,CC11G,CC11M,CC11Q,
         DD00,DD02B,MF,MG30B,MH07,MU70,NA,NH59B,NH59D,NH63,NH74B,NL,PE10,PI07,
         SH04B,SH11,SH59D,SH74B,SI57B,TA80,TB42,TB78,TB93,TB95.

27270   De Fronzo, J. Economic assistance to impoverished Americans: Relation-
         ship to incidence of crime. Criminology, February 1983, 21(1), 119-136.
         Topic Codes: CG11,CT57F,CT68,SW11.

27300   De Hirsch, K. Early language development and minimal brain dysfunction.
         New York Academy of Sciences - Annals, 1973, 205, 158-163. Topic Codes:
         BL11,BL48B,DK09B,DK46B,DT42B,DT48B,MG30,ML02,MM07,MO07,MT48B,NA07I,
         PE44B,PE48B,PG,PN07,PP07,PR07.

27400   De la Burde, B., and Choate, M.S. Early asymptomatic lead exposure and
         development at school age. Journal of Pediatrics, October 1975, 87(4),
         638-642. Topic Codes: BL11,BN70,DA44MB,DT67,DT71,MG,MY,NA07D,NA07I,
         NA44D,NC22,NC44,NC70,NJ06,PE64,PE70,PG,PM,SC70,TA52,TB09K,TB27,TB33G,TB53,
         TB84,TB95,TB98.

27430   De la Burde, B., and Shapiro, I.M. Dental lead, blood lead, and pica in

urban children. <u>Archives of Environmental Health</u>, 1975, 30, 281-284.
Topic Codes: BD,DA44,NA07,NA44D,NC,NJ06,NL07,SF26,SM.

27460   De la Cruz, F.F., Fox, B.H., and Roberts, R.H. (eds.). Minimal brain dysfunction, <u>New York Academy of Sciences – Annals</u>, 1973, 205, 1-396. Topic
Codes: DK48B,MG30,MG48B.

27480   Delamater, A.M., and Lahey, B.B. Physiological correlates of conduct
problems and anxiety in hyperactive and learning-disabled children. <u>Jour-
nal of Abnormal Child Psychology</u>, March 1983, 11(1), 85-100. Topic Codes:
BK04B,BL25B,DT44,ME,TA02,TA74.

27500   Dembo, R. Critical factors in understanding adolescent aggression. <u>So-
cial Psychiatry</u>, 1973, 8, 212-219. Topic Codes: CC81L,CC81S,CG11T,CT57,
MC,NA07B,PA,PE04,PE10,PE64,PT,SB,SC70,SF,SR03,SS,SW,TA57,TA70,TA74.

27600   Dengerink, H.A., and Bertilson, H.S. Psychopathy and physiological arousal in an aggressive task. <u>Psychophysiology</u>, November 1975, 12(6), 682-
684. Topic Codes: BI07B,BL25BB,BL29,BN04BB,MC,MS04,MS04B,PC07B,PE04,
SR03.

27700   Denhoff, E. The natural life history of children with minimal brain dys-
function. <u>New York Academy of Sciences – Annals</u>, 1973, 205, 188-204.
Topic Codes: BL11,BL31,CV15B,DK48B,MG,MG30,MG30B,MG48B,NA07D,NA07I,NA31D,
NA31F,NA31R,NC44,NC70,PE32,PE64B,PG,PK,SC70B,TA02,TA52K,TA80,TB02,TB35B,
TB78B,TB95B.

27800   Denhoff, E. Precursive factors to early and identified learning disabilities. <u>Australian Journal on the Education of Backward Children</u>, July
1972, 19(2), 79-85. Topic Codes: BL11,DF,DF34,DT44,MG,MG30,MM,NA07D,
NA07I,NA31A,NA31C,NA31R,NA33B,NA33I,NA44D,NC44,NC70,NJ06,PE64B,PG,PP,
SC70B,TA02,TA52,TA52K,TA52M.

27900   Denhoff, E., Hainsworth, P.K., and Hainsworth, M.L. The child at risk for
learning disorder: Can he be identified during the first year of life?
<u>Clinical Pediatrics</u>, March 1972, 11(3), 164-170. Topic Codes: BD30,
BD30B,BL07BB,BP02B,DF,DF06BB,DF67B,DT44,MG,MM,NA07D,NA31C,NA31R,NA33I,
NA44D,NC44,NC70,NJ06,PP,TA02,TA52K,TA52M,TA80,TB02,TB95B,TB98B.

27910   Denno, D. Neuropsychological and early environmental correlates of sex
differences in crime. <u>International Journal of Neuroscience</u>, June 1984,
23(3), 199-213. Topic Codes: BA,BL70D,CC11C,CC11S,CC11U,CC37B,CC371,
NA44F,NC04,NJ09,SQ11,TA03,TA55.

27915   Denno D. Sex differences in cognition and crime: Early developmental,
biological, and sociological correlates. Doctoral dissertation, Universi-
ty of Pennsylvania, 1982. Topic Codes: BB11,BB48D,BE11,BK11,BL04D,
BL07BD,BL08BD,BL11C,BL22,BL27KL,BL48D,BL52DD,BL70D,BN44D,BN44H,BP02D,
BP26GD,BP44,BP46,BP47,BP53,BP57,BP63,BP70,CC24B,CC37A,CC37B,CC37D,CC37E,
CC37F,CC37G,CC37H,CC37J,CC37K,CC37M,CC37Q,CC37R,CC37X,CC37Z,CC371,CC67B,
CC81A,CC81E,CC81F,CC81G,CC81J,CC81L,CC81N,CC81Q,CC81T,CC81V,CC81W,CC81Y,
CG11P,CL,CQ22,CQ67,CQ81,CT57,CT59,CT70,CT81,CY,DD08KC,DD28D,DF06BD,DK09D,
DP11D,DP44,DP46,DP48,DP81,DT02B,DT04ED,DT13D,DT44D,MF11,MG11B,MH11,MM11,
NA07DF,NA07ID,NA31B,NA31R,NA33A,NA44F,NC04,NC44,NC59,NC70,NE11,NE22,NE37,
NE81,NH04D,NH59D,NH59PA,NH59PF,NH59PH,NJ09,NL07D,NL22D,PE01,PE64D,PG11,
PI11,PK,PL,PM11,PM70B,PO11,PP11,PR11,SA11,SC18D,SC70D,SF11,SH04D,SH59H,
SH59RA,SH59RF,SH59RH,SH59RL,SI11,SI46D,SI59D,SJ07D,SJ09D,SJ22D,SQ11,SR02,
SW11,SW16,SW33,TA03,TA04,TA52M,TA55,TA59D,TB02,TB09D,TB09K,TB21D,TB33GD,
TB95D,TB96D,TB98D.

27920   Denno, D., Meijs, B., Nachshon, I., and Aurand, S. Early cognitive functioning: Sex and race differences. <u>International Journal of Neurosci-
ence</u>, 1982, 16, 159-172. Topic Codes: BN44H,DT13,DT48,MH,NA07,NA44K,
NC22,NC44,NC70,NJ17,NJ20,NL07,NL22,NL48,PG,PI,PL,PM70,PO33,PP,SN,SQ,SW,
SW16,SW33,TA04,TA52M,TA59D,TB05,TB78,TB95.

27930   Derkson, G.D., and Catalanotto, F.A. The lateral tongue reflex in human

neonates. Perceptual and Motor Skills, February 1978, 46(1), 331-337.
Topic Codes: BK,BL07,BL18,BL27,BL33,BP02,BP26,BP44,BP57,NA33I,TA52M,TB02.

27950   De Rosis, H. Violence: Where does it begin? Family Coordinator, October
1971, 20(4), 355-362. Topic Codes: CC81,CC81D,CC81F,CC81N,CC81S,CQ81,
CT81,NE81,SI57D.

28000   Devore, J.E., and Fryrear, J.L. Analysis of juvenile delinquents' hole
drawing responses on the tree figure of the House-Tree-Person Technique.
Journal of Clinical Psychology, July 1976, 32(3), 731-736. Topic Codes:
CC37B,CC37W,CC371,PM,TA02,TA03,TA59,TB61,TB95.

28050   De Wolfe, A.S., and Ryan, J.J. Wechsler IQ > Verbal IQ index in a forensic sample: A reconsideration. Journal of Clinical Psychology, January
1984, 40(1), 291-294. Topic Codes: BL67B,BL67D,CC81G,CC81R,CC81Y,CT57F,
CT68,DT44D,TB96D.

28100   Diaz, J., and Schain, R.J. Phenobarbital: Effects of long-term administration on behavior and brain of artificially reared rats. Science, 1978,
199, 90-91. Topic Codes: BK11B,BL31,BL52D,BN04,CV15,NA31D,NA31F,PC,PE32,
PK.

28200   Di Cara, L.V. Learning in the autonomic nervous system. Scientific American, January 1970, 222(1), 30-39. Topic Codes: BK04,BL08,BL29,DD,DT44,
MM,PP.

28250   Dielman, T.E., and Cattell, R.B. The prediction of behavior problems in
6- to 8-year-old children from mothers' reports of child-rearing prac-
tices. Journal of Clinical Psychology, January 1972, 28(1), 13-17. Topic
Codes: MG11,NA07D,PE10,PE64,PE68,PG,SC70,SI46B,SI48B,SR,TA02B,TA74.

28300   Dierks, D., and Cushna, B. Sex differences in the Bender Gestalt performance of children. Perceptual and Motor Skills, 1969, 28, 19-22. Topic
Codes: BL04,BL11,BL70,MG,NA07D,NA07I,PG,SQ,TB09K,TB74,TB78,TB86,TB95.

28330   Dietz, G.A. The relationship between risk status at birth and later be-
havior disorders [doctoral dissertation, Indiana State University, 1982].
Dissertation Abstracts International, December 1983, 44(6), 1730A. Topic
Codes: BB,DF60BB,DF67B,MF,MG.

28400   Diller, L. A comparison of the test performances of delinquent and non-
delinquent girls. Journal of Genetic Psychology, 1952, 81, 167-183.
Topic Codes: CC24,CC37J,CC37Q,CC37W,CC371,CQ22,DT42D,ML03,NE22,NL22,
PE44D,PE64D,PM11,PN11,PT11,SC70D,TB93D,TB95D,TB96D,TB98D.

28450   Dimond, S.Y., and Beaumont, Y.G. Hemispheric function and color naming.
Journal of Experimental Psychology, 1972, 96, 87-91. Topic Codes: BK11B,
BN44,NL,PO,TA02,TA55,TA80,TB49.

28500   Dinges, D.F., Davis, M.M., and Glass, P. Fetal exposure to narcotics:
Neonatal sleep as a measure of nervous system disturbance. Science,
August 1, 1980, 209, 619-621. Topic Codes: BL06,BL27,BN68,BP02,BP04,
BP26,DF34,DK07,DT69,MW,NA33B,NA33I,TA52M,TB02.

28550   Di Tullio, B. The relationship between mental illness and criminal behavior. Monographs of the Criminal Law Education and Research Center, 1969,
3, 37-52. Topic Codes: CC11C,CC11F,CC11P,CQ11,CV06,DD01,DK07D,MB11,ME07,
MQ11,MSO4B,MU11,MX11,NE11,PEO1,PEO8D,PE30D,PT11,SRO1,SRO4B,TA03.

28560   Dituri, F. Another thyrotoxic criminal? Annals of Internal Medicine,
September 1971, 75(3), 478-479. Topic Codes: BD30,BK11B,CC11D,CC67B,
CV15B,CV15D,DD00,DD01,DK07B,DK07D,NE67.

28580   Dix, G.E. Determining the continued dangerousness of psychologically abnormal sex offenders. Journal of Psychiatry and Law, Fall 1975, 3(3),
327-344. Topic Codes: CC11C,CC67B,CC81D,CG11CC,CQ59,CQ67,CT68,CV06C,
CV13DA,CV30D,CY,MF11,MV11,NE59,NE67,NL,PEO8D,PE66D,SL11,SR69D.

28590   Dobbs, D.S., and Speck, L.B. Visual evoked response and frequency density spectra of prisoner-patients. Comprehensive Psychiatry, January 1968, 9(1), 62-70. Topic Codes: BK11B,BL18B,BL18D,CC11F,CC11O,CV06,DD,DK07B, DK07D,MU11,NE11,NE59,PC07,PC11,TA02,TA55,TA80,TB35B,TB35D,TB37B,TB37D.

28700   Docter, R.F., and Winder, C.L. Delinquent vs. non-delinquent performance on the Porteus Qualitative Maze Test. Journal of Consulting Psychology, 1954, 71-72. Topic Codes: CC37W,NA07B,NA07ID,NE37,PE10,PG11,TA03,TA59D, TB66.

28750   Docter, R.M., and Craine, W.H. Modification of drug language usage of primary and neurotic psychopaths. Journal of Abnormal Psychology, 1971, 77, 174-180. Topic Codes: CV06C,DA15B,DD02B,DT42BB,MI04,MM07,MS04,MU70, NE59,NL,PE15B,PP07,TA02,TA59D,TA80.

28760   Dodge, K.A., and Frame, C.L. Social cognitive biases and deficits in aggressive boys. Child Development, June 1982, 53(3), 620-635. Topic Codes: DT13B,MC,MH07,MX07,PE04,PE66B,PI11,SR01,SR03.

28800   Dorn, H.F. Methods of analysis for follow-up studies. Human Biology, December 1950, 22, 238-248. Topic Codes: NA44,NJ,NL.

28840   Dorros, K.G. A comparison of auditory behavior in the premature and full-term infant: The effects of intervention [doctoral dissertation, New School for Social Research, 1976]. Dissertation Abstracts International, December 1977, 38(6), 2900B-2901B. Topic Codes: BL27,BP22F,BP26,DF60B, NA33B,PL,TA52M.

28870   Douglas, J.W. Early hospital admissions and later disturbances of behavior and learning. Developmental Medicine and Child Neurology, August 1975, 17(4), 456-480. Topic Codes: DD00,DD02B,MG,NA44H,PE64,SL07,TA02, TA57,TA59,TB.

28900   Dowis, R.T. The effect of a visual training program on juvenile delinquency. Journal of the American Optometric Association, September 1977, 48(9), 1173-1176. Topic Codes: CC37H,CC37J,CC371,DD81D,MG11,PE64D,SC70D, TA03,TA59D.

29040   Drage, J.S., and Berendes, H. Apgar scores and outcome of the newborn. Pediatric Clinics of North America, August 1966, 13, 635-643. Topic Codes: BL06,BL07B,BL27K,BL33,DD,DF06B,DF34,DF48,NA33A,NC44,PL,TA52K, TA52M,TB02.

29050   Drage, J.S., Berendes, H.W., and Fisher, P.D. The Apgar scores and four-year psychological examination performance. Perinatal Factors Affecting Human Development; proceedings of the special session held during the eighth meeting of the PAHO (Pan American Health Organization) Advisory Committee on Medical Research, 1969, scientific publication no. 185, 222-227. Topic Codes: BL33,BP02B,DF34,DP11B,DT04EB,DT13,MH,NA07D,NA31A, NA33A,NA44B,NC22,NC44,NJ03,NL48,PI,PL,PM,TA52M,TA59D,TB02,TB78.

29060   Drage, J.S., Kennedy, C., Berendes, H., Schwarz, B.K., and Weiss, W. The Apgar score as an index of infant morbidity. Developmental Medicine and Child Neurology, April 1966, 8, 141-148. Topic Codes: BL33,DF34,DF48, DP48,DT04E,NA33B,NC44,NL48,TA52M,TB02.

29070   Drage, J.S., Kennedy, C., and Schwarz, B.K. The Apgar score as an index of neonatal mortality: A report from the Collaborative Study of Cerebral Palsy. Obstetrics and Gynecology, August 1964, 24, 222-230. Topic Codes: BL06,BL07BB,BL27KL,BL29,BL33,BP26G,BP26GD,DD,DF06B,DF34,DF70B,NA33B,NC44, PL,TA52M,TA80,TB02.

29080   Draper, R.J. Evidence for an alcohol brain damage syndrome. Irish Medical Journal, July 1978, 71(10), 350-352. Topic Codes: BK11B,DA04B,DD03B, DK07B,DT46,DT48B,MA07,MD07,PE02B,PE06B,TA.

29100   Drillien, C.M. Aetiology and outcome in low-birthweight infants. Developmental Medicine and Child Neurology, 1972, 14, 563-584. Topic Codes:

BB,BB48,BL07B,BL27K,BL31,BP26G,DD02,DD02K,DF,DF06B,DF70,DK,DP,DP11,DP22P,
MG,NA07D,NA31C,NA31D,NA31F,NA31R,NA44B,NJ03,PE32,PK,SW,TA52K.

29200   Drillien, C.M. The incidence of mental and physical handicaps in school-
age children of very low birth weight. Pediatrics, March 1961, 27, 452-
464. Topic Codes: BB,BL07B,BL07BB,BL70,BP02,BP57,DD02,DF06B,DF06BB,DK46,
MG,MO,NA07D,NA44D,NH65B,NH74,NJ06,PE64,PM,SC70,SF07,SH74,SQ,SW07,TA59D,
TA74,TB42,TB95.

29250   Driver, M.V., West, L.R., and Faulk, M. Clinical and EEG studies of prisoners charged with murder. British Journal of Psychiatry, December 1974,
125, 583-587. Topic Codes: BA,BB07,BB11,BK11B,CC11C,CC11D,CC11F,CC11O,
CC11U,CC81D,CC81E,CC81K,CC81R,CE,CG,CQ11,CQ59,CQ67,CT81,DD,DK07B,DKO7D,
MF11,MU11,MU70B,NE11,NE59,NE81,NL,PE01,TA02,TA03,TA80,TB35B,TB35D.

29300   Drorbaugh, J.E., Moore, D.M., and Warram, J.H., Jr. Association between
gestational and environmental event and central nervous system function in
7-year-old children. Pediatrics, October 1975, 56(4), 529-537. Topic
Codes: BL07B,BP,BP02,BP47,DF06B,DF34,DF48,DF60B,DK09,DP,DP11,DP22H,DP44,
DP48,DT52,NA33B,NA33I,NA44D,NC44,NC70,NJ06,SW,TA52M,TB02,TB09,TB27,TB33G,
TB53,TB84,TB95,TB98.

29400   Dubey, D.R. Organic factors in hyperkinesis: A critical evaluation.
American Journal of Orthopsychiatry, April 1976, 46(2), 353-365. Topic
Codes: BB48B,BD07,BI07,CV15B,DA44MB,DD02KB,DK48B,DP11B,DT52B,MG30,MG48B,
NH04B,NH59B,NH59D,NH59E,NH59F,NH74B,SF07,SH04B,SH59B,SH59D,SH59F,SH59H,
SH74B,TB35B.

29500   Duke, D.L., and Duke, P.M. The prediction of delinquency in girls. Journal of Research and Development in Education, November 2, 1978, 11(2), 18-
33. Topic Codes: CC37B,CC37I,CC37L,CC37O,CC37X,CC37Y,CC37I,CJ,CL,NH59D,
NH59F,NL22,PE64D,SC70D,SH59D,SI57D,SJ09D.

29550   Duncan, P., and Hobson, G.N. Toward a definition of aggression. Psychological Record, Summer 1977, 27(3), 545-555. Topic Codes: BL70,NA,NL48,
PE04,SQ,TA80.

29555   Dunham, E.C., Jenss, R.M., and Christie, A.U. A consideration of race and
sex in relation to the growth and development of infants. Journal of Pediatrics, 1939, 14, 156-160. Topic Codes: BL06,BL33,BL67,BL70,NA33F,
NA33I,TA52M,TA80.

29560   Dunne, M. Drug intervention in the management of aggression and explosive
behavior. Australian Family Physician, November 1978, 7(11), 1442-1448.
Topic Codes: CV15B,MC,PE04,SR03.

29600   Dusewicz, R.A., and Kershner, K.M. A scale for the measurement of lateral
dominance. Journal of Educational Measurement, Fall 1969, 6(3), 187-188.
Topic Codes: BN44,PO,TA55.

29700   Dykman, R.A., Peters, J.E., and Ackerman, P.T. Experimental approaches to
the study of minimal brain dysfunction: A follow-up study. New York
Academy of Sciences - Annals, 1973, 205, 93-108. Topic Codes: BL04;
DK48B,DT44B,DT52B,MG30,MG48B,MM07,NA44S,NJ27,PE64B,PP07,SC70B,SJ07B,SJ09B,
TA02,TA04,TA52,TA57,TA74,TB09B,TB09K,TB55,TB95B,TB96B,TB98B.

29800   Dzik, D. Vision and the juvenile delinquent. Journal of the American Optometric Association, May 1966, 37(5), 461-468. Topic Codes: CC37A,
CC37H,CC37J,DD81B,DT59D,MR11,PE64D,PS11,SC18D,SC70D,TA03,TA04.

29900   Eagle, D.B., and Brazelton, T.B. The infant at risk: Assessment and im-
plications for intervention. In M. McMillan and S. Henao (eds.), Child
Psychiatry: Treatment and Research. New York: Brunner-Mazel, 1977.
Topic Codes: DF34,DK09,NA33B,NA33D,NA33I,PE34,TA52M,TB02.

30000   Easson, W.M., Steinhilber, R.M., and Minn, R. Murderous aggression by
children and adolescents. Archives of General Psychiatry, January 1961,

4, 27-35. Topic Codes: CC37B,CC37K,CC37L,CT57BD,CT57F,CZ07,DD10D,MG18D,
MZ,SI57D,SI57GD,SY11,TB74B.

30100   Eaton, J.W., and Polk, K. Measuring Delinquency: A Study of Probation
Department Referrals. Pittsburgh: University of Pittsburgh Press, 1961.
Topic Codes: CC37B,CC37K,CC67B,CG11CC,CL,CQ37,CQ67,CV13D,MF11,MX11,
NA07DF,NE37,NE67,NL,PE02,SF07,SR02,TA03.

30180   Edelhoch, M.J. Biosociology of criminal action. Doctoral dissertation,
Florida State University, 1980. Topic Codes: BA,BI11,CG,PY11,SF11,
SI57PB,SU11.

30200   Edelston, H. The impervious character: A clue to the genesis of persistent delinquency and its early recognition. Community Health, 1977,
9(20), 20-28. Topic Codes: CC11G,CC11P,CC37B,CC37G,CC37K,CC37M,CC37W,
CC37Z,CQ37,CV06,NA07,PA,PG,SF,SH.

30230   Editorial: What becomes of the XYY male? Lancet, November 30, 1974,
7892, 1297-1298. Topic Codes: BB70D,BD70B,BI11,CC11D,CC11M,CC67B,CL,
CV13,DD02D,DD02NF,MF11,MV11,NE67,PE01,PE66D,SR69D.

30260   Egger, G.J., Webb, R.A.J., and Reynolds, I. Early adolescent antecedents
of narcotic abuse. International Journal of the Addictions, 1978, 13(5),
773-781. Topic Codes: DA15,MI,NL,SF07,SJ09,TA02,TA59,TB.

30300   Ehlers, C.L., Rickler, K.C., and Hovey, J.E. A possible relationship be-
tween plasma testosterone and aggressive behavior in a female outpatient
population. In M. Girgis and L.G. Kiloh (eds.), Limbic Epilepsy and the
Dyscontrol Syndrome; proceedings of the First International Symposium on
Limbic Epilepsy and the Dyscontrol Syndrome held in Sydney, Australia,
February 6-9, 1980. New York: Elsevier/North-Holland Biomedical Press,
1980. Topic Codes: BD70B,BL70B,CC81D,CC81I,CT57,CT59,MC,MC11,NL22,PE04,
PE04D,SQ07,SR03,SR03B,TA02,TA03,TA59.

30400   Ehrenkranz, J., Bliss, E., and Sheard, M.H. Plasma testosterone: Correlation with aggressive behavior and social dominance in man. Psychosomatic Medicine, November-December 1974, 36(6), 469-475. Topic Codes:
BD70B,CC11E,CC11P,CC11U,CC81E,MC,MC11,MX11,PE04,PE04D,PE68D,SR02,SR03,
SR03B,TB19B,TB21D,TB23B.

30470   Eibl-Eibesfeldt, I. Evolution of destructive aggression. Aggressive Behavior, 1977, 3(2), 127-144. Topic Codes: MC,PE04,PP07B,PT,PY11,SB11,
SF07B,SR03,SU11.

30480   Eibl-Eibesfeldt, I. Ontogenetic and maturational studies of aggressive
behavior. UCLA Forum in Medical Sciences, 1967, 7, 57-94. Topic Codes:
MC,PE04,SR03.

30490   Eichelman, B. The limbic system and aggression in humans. Neuroscience
and Biobehavioral Reviews, Fall 1983, 7(3), 391-394. Topic Codes:
BK11BL,MC,PE04,SR03.

30500   Eisen, P. The infantile roots of adolescent violence. American Journal of Psychoanalysis, 1976, 36, 211-218. Topic Codes: BL11C,CC37G,
CC37L,CC81F,CC81N,NA07ID,PG11,SI57D.

30600   Eisenberg, J.R. Criminality and heart rate: A prospective study [doctor-
al dissertation, New School for Social Research, 1977]. Dissertation Abstracts International, December 1977, 38(6), 2924B. Topic Codes: BK04D,
BL29D,BN04D,CV13D,DT44,MM,PC11,PP.

30670   Eldridge, R., Sweet, R., Lake, R., Ziegler, M., and Shapiro, A.K. Gilles
de la Tourette's Syndrome: Clinical, genetic, psychological, and biochemical aspects in 21 selected families. Neurology, February 1977, 27(2),
115-124. Topic Codes: BD,BI,DD,DT48,DT52,MC,MF,MG,MK,MQ,MT,MV,NH,NL,
PE68,PT,SH,SR,TA52.

30700   El-Guebaly, N., and Offord, D. The offspring of alcoholics: A critical

review. _American Journal of Psychiatry_, April 1977, 134(4), 357–365.
Topic Codes: BI07,BL04,BL70B,CC37I,CC37L,CT57B,DA04,DD10,DP22D,MD,MG,
MG30,MG30B,NA07D,NH04B,NH59B,NH59D,NH59E,NH59F,NH65B,NH74B,PE06,SH04B,
SH59B,SH59D,SH59F,SH59H,SH74B,SI57G,SJ09D,SQ07.

30830   Elkind, D., and Dabek, R.F. Personal injury and property damage in the
moral judgments of childhood. _Child Development_, June 1977, 48(2), 518–
522. Topic Codes: BL11,CE,CT57,CT59,DT13,NA07B,NA07I,PE10,PG,TA59,TA80,
TB.

30860   Ellingson, R.J. The incidence of EEG abnormality among patients with mental disorders of apparently nonorganic origin: A critical review. _Ameri-
can Journal of Psychiatry_, 1955, 111, 263–275. Topic Codes: BK11B,DK07,
TB35.

30900   Elliott, D.S., and Ageton, S.S. Reconciling race and class differences in
self-reported and official estimates of delinquency. _American Sociological Review_, February 1980, 45, 95–110. Topic Codes: BL67,BL67D,CC37Y,
CC37Z,CC67,CG,CG11P,CQ67,CT57,CT59,MG11,NE67,SN,SN11,SW11.

30970   Ellis, D.E. The assessment of self-instructional training in developing
self-control of aggressive behavior in impulse-aggressive boys [doctoral
dissertation, North Carolina State University at Raleigh, 1976]. _Disser-
tation Abstracts International_, December 1976, 37(6), 3070B. Topic Codes:
MC,MK,MM,NA07B,PE04,PE30,PP,SR03.

31000   Ellis, K.J., Vartsky, D., Zanzi, I., Cohn, S.H., and Yasumura, S. Cadmium: In vivo measurement in smokers and nonsmokers. _Science_, July 20,
1979, 205, 323–325. Topic Codes: BE,BP70.

31100   Ellis, L. Androgens and criminality: Recent research and theoretical im-
plications. Paper presented at the annual meeting of the American Society
of Criminology, Dallas, Texas, November 11, 1978. Topic Codes: BD70B,
BI11,BL04D,BL22,BL52,BL52DD,BL70,BL70D,BP22F,CC11A,CC11D,CC11S,CC37,CC37A,
CC37C,CC67,CC81A,CC81V,CQ37,CQ67,CT59,DP,DP11D,DT44D,MC,MM11,MV,NE37,NE67,
PE04,PE66,PP11,SQ,SQ11,SR03,SR69.

31105   Ellis. L. Genetics and criminal behavior: Evidence through the end of
the 1970s. _Criminology_, May 1982, 20(1), 43–66. Topic Codes: BB70D,
BI11,BL11,CC11L,CC11M,CG,NH,NH04D,NH67D,NH74D,PG11,SH,SH04D,SH11,SH74D.

31130   Ellis, N.R. (ed.). _Aberrant Development in Infancy: Human and Animal
Studies_. Hillsdale, New Jersey: Lawrence Erlbaum Associates, 1975.
Topic Codes: BB,BK04,BK11,BL07B,BL22,BL27KL,BL33,BL52D,BN04,BP02,BP03,
BP04,BP22F,BP26GD,BP47,BP48,DA,DA15,DD08K,DD26,DD81,DF06B,DF34,DF60B,
DF70B,DK07,DK09,DK46,DP11,DP22P,DP46,DT04,DT13,DT42,DT44,DT48,MG30,MH,MI,
ML,MM,MO,NA31C,NA31F,NA33B,NA33F,NL,PE15,PE34,PE44,PI,PL,PM,PN,PP,SI46,
SI59,TA52K,TA52M.

31160   Ellis, R.W.B. Height and weight in relation to onset of puberty in boys.
Archives of Disease in Childhood, 1946, 21, 181–189. Topic Codes: BE,
BL04,NA,NL,TA52.

31200   Emler, N.P., Heather, N., and Winton, M. Delinquency and the development
of moral reasoning. _British Journal of Social and Clinical Psychology_,
1978, 17, 325–331. Topic Codes: BL11C,CC37,CC37F,CG11P,CL,CQ37,DT13D,
MH11,NA07ID,NE37,PG11,PI11,TA03.

31300   Emond, S.M. The relationships among scores on the reading subtests of the
Metropolitan Achievement Tests and achievement of the reading standards on
the Third Grade Florida Statewide Assessment Test according to pupil,
race, sex and intelligence [doctoral dissertation, University of Florida,
1978]. _Dissertation Abstracts International_, April 1979, 39(10), 5899A–
5900A. Topic Codes: BL67,BL70,NA07,NL48,PE64,PM,SC70,SN,SQ,TA04,TA80.

31400   Engel, R. EEG in prematures and subsequent development. In C.R. Angle
and E.A. Bering (eds.), _Physical Trauma as an Etiological Agent in Mental
Retardation_. Proceedings of a Conference on the Etiology of Mental Re-

tardation. Washington, D.C.: U.S. Government Printing Office, 1970.
Topic Codes: BL04,BL22,BL27,BL31,BL33,BL48,BL70,BP22F,DF60B,DK11,DP,DT42,
DT48,ML,MT48,NA31F,NA33I,NC44,PE32,PE44,PE48,PK,PN,PR,SQ,TA52K,TA52M,TB05,
TB35.

31500   Engel, R., Butler, B., Fay, W., and Clarkson, D. Visual evoked responses,
developmental and intelligence scores from birth to seven. Developmental
Medicine and Child Neurology, 1972, 14, 114-115 (abstract). Topic Codes:
BL18,BL31,DT42,ML,NA31F,NA33I,NA44D,NC22,NC44,NC70,NJ06,PE44,PK,PN,TA52M,
TB05,TB09,TB37,TB78,TB95.

31530   Engel, R., and Fay, W. Are electroencephalographic-evoked response laten-
cies in neonates predictors of language performance at 1 and 3 years of
age? Electroencephalography and Clinical Neurophysiology, 1971, 30, 159-
160. Topic Codes: BK11B,DK07,DT42B,ML02,NL,PN07,TB35B.

31560   Engel, R., and Fay, W. Neonatal visual evoked potentials as predictors of
language performance test scores at age eight. Electroencephalography and
Clinical Neurophysiology, 1976, 40, 332 (abstract). Topic Codes: BL18,
NA33,NC44,NC70,PM,PN,TA,TB95.

31600   Engel, R., and Fay, W. Visual evoked responses at birth, verbal scores at
three years and IQ at four years. Developmental Medicine and Child Neurology, 1972, 14, 283-289. Topic Codes: BL04,BL11,BL18,BL31,BL67,BL70,
DT42,ML,NA07I,NA31F,NA33I,NA44B,NC22,NC44,NJ03,PE44,PG,PK,PM,PN,SN,SQ,
TA52M,TB02,TB37.

31700   Engel, R., and Henderson, N.B. Visual evoked responses and IQ scores at
school age. Developmental Medicine and Child Neurology, 1973, 15, 136-
145. Topic Codes: BL11,BL18,BL67,BL70,DK07,NA07I,NC70,PG,PM,SN,SQ,TB09K,
TB35,TB37,TB95.

31750   English, P.C. Failure to thrive without organic reason. Pediatric Annals, November 1978, 7(11), 774-778. Topic Codes: BB,BD,DD02,NA07I,PG,
PK,SI46,SI48,SI57,SI59,SS.

31800   Epilepsy and Learning. British Medical Journal, March 1979, 1(6163), 576.
Topic Codes: BL52D,CV15,DK07,DK18,DT44B,MM07,PE10,PP.

31900   Epps, P., and Parnell, R.W. Physique and temperament of women delinquents
compared with women undergraduates. British Journal of Medical Psychology, 1952, 25(4), 249-255. Topic Codes: BE11,CC24,CQ22,NE22,PT11,PT74B.

31930   Epstein, A.W. Disordered human sexual behavior associated with temporal
lobe dysfunction. Medical Aspects of Human Sexuality, 1969, 3(2), 62-68.
Topic Codes: BK11B,CC11F,CT68,DD00,DD01,DD02B,DD02D,DK07B,DK07D,DT67B,
MV07,MV11,PE66B,PE66D.

31950   Epstein, M.H., and Cullinan, D. Academic performance of behaviorally disordered and learning-disabled pupils. Journal of Special Education, Fall
1983, 17(3), 303-307. Topic Codes: DT44,MG,PE64B,TB98B.

32030   Erhardt, C.L., Joshi, G.B., Nelson, F.G., Kroll, B.H., and Weiner, L.
Influence of weight and gestation on perinatal and neonatal mortality by
ethnic group. American Journal of Public Health, November 1964, 54, 1841-
1855. Topic Codes: BL06,BL22,BL27KL,BP02,BP22,BP26GD,BP44,BP46,BP53,
NL48.

32050   Erickson, M.T. Reading disability in relation to performance on neuro-
logical tests for minimal brain dysfunction. Developmental Medicine and
Child Neurology, December 1977, 19(6), 768-775. Topic Codes: BB,BE30C,
BK11B,DK07,DK48,DT44,DT46,DT52,MQ,NA07B,PM,PP,TA04,TA55,TA80.

32100   Ernhart, C.B., Graham, F.K., Eichman, P.L., Marshall, J.M., and Thurston,
D. Brain injury in the preschool child: Some developmental considerations: II. Comparison of brain injured and normal children. Psychological Monographs: General and Applied, 1963, 77(11, whole no. 574).

Topic Codes: BL04B,BL11,BL48,DK07,DK07B,DT04EB,DT13,DT48,MG,MG30,MH,MT48,
NA07D,NA07I,PE48,PG,PI,PM,PR,TA52,TA57,TA59,TA59D,TA80,TB25,TB44,TB78.

32200   Eron, L.D., Walder, L.O., Toigo, R., and Lefkowitz, M.M. Social class,
parental punishment for aggression, and child aggression. Child Development, 1963, 34, 849-867. Topic Codes: BL70,MC,NA07B,PE04,PE10,PY,SI22,
SI48,SI57,SI57J,SI57P,SQ,SR03,SU,SW56.

32300   Ervin, F.R. Evaluation of organic factors in patients with impulse disor-
ders and episodic violence. In W.L. Smith and A. Kling (eds.), Issues in
Brain/Behavior Control. New York: Spectrum, 1976. Topic Codes: CC81F,
CC81I,CC81R,DK07D,MK11,PE30D.

32330   Erwin, B.J. Body image and proprioceptive dysfunction in schizophrenic
and brain damaged subjects: Weight discrimination, size estimation and
tactile recognition [doctoral dissertation, Wayne State University, 1973].
Dissertation Abstracts International, December 1973, 34(6), 2927B. Topic
Codes: DT59B,MR07,MU70,NL,PS07,TA59,TA80.

32500   Escalona, S.K., and Moriarty, A. Prediction of school-age intelligence
from infant tests. Child Development, 1961, 32, 597-605. Topic Codes:
BL31,NA07B,NA31F,NA31R,PA,PE10,PK,PM,TA52K,TB25,TB42,TB95.

32540   Escobar, J.I., and Koch, M. Psychiatric aspects of a family with a chromosome translocation. Diseases of the Nervous System, April 1976, 37(4),
184-187. Topic Codes: BI07,MG,NL,TB78B,TB95B.

32600   Eshraghi-Tabri, G.A. Structures in the development of moral judgments
in delinquent children [doctoral dissertation, University of Texas at
Austin, 1975]. Dissertation Abstracts International, November 1975,
36(5), 2710A-2711A. Topic Codes: BL11C,CC37G,CC37W,NA07ID,PG11.

32700   Estes, B.W. Relationships between the Otis, 1960 Stanford-Binet and WISC.
Journal of Clinical Psychology, 1965, 21, 296-297. Topic Codes: NA07B,
PE10,PG,TA59,TB78,TB95.

32800   Etaugh, C. Effects of nonmaternal care on children: Research evidence
and popular views. American Psychologist, April 1980, 35(4), 309-319.
Topic Codes: BL04,BL11,BL70,MX,NA07B,NA07I,PE10,PE68,PG,SC59,SI46,SI48,
SQ,SR.

32870   Evans, E.G. Behavior problems in children. Child Care, Health and Development, February 1976, 2(1), 35-43. Topic Codes: MB,NA07D.

32900   Evans, J.H. Attitudes of adolescent delinquent boys. Psychological Reports, 1974, 34, 1175-1178. Topic Codes: BL04,CC37W,CC37Z.

32930   Evans, J.R., and Smith, C.J. Common behavioral SLD characteristics.
Academic Therapy, Summer 1977, 12(4), 425-427. Topic Codes: CC37B,CC37H,
DT44B,MF,MH07,MM07,PE10,PI07,PM07,PP07.

32950   Evseeff, G.S. A potential young murderer. Journal of Forensic Science,
April 1976, 21(3), 441-450. Topic Codes: BL04B,CC81A,CC81F,CL,CQ81,
CT57F,CT81,CY,MG02D,NA07DF,NE81,PE68D,SR02.

32970   Eysenck, H.J. Crime and Personality. Boston: Houghton Mifflin, 1964.
Topic Codes: BA,BE11,BI11,BK04D,BK11B,BN04D,CC11A,CC11C,CC11D,CC11E,
CC11F,CC11G,CC11M,CC11N,CC11P,CC37A,CC37E,CC37F,CC37H,CC37M,CC37N,CC37O,
CC37Q,CC37W,CG11,CQ11,CQ37,CV06C,CV13D,DD02D,DK07D,DK09D,DT13D,DT44D,MB11,
MH11,MK11,MM11,MS02,MX11,NE11,NE37,NE59,NH70D,NH74D,NL,PA11,PC11,PE01,
PE08D,PE68D,PI11,PM11,PP11,PT74B,PY11,SH70D,SH74D,SI57PB,SR02,SU11,TA03,
TA52,TA59D,TB38B,TB61B,TB66D.

32973   Eysenck, H.J. Personality, conditioning, and antisocial behavior. In W.
Slaufer and J.M. Day (eds.), Personality Theory, Moral Development and
Criminal Behavior. Lexington, Massachusetts: Lexington Books, 1983,
51-80. Topic Codes: BL11,ME,NA07I,PE08,PG,PT11,PY11,SI57PB,SR04,SU11.

32980   Eysenck, S.G., White, O., and Eysenck, H.J. Personality and mental ill-
          ness. Psychological Reports, December 1976, 39(3, part 1), 1011-1022.
          Topic Codes: CC11U,CC24B,DD00B,DD01,MF,MQ,MU,N,TA02,TA59,TB38.

33000   Fagan, T.J. Aggressive responding in convicted felons as a function of
          sociopathy and anxiety [doctoral dissertation, Virginia Polytechnic Insti-
          tute and State University, 1977]. Dissertation Abstracts International,
          March 1978, 38(9), 4452B. Topic Codes: CC11C,CC11P,CC11U,MC11,MS04B,
          PE04D,PT11,SR03B,TA02B,TA03,TA59,TB61B.

33050   Fagan-Dublin, L. Lateral dominance and development of cerebral special-
          ization. Cortex, March 1974, 10(1), 69-74. Topic Codes: BL11,BL70,BN44,
          DT13,MH,NA07I,PG,PI,PO,SQ,TB95,TB96.

33100   Fahmy, M. Initial exploring of intelligence of Shilluk children: Studies
          in Southern Sudan. Vita Humana, 1964, 7, 164-177. Topic Codes: NA07,NL,
          PM,TA80,TB33,TB66.

33150   Faigel, H.C. The adolescent with a learning problem experience and in-
          sight with delinquent boys. Acta Paediatrica Scandinavia, 1975, supple-
          ment 256, 56-61. CC37H,CC37J,CC37I,DT59D,MR11,PE64D,TA03,TA04,TA59,TA59D,
          TA80,TB09D,TB33GD,TB53B,TB74B,TB86C,TB95D,TB98D.

33200   Fairchild, L., and Erwin, W.M. Physical punishment by parent figures as a
          model of aggressive behavior in children. Journal of Genetic Psychology,
          1977, 130, 279-284. Topic Codes: MC,NA07B,PE04,PE10,SI57,SI57J,SR03,
          TA59.

33250   Falconer, M.A. Brain mechanisms suggested by neurophysiologic studies.
          In F.L. Darley (ed.), Brain Mechanisms Underlying Speech and Language.
          New York: Grune & Stratton, 1967. Topic Codes: BN44,DK07,DK18S,DT02,

33265   Faretra, G. A profile of aggression from adolescence to adulthood: An
          18-year follow-up of psychiatrically disturbed and violent adolescents.
          American Journal of Orthopsychiatry, July 1981, 51(3), 439-453. Topic
          Codes: MC11,MG02D,NA07DD,PE04D,SR03B.

33270   Farley, F.H., and Sewell, T. Test of an arousal theory of delinquency:
          Stimulation-seeking in delinquent and non-delinquent black adolescents.
          Criminal Justice and Behavior, December 1976, 3(4), 315-320. Topic Codes:
          BN04D,CC37P,CQ37,DK09D,NE37,NL07D,PC11,PT74B,SR02.

33300   Farrington, D.P., and West, D.J. A comparison between early delinquents
          and young aggressives. British Journal of Criminology, 1971, 11, 341-358.
          Topic Codes: CC37B,CC37L,CC37Q,CC37W,CC37Z,CC37I,CG11P,MC11,NH59E,NH59F,
          PE04D,PE64D,PT11,SC70D,SH59,SH59F,SH59H,SI46D,SI48D,SI57D,SI59D,SJ09D,
          SJ22D,SR03B,SW11,TA57,TA59,TA74,TB72B.

33500   Feldhusen, J.F., Aversano, F.M., and Thurston, J.R. Prediction of youth
          contacts with law enforcement agencies. Criminal Justice and Behavior,
          1976, 3, 235-253. Topic Codes: BL04D,BL70D,CC37A,CC37J,CC37L,CC37Q,
          CC37W,CC37I,CL,MC11,NH59P,NH59PL,PE04D,PE64D,PM11,PT11,SC70D,SF26D,SH59R,
          SH59RL,SI57D,SQ11,SR03B,TA04,TA59,TA59D,TA74.

33600   Feldman, M.P. Criminal Behavior: A Psychological Analysis. New York:
          John Wiley & Sons, Inc., 1977. Topic Codes: BB70D,BE11,BI11,BK11B,BL11,
          BL70D,CC11C,CC11D,CC11E,CC11F,CC11G,CC11H,CC11L,CC11M,CC11N,CC11O,CC11P,
          CC11S,CC11T,CC11U,CE81,CQ11,CQ22,CQ37B,CQ81,CV,CX,CY,DK07D,MC11,N,PE66,PG,
          S,TB38B,TB61B.

33700   Fenton, G.W., Tennent, T.G., Fenwick, P.B.C., and Rattray, N. The EEG in
          antisocial behavior: A study of posterior temporal slow activity in spe-
          cial hospital patients. Psychological Medicine, 1974, 4, 181-186. Topic
          Codes: BL04B,BL04D,CC11F,CC81K,CE,CT57,CT59,CY,DD26B,DD26D,ME07,MS04B,
          NH59E,NH59F,PE08D,SH59F,SH59H,SI46,SI59,SR04B,SW07,SW11,TB35BB,TB35D,
          TB61B,TB93B,TB93D.

33800   Ferdman, J. Differential sex learning in early childhood. Journal of

Asthma Research, June 1974, 11(4), 151-158. BL11,BL29,BL31,BL70,DT13,
DT44,MH,MM,NA07B,NA07I,NA31F,NA31R,PE10,PG,PI,PK,PP,PY,SI57P,SQ,SQ70,SU,
TA52K,TA59D.

33900   Ferdon, N.M. Chromosomal abnormalities and antisocial behavior. Journal of Genetic Psychology, 1971, 118, 281-292. Topic Codes: BB70B,
BB70D,BE11,CC37N,DD02ND,DD02NF,ME07,PE08D,PM11,SR04B,TB35.

34000   Ferracuti, F., and Newman, G. Assaultive offenses. In D. Glaser (ed.),
Handbook of Criminology. Chicago: Rand McNally Co., 1974. Topic Codes:
BL04D,BL67D,BL70D,CC37L,CC37Y,CC81,CC81A,CC81L,CC81N,CC81U,CC81V,CC81W,CE,
CG,CG11P,CQ81,CT57,CT57B,CT57F,CT81,CX,DD10,MC11,MZ,NE79,NE81,NH67,PE04D,
SF11,SI57G,SN11,SQ11,SR03B,SW11.

34100   Ferreira, A.L. Emotional factors in prenatal environment. Journal of
Nervous and Mental Disease, 1965, 141(1), 108-118. Topic Codes: BL22,BP,
BP02B,BP22F,DF48,DF60,DP,DP22H,DP48,MG,MG30,NA07D,NA31D,PE32.

34140   Feshbach, N.D. Studies of empathic behavior in children. Progress in
Experimental Personality Research, 1978, 8, 1-47. Topic Codes: MC,MG11,
NA07B,PE04,PE08,PE10,PG,PI,PP,PT,SC70,SF,SI57,SQ07,SU,TA59D,TA80.

34200   Fianu, S. Fetal mortality and morbidity following breech delivery. Acta
Obstetrica et Gynecologica, 1976, 56 (supplement). Topic Codes: BL22,
BL70,BP02,BP22F,BP26G,BP26GD,BP44,BP46,BP57,DF06B,DF34,DF48,DF60B,DP11,
DP44,DP48,NA33B,NA33F,PL,SQ,TA80.

34300   Fiedler, M., and Schmidt, E.P. Sex differences in Bender Gestalt drawings
of seven-year-old children. Perceptual and Motor Skills, 1969, 29, 753-
754. Topic Codes: BL70,NA07B,NC70,PE10,SQ,TB09K.

34350   Fields, M. The relationship between problem behavior and food allergies:
One family's story. Journal of Autism and Childhood Schizophrenia, March
1976, 6(1), 75-84. Topic Codes: BE30,BK11B,BL11,DD03,DK07BB,MA,MG11.

34400   Fieve, R.R., Rosenthal, D., and Brill, H. (eds.). Genetic Research in
Psychiatry; proceedings of the 63rd annual meeting of the American Psychopathological Association. Baltimore: Johns Hopkins University Press,
1975.

34500   Figlio, R.M. The biological bases of criminal behavior policy implica-
tion. Paper presented at the annual meeting of the American Society of
Criminology, Tucson, Arizona, 1976. Topic Codes: BB70B,BB70D,BD52B,BE11,
BI11,BL04B,BL70D,CC81I,CC81K,CC81M,CC81O,CC81R,CG,CT57FT,CV52B,DD02NF,
DK07D,DK18SD,DK48D,DP11B,DP11D,DT04EB,DT44,MG30D,MG48D,MM,PP,SF11,SH74D,
SQ11,TB35BB,TB35D.

34600   Figueira-McDonough, J., and Selo, E. A reformulation of the "equal oppor-
tunity" explanation of female delinquency. Crime and Delinquency, July
1980, 26(3), 333-343. Topic Codes: BL70,BL70D,CC24,CC37A,CC37L,CC37M,
CC37W,CC37Z,CQ22,MS02,NE22,NH59F,PE10,PG,SF11,SH59H,SI46,SI59,SJ09D,SQ,
SQ11,SQ70D,SW11.

34660   Finch, A.J., and Nelson, W.M. Reflection-impulsivity and behavioral problems in emotionally disturbed boys. Journal of Genetic Psychology, June
1976, 128(2), 271-274. Topic Codes: DD02B,MG02B,NA07B,NA07D,PG,TA02,
TA80.

34670   Finch, A.J., Spirito, A., and Brophy, C.J. Reflection-impulsivity and
WISC-R performance in behavior-problem children. Journal of Psychology,
July 1982, 111(2), 217-221. Topic Codes: DT13B,MG,MK,TB96B.

34700   Finegan, J., and Quarrington, B. Pre-, peri-, and neonatal factors and
infantile autism. Journal of Child Psychology and Psychiatry and Allied
Disciplines, 1979, 20, 119-128. Topic Codes: BD30,BD30B,BL70B,BP,BP02B,
DF67B,DK09B,DP,DP11B,MG04,NA33A,NH65,PM07,SQ07,SW07,TA02,TA52,TA59D,TB02,
TB78B.

34750   Finley, W.H., McDanal, C.E., Finley, S.C., and Rosecrans, C.J. Prison
         survey for the XYY karyotype in tall inmates. Behavior Genetics, March
         1973, 3(1), 97-100. Topic Codes: BB70D,BE11,CC11D,CC11E,CG11CC,CQ59,
         DD02NF,MV11,NE59,NL,PE66D,SR69D,TA52.

34800   Finnerty, F.A., Jr. Hypertension is different in blacks. Journal of the
         American Medical Association, 1971, 216(10), 1634-1635. Topic Codes:
         BL08B,BL67,DD,DD28,SN.

35000   Firestone, P., Peters, S., Rivier, M., and Knights, R.M. Minor physical
         anomalies in hyperactive, retarded and normal children and their families.
         Journal of Child Psychology and Psychiatry and Allied Disciplines, 1978,
         19, 155-160. Topic Codes: BB48B,BL04B,DD02KB,DK46,MG,MG30,MO,NA07D,NH65,
         SI59B,TA74.

35100   Fisch, R.O., Bilek, M.K., Deinard, A.S., and Chang, P. Growth, behavioral
         and psychological measurements of adopted children: The influences of ge-
         netic and socioeconomic factors in a prospective study. Journal of Pe-
         diatrics, September 1976, 89(3), 494-500. Topic Codes: BE30C,BI,BL11,
         BP02,BP46,BP53,BP70,MG,NA07B,NA07D,NA07I,NA44D,NC22,NC44,NC59,NC70,NH04,
         NH04B,NJ06,PE10,PE64,PG,PM,SC70,SH04,SH04B,SW,TA52,TB05,TB09,TB27,TB33G,
         TB76,TB78,TB95,TB98.

35200   Fisch, R.O., Bilek, M.K., Horrobin, J.M., and Chang, P. Children with su-
         perior intelligence at 7 years of age. American Journal of Diseases of
         Children, May 1976, 130, 481-487. Topic Codes: BE30C,BL06,BL11,BL27,
         BL48,BP02,BP26,DT48,MT48,NA07B,NA07I,NA31R,NA33I,NA44D,NC22,NC44,NC59,
         NC59G,NC70,NH59B,NH59F,NH59PB,NJ06,PE10,PE48,PG,PM,PR,SH59B,SH59H,SH59RB,
         SJ09D,SW,TA52,TA52K,TA52M,TB02,TB05,TB09,TB33GD,TB53,TB66,TB76,TB78,TB95,
         TB98.

35300   Fisch, R.O., Bilek, M.K., Miller, L.D., and Engel, R.R. Physical and men-
         tal status at 4 years of survivors of the respiratory distress syndrome.
         Journal of Pediatrics, April 1975, 86(4), 497-503. Topic Codes: BE30,
         BL05,BL06,BL11,BL31,DF67B,NA07I,NA31F,NA31R,NA44B,NC22,NC44,NJ03,PG,PK,PM,
         TA52,TA52K,TB05,TB27,TB44,TB66,TB78.

35350   Fisch, R.O., Gravem, H.J., and Engel, R.R. Neurological status of survi-
         vors of neonatal respiratory distress syndrome. Journal of Pediatrics,
         September 1968, 73, 395-403. Topic Codes: BK11B,BL07B,BL27K,BL31,BL33,
         BL52D,DF67B,DF70B,DK07,NC44,PE32,PE34,PM,TA52,TA52K,TA52M,TA59,TB02.

35360   Fish, B. An approach to prevention in infants at risk for schizophrenia:
         Developmental deviations from birth to 10 years. Journal of the American
         Academy of Child Psychiatry, Winter 1976, 15(1), 62-82. Topic Codes:
         BL11,BL31,BL52DB,DD02B,MB,MG04GB,MU70,NA31A,NA44D,NJ06,NL,PE10,PG,PK,SR01.

35370   Fish, B. Treating hyperactive children. Journal of the American Medical
         Association, 1971, 218, 1427. Topic Codes: DT44,MG30B,PE10,PE66B.

35380   Fishbein, D.H. The contribution of refined carbohydrate consumption to
         maladaptive behaviors [doctoral dissertation, Florida State University,
         1980]. Dissertation Abstracts International, July 1981, 42(1), 399A-400A.
         Topic Codes: BD30H,CC11D,CQ59,DT44,MF,MG30.

35400   Fitzhardinge, P.M., and Steven, E.M. The small-for-date infant: II.
         Neurological and intellectual sequelae. Pediatrics, July 1972, 50(1), 50-
         57. Topic Codes: BL07BB,BL11,BL27K,BL31,BL70,BP,BP26G,DD81,DF06BB,DF70,
         DK09,DK48,DP,DP22P,MG48,NA07I,NA31F,NA44D,NJ06,PE64,PG,PK,PM,SC70,SQ,SW,
         TA52,TB02,TB09,TB33G,TB35,TB78,TB89,TB95.

35500   Fitzhugh, K.B. Some neuropsychological features of delinquent subjects.
         Perceptual and Motor Skills, 1973, 36, 494. Topic Codes: BN44D,CC37F,
         CC37R,CC37T,CC37I,PO11,TA03,TA80,TB40D,TB95D.

35600   Fledelius, H. Prematurity and the eye. Acta Opthalmologica Supplemen-
         tum, 1976, 128, 1-18. Topic Codes: BL07B,DF06B,DF48,DF60B,DK07,DP48,SW.

35650   Flick, G. Sinistrality revisited: A perceptual—motor approach. <u>Child</u>
<u>Development</u>, 1966, 37, 613-622. Topic Codes: BK11B,BL11,BN44H,NA07B,
NA07I,NL07,PE10,PE48,PO33,PR,TA80,TB78.

35700   Flor-Henry, P. Gender, hemispheric specialization and psychopathology.
<u>Sociology of Science and Medicine</u>, 1978, 12B, 155-162. Topic Codes:
BB70,BD70,BI,BI07,BK11BL,BL11,BL22,BL52D,BL70,BL70B,BL70BB,BN44,BN44B,
BN44BB,BP22F,DD02N,DK07B,DK18B,DT13,MB,MC,MG,MH,MS04,MU70,NA07D,NA07I,
NH74B,PE04,PG,PI,PM,PO,PO07,PO07B,SH74B,SQ,SQ07,SQ07B,SR03,TB93,TB96B.

35800   Fodor, E.M. Moral development and parent behavior antecedents in adoles-
cent psychopaths. <u>Journal of Genetic Psychology</u>, 1973, 122, 37-43. Topic
Codes: BL11C,CC37B,CC37G,CC37L,CC37W,MS04B,NA07ID,NL48,PG11,SI22B,SI22D,
SI48B,SI48D,SI57BB,SI57D,TA02B,TA03,TA59.

35900   Fogel, R.L., Hunt, J., Bauer, R., and Brockway, M. The relationship of
learning problems to juvenile delinquency. Paper presented at the International Conference of the Association for Children with Learning Disabilities, Seattle, Washington, March 4, 1976. Topic Codes: CC37B,CC37Q,
CC37I,CQ59,CV13DA,DT44D,MM11,NE59,PE64D,PP11,SC,SC70D,TA03,TA04,TB09D,
TB33B,TB95D,TB98D.

36000   Folstein, S., and Rutter, M. Genetic influences and infantile autism.
<u>Nature</u>, February 24, 1977, 265, 726-728. Topic Codes: BI07,DK07B,DK46B,
DT13B,MG04,MH07,MO07,NA33A,NH74B,PI07,SH74B.

36100   Foodman, A., and Estrada, C. Adolescents who commit accidental homicide.
<u>Journal of the American Academy of Child Psychiatry</u>, 1977, 16(2), 314-326.
Topic Codes: CC37B,CC37L,DD26BB,DT44,MG,MM,NA07B,NA07D,NH59E,NH59F,PE10,
PE64B,PP,SC70B,SH59F,SH59H.

36200   Fooks, G., and Thomas, R.R. Differential qualitative performance of delinquents on the Porteus Maze. <u>Journal of Consulting Psychology</u>, 1957,
21, 351-353. Topic Codes: BL11,CC24,CC37BB,CC37I,CQ37,CQ59,CV13DA,NA07,
NE37,NE59,PE10,SQ70,TB66D.

36300   Ford, F.R. Cerebral birth injuries and their results. <u>Medicine</u>, May
1926, 5(2), 121-139. Topic Codes: BP02,BP47,DD08K,DF48,DF60B,DK07,DK09,
DP44,DP48,DT04E,NA33I, TA52M.

36330   Forness, S.R. Concepts of learning and behavior disorders: Implications
for research and practice. <u>Exceptional Children</u>, September 1981, 48(1),
56-64. Topic Codes: DK46,DT44,MG,SC.

36380   Forssman, H. The mental implications of sex chromosome aberrations.
<u>British Journal of Psychiatry</u>, October 1970, 117(539), 353-363. Topic
Codes: BB70B,BB70D,DD02ND,DD02NF,MF,MO07,PM07.

36400   Forssman, H., and Frey, T.S. Electroencephalograms of boys with behavior
disorders. <u>Acta Psychiatrica Neurologica Scandinavica</u>, 1953, 28, 61-73.
Topic Codes: CC37B,CC37F,CC37O,CC37W,MC,MG,NA07D,PE04,SR03,TB35B,TB35BB.

36430   Forssman, H., and Hambert, G. Chromosomes and antisocial behavior. <u>Ex-</u>
<u>cerpta Criminologica</u>, 1967, 7, 113-117. Topic Codes: BB70B,BB70D,CC11M,
DD02ND,DD02NF,ME07,PE08D.

36450   Fort, A.T., and Harlin, R.S. Pregnancy outcome after noncatastrophic maternal trauma during pregnancy. <u>Obstetrics and Gynecology</u>, June 1970, 35,
912-915. Topic Codes: BP02,DP11,DP46,NC59G,T.

36500   Foster, R.M., Margolin, L., Alexander, C., Benitez, O., and Carr, F.
Equivocal neurological signs, child development, and learned behavior.
<u>Child Psychiatry and Human Development</u>, Fall 1978, 9(1), 28-32. Topic
Codes: DT52B,MG,NA07D,TA02,TA80,TB57.

36530   Fottrell, E. Violent behavior by psychiatric patients. <u>British Journal</u>
<u>of Hospital Medicine</u>, January 1981, 25(1), 28-28. Topic Codes: CC81D,
CC81H,CC81S.

36600   Fowler, I. The relationship of certain perinatal factors to behavior, speech, or learning problems in children. Southern Medical Journal, October 1965, 58, 1245-1248. Topic Codes: BL67,BL70,BN44,BN44B,BP02B,BP47, DD05,DK48,DK48B,DP,DP11B,DP60,DP81,DT44,DT52B,MG,MG30,MG48,MG48B,MM,NA07D, PO,PO07,PP,SN,SQ,TB02,TB09,TB33G,TB42,TB95.

36700   Fox, S.J. Delinquency and biology. University of Miami Law Review, 1961, 16, 65-91. Topic Codes: BD30HD,BE11,BL11C,CC37B,CC37C,CC37E,CC37G,CC37L, CC37W,CG,CL,CV13D,DD30D,NA07ID,NH59F,PG11,PT11,SF11,SH59H.

36800   Frank, S., and Quinlan, D. Ego development and female delinquency: A cognitive-developmental approach. Journal of Abnormal Psychology, 1976, 85(5), 505-510. Topic Codes: BB70,BL11,BL11C,BL52D,BN44,BP22F,CC24, CC37G,CC37Q,CC37W,CQ22,DD02N,MK11,NA07I,NA07ID,NE22,NL48,PE30D,PG,PG11,PM, PM11,PO.

36860   Fredericksen, L.W., and Peterson, G.L. Schedule-induced aggression in humans and animals: A comparative parametric review. Aggressive Behavior, 1977, 3(1), 57-75. Topic Codes: MC,PE04.

37000   Freedman, B.J., Donahoe, C.P., Rosenthal, L., Schlundt, D.G., and McFall, R.M. A social-behavioral analysis of skill deficits in delinquent and non-delinquent adolescent boys. Journal of Consulting and Clinical Psychology, 1978, 46(6), 1448-1462. Topic Codes: BL04B,CC37B,CC37I,CC37P, CC37U,CC37Y,PM,PT11,PY11,SI57PB,SU11,SW07B,TA03,TA59,TA59D,TB35,TB98D.

37100   Freeman, R.D. Minimal brain dysfunction, hyperactivity and learning disorders: Epidemic or episode? School Review, November 1976, 85(1), 5-30. Topic Codes: BI07,BN44B,BP02B,BP70,CV06,CV15B,DK48D,DP11B,DT04EB,DT44, DT44B,DT52B,MG30,MG48B,MM,MM07,PE64B,PO07,PP,PP07,SC70B,TB35B.

37150   Freeman, T. Childhood Psychopathology and Adult Psychoses. New York: International University Press, 1976. Topic Codes: BB11,BI07B,BL11, CC37B,CC37G,CC37N,CC37V,DD02B,MB11,MF11,MG02,MS02,MU,MX07,NA07DB,NA44V, NJ30,NL,PE,PE10,PE68B,PG11,SR01,TA02,TA59.

37200   French, A., and Steward, M.S. Family dynamics, childhood depression, and attempted suicide in a 7-year-old boy. Suicide, Spring 1975, 5(1), 29-37. Topic Codes: CV06,DD03B,MA07,MG,MG30,MZ,NA07D,NH65B,PE02B,SI57B,TB35B, TB61.

37300   Friedman, E.A., and Kroll, B.H. Computer analysis of labor progression: IV. Diagnosis of secondary arrest of dilatation. Journal of Reproductive Medicine, October 1971, 7(4), 176-178. Topic Codes: BP44,BP53,DP44, NC59G.

37400   Friedman, E.A., and Kroll, B.H. Computer analysis of labor progression: V. Effects of fetal presentation and position. Journal of Reproductive Medicine, March 1972, 8(3), 117-121. Topic Codes: BP44,DP44,NC44,NC59G.

37500   Friedman, E.A., and Neff, R.K. Hypertension-hypotension in pregnancy. Journal of the American Medical Association, May 26, 1978, 239(21), 2249- 2251. Topic Codes: DF48,DP48,DP60,NC59G.

37550   Friedman, E.A., Sachtleben, M.R., and Bresky, P.A. Dysfunctional labor: XII. Long-term effects on infant. American Journal of Obstetrics and Gynecology, 1977, 127, 779-783. Topic Codes: BP02,BP44,NA33F,NA33I,PM, TA52K,TA55,TA59,TA80,TB78.

37575   Friedman, E.A., Sachtleben, M.R., and Wallace, A.K. Infant outcome following labor induction. American Journal of Obstetrics and Gynecology, March 15, 1979, 133(6), 718-722. Topic Codes: BL11,DF60B,DP11,NA07B, NA07I,PE10,PG,TA52K,TB02.

37600   Friedman, R.C., Richart, R.M., and Vande Wiele, R.L., (eds.). Sex Differences in Behavior. New York: John Wiley & Sons, Inc., 1974. Topic Codes: BB70B,BB70D,BD70,BE11,BI,BK11B,BL33,BL52D,BL70BB,BL70D,BN44,BN68, CC11D,CC11E,CC11M,CC11N,CC37E,CC37H,CC37N,CC81E,CC81G,CC81Q,CC81V,CG11CC,

CQ59,DD02NF,DT13,DT42,DT44D,DT69,MC,MG,MH,ML,MM11,MV,MW,NA07D,NA33D,NA33F,
NE59,NL,PE34,PE44,PE66,PI,PK,PL,PM,PN,PO,PP11,SF,SH59,SI46,SI57,SQ07,SQ11,
SQ70,SR69,SU,SW11,TA80,TB66,TB93,TB95.

37700   Friedman, S.L., Brackbill, Y., Caron, A.J., and Caron, R.F. Obstetric
medication and visual processing in 4- and 5-month-old infants. Merrill-
Palmer Quarterly of Behavior and Development, 1978, 24(2), 111-128. Topic
Codes: BL04,BL31,BL52D,BP04,BP44,DD81,DF34,DK09,DP44,DT59,MR,NA31D,NA31F,
NA31R,NA33A,PE32,PK,PL,PS,TA52K,TB02.

37830   Friedrich, W.N., and Wheeler, K.K. The abusing parent revisited: A dec-
ade of psychological research. Journal of Nervous and Mental Disease,
October 1982, 170(10), 577-587. Topic Codes: CT57BB,CT57BD,DD10B,DD10D,
NH11,NH59B,NH59D,SH11,SH59B,SH59D,SI57GB,SI57GD.

37900   Frodi, A., Macaulay, J., and Thome, P.R. Are women always less aggressive
than men? A review of the experimental literature. Psychological Bulletin, 1977, 84(4), 634-660. Topic Codes: BL08,BL25,BL70,BN04,CC24,CQ22,
CX,CZ07,MC,NE22,NE79,PC,PE04,PT,PY,SA,SI57J,SI57P,SQ,SR03,SU,SY11,TB86.

37970   Frosch, J. The relationship between acting out and disorders of impulse
control. Psychiatry, November 1977, 40(4), 295-314. Topic Codes: BL11,
CC11C,CC11E,CT68,MF,PC.

38000   Fuccillo, D.A., Kurent, J.E., Manne, S.H., Rosenthal, D., Beadle, E., and
Sever, J.L. Lack of association between defective delinquents and anti-
body of herpes virus hominis. Neurology (Minneapolis), March 1977, 27,
304-305. Topic Codes: CC81P,DD00,DD01,DK07D,MC,MG11,PE04,SR03.

38100   Fujikura, T., and Froehlich, L.A. Organ-weight/brain-weight ratios as a
parameter of prenatal growth: A balanced growth theory of visceras.
American Journal of Obstetrics and Gynecology, April 1, 1972, 112(7),
896-902. Topic Codes: BD30,BK11B,BL06,BL22,BL67,BL70,BP02,BP22F,BP47,
DF48,DP,DP22,DP48,DP60,NC44,NC59G,NH74,SN,SQ.

38130   Fuller, G., and Friedrich, D. A diagnostic approach to differentiate
brain-damaged from non-brain-damaged adolescents. Journal of Clinical
Psychology, July 1974, 30(3), 361-363. Topic Codes: BK11B,BL11,DK07B,
DT48,NA07B,NA07D,NA07I,PE10,PG,PR,TA02,TA55,TA80.

38140   Fuller, P.W., Wenner, W.H., and Blackburn, S. Comparison between time-
lapse video recordings of behavior and polygraphic state determinations in
premature infants. Psychophysiology, November 1978, 15(6), 594-598.
Topic Codes: BL27,BL33,BP26,DF60,DF60B,NA33B,NA33D,NA33F,NA33I,PL,TA52M,
TA55,TA80,TB35.

38180   Furnon, B., De Villard, R., Bouvard, C., and Courson, J. Some aspects of
cognitive activity in epileptic children and adolescents: A clinical
study trial. Revue de Neuropsychiatrie Infantile et d'Hygiene Mentale de
l'Enfance, August-September 1975, 23(8-9), 577-590 (in French). Topic
Codes: BL11,DK18,DT13,MH,NA07I,PG,PI.

38200   Furr, K.D. Standard scores for the Koppitz Developmental Scoring System.
Journal of Clinical Psychology, 1970, 26, 78-79. Topic Codes: TB09K,
TB33G,TB95,TB98.

38300   Gabrielli, W.F., and Mednick, S.A. Sinistrality and delinquency. Journal
of Abnormal Psychology, 1980, 89(5), 654-661. Topic Codes: BB48D,BL48D,
BN44D,CC37L,CC37P,CC37Q,CC37S,CC37V,CC37I,CT59,DD02KD,DT48D,DT52D,MG11,
MT48D,MX11,NA44,NH59B,NH59E,NH59F,NJ,PE48D,PE68D,PM11,PO11,PR11,SH59B,
SH59F,SH59H,SR03B,TA03,TA52,TB95D.

38400   Galin, D. Implications for psychiatry of left and right cerebral special-
ization. Archives of General Psychiatry, October 1974, 31, 572-583.
Topic Codes: BK04B,BK11,BL08,BL29,BN44,BN44B,BN68,DK07B,DT13,DT13B,DT42,
DT44,DT59,DT69,MB,MF,MH,MH07,ML,MM,MR,MW,PE,PE44,PI,PI07,PN,PO,PO07,PP,PS,
PT,TA02,TA80,TB35,TB81.

38450   Gambino, V. Psychological abuse related to interruptions in the psychosocial and cognitive development of disturbed children [doctoral dissertation, Northern Illinois University, 1976]. Dissertation Abstracts International, February 1977, 37(8), 4983A. Topic Codes: MG11,MH,NA07B,NA07D,
NA07I,PA,PE10,PE64,PG,PI,SI57B,SI59.

38500   Gannon, D.R. Relationships between 8 month performance on the Bayley
Scales of Infant Development and 48 month intelligence and concept for-
mation scores. Psychological Reports, 1968, 23, 1199-1205. Topic Codes:
NA44B,NC22,NC44,NJ03,PM,TB05,TB44,TB78.

38600   Ganzer, V.J., and Sarason, I.G. Variables associated with recidivism
among juvenile delinquents. Journal of Consulting and Clinical Psychology, 1973, 40(1), 1-5. Topic Codes: BL04B,BL70,BL70D,CC37,CC37A,
CC37B,CC37L,CC37P,CC37U,CC37Y,CC371,CQ37,CT57,CT59,CV13D,MC11,MG,MG11,
MS04B,NA07D,NE37,NH59F,PE04D,PM11,SH59H,SJ09D,SQ,SQ11,SR03B,SW11,TB95D.

38660   Gardner, E. Fundamentals of Neurology: A Psychophysiological Approach.
Philadelphia: W.B. Saunders Company, 1975. Topic Codes: BK04,BK11B,
BL22,BL48,BL52D,BN,BP22F,DD,DD81,DF34,DK07,DK09,DK18,DP22,DT42,DT44,DT48,
MB,MH,ML,MM,MT48,PE44,PE48,PN,PP,PR,TA52M.

38670   Gardner, L. Review: Is brain damage a useful concept? Child Care,
Health and Development, December 1976, 2(6), 395-411. Topic Codes: BL11,
DK07,NA07I,PG.

38680   Gardner, L.I., and Neu, R.L. Evidence linking an extra Y chromosome to
sociopathic behavior. Archives of General Psychiatry, March 1972, 26(3),
220-222. Topic Codes: BA,BB70B,BB70D,CC11D,DD02ND,DD02NF.

38800   Garmezy, N. Observations on research with children at risk for child and
adult psychopathology. In M. McMillan and S. Henao (eds.), Child Psychiatry: Treatment and Research. New York: Brunner-Mazel, 1977. Topic
Codes: BI07,BL04B,BL11,CT57B,DD10,MU70,NA07I,NA31D,NH59PB,NH59PJ,PE32,PG,
PT,PT74,SF07,SH59RB,SH59RJ,SI57,SI57G.

38900   Garmezy, N., and Stroitnan, S. Children at risk: The search for the
antecedents of schizophrenic conceptual models and research methods.
Schizophrenic Bulletin, 1974, 8, 28-30. Topic Codes: BI07,BL07BB,BL11,
BL22,BP02,BP02B,BP44,DD00,DP11B,DP22P,MG,MG02,MG02B,MU70,PE10,PG,SF07,
SI07,SI48B.

38950   Garn, S.M., Clark, D.C., and Trowbridge, F.L. Tendency toward greater
stature in American black children. American Journal of Diseases of
Children, August 1973, 126, 164-166. Topic Codes: BL04,BL05,BL11,BL67,
NA07,NL48.

39000   Garn, S.M., Shaw, H.A., and McCabe, K.D. Birth size and growth appraisal.
Journal of Pediatrics, June 1977, 90(6), 1049-1051. Topic Codes: BL05,
BL06,BL11,BL27K,BL67,BL70,BP02,BP26G,DF70,DP22P,NA07I,NA33I,NA44D,NC44,
NC70,NJ06,PG,SN,SQ,TA52M.

39050   Garn, S.M., Shaw, H.A., Cole, P.E., Owen, G.M., and McCabe, K.D. Reply to
Hoobler and Hunscher. American Journal of Clinical Nutrition, December
1977, 30, 1935-1937. Topic Codes: BD30,BD52,BL67,NA07,NC,NL.

39100   Garn, S.M., Shaw, H.A., and McCabe, K.D. Dose-response effect of maternal
smoking. Pediatrics, November 1978, 62(5), 861-862. Topic Codes: BD30,
BL06,BL07,BL67,BP02,BP70,DF06,DF60,NA33I,NC44,NC59G,SN,TA52M.

39200   Garn, S.M., Shaw, H.A., and McCabe, K.D. Effect of maternal smoking on
hemoglobins and hematocrits of the newborn. American Journal of Clinical
Nutrition, April 1978, 31, 557-558. Topic Codes: BD30,BP02,BP70,NA33I,
NC44,NC59G,TA52M.

39350   Garn, S.M., Shaw, H.A., and McCabe, K.D. Effect of socioeconomic status
on early growth as measured by three different indicators. Ecology of

Food and Nutrition, 1978, 7, 51-55. Topic Codes: BE30,BL05,BL06,BL11,
BL67,NA07I,NA44D,NC,SH59RF,SW33.

39400   Garn, S.M., Shaw, H.A., and McCabe, K.D. Effects of socioeconomic status
and race on weight-defined and gestational prematurity in the United
States. Epidemiology of Prematurity, 1977, 31(4), 127-143. Topic Codes:
BI,BL07,BL67,BL70,BP70,DF06,DF60,NC44,NC59G,NH59PP,SC18,SH59RP,SN,SQ,SW,
SW33,SW56.

39500   Garn, S.M., Shaw, H.A., and McCabe, K.D. Relative effect of smoking and
other variables on size of newborn. Lancet, September 24, 1977, 8039,
667. Topic Codes: BL07,BL67,BP70,DF06,NC44,NC59G,NH59PP,SH59RP,SN,SW33.

39600   Gastil, R.D. Homicide and a regional culture of violence. American
Sociological Review, 1971, 36, 412-427. Topic Codes: BL04D,BL67,BL67D,
CC81A,CC81L,CC81U,CT57F,CV13D,CZ07,SC18D,SF11,SF26D,SF26DD,SN,SN11,SW11,
SY11.

39700   Gath, D., Tennent, G., and Pidduck, R. Criminological characteristics of
bright delinquents. British Journal of Criminology, July 1971, 11(3),
275-279. Topic Codes: BL04D,CC37A,CC37B,CC37J,CC37Q,CC37I,CC67,CG11C,
CG11CC,CG11P,CQ67,CT57,CT59,CT68,CV13,MG11,NE67,PE64D,PM11,SC70D,TB95D.

39800   Gazzaniga, M.S. Brain theory and minimal brain dysfunction. New York
Academy of Sciences - Annals, 1973, 205, 89-92. Topic Codes: BN44B,
DK48B,DT42,DT44,MG48B,ML,MM,PE44,PN,PO07,PP.

39850   Gazzaniga, M.S. (ed.). Neuropsychology. New York: Plenum Press, 1979.
Topic Codes: BK11B,BL04B,BL11,BL48,BL52D,BN44B,BN70D,DA04B,DD00,DD02B,
DD26B,DD81,DK07B,DK48B,DT02,DT06,DT13,DT15,DT42B,DT44B,DT46,DT48B,DT52B,
DT59B,MB,MD07,MF,MG,MH07,ML02,ML15,MR,MS,MT,MU70,MY,NA07D,NA07I,PE06B,
PE44,PE48B,PE68B,PG,PI07,PM,PN07,PO07,PP07,PQ,PR07,PS11,PT,SR01,TA80,TB09,
TB33G,TB35B,TB37B,TB57B,TB66,TB68,TB93.

39900   Gazzaniga, M.S. The split brain in man. Scientific American, August
1967, 217(2), 24-29. Topic Codes: BN44B,DK07B,DT42,DT59,ML,MR,PE44,PN,
PO07,PS.

39950   Geen, R.G. Human aggression. Contemporary Issues of Mental Health, December 1976, 1(4) (monograph series). Topic Codes: MC,PE04,SR03.

40000   Geen, R.G. The meaning of observed violence: Real v. fictional violence
and consequent effects on aggression and emotional arousal. Journal of
Research in Personality, 1975, 9, 270-281. Topic Codes: BK04,BL08,BN04,
CC81,CQ81,CT81,MC,NE81,PC,PE04,SI57J,SR03,TA59.

40100   Gehman, I.H., and Matyas, R.P. Stability of the WISC and Binet tests.
Journal of Consulting Psychology, 1956, 20(2), 150-152. Topic Codes:
NA07B,PE10,TB78,TB95.

40200   Gelfand, S. The relationship of birth order to pain tolerance. Journal
of Clinical Psychology, 1963, 19, 406-407. Topic Codes: PT,SJ07.

40220   Geller, B., and Greydanus, D.E. Aggression in adolescents: Aspects of
pathogenesis. Journal of Adolescent Health Care, March 1981, 1(3), 236-
243. Topic Codes: CC37C,CC37F,CC37L,CC81,CQ81,DK07D,DK18D,TB35D.

40230   Gelles, R.J. Violence in the family: A review of research in the seven-
ties. Journal of Marriage and the Family, November 1980, 42(4), 873-885.
Topic Codes: CC81N,NH11,PY11,SH11,SI57PB,SU11.

40300   Gendreau, P., Wormith, J.S., Kennedy, D.J., and Wass, J. Some norms and
validities of the Quick Test for delinquent samples. Psychological Reports, December 1975, 37(3, part 2), 1199-1203. Topic Codes: BL04,CC11N,
CC11U,PM11,SC18,TA03,TA59D,TB15B,TB70B,TB93D.

40330   Genshaft, J.L. Personality characteristics of delinquent subtypes. Journal of Abnormal Child Psychology, June 1980, 8(2), 279-283. Topic Codes: CC37B,CC37BB,CC37W,CC371,TB61B.

40400   Gerson, L.W. Alcohol-related acts of violence: Who was drinking and where the acts occurred. Journal of Studies on Alcohol, 1978, 39(7), 1294-1296. Topic Codes: CC81B,CT57,CX,DA04D,MD11,NE79,NH67,PEO6D,SF11.

40430   Gersten, J.C., Langner, T.S., Eisenberg, J.G., Fagan, O.S., and McCarthy, E.D. Stability and change in types of behavioral disturbance of children and adolescents. Journal of Abnormal Child Psychology, 1976, 4(2), 111-127. Topic Codes: BL04B,CC37A,CC37B,CC37G,CQ37,MF,MG,NA07D,NA07ID,NA44S, NE37,NJ27,NL,PE10,PE68B,PG,SR01.

40500   Geschwind, N. Language and the brain. Scientific American, April 1972, 226(4), 76-83. Topic Codes: BN44B,DK07B,DT06,DT15,DT42,ML,ML04,ML15, PE44,PN,PO07.

40520   Geschwind, N. Neurological functions of language. In H.R. Myklebust (ed.), Progress in Learning Disabilities (vol. 1). New York: Grune & Stratton, 1968, 182-198. Topic Codes: BK11BL,BL52D,BN44H,BN70,DK07,DK09, DT06,DT13,DT42,DT44,MH,ML04,MM,MY,PE70,PI,PN,PO07,PP.

40550   Gevins, A.S., Doyle, J.C., Cutillo, B.A., Schaffer, R.E., Tennehill, R.S., Ghannam, J.H., Gilcrease, V.A., and Yeager, C.L. Electrical potentials in human brain during cognition: New method reveals dynamic patterns of correlation. Science, August 21, 1981, 213, 918-922. Topic Codes: BK11B, NL,TB35,TB37.

40600   Gevins, A.S., Zeitlin, G.M., Doyle, J.C., Yingling, C.D., Schaeffer, R.E., Calloway, E., and Yeager, C.L. EEG correlates of higher correlates of higher cortical functions. Science, February 16, 1979, 203, 665-668. Topic Codes: BK11B,BN44,DT13,MH,NL,PI,PO,TA55,TA59D,TB35.

40670   Gibbens, T.C.N. Female offenders. British Journal of Psychiatry, 1975, 9(special no.), 326-333. Topic Codes: BL70D,CC11S,CC81V,CQ22,NE22,NL22D, SQ11,SQ70D.

40700   Gibbens, T.C.N. The delinquent and his brain. Proceedings of the Royal Society of Medicine, January 1969, 62(1), 57-59. Topic Codes: BP02D, CC110,CC37F,CC37X,DK07B,DK07D,DP,DT10B,MT04B,MV11,PE66D,SR69D.

40730   Gibbens, T.C.N., Briscoe, O., and Dell, S. Psychopathic and neurotic offenders in mental hospitals. International Psychiatry Clinics, 1968, 5(3), 143-151. Topic Codes: CC11C,CV06,CV30B,ME,NE11,PE01,PE08D,SF07,SH, SI07,SI11,SI57BB,SI57D,SL07,SL11,SR01,SR02,SW07.

40750   Gibbens, T.C.N., Pond, D.A., and Stafford-Clark, D. A follow-up study of criminal psychopaths. British Journal of Psychiatry, 1959, 105, 108-115. Topic Codes: BL04BB,BL04D,CC11C,CC67,CQ67,CT57,CT59,DD26BB,DD26D,DK18B, DK18D,MC11,MG11,MS04B,NE67,PE04D,SR03B,TB35BB,TB35D.

40760   Gibbs, J.T. Black adolescents and youth: An endangered species. American Journal of Orthopsychiatry, January 1984, 54(1), 6-21. Topic Codes: BL67,BL67B,BL67D,CC37Y,CC37Z,DA15,NL07,NL07B,NL07D,SN,SNO7,SN11,SW07,SW11.

40763   Gibbs, J.T. Personality patterns of delinquent females: Ethnic and sociocultural variations. Journal of Clinical Psychology, January 1982, 38 (1), 198-206. Topic Codes: CC24B,CC37B,CC37BB,CC37Y,CC37Z,CC371,MQ11, MS04B,SW11,TB74,TB93D,TB95D.

40770   Gilula, M.F., and Daniels, D.N. Violence and man's struggle to adapt. Science, April 25, 1969, 164(878), 396-405. Topic Codes: BA,CC81D,CC81L, CQ81,CT81,CZ07,DD00,DD01,MC11,NE81,PA11,PE04D,PY,SB,SF11,SR03B,SS,SY11.

40800   Gilbert, G. Strength of left-handedness and facial recognition ability. Cortex, 1973, 9, 145-151. Topic Codes: BL52D,BN44H,NL,PI,PM,TA55,TB49.

40830   Gillberg, I.C., and Gillberg, C. Three-year follow-up at age 10 of children with minor neurodevelopmental disorders: I. Behavioral problems. Developmental Medicine and Child Neurology, August 1983, 25(4), 438-449. Topic Codes: BL11,DK48B,MG,TA02,TA57,TA74.

40900   Ginsburg, H.J., Pollman, V.A., and Wauson, M.S. An ethological analysis of nonverbal inhibitors of aggressive behavior in male elementary school children. Developmental Psychology, 1977, 13(4), 417-418. Topic Codes: CX,MC,NA07B,NE79,PE04,PE10,SR03.

41000   Giordano, P.C. Girls, guys and gangs: The changing social context of fe-male delinquency. Journal of Criminal Law and Criminology, 1978, 69(1), 126-132. Topic Codes: BL67,BL67D,CC24,CC37L,CC37X,CC371,CQ22,CQ37B,CT57, CT59,MX11,NE22,NE37D,PE68D,SF11,SN,SN11,SQ70D,SR03B.

41050   Girard, V., and Schadelle, J.M. The clinical and social development of young adults with craniocerebral injury. Annales Medico-Psychologiques, March 1976, 1(3), 321-366 (in French). Topic Codes: BL11,DK07,MF,MX, NA07I,PE,PE68,PG,SR.

41080   Givon, M. Frustration-produced aggression in over-controlled, under-con-trolled and nonassaultive offenders [doctoral dissertation, Southern Illi-nois University, 1975]. Dissertation Abstracts International, August 1975, 36(2), 908B. Topic Codes: CQ11,CQ59,CY,MC,NE59,PE04,PT74,SS,TA80.

41100   Glaser, G.H. Limbic epilepsy in childhood. Journal of Nervous and Mental Disorders, 1967, 144(5), 391-397. Topic Codes: BK11BL,BL11,CV15B,DD26B, DF34,DF60B,DK18SB,DP,DP11B,DT02,DT04EB,DT10,MG,MN04,MT04,NA07D,NA07I, NA33B,PG,PM07,TA02,TA59D,TB35B,TB74.

41200   Glass, D.C., Horwitz, M., Firestone, I., and Grinker, J. Birth order and reactions to frustration. Journal of Abnormal and Social Psychology, 1963, 66, 192-194. Topic Codes: MC,PE04,PT,SJ07,SR03.

41400   Glidewell, J.C., Domke, H.R., and Kantor, M.B. Screening in schools for behavior disorders: Use of mothers' reports of symptoms. Journal of Educational Research, July-August 1963, 56(10), 508-515. Topic Codes: BL70,MG,NA07D,SQ,TA57,TA74.

41500   Glidewell, J.C., Mensh, I.N., and Gildea, M. Behavior symptoms in chil-dren and degree of sickness. American Journal of Psychiatry, 1957, 114 (1), 47-53. Topic Codes: BL70,MG,NA07D,SQ,TA57,TA74.

41530   Gliebe, W.A. Involuntary deviance: Schooling and epileptic children. Journal of School Health, February 1979, 49(2), 88-92. Topic Codes: BK11B,BL11,CC37L,DK18B,MG,PE10,PG,SC70B.

41570   Glueck, S., and Glueck, E. Physique and Delinquency. New York: Harper & Brothers, 1956. Topic Codes: BE11,CC37E,CQ37B,MG,PE10,SI11,TB74B.

41600   Godfrey, E., and Schulman, R. Age and a group test battery as predictors of types of crime. Journal of Clinical Psychology, 1972, 28, 339-342. Topic Codes: BL04D,CC11A,CC11P,CC11U,CC67,CQ67,CT57,CT59,NE67,TA03,TA04, TA59,TA59D,TB15B,TB61B.

41700   Goff, A.F., and Parker, A.W. Reliability of the Koppitz scoring system for the Bender Gestalt test. Journal of Clinical Psychology, 1969, 25, 407-409. Topic Codes: BL11,DK07,NA07B,NA07I,NL48,PE10,PG,TB09K.

41800   Goff, R.M. Problems and emotional difficulties of Negro children due to race. Journal of Negro Education, 1950, 19, 152-158. Topic Codes: BL67, BL70,NA07B,NL07,PE10,SF,SN,SQ.

41900   Goffeney, B., Henderson, N.B., and Butler, B.V. Negro-white, male-female eight-month developmental scores compared with seven-year WISC and Bender test scores. Child Development, 1971, 42, 595-604. Topic Codes: BL48, BL67,BL70,DT48,MT48,NA44K,NC44,NC70,NJ17,PE48,PM,PR,SN,SQ,TB05,TB09K,TB25, TB42,TB95.

41940   Goldberg, L. Aggression in boys in a clinic population [doctoral dissertation, City University of New York, 1973]. Dissertation Abstracts International, December 1973, 34(6), 2929B. Topic Codes: BL11,MC11,MG,NA07B,
NA07I,PE04D,PE10,PG,TA55,TA80,TB51,TB86.

41970   Goldberg, M.E., and Horovitz, Z.P. Antidepressants and aggressive behavior. Modern Problems of Pharmacopsychiatry, 1978, 13, 29-52. Topic
Codes: BD30,BK11B,CV15,DK07B,MC,PE04,TA80.

41980   Goldman, H., Lindner, L.A., Dinitz, S., and Allen, H.E. The simple sociopath: Physiologic and sociologic characteristics. Biological Psychiatry,
1971, 31, 77-83. Topic Codes: CC11C,CC11U,CG,CQ59,CV15B,ME07,NA,NE11,
NE59,PE08D,TB.

41990   Goldsmith, A.J. Eysenck's theory of criminal personality: A review of
recent evidence and the implications for criminological theory and social
practice. Canadian Criminology Forum, Spring 1982, 4(2), 88-102. Topic
Codes: BI11,DT13D,MH11,MQ11,MS04B,MU11,PI11,PT11,SB11,SS09,SW11.

42000   Goldstein, H. Factors influencing the height of seven-year-old children:
Results from the National Child Development Study. Human Biology, 1971,
43, 92-111. Topic Codes: BE,BL06,BL11,BL27,BL70,BP02,BP26,BP46,BP53,BP70,
NA07I,NA44D,NH59PP,NJ06,PG,SH59RP,SJ07,SQ,SW.

42100   Goldstein, H. Smoking in pregnancy: Some notes on the statistical con-
troversy. British Journal of Preventive and Social Medicine, 1977, 31,
13-17. Topic Codes: BE,BL07,BL11,BP02,BP70,DF06,DF48,DP48,NA07I,NA44F,
NJ09,PG.

42200   Goldstein, M. Brain research and violent behavior. Archives of Neurology,
January 1974, 30, 1-35. Topic Codes: BB70D,BD07,BD11,BD70B,BI11,BK11B,
BK11BL,CC81,CC81D,CC81I,CC81J,CC81K,CC81M,CC81R,CQ81,CT57F,CT81,CV06,
CV15D,DD02NF,DD26BB,DK07B,DK07D,DK18D,DK18SB,DK18SD,MC,MS04B,MU70B,NE81,
NH74D,PE04,SH74D,SR03,TB19,TB35B,TB35BB,TB35D.

42370   Goldstein, M.J., and Rodnick, E.H. The family's contribution to the etiology of schizophrenia: Current status. Schizophrenia Bulletin, Fall
1975, 14, 48-63. Topic Codes: DD02B,MU70,PG,SH,SH70,SI07,SI57B,SJ.

42380   Golla, F.L., and Hodge, R.S. Hormone treatment of the sexual offender.
Lancet, June 11, 1949, 256, 1006-1007. Topic Codes: CC11D,CT68,CV15B,
CV15D,MV07,MV11,NE59,PE66B,PE66D.

42390   Gollnitz, G., and Rosler, H.D. A dynamic approach to disorders in intellectual development. International Journal of Mental Health, Winter 1975-
1976, 4(4), 6-18. Topic Codes: BL11,DK46B,MG02,PE10,PG,PM07,SC18B.

42393   Gonzalez, E.R. Premenstrual syndrome: An ancient woe deserving of modern
scrutiny. Journal of the American Medical Association, April 10, 1981,
245(14), 1393-1396. Topic Codes: BL70,BL70D,CC24,CQ22,CV15B,DD00,NE22,SQ,
SQ11.

42396   Gonzalez, J.L. A psychotherapy analogue study: Changes in autonomic and
behavioral functioning of incarcerated young offenders as a function of
predominant response to interpersonal stress and a brief exposure to one
of four therapy tapes and a conditioning procedure [doctoral dissertation,
Florida State University, 1976]. Dissertation Abstracts International,
December 1976, 37(6), 3073B. Topic Codes: CC81,CQ59,MC11,NE59,PE04D,
TA80.

42400   Goodman, J.D. The behavior of hypersexual delinquent girls. American
Journal of Psychiatry, June 1976, 133(6), 662-668. Topic Codes: BD70B,
BE11,BL11C,BP04,CC24,CC37B,CC37E,CC37G,CC37Q,CC37X,CQ22,CV15D,MC,MV11,
NA07ID,NE22,PE04,PE66D,PG11,PM11,SR03,SR69D.

42700   Goodwin, D.W., Schulsinger, F., Knop, J., Mednick, S., and Guze, S.B.
Psychopathology in adopted and nonadopted daughters of alcoholics. Archives of General Psychiatry, September 1977, 34(9), 1005-1009. Topic

Codes: BI07,BL04B,BL70B,DA04B,MD07,MG,NA07D,NH04B,NH59,NH59B,NH59E,NL22,
PE06B,SC18B,SF07,SH04B,SH59,SH59B,SH59F,SJ09D,SQ07,SW07.

42800   Gora, J.G. A longitudinal analysis of female crime trends in an American
        city. Sociological Abstracts, 1979, 27(supplement 94), abstract S10980.
        Topic Codes: BL67,BL67D,CC11S,CC24,CQ22,NE22,SN,SN11,SQ70D,SW11,SW33.

42900   Gordis, L., and Gold, E. Privacy, confidentiality and the use of medical
        records in research. Science, January 1980, 207, 153-156. Topic Codes:
        BB,BP02,CG,CV15,DD02.

43000   Gordon, M., Rich, H., Deutschberger, J., and Green, M. The immediate and
        long-term outcome of obstetric birth trauma. American Journal of Obstet-
        rics and Gynecology, September 1, 1973, 117(1), 51-56. Topic Codes:
        BL07,BL31,BL70,BP,BP02,DD08K,DF06,DF60,DK09B,DP,DP11,DP22H,DT04E,NA31F,
        NA31R,NC22,NC44,NC59G,PK,SQ,TA52K,TB02,TB05,TB78.

43030   Gordon, R.A. Cognitive functioning in children at high risk for schizo-
        phrenia as a function of perinatal and environmental factors [doctoral
        dissertation, New School for Social Research, 1976]. Dissertation Ab-
        stracts International, December 1977, 38(6), 2860B-2861B. Topic Codes:
        BL11,DP11B,DT13,MH,MU70,NA07I,NA44F,NH59PB,NJ09,PG,PI,SH59RB.

43090   Gossop, M. Drug dependence, crime and personality among female addicts.
        Drug-Alcohol Dependence, September 1978, 3(5), 359-364. Topic Codes:
        CC11H,CC11P,CC24,CC37I,CC37W,CQ22,DA15D,MI07,NE22,PE15D,PT11.

43100   Gossop, M., and Roy, A. Hostility, crime and drug dependence. British
        Journal of Psychiatry, 1977, 130, 272-278. Topic Codes: BL04D,CC11A,
        CC11H,CC11P,CC67,CC81H,CC81S,CG11P,CQ67,CT57,DA15D,MI04,NE67,PE15D,PT11,
        TA03,TA59.

43160   Gottsagen, M.L. An analysis of the relationship between frustration, in-
        hibition, and aggressive cue with overt aggressive behavior in delinquents
        [doctoral dissertation, Temple University, 1973]. Dissertation Abstracts
        International, February 1974, 34(8), 4040B. Topic Codes: CC37,CC37K,
        CQ37,MC11,NE37,NL07D.

43180   Graber, B., Hartmann, K., Coffman, J.A., Huey, C.J., and Golden, C.J.
        Brain damage among mentally disordered sex offenders. Journal of Foren-
        sic Sciences, January 1982, 27(1), 125-134. Topic Codes: CT68,DK07D,
        TA03,TA52.

43200   Graham, E.E., and Kamano, D. Reading failure as a factor in the WAIS sub-
        test patterns of youthful offenders. Journal of Clinical Psychology, 1959,
        14, 302-305. Topic Codes: BL04D,CC37BB,CC37J,CC37I,CQ59,CV13DA,MS04B,
        NE59,PE64D,PM11,SC70D,TB93BB,TB93D,TB96D,TB98D.

43250   Graham, F.K. Behavioral differences between normal and traumatized new-
        borns: I. The test procedures. Psychological Monographs: General and
        Applied, 1956, 70(20, whole no. 427). Topic Codes: BL33,DD08K,DK07,
        NA33D,NA33F,NA33I,PE34,PL,TA52M.

43300   Graham, F.K., Ernhardt, C.B., Craft, M., and Berman, P.W. Brain injury in
        the preschool child: Some developmental considerations: I. Performance
        in normal children. Psychological Monographs: General and Applied, 1963,
        77(10, whole no. 573), 1-16. Topic Codes: BL11,DK07,DK07B,MG,NA07D,NA07I,
        PG.

43400   Graham, F.K., Ernhart, C.B., Thurston, D., and Craft, M. Development three
        years after perinatal anoxia and other potentially damaging newborn expe-
        riences. Psychological Monographs: General and Applied, 1962, 76(3, whole
        no. 522). Topic Codes: BL11,DD08K,DF34,DP11,DT04EB,NA07I,NA33A,NA33B,PG.

43500   Graham, F.K., Matarazzo, R.G., and Caldwell, B.M. Behavioral differences
        between normal and traumatized newborns: II. Standardization, reliabili-
        ty, and validity. Psychological Monographs: General and Applied, 70(21,
        whole no. 428). Topic Codes: DD08K,DF34,DK07,DP11,DT04E,NA33D.

43600   Graham, P., Rutter, M., and George, S. Temperamental characteristics as predictors of behavior disorders in children. American Journal of Orthopsychiatry, April 1973, 43(3), 328-339. Topic Codes: BL04B,BL70B,NA07B, NA44,NH59B,NJ,PE10,PT74,SH59B,SI48B,SQ07,TA74.

43700   Graham, P.J. Epidemiologic perspectives on maladaptation in children: Neurological, familial and social factors. Journal of the American Academy of Child Psychiatry, Spring 1978, 17(2), 197-208. Topic Codes: BL04B, BL70B,MG,NA07D,NA44,NH59,NH59B,NH59E,NJ,SH59,SH59B,SH59F,SI48B,SQ07,TA57, TA74.

43750   Graham, P.J. (ed.). Epidemiological Approaches in Child Psychiatry. New York: Academic Press, 1977. Topic Codes: BL70B,BL70D,CC37J,CC37L,CC37W, CC37Z,CC371,CC67,CE,CG11P,CG11T,CJ,CQ37,CQ67,DA04,DA15,MC11,MD,MG,MG11,MI, MQ,MS02,NA07D,NE37,NE67,NH59E,NH59P,NH59PB,NH59PJ,NH65,PE04D,PE06,PE15, PE64B,PE64D,SC70B,SC70D,SF26B,SF26D,SH59F,SH59R,SH59RB,SH59RJ,SI57B,SJ07B, SJ09D,SJ22B,SQ07,SQ11,SR03B,SW,SW07,SW11,SW56,TA03,TA04,TA57,TA59,TA70, TA74.

43800   Grajales, M.C. Porteus' qualitative maze test as a measure of delinquency. Master's thesis, Fordham University, 1945. Topic Codes: CC37H, CC37Q,CL,CQ37,DT13D,MH11,NE37,PI11,PM11,TA03,TA59D,TB66D.

43870   Green, A.H., Liang, V., Gaines, R., and Sultan, S. Psychopathological assessment of child-abusing, neglecting, and normal mothers. Journal of Nervous and Mental Disease, June 1980, 168(6), 356-360. Topic Codes: CT57B,DD10,NH59PB,NH59PF,SH59RB,SH59RD,SI57G.

43900   Green, J.B. Association of behavior disorder with an electroencephalographic focus in children without seizure. Neurology, 1961, 11, 337-344. Topic Codes: BL31,BP,BP02B,CV15B,DK18B,DP,DP11B,DT30,DT67,MG,MG18,MG30, NA07D,NA31F,PK,TB35B,TB78B.

43905   Green, M., Alston, F.K., and Rich, H. Prenatal exposure to narcotics: What is the risk of long-term damage to the central nervous system? Pediatric Annals, July 1975, 4, 78-85. Topic Codes: BL07B,BP04,DF06B,DK09, NC44,NC59G,NC70,TB95.

43925   Greenberg, R.N. Fluid and crystallized intelligence, age, socioeconomic status, and mathematics achievement of children with special learning and behavior problems [doctoral dissertation, New York University, 1980]. Disertation Abstracts International, June 1981, 41(12, pt. 1), 4717B. Topic Codes: BL04B,DT44,MG,PE64,PM07,SW07.

43930   Greenberg, S.W. The relationship between crime and amphetamine abuse: An empirical review of the literature. Contemporary Drug Problems, Summer 1976, 5(2), 101-130. Topic Codes: CC11H,DA15D,MI07,PE15D.

43940   Greene, R.S. Brief case presentation on the nature of psychopathy in structural analysis theory. Perceptual and Motor Skills, December 1978, 47(3, part 2), 1213-1214. Topic Codes: MS04,TB61.

43950   Greenland, C. Evaluation of violence and dangerous behavior associated with mental illness. Seminars in Psychiatry, August 1971, 3(3), 345-356. Topic Codes: CC81D.

43960   Greenstein, M.G. The influence of cognitive role-taking ability and maternal regulatory style upon aggressive and withdrawn children [doctoral dissertation, Washington University, 1976]. Dissertation Abstracts International, June 1977, 37(12, part 1), 6325B. Topic Codes: MG,NA07B,SI48B.

43970   Greer, G.R. The roles of basal arousal, anticipatory anxiety and incubation in primary sociopathic delinquents, secondary sociopathic delinquents, high-anxious normal delinquents and low-anxious normal delinquents [doctoral dissertation, University of Pittsburgh, 1973]. Dissertation Abstracts International, May 1974, 34(11), 5677B. Topic Codes: BK04BB, BK04D,BL25BB,BL25D,CC37BB,CC37T,MS04.

43980   Greer, J.G., Davis, T.B., and Yearwood, K. Drug treatment: Factors contributing to high risk in institutions. Exceptional Children, April 1977, 43(7), 451-453. Topic Codes: CV15B,DK46,DT44,MG,MM,MO,NA07D,PP.

43990   Gregg, R.E. Passivity, assertion and aggression: Assertive training with two types of institutionalized criminal offenders [doctoral dissertation, University of Texas Health Science Center at Dallas, 1976]. Dissertation Abstracts International, February 1977, 37(8), 4139B-4140B. Topic Codes: CC11,CQ11,CV06C,NE11.

44100   Greguras, F.M., Broder, P.K., and Zimmerman, J. Establishing an Operational Definition of Juvenile Delinquency (report no. 13). Omaha, Nebraska: Creighton University, Institute for Business, Law and Social Research, March 1978. Topic Codes: CC37H,CG11CC,CG11P,CJ,CT70,CV13,DT44D,MM11, PP11.

44200   Griffiths, A.W. Psychological and sociological investigation of XYY prisoners. Nature, July 18, 1970, 227, 290-292. Topic Codes: BB70D,BE11, BP46,CC11C,CC11D,CC11E,CC11I,CC11J,CC11L,CC11N,CC11P,CC11U,CC67,CQ67, CT57,CT59,DD02NF,DD03D,DP22,MA11,MG11,MV11,MX11,NE67,NH59GI,NH59PL,NH67B, NH67D,PE02D,PE66D,PE68D,PM11,PT11,SD11,SH59JL,SH59RL,SJ07D,SJ22D,SR02, SR69D,TA03,TA04,TA52,TB38B,TB93D.

44220   Griffiths, A.W., Marks, V., Fry, D., Morley, G., and Lewis, G. Prisoners of XYY constitution: Biochemical studies. British Journal of Psychiatry, October 1972, 121(563), 365-368. Topic Codes: BB70D,BD11,CC11M,CQ11, CQ59,CV13DA,NE11,NE59.

44300   Grissom, R.J. An analysis of a curriculum supplement especially designed for Tucker Prison inmates, Arkansas Department of Corrections (chapters 3-5). Doctoral dissertation, University of Florida, 1977. Topic Codes: BL04D,CC11A,CC11I,CC11U,SC,TB21D,TB98D.

44380   Groden, G., Domingue, D., Pueschel, S.M., and Deignan, L. Behavioral/emotional problems in mentally retarded children and youth. Psychological Reports, August 1982, 51(1), 143-146. Topic Codes: DK46B,MG.

44410   Grody, G.L. The effects of exposing derisive humor to juvenile delinquent males as a cathartic tool to reduce aggressive impulse strength [doctoral dissertation, United States International University, 1976]. Dissertation Abstracts International, November 1977, 37(5), 2477B-2478B. Topic Codes: CC37,CV06C.

44412   Groh, T.R. Infant stimuli as aggression-inhibiting cues [doctoral dissertation, University of Connecticut, 1976]. Dissertation Abstracts International, March 1977, 37(9), 4681B-4682B. Topic Codes: MC,NA31,PE04,SR03.

44414   Gross, A.D. Sex differences in an Israeli kibbutz system: Reading disabilities, maturation, and sex-role standards [doctoral dissertation, Boston University School of Education, 1977]. Dissertation Abstracts International, October 1977, 38(4), 1998A. Topic Codes: BL70B,DT44,MM,PP, SQ07,SQ70B.

44416   Gross, H., and Kaltenback, E. Epilepsy and delinquent aggressive behavior. Nervenarzt, August 1975, 46(8), 472-474 (in German). Topic Codes: CC37L,DK18D,MC,PE04,SR03.

44417   Gross, M. Violence associated with organic brain disease. In J. Fawcett (ed.), Dynamics of Violence. Chicago: American Medical Association, 1971. Topic Codes: BK11BL,BL52DD,CC81E,CC81G,CQ81,CT81,CY,DK07D,DK09D, DT13D,MH11,NE81,NL,PI11,SR02,TA03,TA52.

44418   Grube, M., and Hartwich, P. The potential of aggressiveness in families of schizophrenics in relation to the danger of relapse. Archiv für Psychiatrie und Nervenkrankheiten, 1983, 233(2), 247-251. Topic Codes: MC, NH65,NH65B,PE04,SR03.

44419   Gruenberg, E.M. Some epidemiological aspects of congenital brain damage.

In H.G. Birch (ed.), Brain Damage in Children: The Biologic and Social Aspects. Baltimore: The Williams & Wilkins Co., 1964. Topic Codes: BK11B,BL52D,BP02B,DD08K,DF34,DK07,DK09,DP11,NA33B,PL,SF07.

44420   Gruenberg, F., and Pond, D.A. Conduct disorders in epileptic children. Journal of Neurology, Neurosurgery and Psychiatry, 1957, 20, 65-68. Topic Codes: DK18B,MG11.

44430   Gruzelier, J.H. Bilateral asymmetry of skin conductance orienting activity and levels in schizophrenics. Biological Psychology, 1973, 1, 21-41. Topic Codes: BL25B,BN44B,MU11.

44460   Gruzelier, J.H., and Venables, P.H. Skin conductance orienting activity in a heterogeneous sample of schizophrenics. Journal of Nervous and Mental Disease, 1972, 155, 277-287. Topic Codes: BL25B,MU11.

44480   Gulkin, R. Sociopathy: A test of two theories [doctoral dissertation, Memphis State University, 1975]. Dissertation Abstracts International, May 1976, 36(11), 5792B. Topic Codes: CC37BB,MS04.

44481   Gully, K.J., and Hosch, H.M. Adaptive behavior scale: Development as a diagnostic tool via discriminant analysis. American Journal of Mental Deficiency, March 1979, 83(5), 518-523. Topic Codes: NA07B,PA,TA74.

44500   Gumnit, R.J., and Mavor, H. Society proceedings: Central Association of Electroencephalographers and Western Association of Electroencephalographers, Aspen, Colorado, March 12-15, 1970. Electroencephalography and Clinical Neurophysiology, 1971, 30, 159-165. Topic Codes: BL04,BL18, BL18B,BL70,BN44,BN68,CV15,DK18,DK18B,DT42,DT67,DT69,ML,MW,NA31R,NA33I, NA44B,NC22,NC44,NH74,NJ03,PE44,PN,PO,SH74,SQ,TA52K,TA52M,TB05,TB35,TB35B, TB37,TB37B,TB46,TB93.

44600   Gunn, J. Criminal behaviour and mental disorder. British Journal of Psychiatry, 1977, 130, 317-329. Topic Codes: BL70B,BL70D,CC11C,CC67,CC81D, CG,CQ67,CT57,CT59,DA04D,DA15D,DK18D,MD11,MG11,MI07,MQ11,MS02,MS04B,MU11, MU70B,MZ,NE67,PE06D,PE15D,SQ07,SQ11.

44700   Gunn, J. Social factors and epileptics in prison. British Journal of Psychiatry, 1974, 124, 509-517. Topic Codes: BL04D,BN44B,BN44D,CC11A, CC11C,CC11G,CC11J,CC11K,CC11L,CC11O,CC37K,DA04B,DA04D,DD26B,DD26D,DK07D, DK09B,DK09D,DK18B,DK18D,MD07,MD11,NH59F,PE06B,PE06D,PO07,PO11,SD11,SF11, SH59H,SJ09D,SJ22D,SW11.

44800   Gunn, J., and Bonn, J. Criminality and violence in epileptic prisoners. British Journal of Psychiatry, 1971, 118, 337-343. Topic Codes: CC11K, CC81M,CE,CT57,CT59,CT68,CY,DK18D,DK18SD,MK11,PE30D.

44900   Gunn, J., and Fenton, G. Epilepsy, automatism and crime. Lancet, June 5, 1971, 7710, 1173-1176. Topic Codes: CC11B,CC11K,CC37F,CC81C,CC81K,CC81M, CT68,DK18D,DK18SD,DT02B,DT10B,DT67,MN04B,MT04B,TB35D.

44920   Gunthey, R.K., and Upadhyaha, S. Adaptive behavior in retarded and nonretarded children. Indian Journal of Clinical Psychology, September 1982, 9(2), 163-166. Topic Codes: CC37,CC37Q,DK46,PA.

45000   Gupta, C., Sonaware, B.R., and Yaffe, S.J. Phenobarbital exposure in utero: Alterations in female reproductive function in rats. Science, May 2, 1980, 208, 508-510. Topic Codes: BP04,DP11.

45050   Gur, R.C. Motoric laterality imbalance in schizophrenia. Archives of General Psychiatry, 1977, 34, 33-37. Topic Codes: BL48B,BN44,DT48,MU11.

45100   Gur, R.C., Levy, J., and Van Auken, C.L. Eyedness, handedness and perinatal stress. Unpublished manuscript, Department of Psychology, University of Pennsylvania, 1978. Topic Codes: BL70,BN44,BP,BP02,DK07,DP,DP11, PO,SQ.

45200   Gutgesell, M., Terrell, G., and Darwin, L. Pediatric blood pressure:

Ethnic comparisons in a primary care center. Hypertension, January–February 1981, 3(1), 39–46. Topic Codes: BE,BL04,BL08B,BL67,BL70,DD28,SN,SQ.

45300   Guth, L. History of central nervous system regeneration research. Experimental Neurology, 1975, 48(3, part 2), 3–15. Topic Codes: BD,BL52D, CV15,DK09.

45330   Guthrie, R.D., and Wyatt, R.J. Biochemistry and schizophrenia: III. A review of childhood psychosis. Schizophrenia Bulletin, Spring 1975, 12, 18–32. Topic Codes: BD07,MG,MU11,NA07D.

45400   Guze, S.B. A study of recidivism based upon a follow-up of 217 consecutive criminals. Journal of Nervous and Mental Disorders, 1964, 138, 575–580. Topic Codes: BL04D,BL67,BL67D,CC11A,CC11C,CC11H,CC11I,CC11L, CC11R,CC67,CG11C.CG11P,CQ67,CT57,CT59,CV13,DA04D,DA15D,MD11,MG11,MI04, MQ11,MS04B,NE67,NH59D,NH59F,PE06D,PE15D,SC18D,SH59D,SH59H,SN,SN11.

45500   Guze, S.B., Goodwin, D.W., and Crane, J.B. Criminality and psychiatric disorders. Archives of General Psychiatry, May 1969, 20, 583–591. Topic Codes: CC11C,CC11H,CG11P,DA04D,DA15D,MB11,MD11,MI04,MQ11,MS04B,MU11, MU70B,NL48,PE06D,PE15D.

45600   Guze, S.B., Wolfgram, E.D., McKinney, J.K., and Cantwell, D.P. Psychiatric illness in the families of convicted criminals: A study of 519 first-degree relatives. Diseases of the Nervous System, October 1967, 28(10), 651–659. Topic Codes: BL67D,BL70D,CC11C,CC11H,CC11L,CG11CC,CV13,DA04D, DA15D,DD26BB,MB11,MD11,MI07,MQ11,MS04B,MU70B,NH67B,NH67BB,PE06D,PE15D, SN11,SQ11.

45700   Guze, S.B., Woodruff, R.A., and Clayton, P.J. Psychiatric disorders and criminality. Journal of the American Medical Association, February 11, 1974, 227(6), 641–642. Topic Codes: BL67D,BL70D,CG11P,CT57,CT59,CT68, DA04D,DA15D,DK46D,MB11,MD11,MI07,MO11,MQ11,MS04B,MU70B,PE06D,PE15D,SN11, SQ11.

45800   Haertzen, C.A., Martin, W.R., Hewett, B.B., and Sandquist, V. Measurement of psychopathy as a state. Journal of Psychology, November 1978, 100(2), 201–214. Topic Codes: MS04,TB61.

45900   Hagan, J., Gillis, A.R., and Chan, J. Explaining official delinquency: A spatial study of class, conflict and control. Sociological Quarterly, Summer 1978, 19, 386–398. Topic Codes: CC37L,CC37Y,CG,CG11C,CG11P,CV13, CX,NE79,NH59F,SA11,SF11,SF26D,SH59H,SJ09D,SW11.

46000   Hahn, N.F. Crime and intelligence. In J.A. Inciardi and K.C. Haas (eds.), Crime and the Criminal Justice Process. Dubuque, Iowa: Kendall/ Hunt Publishing Company, 1978. Topic Codes: BI07,BI11,CG,DK46D,MO11, PM11,SW11,TA03,TA59D.

46010   Hahn, Y.S., Raimondi, A.J., McLone, D.G., and Yamanouchi, Y. Traumatic mechanisms of head injury in child abuse. Child's Brain, 1983, 10(4), 229–241. Topic Codes: CT57B,CT57BB,DD10,DD26,DK07,SI57G.

46030   Haier, R.J., Rosenthal, D., and Wender, P.H. MMPI assessment of psychopathology in the adopted-away offspring of schizophrenics. Archives of General Psychiatry, February 1978, 35(2), 171–175. Topic Codes: MU11, NH04B,NH59PB,NH59PJ,SH04B,SH59RB,SH59RJ,TB61.

46040   Hains, A.A. The development of social cognitive processes among juvenile delinquents and nondelinquent peers [doctoral dissertation, Notre Dame University, 1980]. Dissertation Abstracts International, May 1981, 41 (11), 4284B. Topic Codes: BL11C,CC37G,CC37H,MX11.

46060   Haldeman, C.F. Reactivity to anxiety-provoking stimuli in criminal sexual psychopaths [doctoral dissertation, Purdue University, 1973]. Dissertation Abstracts International, January 1974, 34(7), 3498B. Topic Codes: CC11P,CT68,MS04,SF07B.

46100   Halsey, J.H., Blauenstein, V.W., Wilson, E.M., and Wills, E.H. Regional
cerebral blood flow comparison of right and left hand movement. Neurology, January 1979, 29, 21-28. Topic Codes: BL08,BN44,CV15,DT13,MH,PI,
PO,TA52.

46200   Hamburg, B.A. The psychobiology of sex differences: An evolutionary perspective. In R.C. Friedman, R.M. Richart and R.L. Vande Wiele (eds.),
Sex Differences in Behavior. New York: John Wiley & Sons, Inc., 1974,
373-392. Topic Codes: BD70,BI,BK11B,BL52D,BL70,BN44,DT13,DT42,MH,ML,MV,
PE44,PE66,PI,PN,PO,SF,SQ,SQ70,SR69,TB66.

46250   Hamilton, G.R. The effects of intoxication on aggressive behavior in al-
coholics [doctoral dissertation, Tufts University, 1975]. Dissertation
Abstracts International, September 1976, 37(3), 1459B. Topic Codes:
BL11,DT13,MH,NA07I,PG,PI.

46300   Hammer, M., and Turkewitz, G. A sensory basis for the lateral difference
in the newborn infant's response to somesthetic stimulation. Journal of
Experimental Child Psychology, 1974, 18, 304-312. Topic Codes: BL29,
BN44,NA33I,NL22,PO,TA52M,TB02.

46350   Hammer, R.H. Cumulative school records as early predictors of behavior
problems in eighth grade [doctoral dissertation, Boston College, 1976].
Dissertation Abstracts International, August 1976, 37(2), 881A-882A.
Topic Codes: MG,NA07D,PE64B,SC70B,TA74.

46400   Handford, H.A. Brain hypoxia, minimal brain dysfunction, and schizo-
phrenia. American Journal of Psychiatry, February 1975, 132(2), 192-194.
Topic Codes: BD07,BK11BL,BL48B,BP02B,DD08K,DF60B,DK07B,DK09B,DK11,DK48B,
DP,DT04EB,DT48B,MG48B,MT48B,MU70,NA33A,NH74B,PE48B,PR07,SH74B,TB02.

46500   Hansman, C.F., and Maresh, M.M. A longitudinal study of skeletal maturation. American Journal of Diseases of Children, March 1961, 101, 305-321.
Topic Codes: BE,BL11,BL70,NA07I,PG,SQ.

46530   Hanson, D.R. Children of schizophrenic mothers or fathers compared to
children of other psychiatric controls: Their first eight years [doctoral
dissertation, University of Minnesota, 1974]. Dissertation Abstracts International, December 1974, 35(6), 3015B-3016B. Topic Codes: MU11,NA44D,
NH59B,NH59E,NJ06,SH59B,SH59F.

46560   Hanson, D.R., and Gottesman, I.I. The genetics, if any, of infantile autism and childhood schizophrenia. Journal of Autism and Childhood Schizophrenia, September 1976, 6(3), 209-234. Topic Codes: BI07,MG04,MU11,
NA07B,NH59B,NH59E,SH59B,SH59F.

46600   Hardy, J.B. Birth weight and subsequent physical and intellectual development. New England Journal of Medicine, November 1, 1973, 289(18), 973-
974. Topic Codes: BL07B,BL11,BL27K,BL67,BP,BP02,BP26G,DF06B,DF48,DF70,
DP22P,DP48,NA07I,NA31R,NC44,NH74,PG,PM,SH74,SN,TA52K.

46650   Hardy, J.B. The Johns Hopkins Collaborative Perinatal Project: A symposium. Johns Hopkins Medical Journal, 1971, 128, 237-243. Topic Codes:
BP,BP02,CG,DF48,DP,DP11,DP48,NC,NC22,NC44,NC59G,NC70,NC80.

46675   Hardy, J.B., Drage, J.S., and Jackson, E.C. The First Year of Life: The
Collaborative Perinatal Project of the National Institute of Neurological
and Communicative Disorders and Stroke. Baltimore: Johns Hopkins Uni-
versity Press, 1979. Topic Codes: BD30BA,BE30,BK11,BL04,BL05,BL06,BL07B,
BL22,BL27KL,BL33,BL48,BL52D,BL67,BL70,BP02,BP04,BP26GD,BP44,BP46,BP47,
BP53,BP57,BP59,BP63,BP70,DA,DD00,DD05,DD08K,DF06B,DF34,DF48,DF60B,DF67B,
DF70B,DK07,DK09,DP11,DP44,DP46,DP48,DP60,DP81,DT04,NA33B,NA33I,NC44,
NH59PP,NL48B,PE34,PE48,PE68B,PL,PR07,SN,SQ,SW07,TA52K,TA52M,TB02,TB05.

46676   Hardy, J.B., and Mellits, E.D. Does maternal smoking during pregnancy
have a long-term effect on the child? Lancet, December 23, 1972, 7791,
1332-1336. Topic Codes: BD30,BE30,BL05,BL06,BL07,BL11,BL27K,BL48,BL67,
BP26G,BP70,DF06,DF48,DF70,DP22P,DP48,DT48,MT48,NA07I,NA31R,NA33I,NC22,

NC44,NC59G,NC70,PE48,PG,PR,SN,TA52,TA52K,TA52M,TB02,TB09,TB33G,TB44,TB53,
TB78,TB95,TB98.

46677   Hardy, J.B., and Mellits, E.D. Relationship of low birth weight to maternal characteristics of age, parity, education and body size. Epidemiology
of Prematurity, 1977, 31(4), 105-117. Topic Codes: BL07,BP57,DF06,
NH59PA,NH59PF,NH59PP,SH59RA,SH59RF,SH59RP.

46678   Hardy, M.P., Mellits, E.D., and Willig, S.N. Reading: A function of
language usage. Johns Hopkins Medical Journal, 1971, 129, 43-53. Topic
Codes: DT15,DT42,ML15,NC70,PE44,PN,TA59D,TB95,TB98.

46679   Hardy, J.B., Welcher, D.W., Mellits, E.D., and Kagan, J. Pitfalls in the
measurement of intelligence: Are standard intelligence tests valid in-
struments for measuring the intellectual potential of urban children?
Journal of Psychology, 1976, 94, 43-51. Topic Codes: PM,TB95.

46680   Hardy, J.B., Welcher, D.W., Stanley, J., Wessel, K.W., Dallas, J.R., and
Blaustein, R. Socialization of the urban child: The Johns Hopkins Child
Development Study. Unpublished manuscript, Johns Hopkins University
School of Medicine, 1978. Topic Codes: BL11,DT42,MG,ML,NA07D,NA07I,NA44,
NC70,NJ,NL48,PE44,PE64B,PG,PN,SC70B,SF07,TA04,TB53,TB98.

46730   Hardyck, C., and Petrinovich, L.F. Left-handedness. Psychology Bulletin,
May 1977, 84(3), 385-404. Topic Codes: BN44,PO.

46760   Hardyck, C., Petrinovich, L.F., and Goldman, R.D. Left-handedness and
cognitive deficit. Cortex, 1976, 12, 266-279. Topic Codes: BE,BE30,
BL06,BL07B,BL11,BL22,BL27,BL67,BL70,BN44,BN44B,BP,BP02,BP22F,BP26,BP46,
BP57,DF06B,DF48,DF60B,DK,DP,DP11,DP48,DT13,MG,MH,NA07D,NA07I,NA44D,NC44,
NC59G,NC70,NH59PF,NH59PP,NJ06,PE64,PG,PI,PM,PO,POO7,SC70,SH59RF,SH59RP,SN,
SQ,SW,TA04,TA52,TA59,TA59D,TB09,TB95.

46780   Hare, R.D. The assessment of psychopathy in criminal populations. Paper
presented at the VII International Seminar in Comparative Clinical Criminology, Montreal, Quebec, June 5-7, 1979. Topic Codes: CC11C,CC11U,MS04,
MS04B,TA02B,TA59.

46785   Hare, R.D. Diagnosis of antisocial personality disorder in two prison
populations. American Journal of Psychiatry, July 1983, 140(7), 887-890.
Topic Codes: CC11C,CQ59,MS04B.

46790   Hare, R.D. Psychopathy and choice of immediate versus delayed punishment.
Journal of Abnormal Child Psychology, February 1966, 71(1), 25-29. Topic
Codes: BN04D,BN44B,CC11D,CC81E,CQ59,CV06C,CV13D,MB11,MS02,NE59,PC11,PT11,
PY11,TA03,TA80.

46795   Hare, R.D. Psychopathy and crime. Paper presented at the Colloquium on
the Correlates of Crime and Determinants of Criminal Behavior, Washington,
D.C., March 30-31, 1978. Topic Codes: CC11C,CC37BB,MS04B,PY11,SI57D,
SI57PB,SU11.

46900   Hare, R.D. Psychopathy and electrodermal responses to nonsignal stimulation. Biological Psychology, 1978, 6, 237-246. Topic Codes: BL25BB,
BN44BB,BN44D,CC11C,CC11O,CC11U,MS04B,POO7B,PO11,PY11,SI57PB,SU11,TB23B.

47000   Hare, R.D. Psychopathy and laterality of cerebral function. Journal of
Abnormal Psychology, 1979, 88(6), 605-610. Topic Codes: BL04BB,BN44,
BN44BB,BN44D,CC11A,CC11C,CC11I,CC11O,CC11T,DK07BB,PO,POO7B,PO11,TA02B,
TA80,TB15B,TB23B,TB35BB,TB81.

47100   Hare, R.D. Psychopathy: Theory and Research. New York: John Wiley &
Sons, Inc., 1970. Topic Codes: BK11B,BL25BB,CC11C,CC11F,CC11G,CC11H,
CC11L,CC11P,CC11U,CC67B,CC81,CQ59,CQ67,CV06C,CV13DA,CV15B,CV15D,DD02B,
DD02D,DT44BB,DT44D,ME07,MF11,MK11,MM07B,MM11,MS04B,NE59,PE08D,PPO7B,PP11,
PT11,SI07,SI11,SI57BB,TA80,TB35BB,TB37B,TB37D,TB59B,TB61B,TB66B,TB66D,
TB74B,TB93BB.

47200   Hare, R.D., and Schalling, D., (eds.). Psychopathic Behavior: Approaches to Research. New York: John Wiley & Sons, Inc., 1978. Topic Codes: BA, BB70B,BB70D,BD07,BD11,BD70B,BE07,BE11,BI07,BI11,BK04D,BK11BL,BL04BB, BL04D,BL08BB,BL08BD,BL11C,BL18B,BL18D,BL22,BL25B,BL25D,BL29B,BL29D,BL67B, BL67D,BL70BB,BL70D,BN04B,BN04D,BN68B,BP63,CC11A,CC11C,CC11D,CC11G,CC11H, CC11I,CC11L,CC11M,CC11N,CC11O,CC11P,CC11Q,CC11R,CC11S,CC11T,CC11U,CC24, CC37A,CC37BB,CC37G,CC37J,CC37L,CC37M,CC37S,CC37W,CC371,CC67B,CC81E,CC81J, CE81,CG,CJ,CL,CQ11,CQ22,CQ37B,CQ59,CQ67,CQ81,CT81,CV06C,CV13DA,CV15B, CV15D,DA04,DD00B,DD01,DD02B,DD02D,DD02ND,DD02NF,DD10B,DD10D,DD28B,DD28D, DK07B,DK46B,DK46D,DK48B,DK48D,MB11,MC11,MD07B,MD11,ME07,MF11,MG02B,MG02D, MG11B,MG30BB,MG30D,MI04,MI07,MK11,ML,MM,MO07,MO11,MS04B,MU11,MU70B,MW, MX07,MX11,MY,NA07,NA44,NE,NH04BA,NH04D,NH59B,NH59E,NH59GB,NH59GD,NH59GG, NH59GI,NH63B,NH65B,NH67D,NH70,NH74BB,NH74D,NJ,NL,PA11,PC07B,PC11,PE01, PE04D,PE06BB,PE06D,PE08D,PE10,PE15B,PE15D,PE64,SC,SC70,SF,SH04D,SH59,SH70, SH74,SQ,SRO3,SRO4B,TA02B,TA03,TA52,TA59D,TA80,TB23B,TB35BB,TB35D,TB38B, TB61B,TB66.

47300   Harlap, S., and Davies, A.M. Infant admission to hospital and maternal smoking. Lancet, March 30, 1974, 7856, 529-532. Topic Codes: BL06, BL48,BP70,CV30,DD,DT48,DT59,MR,MT48,NA31R,PE48,PR,PS,SJ07,SL,SW,TA52K.

47400   Harlap, S., and Davies, A.M. Smoking in pregnancy and child development. British Medical Journal, June 15, 1974, 2, 610. Topic Codes: BL11,BP70, NA07I,NA31R,PG,TA52K.

47500   Harlap, S., Davies, A.M., Grover, N.B., and Prywes, R. The Jerusalem Perinatal Study: The first decade, 1964-1973. Israel Journal of Medical Sciences, November 1977, 13(11), 1073-1091. Topic Codes: BB,BD30,BL07, BP,BP02,CV30,DD,DD02,DD81,DF06,DF48,DP,DP48,NA31,NA31R,NA44D,NH59P,NJ06, PV,SF,SH59R,SJ07,SL,SO,SW,TA52K.

47550   Harper, M.A., Morris, M., and Bleyerveld, J. The significance of an abnormal EEG in psychopathic personalities. Australian Journal of Psychiatry, December 1972, 6(4), 215-224. Topic Codes: MS04,TB35BB.

47600   Harper, P.A., and Wiener, G. Sequelae of low birth weight. Annual Review of Medicine, 1965, 16, 405-420. Topic Codes: BA,BD30,BE,BL07B,BL11,BL27, BL67,BP26,DD,DD02,DD08,DD81,DF06B,DF34,DF48,DF60B,DF67,DK,DK11,DP,DP11, DP48,MG18,NA07I,NA33B,NA44D,NH74,NJ06,PE64,PG,PM,SC70,SH74,SN,TA52,TB09, TB57,TB78,TB95.

47700   Harrington, D.M., Block, J.H., and Block, J. Intolerance of ambiguity in preschool children: Psychometric considerations, behavioral manifestations, and parental correlates. Developmental Psychology, 1978, 14(3), 242-256. Topic Codes: BL70,DT13,MH,NA07B,NA44N,NJ20,NL48,PA,PE10,PI,PT, SI22,SI48,SI57,SQ,TA59,TA74.

47800   Harris, L.J. Left handedness: Early theories, facts and fancies. In J. Herron (ed.), Neuropsychology of Left Handedness. New York: Academic Press, 1980. Topic Codes: BE,BL70,BN44,BN44B,BN44D,DK07B,DT13,MH,MV11, PE66D,PI,PM70,PO,PO07,PO11,PT,SQ,SR69D.

47900   Harris, L.J. Sex differences in spatial ability: Possible environmental, genetic, and neurological factors. In M. Kinsbourne (ed.), Asymmetrical Function of the Brain. New York: Cambridge University Press, 1978. Topic Codes: BB70,BD70,BI,BK11B,BL11,BL48,BL52D,BL70,BN44,DD02N,DK07B, DP22,DT06,DT13,DT42,DT48,DT59,MH,ML,ML04,MR,MT48,NA07B,NA07I,NH59,NH59B, NH59GB,NH59P,NH59PB,PE10,PE44,PE48,PG,PI,PM70,PN,PO,PR,PS,PY,SF,SH59, SH59B,SH59JB,SH59R,SH59RB,SI57P,SQ,SQ70,SU,TA59D,TB09,TB12,TB33,TB35,TB66, TB68,TB72,TB81,TB95,TB96.

48000   Harris, L.J., and Gitterman, S.R. Sex and handedness differences in well-educated adults' self-descriptions of left-right confusability. Archives of Neurology, November 1978, 35, 773. Topic Codes: BL70,BN44,DT13,MH,PI, PM70,PO,SQ.

48050   Harris, R. Relationship between EEG abnormality and aggressive and antisocial behavior: A critical appraisal. Journal of Child Psychology and

Psychiatry and Allied Disciplines, 1978, 1(book supplement), 13-27. Topic Codes: BK11B,BL52DD,BN04D,CC11F,CC11M,DK09D,PC11,PE04D,SR03B.

48200   Harris, R. Tampering with genes: A new threat to blacks? *Ebony*, September 1980, 35(11), 31-34. Topic Codes: BI,BL67,DD,MF,PE,SN.

48250   Harris, S.L., and Ersner-Hershfield, R. Behavioral suppression of seriously disruptive behavior in psychotic and retarded patients: A review of punishment and its alternatives. *Psychological Bulletin*, November 1978, 85(6), 1352-1375. Topic Codes: DK46,MF,MU,SI57J.

48260   Harris, W.J., and King, D.R. Achievement, sociometric status, and personality characteristics of children selected by their teachers as having learning and/or behavior problems. *Psychology in the Schools*, October 1982, 19(4), 452-457. Topic Codes: DT44,MG,PE64,PM.

48300   Hartlage, L.C. Sex-linked inheritance of spatial ability. *Perceptual and Motor Skills*, 1970, 31, 610. Topic Codes: BI,BL70,BP47,DP22,NH59B, NH59GB,NH59P,NH59PB,PM70,SH59B,SH59JB,SH59R,SH59RB,SQ.

48400   Hartlage, L.C., and Tollison, C.D. MMPI correlates of looking left or right during mental tasks. *Journal of Clinical Psychology*, January 1979, 35(1), 92-94. Topic Codes: BL70,BN44,DT13,DT42,MH,ML,PE44,PI,PM70,PN,PO, PT,SQ,TB61.

48460   Hartmann, K., and Allison, J. Sexual sociopaths in Nebraska. *Nebraska Medical Journal*, March 1979, 64(3), 59-60. Topic Codes: CC37BB,CT68, MS04.

48490   Hartshorn, M.A. Genetic aspects of misbehavior. *New England Journal of Medicine*, November 5, 1970, 283(19), 1056. Topic Codes: BB70D,CC37N.

48495   Harvey, A.R., and Carr, T.L. Need for a holistic approach to analysis and treatment of the black mentally retarded offender. In A.R. Harvey and T. L. Carr (eds.), *Black Mentally Retarded Offender: A Holistic Approach to Prevention and Habilitation*. New York: United Church of Christ, Commission of Racial Justice, 1982, 3-13. Topic Codes: BA,BL67D,CG11CC,CV13, DK46D,MO11,SB11,SF11,SM11,TB78,TB95.

48500   Hastings, J.E., and Barkley, R.A. A review of psychophysiological research with hyperkinetic children. *Journal of Abnormal Child Psychology*, 1978, 6(4), 413-447. Topic Codes: BK04B,BL18B,BL25B,BL29B,BL70,BN04B, BN68,CV15B,DK09B,DK48B,DT52B,DT69,MG,MG30,MG48B,MW,NA07D,PC07,SQ,TA02, TA52,TB35B,TB37B.

48600   Hatfield, J.S., Ferguson, L.R., and Alpert, R. Mother-child interaction and the socialization process. *Child Development*, 1967, 38, 356-414. Topic Codes: BL70,MC,MK,NA07B,PE04,PE10,PE30,PT,PY,SI48,SI57P,SQ,SQ70, SR03,SU,TA59.

48620   Hawk, S.S., and Peterson, R.A. Do MMPI psychopathic deviancy scores reflect psychopathic deviancy or just deviancy? *Journal of Personality Assessment*, August 1974, 38(4), 362-368. Topic Codes: MS04,TB61.

48640   Hays, J.R., and Solway, K.S. Violent behavior and differential Wechsler Intelligence Scale for Children characteristics. *Journal of Consulting and Clinical Psychology*, December 1977, 45(6), 1187. Topic Codes: CC37Q, CC37I,CC81Q,CC81Y,PM11,TB95D.

48660   Hays, J.R., Solway, K.S., and Schreiner, D. Intellectual characteristics of juvenile murderers versus offenders. *Psychological Reports*, August 1978, 43(1), 80-82. Topic Codes: CC37I,CC81Y,TB95D.

48680   Haywood, H.C. Experiential factors in intellectual development: The concept of dynamic intelligence. *Proceedings of the American Psychopathological Association*, 1976, 56, 69-104. Topic Codes: BL11,NA07I,PG,PM.

48690   Heath, G.A., Gayton, W.F., and Hardesty, V.A. Childhood firesetting.

Canadian Psychiatric Association Journal, June 1976, 21(4), 229-237. Topic Codes: CT59B,CV,MG18,SI57D.

48700   Heath, R.G. Subcortical brain function correlates of psychopathology and epilepsy. In C. Shagass, S. Gershon, and A.J. Friedhoff (eds.), *Psychopathology and Brain Dysfunction*. New York: Raven Press, 1977. Topic Codes: BK11B,BK11BL,DK07B,DK18B,DT67,MB,MU,MU70,PT74,TB35B.

48800   Heather, N. The structure of delinquent values: A repertory grid investigation. *British Journal of Social and Clinical Psychology*, 1979, 18, 263-275. Topic Codes: CC37W,CC37Z,CC37I,CG11P,PT11,SW11,TA59.

48850   Hecaen, H., and Piercy, M. Parotysmal dysphasia and the problem of cerebral dominance. *Journal of Neurology, Neurosurgery and Psychiatry*, 1956, 19, 194-201. Topic Codes: BN44,DT06,DT67.

48900   Hecaen, H., and Sauguet, J. Cerebral dominance in left-handed subjects. *Cortex*, 1971, 7, 19-48. Topic Codes: BL48,BN44,BN44B,DK07B,DT06,DT13, DT15,DT42,DT48,DT59,MH,ML,ML04,ML15,MR,MT48,NH,PE44,PE48,PI,PM70,PN,PO, PO07,PR,PS,SH,TB02.

48915   Hechtman, L., Weiss, G., and Perlman, T. Hyperactives as young adults: Past and current substance abuse and antisocial behavior. *American Journal of Orthopsychiatry*, July 1984, 54(3), 415-425. Topic Codes: DA04B, DA15,MD07,ME,MG02B,MG30B,MI,NA07DD,PE06,PE08,PE15,SR04.

48950   Heijbell, J., and Bohman, M. Benign epilepsy of children with centrotemporal EEG foci: Intelligence, behavior, and school adjustment. *Epilepsia*, December 1975, 16(5), 679-687. Topic Codes: DK18,NA07B,PE64,PM.

49000   Heilbrun, A.B., Jr. Psychopathy and violent crime. *Journal of Consulting and Clinical Psychology*, 1979, 47(3), 509-516. Topic Codes: BL04D,CC11A, CC11C,CC11I,CC11N,CC11U,CC81A,CC81D,CC81J,CC81Y,CG11P,CT57,CT59,CY,MK11, MS04B,PE30D,PM11,SC18D,TA02B,TA03,TA59D,TB23B,TB61B,TB98D.

49005   Heilbrun, A.B., Jr. Toward two models of psychopathic violence. *Medical Law*, 1984, 3(2), 119-125. Topic Codes: CC81D,MS04B.

49100   Heinonen, O.P., Slone, D., Monson, R.D., Hook, E.B., and Shapiro, S. Cardiovascular birth defects and antenatal exposure to female sex. *New England Journal of Medicine*, January 13, 1977, 296(2), 67-70. Topic Codes: BB,BD70,BL06,BL22,BL67,BP,BP02,BP04,BP22F,DD02,DF48,DP,DP11,DP48, NC44,NC59G,SN.

49150   Heinonen, O.P., Slone, D., and Shapiro, S. *Birth Defects and Drugs in Pregnancy*. Lexington, Massachusetts: PSG Publishing Company, 1977. Topic Codes: BB,BP04,DD02,DF,NA31C.

49170   Hellman, D.S., and Blackman, N. Enuresis, firesetting and cruelty to animals: A triad predictive of adult crime. *American Journal of Psychiatry*, June 1966, 122(12), 1431-1435. Topic Codes: CC37V,CT59B,MG02D,MG18B, MG18D,MS04.

49190   Hellon, C.P. Crime, malnutrition, and other forms of cerebral trauma. *Journal of Orthomolecular Psychiatry*, 1975, 4(4), 256-260. Topic Codes: BD52D,DK07D.

49200   Helzer, B., and Yard, G.J. A study of educational needs and competencies for institutionalized juvenile delinquents. Unpublished manuscript, Programs for Behavior Disordered Children, University of Missouri, St. Louis, n.d. Topic Codes: CC37A,CC37B,CC37G,CC37H,CC37I,CC37J,CC37I,CQ37,CT57F, DT42BB,DT42D,MG,ML02B,ML03,MQ11,MS04B,MZ,NA07D,NE37,PE44BB,PE44D,PE64B, PE64D,PNO7B,PN11,SC70B,SC70D,TA03,TA59,TB21B,TB21D.

49300   Henderson, N.B., Butler, B.V., and Clark, W.M., Jr. Relationships between selected perinatal variables and seven-year intelligence. *Proceedings of the 79th Annual Convention of the American Psychological Association*,

1971, 6, 139–140. Topic Codes: BL70,BP02,DP11,NA44D,NC44,NC59G,NC70,
NJ06,PM,SQ,SW,TB02,TB95.

49350   Henderson, N.B., Butler, B.V., and Goffeney, B. Effectiveness of the WISC
and Bender Gestalt test in predicting arithmetic and reading achievement
for white and nonwhite children. Journal of Clinical Psychology, July
1969, 25, 268–271. Topic Codes: BL11,BL67,PE64,TB95.

49400   Henderson, N.B., and Engel, R. Neonatal visual evoked potentials as predictors of psychoeducational tests at age seven. Developmental Psychology, 1974, 10(2), 269–276. Topic Codes: BL18,BL67,BL70,NA31A,NA44D,
NC44,NC70,NJ06,PE64,PM,SC70,SN,SQ,TA52M,TB09K,TB37,TB84,TB95,TB98.

49450   Henderson, N.B., Goffeney, B., Butler, B.V., and Clarkson, Q.D. Differential rates of school promotion from first grade for white and Negro,
male and female 7-year-olds. Psychology in the Schools, 1971, 8, 101–109.
Topic Codes: BL67,BL70,NC70,PE64,SC70,SN,SQ,SW,TB09K,TB27,TB53,TB95,TB98.

49500   Henig, R.M. The child savers. New York Times Magazine, March 22, 1981,
34–44. Topic Codes: BL22,BL31,BP22F,CT57B,DD,DD10,DF06B,DF48,DP22,DP48,
NA31D,NA31F,NA33A,NA33I,PE32,PK,SI57,SI57G,TA52M.

49590   Henn, F.A., Bardwell, R., and Jenkins, R.L. Juvenile delinquents revisited: Adult criminal activity. Archives of General Psychiatry, October
1980, 37(10), 1160–1163. Topic Codes: CC37B,CC37V,CC37W,MG11B,PY11,
SI57PB,SU11.

49600   Henn, F.A., Herjanic, M., and Vanderpearl, R.H. Forensic psychiatry:
Diagnosis and criminal responsibility. Journal of Nervous and Mental
Disease, 1976, 162 (6), 423–429. Topic Codes: CC81D,CT57,CT57F,CT59,
CT59B,CT68,DA04D,DA15D,DK18D,DK46D,MB11,MD11,MI04,MO11,MS02,MU70B,MV11,MZ,
PE06D,PE15D,PE66D,SR69D,TB35D.

49700   Henning, J., and Levy, R. Verbal-performance IQ differences of white
and Negro delinquents on the WISC and WAIS. Journal of Clinical Psychology, 1967, 23, 164–168. Topic Codes: BL04D,BL67,BL67D,CC37,CC37A,CC37I,
CC37P,CC37I,CQ37,DT44D,MM11,MS04B,NE37,PE64D,PM11,PP11,SC70D,SN,SN11,
TB93D,TB95D,TB96BB,TB96D.

49760   Hermann, B.P. Psychological effects of epilepsy: A review. Catalog of
Selected Documents in Psychology, February 1977, 7, 16. Topic Codes:
DK18B.

49790   Herrnstein, R.J. Some criminogenic traits of offenders. In J.Q. Wilson
(ed.), Crime and Public Policy. San Francisco, California: ICS Press,
1983, 31–49. Topic Codes: BE11,CC37E,CC37Q,CC37W,PM11,PT11.

49800   Herron, J. (ed.). Neuropsychology of Left-Handedness. New York: Aca-
demic Press, 1980. Topic Codes: BD70,BE,BI,BK11B,BL04,BL11,BL22,BL48,
BL52D,BL70,BN44B,BN44D,BN44H,BP02,BP22F,DD00,DD02B,DD08K,DF34,DK07B,DP11,
DP44,DT13,DT15,DT42,DT44,DT46,DT59,MG,MH,ML04,ML15,MM,MN,MR,MU70,MV11,NA,
NA07D,NH59B,NH74B,NL,PE44,PE48,PE66D,PE70,PG,PI,PM70,PN,PO07,PO11,PO33,PP,
PQ,PS,PT,SB,SC,SF,SH,SQ,SRO1,SR69D,TA02,TA52,TA55,TA59D,TA80,TB35,TB37,
TB49,TB68,TB72,TB81,TB93,TB95B.

49900   Herron, J., Galin, D., Johnstone, J., and Ornstein, R.E. Cerebral specialization, writing posture, and motor control of writing in left-
handers. Science, September 1979, 205(21), 1285–1289. Topic Codes:
BL70,BN44,PO,SQ,TB35,TB81.

49950   Herrschaft, H. Early diagnosis of brain tumors. Fortschritte der Neurologie, Psychiatrie und Ihrer Grenzgebiete, July 1977, 45(7), 383–404 (in
German). Topic Codes: DK07,DK09B.

50000   Hersher, L. Minimal brain dysfunction and otitis media. Perceptual and
Motor Skills, 1978, 47, 723–726. Topic Codes: BD07,CV15B,DD00,DK48B,
DT44,MG,MG30,MG48B,MM,NA07D,NH65B,PP,TB95B,TB98B.

50030   Hertzig, M.E., and Birch, H.G. Neurologic organization in psychiatrically disturbed adolescents: A comparative consideration of sex differences. Archives of General Psychiatry, November 1968, 19(5), 528-537. Topic Codes: BL04B,BL70B,DT52B,DT59B,MG,MR07,MS,MU70,NA07B,PE10,PM07,PS07,SQ07, TA52.

50060   Herzberg, B., and Herzberg, L. Brain damage and abnormal behaviour in children. Medical Journal of Australia, June 4, 1977, 23, 853-855. Topic Codes: BK11B,BL52D,DK07B,MG.

50090   Hess, A.K. Indoctrination of two types of criminal offenders as a function of altered arousal conditions [doctoral dissertation, University of Kentucky, 1973]. Dissertation Abstracts International, April 1974, 34 (10), 5193B-5194B. Topic Codes: BN04BB,BN04D,CC11C,CC11D,MQ11,MS04B.

50100   Heston, L.L. The genetics of schizophrenia and schizoid disease. Science, January 16, 1970, 167, 249-256. Topic Codes: BD07,BE07,BI07,BK04B, DK46B,MO07,MU70,MU70B,NH04B,NH59B,NH59E,NH59PB,NH59PJ,NH59PL,NH65B,NH74B, PM07,SF07,SH04B,SH59B,SH59F,SH59RB,SH59RJ,SH59RL,SH74B.

50200   Hetherington, E.M. A developmental study of the effects of sex of the dominant parent on sex-role preference, identification, and imitation in children. Journal of Personality and Social Psychology, 1965, 2, 188-194. Topic Codes: BL11,BL70,NA07B,NA07I,PE10,PG,PT,SI22,SI48,SI57,SQ,SQ70, TA59.

50300   Hetherington, E.M., Stouwie, R.J., and Ridberg, E.H. Patterns of family interaction and child-rearing attitudes related to three dimensions of juvenile delinquency. Journal of Abnormal Psychology, 1971, 78(2), 160-176. Topic Codes: BL70D,CC37,CC37B,CC37L,CC371,CQ37,CT57F,MG,MX11,MZ, NA07D,NE37,PE68D,SI22D,SI48D,SI57BB,SI57D,SQ11,SR02,TA59.

50350   Heuser, J.P. The methodological adequacy of deviant behavior research: Problems and prospects for the conventional study of unconventional behavior [doctoral dissertation, University of Oregon, 1973]. Dissertation Abstracts International, September 1973, 34(3), 1382A. Topic Codes: CG,MF.

50400   Hickey, R.J., and Clelland, R.C. Causes of carboxyhemoglobinemia and associated atherosclerotic disease: Environmental and constitutional factors. In 1975 Symposium Nicotine and Carbon Monoxide, presented by the Tobacco and Health Research Institute and the Kentucky Tobacco Research Board, Lexington, Kentucky, November 17-18, 1975, 162-172. Topic Codes: BI,BP70,DD,DT04E,SF.

50500   Hickey, R.J., Clelland, R.C., and Bowers, E.J. Essential hormones as carcinogenic hazards. Journal of Occupational Medicine, April 1979, 21(4), 265-268. Topic Codes: BD,BD52,BD70,CV52,DD.

50600   Hickey, R.J., Clelland, R.C., and Bowers, E.J. Maternal smoking, birth weight, infant death, and the self-selection problem. American Journal of Obstetrics and Gynecology, August 1, 1978, 131(7), 805-811. Topic Codes: BD,BI,BL07,BL27K,BL52D,BL67,BP,BP02,BP26G,BP70,DD30,DF06,DF48,DF70,DP22P, DP48,DT04E,NA33D,NC44,NC59G,PE34,SF,SH59RP,SN,SW.

50660   Higgins, J. Inconsistent socialization. Psychological Reports, August 1968, 23(1), 303-336. Topic Codes: CC37M,MG,PY11,SI57B,SI57D.

50750   Hill, B.K., and Bruininks, R.H. Maladaptive behavior of mentally retarded individuals in residential facilities. American Journal of Mental Deficiency, January 1984, 88(4), 380-387. Topic Codes: DK46B,MO07,PA.

50800   Hillenbrand, E. Father absence in military families. Family Coordinator, October 1976, 25, 451-458. Topic Codes: BL70,MC,MK,NA07B,PE04,PE10,PE30, PE64,PM,PT,SC70,SI57,SI59,SJ07,SQ,SR03,TA59D,TA74,TB95.

50900   Hilton, I. Differences in the behavior of mothers toward first- and later-born children. Journal of Personality and Social Psychology, 1967, 7(3), 282-290. Topic Codes: BL70,NA07B,PE10,PT,SI48,SJ07,SQ.

51000   Hindelang, M.J. Race and involvement in common law personal crimes. _American Sociological Review_, February 1978, 43, 93-109. Topic Codes: BL67,BL67D,CC37Y,CC81L,CC81U,CG11P,CT57,CT59,CX,NE79,SF11,SN,SN11.

51100   Hindelang, M.J. Sex differences in criminal activity. _Social Problems_, December 1979, 27(2), 143-156. Topic Codes: BL70D,CC81V,CE,CG11P,CT57, CT59,CX,NE79,SF11,SQ11.

51200   Hindelang, M.J., Hirschi, T., and Weis, J.G. Correlates of delinquency: The illusion of discrepancy between self-report and official measures. _American Sociological Review_, December 1979, 44, 995-1014. Topic Codes: BL67,BL67D,BL70,BL70D,CC37X,CC37Y,CC81U,CE,CG,CG11P,CT57,CT59,CT70,SN, SN11,SQ,SQ11,SW11.

51300   Hindley, C.B., and Owen, C.F. The extent of individual changes in IQ for ages between 6 months and 17 years in a British longitudinal sample. _Journal of Child Psychology and Psychiatry and Allied Disciplines_, 1978, 19, 329-350. Topic Codes: BL04,BL11,BL31,BL70,NA07B,NA07I,NA31F,NA44F, NH59P,NH59PB,NJ09,PE10,PG,PK,PM,SH59R,SH59RB,SQ,SW,TA59D,TB78.

51350   Hines, D., and Satz, P. Superiority of right visual half fields in right handers for recall of digits presented at varying rates. _Neuropsychologia_, 1971, 9, 21-25. Topic Codes: BN44,DT46,DT59.

51370   Hinton, J., O'Neill, M., Hamilton, S, and Burke, M. Psychophysiological differentiation between psychopathic and schizophrenic abnormal offenders. _British Journal of Social and Clinical Psychology_, 1980, 19(3), 257-269. Topic Codes: BL25B,BL25BB,MS04,MU70.

51400   Hippchen, L.J. The biochemistry of stress reactions and crime. _Journal of Offender Counseling_, Winter 1980, 5(2), 19-38. Topic Codes: BB70D, BD11,BD30HD,BD52D,BI11,CC81E,CV52D,DA04D,DA15D,DA44MB,DD30D,DK07D,DT44,MC, MD11,MG,MG30,MI04,MM,NA07D,PE04,PE06D,PE15D,PP,SF11,SR03.

51500   Hippchen, L.J. (ed.). _Ecologic-Biochemical Approaches to Treatment of Delinquents and Criminals_. New York: Van Nostrand Reinhold Company, 1978. Topic Codes: BB70D,BD11,BD30D,BD30HD,BD52D,BD70B,BI11,CC11C,CC11D,CC11M, CC11Q,CC37B,CC37BB,CC37H,CC37U,CC371,CC81,CG11,CQ11,CQ37,CQ81,CT81,CV52D, CY,DA04D,DA44,DD00,DD01,DD15,DD30D,DD81D,DT15B,DT59D,MC11,MG02D,MI07, ML15B,MM11,MR11,MU70B,NE37,PE04D,PE06D,PE08D,PP07B,PS11,SF11,TA80,TB98D.

51600   Hirschi, T., and Hindelang, M.J. Intelligence and delinquency: A revisionist review. _American Sociological Review_, August 1977, 42, 571-587. Topic Codes: BL67D,CC37J,CC37L,CC37Q,CC37Y,CC37Z,CG,CG11P,DP22,MG11, NH59GI,PE64D,PM11,SC18,SC70D,SF11,SH59JL,SN11,SW11,TB78D,TB93D.

51700   Hobby, E.E. The psychopathic code and the therapeutic community. _Hospital and Community Psychiatry_, January 1972, 23(1), 25-27. Topic Codes: CC11C,CC67B,CV06C,CV13D.

51800   Hodgkinson, R., Wang, C.N., and Marx, G.F. Evaluation of the effects of general anesthesia and pethedine on neurobehavioral tests during the first two days of life. _Anesthesia_, 1976, 31, 143-144. Topic Codes: BP04, NA33I,TA52M,TB02.

51900   Hoffer, A. Crime, punishment, and treatment. _Orthomolecular Psychiatry_, 1979, 8(3), 193-199. Topic Codes: BD30HD,BL52D,CT57,CV06C,CV13D,CV15D, CV52D,CX,DA04D,DD30D,DK09D,MD11,MG11,MU11,NE79,PE06D.

51930   Hoffman, B.F. Two new cases of XYY chromosome complement and a review of the literature. _Canadian Psychiatric Association Journal_, December 1977, 22(8), 447-455. Topic Codes: BB70B,BB70D,CC11M.

51950   Hofmann, A.D. The impact of illness in adolescence and coping behavior. _Acta Paediatrica Scandinavica_, 1975, supplement 256, 29-38. Topic Codes: BL11,CV30,DA15,DD,MG,MI,MZ,NA07B,NA07D,NA07I,PE10,PE15,PG,SL,TB33.

51970   Hokanson, J.E., Megargee, E.I., O'Hagan, J.E., and Perry, A.M. Behavioral, emotional, and autonomic reactions to stress among incarcerated, youthful offenders. Criminal Justice and Behavior, September 1976, 3(3), 203-234. Topic Codes: BK04D,BN04D,CC37B,CG11CC.CQ37,CQ59,DD00,MB11,MF11, MX11,NE37,NE59,PA11,PC11,PE01,SR02.

51990   Holcomb, W.R., Adams, N.A., Ponder, H.M., and Anderson, W.P. Cognitive and behavioral predictors of MMPI scores in pretrial psychological evaluations of murderers. Journal of Clinical Psychology, March 1984, 40(2), 592-597. Topic Codes: CC11H,CC11N,CC11P,CC11U,CT57F,TB61B.

52000   Holden, C. The criminal mind: A new look at an ancient puzzle. Science, February 3, 1978, 199, 511-514. Topic Codes: CC81S,CV06C,MG11,MS04B, MU11,PT11.

52050   Holden, R.H., and Willerman, L. Neurological abnormality in infancy, intelligence, and social class. In E.P. Trapp and P. Himelstein (eds.), Readings on the Exceptional Child (2nd ed.). New York: Appleton-Century-Crofts, 1972. Topic Codes: BL11,DK09,DK46,MO,NA31A,NA31R,NA44B,NC22, NC44,NJ03,PM,SW,TA52K,TB05,TB25,TB78.

52100   Holden, R.M., Mendelson, M.A., and De Vault, S. Relationship of the WAIS to the SRA Non-Verbal Test scores. Psychological Reports, 1966, 19, 987-990. Topic Codes: NC59G,NC80,TB76,TB93.

52130   Hollander, L., and Karp, E. Youth psychopathology and family process research. American Journal of Psychiatry, July 1973, 130(7), 814-817. Topic Codes: MG,NH65,SI07.

52160   Holstein, C.B. Irreversible, stepwise sequence in the development of moral judgment: A longitudinal study of males and females. Child Development, March 1976, 47(1), 51-61. Topic Codes: BL11,BL70,DT13,MH,NA07I, NA44,NH59G,NH59P,NJ,PG,PI,PM,SH59J,SH59R,SQ,TA59D.

52180   Holzman, H.R. Learning disabilities and juvenile delinquency: Biological and sociological theories. In C.R. Jeffery (ed.), Biology and Crime. Beverly Hills, California: Sage Publications, Inc., 1979, 77-86. Topic Codes: BA,BL48D,CC37H,CC37J,CG,DT44D,DT48D,MM11,MT48D,PE48D,PE64D,PP11, PR11,SC70D.

52200   Hoobler, I.M., and Hunscher, H. Hemoglobin differences between blacks and whites. American Journal of Clinical Nutrition, December 1977, 30, 1935-1937. Topic Codes: BD30,BD52,BL67,BP,CV52,NA31R,NC59G,SN,SW,TA52K.

52230   Hook, E.B. Behavioral implications of the human XYY genotype. Science, January 12, 1973, 179(69), 139-150. Topic Codes: BB70B,BB70D.

52250   Hook, E.B., Heinonen, O.P., Shapiro, S., and Slone, D. Maternal exposure to oral contraceptives and other female sex hormones: Relation to birth defects in a prospectively ascertained cohort of 50,282 pregnancies. Teratology, 1974, 9, A21-A22 (abstract). Topic Codes: BB,BP04,DF.

52300   Hoppe, C.M., and Singer, R.D. Interpersonal violence and its relationship to some personality measures. Aggressive Behavior, 1977, 3, 261-270. Topic Codes: CC11C,CC11P,CC11U,CC81D,CC81S,CC81Y,CT57,CT59,CT68,MC11, MS02,MU11,PE04D,PT11,SR03B,TA03,TA59,TB61B.

52400   Horney, J. Menstrual cycles and criminal responsibility. Law and Human Behavior, 1978, 2(1), 25-36. Topic Codes: BD70B,CC24,CC37C,CQ22,MC,NE22, PE04,SR03.

52500   Horton, A.M., Jr., and Whitesell, L.J. Prediction of recidivism by sex and number of siblings. Psychological Reports, 1979, 45(1), 98. Topic Codes: CC11L,MG11,SJ07D,SJ22D.

52600   Horton, C.P., and Crump, E.P. Growth and development: III. Skin color in Negro infants and parents: Its relationship to birth weight, reflex maturity, socioeconomic status, length of gestation, and parity. Journal of Pediatrics, May 1958, 52, 547-558. Topic Codes: BE,BI,BL06,BL27,BL70,

BP,BP02,BP26,DP22,NA33I,NA44D,NH59B,NH59GB,NH59P,NH59PB,NJ06,NL07,SH59B,
SH59JB,SH59R,SH59RB,SQ,SW,TA52M.

52650   House, T.H., and Milligan, W.L. Autonomic responses to modeled distress
in prison psychopaths. Journal of Personality and Social Psychology,
October 1976, 34(4), 556-560. Topic Codes: BK04D,BL25D,BL29D,CC11O,CQ59,
MS04B.

52700   Hovey, J.E. Neurobehavioral evaluation of aggressive patients in an outpatient clinic. Paper presented to the American Academy of Criminal Justice Sciences, Oklahoma, March 1980. Topic Codes: CC81,CC81B,CC81D,
CC81E,CC81F,CC81H,CC81I,CC81J,CC81K,CC81M,CC81O,CC81R,CC81T,CC81V,CC81W,
CC81Y,CQ81,CT81,CZ07,NE81,SY11,TB61B.

52730   Hreidarsson, A.B., Nielsen, J., and Berggreen, S. Presumptive Y/15 translocation and mental retardation in a family with a case of Klinefelter's
syndrome. Journal of Mental Deficiency Research, September 1973, 17(3-4),
163-170. Topic Codes: BB70,BI.

52740   Hubble, L.M. Comparability and equivalence of estimates of IQs from re-
vised Beta Examination and Wechsler Adult Intelligence Scale among older
male delinquents. Psychological Reports, June 1978, 42(3, part 2), 1030.
Topic Codes: TB15,TB93.

52745   Hubble, L.M., and Groff, M. Factor analysis of WISC-R scores of male de-
linquents referred for evaluation. Journal of Consulting and Clinical
Psychology, October 1981, 49(5), 738-739. Topic Codes: CC37Q,CC37I,
TB95D.

52748   Hubble, L.M., and Groff, M. Magnitude and direction of WISC-R verbal-per-
formance IQ discrepancies among adjudicated male delinquents. Journal of
Youth and Adolescence, April 1981, 10(2), 179-184. Topic Codes: CC37Q,
CC37I,PM11,TB96D.

52760   Huesmann, L.R., Lefkowitz, M.M., and Eron, L.D. Sum of MMPI scales F, 4,
and 9 as a measure of aggression. Journal of Consulting and Clinical Psychology, October 1978, 46(5), 1071-1078. Topic Codes: MC,TB61.

52770   Huey, L.Y., Zetin, M., Janowsky, D.S., and Judd, L.L. Adult minimal brain
dysfunction and schizophrenia: A case report. American Journal of Psychiatry, December 1978, 135(12), 1563-1565. Topic Codes: CV15B,DK48B,
MG48B,MU11,MU70.

52780   Humes, C.E., Siles, P.M., and Savage, W.M. Early learning disabilities
identification: A report. Academic Therapy, Summer 1975, 10(4), 419-425.
Topic Codes: DT44,MG,TA59D,TB33.

52800   Humphrey, J.A., and Kupferer, H.J. Pockets of violence: An exploration
of homicide and suicide. Diseases of the Nervous System, October 1977,
38(10), 833-837. Topic Codes: BL67,BL67D,CC81L,CC81W,CT57F,MC11,MX11,MZ,
NH59F,PE04D,PE68D,SF11,SH59H,SJ09D,SN,SN11,SR02,SR03B,SW11.

52900   Hunt, D.E., and Hardt, R.H. Developmental stage, delinquency, and differential treatment. Journal of Research in Crime and Delinquency, 1965,
2, 20-31. Topic Codes: BL11C,CC37F,CC37U,CC37I,CV06C,NA07ID,PG11,PY11,
SI57PB,SU11,TA03,TA59,TA59D.

53000   Hunt, J.V., and Bayley, N. Explorations into patterns of mental develop-
ment and prediction from the Bayley Scales of Infant Development. Minne-
sota Symposia on Child Psychology, 1971, 5, 52-71. Topic Codes: BL11,
BL31,BL48B,BL70,DK46,DT42,DT48B,ML,MO,MT48B,NA07B,NA07I,NA31D,NA31F,NA31R,
NA44H,NJ12,PE10,PE32,PE44,PE48B,PG,PK,PM,PN,PR07,SQ,TA52K,TB05,TB78,TB93,
TB95.

53060   Hunter, H. Kleinfelter's syndrome and delinquency. British Journal of
Criminology, 1968, 8(2), 203-207. Topic Codes: BB70B,DD02ND,NL,TA80.

53070   Hunter, H. XYY males: Some clinical and psychiatric aspects deriving from a survey of 1,811 males in hospitals for the mentally handicapped. British Journal of Psychiatry, November 1977, 131, 468-477. Topic Codes: BB70B,DK46,MX.

53090   Huntsinger, G.M. Teaching self-control of verbal and physical aggression to juvenile delinquents [doctoral dissertation, Virginia Commonwealth University, 1976]. Dissertation Abstracts International, January 1977, 37 (7), 3612B. Topic Codes: CC37,CQ59,CV06C,MC.

53100   Hurwitz, I., Bibace, R.M.A., Wolf, P.H., and Rowbotham, B.M. Neuropsychological function of normal boys, delinquent boys, and boys with learning problems. Perceptual and Motor Skills, 1972, 35, 382-394. Topic Codes: BL11C,BL48B,BL48D,CC37H,CC37Q,CC37T,CC37I,DT44,DT48B,DT48D,MM,MT48B,MT48D, MV,NA07ID,PE48B,PE48D,PE66,PG11,PM70B,PP,PR07,PR11,SR69,TA03,TA59D,TB57, TB57B,TB57D,TB72B,TB78B,TB95D.

53110   Hurwitz, S., and Christiansen, K.O. Criminology. Winchester, Massachusetts: Allen & Unwin, 1983. Topic Codes: BA,BI11,CC11C,CC11D,CC11L, CC11M,CG,SB11,SF11.

53150   Husain, A., and Kashani, J. Maternal medication and minimal brain dysfunction. Missouri Medicine, October 1978, 75(10), 508-511. Topic Codes: BA,BB07,BL07,BP02,BP02B,BP04,DD02,DD02B,DF,DF06,DK09B,DK48B,DT44,MG,MG30, MG48B,MM,NA07D,NA31A,NA31B,PP,TB95.

53200   Husband, P., and Hinton, P.E. Families of children with repeated accidents. Archives of Diseases in Childhood, 1972, 47, 396-400. Topic Codes: BL04,BL70B,DD00,DD03B,MA07,MG,NA07D,NH59,NH59E,NH65,NH65B,PE02B, SF07,SH59,SH59F,SJ07,SJ09D,SQ07,SW07.

53220   Hutchinson, T.P., and Satterthwaite, S.P. Mathematical models for describing the clustering of sociopathy and hysteria in families: A comment on the recent paper by Cloninger, et al. British Journal of Psychiatry, March 1977, 130, 294-297. Topic Codes: MS04,NH63.

53230   Ilfeld, F.W., Jr. Overview of the causes and prevention of violence. Archives of General Psychiatry, June 1969, 20(6), 675-689. Topic Codes: BL11,CC81F,CC81L,CY,MC,PE04,PG,SU.

53235   Inamdar, S.C., Lewis, D.O., Siomopoulos, G., Shanok, S.S., Lamela, M. Violent and suicidal behavior in psychotic adolescents. American Journal of Psychiatry, July 1982, 139(7), 932-935. Topic Codes: CC37B,CC81, CC81D,MU11,MZ.

53240   Inciardi, J.A., and Haas, K.C., (eds.). Crime and the Criminal Justice Process. Dubuque, Iowa: Kendall/Hunt Publishing Company, 1978. Topic Codes: BI07,BI11,CC11D,CC11G,CC11I,CC11L,CC11N,CG11CC,CG11P,CV13D,DK46D, MO11,PM11,SW11,TA03,TA59D.

53260   Ingram, T. A characteristic form of overactive behavior in brain-damaged children. Journal of Mental Science, 1956, 102, 550-558. Topic Codes: BK11B,BL11,CV,DF,MG,MG30B,NA07B,NA07I,PE10,PG,TA80,TB35B.

53400   Ingram, T.T.S. The development of higher nervous activity in childhood and its disorders. In R.B. Johnston and P.R. Magrab (eds.), Developmental Disorders. Baltimore: University Park Press, 1976. Topic Codes: BL11, BL31,BL33,BL48,BN44,DK07B,DT48,MG,MG30,MT48,NA07B,NA07D,NA07I,NA31D,NA31F, NA31R,NA33D,NA33F,NA33I,PE10,PE32,PE34,PE48,PG,PK,PL,PO,PR,TA52K,TA52M, TB02.

53500   Ingvar, D.H., and Philipson, L. Distribution of cerebral blood flow in the dominant hemisphere during motor ideation and motor performance. Annals of Neurology, September 1977, 2(3), 230-237. Topic Codes: BL08, BN44B,DK07B,MU70,PO07.

53600   Ireton, H., Thwing, E., and Gravem, H. Infant mental development and neurological status, family socioeconomic status, and intelligence at age

four. <u>Child Development</u>, 1970, 41, 937-945. Topic Codes: BL70,NA31R,
NA44B,NC22,NC44,NJ03,PM,SQ,SW,TA52K,TB05,TB25,TB42,TB68,TB78.

53650   Isom, J.B. Neurological research relevant to reading. <u>Proceedings of the</u>
<u>12th Annual Convention, International Reading Association</u>, 1968, 12(4),
61-67. Topic Codes: DT44,DT52,MM,PE64,PP.

53670   Isom, J.B. Reading disabilities. In V.C. Vaughan, III and R.J. McKay
(eds.), <u>Nelson's Textbook of Pediatrics</u> (10th ed.). Philadelphia: W.B.
Saunders Company, 1975. Topic Codes: BL11,DT44,ML15,MM,NA07B,PE10,PE64,
PG,PP,TB96B.

53690   Isom, J.B. Some neuropsychological findings in children with reading
problems. In M.P. Douglas (ed.), <u>Claremont Reading Conference, 32nd</u>
<u>Yearbook</u>. Claremont, California: Claremont University Center, 1968.
Topic Codes: DT15,MG,ML15,NA07D,PE64,SC70,TA02,TA55.

53700   Itil, T.M., and Mukhopadhyay, S. Pharmacological management of human vio-
lence. <u>Modern Problems in Pharmacopsychiatry</u>, 1978, 13, 139-158. Topic
Codes: CC81,CC81B,CC81D,CC81H,CC81I,CC81M,CC81R,CQ81,CT81,CV15B,CV15D,
DK18D,MC,MG,NA07D,NE81,PE04,SR03.

53750   Itil, T.M., and Wadud, A. Treatment of human aggression with major tran-
quilizers, antidepressants, and newer psychotropic drugs. <u>Journal of Ner-</u>
<u>vous and Mental Disease</u>, February 1975, 160(2-1), 83-99. Topic Codes:
BK11B,CV15B,CV15D,MC,PE04.

53800   Jackson, A.M., Farley, G.K., Zimet, S.G., and Gottman, J.M. Optimizing
the WISC-R test performance of low- and high-impulsive emotionally disturbed children. <u>Journal of Learning Disabilities</u>, November 1979, 12(9),
622-628. Topic Codes: BL04,BL70B,MG,MK,NA07D,PE30,SQ07,TB66B,TB95B.

53900   Jacobs, D.H. The borderline or psychotic character in the prison setting.
In J.E. Mack (ed.), <u>Borderline States in Psychiatry</u>. New York: Grune
& Stratton, 1975. Topic Codes: CV13D,MS04B,MU11.

53950   Jacobs, D.H. Psychiatric examinations in the determination of sexual
dangerousness in Massachusetts. <u>New England Law Review</u>, Fall 1974, 10(1),
85-103. Topic Codes: CC11C,CT68,DD01,MV07,MV11,PE66B,PE66D.

53980   Jacobson, J.W. Problem behavior and psychiatric impairment within a de-
velopmentally disabled population: I. Behavior frequency. <u>Applied Re-</u>
<u>search in Mental Retardation</u>, 1982, 3(2), 121-139. Topic Codes: DK46B,
DT44B,MG,MM07,MO07,NA07D,PP07.

54000   Jacobson, M. <u>Developmental Neurobiology</u> (2nd ed.). New York: Plenum
Press, 1978. Topic Codes: BD52,BD70,BI,BK04,BK11B,BL52D,BN,BP52,DD81,
DK07,DK09,DT59,PS,TA52.

54100   Jahoda, G. On the nature of difficulties in spatial-perceptual tasks:
Ethnic and sex differences. <u>British Journal of Psychology</u>, 1979, 70,
351-363. Topic Codes: BL11,BL67,BL70,MH,NA07B,NA07I,PE10,PG,SB,SN,SQ,
TA59D.

54200   Jahoda, G. Sex and ethnic differences on a space-perceptual task: Some
hypotheses tested. <u>British Journal of Psychology</u>, 1980, 71, 425-431.
Topic Codes: BI,BL70,BN44,NA07B,PE10,PM70,PO,SC18,SQ,SQ70.

54230   Janes, C.L. Hesselbrock, V., and Stern, J.A. Parental psychopathology,
age, and race as related to electrodermal activity of children. <u>Psycho-</u>
<u>physiology</u>, January 1978, 15(1), 24-34. Topic Codes: BK04,BL11,BL67,MF,
NA07,NH59B,NL48,PE10,SH59B,SN,TA80.

54300   Jeffery, C.R. Criminal behavior and the physical environment. <u>American</u>
<u>Behavioral Scientist</u>, November-December 1976, 20(2), 149-174. Topic
Codes: BD,BI11,BK04BB,BK11B,BN04BB,CG,CV06C,DT44,DT59,MF,MM,MR,MS04,
PC07B,PE,PP,PS,PY11,SF11,SF26D,SI57PB,SU11.

54310   Jeffery, C.R. Criminology as an interdisciplinary behavioral science. In F.H. Marsh and J. Katz (eds.), Biology, Crime and Ethics. Cincinnati, Ohio: Anderson Publishing Co., 1985, 44-54. Topic Codes: BB70D,BI11, CC11C,CC67,CV,CV13D,CV13DA,CV15,CV30,CV30B,CV30D.

54330   Jeffery, C.R. Sociobiology and criminology: The long lean years of the unthinkable and the unmentionable. In E. Sagarin (ed.), Taboos in Criminology. Beverly Hills, California: Sage Publications, Inc., 1980, 115-124. Topic Codes: BA,CG,SF11.

54340   Jeffery, C.R. (ed.). Biology and Crime. Beverly Hills, California: Sage Publications, Inc., 1979. Topic Codes: BA,BD11,BL48D,CC11C,CC11D,CC37H, CC37J,CG,CV13D,CV15D,DK09D,DK18SD,DT44D,DT48D,MC11,MM11,MS04B,MT48D,PE04D, PE48D,PE64D,PP11,PR11,SC70D,SI57J,SR03B.

54400   Jenkins, S., Bax, M., and Hart, H. Behaviour problems in pre-school children. Journal of Child Psychology and Psychiatry and Allied Disciplines, 1980, 21, 5-17. Topic Codes: BL11,BL70B,BN68,CV30B,DD00,DT42B, DT69,MG,ML02,MW,NA07D,NA07I,NA31D,NA44B,NJ03,PE32,PE44B,PG,PNO7,PT74, SF07B,SL07,SQ07.

54450   Jensen, A.R. Estimation of the limits of heritability of traits by comparison of monozygotic and dizygotic twins. Proceedings of the National Academy of Sciences of the United States of America, July 1967, 58(1), 149-156. Topic Codes: BI,NH74,PM,SH74.

54500   Jensen, A.R. How much can we boost IQ and scholastic achievement? Harvard Educational Review, Winter 1969, 39(1), 1-123. Topic Codes: BI, BL11,PE10,PE64,PG,PM,SB,SC59,SC70,SS.

54600   Jensen, A.R. Sex linkage and race differences in spatial ability: A reply. Behavior Genetics, 1978, 8(2), 213-217. Topic Codes: BD70,BI, BL67,BL70,PM70,SF,SN,SQ,TB95.

54630   Jensen, O.N. The mask of psychopathy. International Journal of Law and Psychiatry, 1978, 1(2), 153-166. Topic Codes: MS04.

54700   Jessor, S.L., and Jessor, R. Maternal ideology and adolescent problem behavior. Developmental Psychology, 1974, 10(2), 246-254. Topic Codes: BL70B,DA04,DA15,DP22,MD,MG,MI,NA07D,NH59GG,NH59P,NH59PJ,PE06,PE15,PT,PV07, PY,SH59JJ,SH59R,SH59RJ,SI48B,SI57P,SOO7,SQ07,SU.

54730   Jew, J.Y., and Sandquist, D. CNS changes in hyperbilirubinemia: Functional implications. Archives of Neurology, March 1979, 36(3), 149-154. Topic Codes: BD30BA,BK11B,DK07,NA,NL,TA80.

54740   Jeyasingh, J.V. Influence of family size, birth order and occupation on criminal behavior. Asian Journal of Psychology and Education, April 1983, 11(3), 19-24. Topic Codes: CC11L,CC11T,SJ07D,SJ22D,SW11,SW56.

54750   Johanson, E. Conditions of birth, disease and injury during years of growth among inmates of youth prisons, compared with subjects matched for sex, age and place of birth. Acta Psychiatrica Scandinavica, 1968, 203 (supplement), 75-80. Topic Codes: BP02D,CC37O,CC37P,CC37X,CV30D, DD01,DD26D,SL11.

54900   John, E.R., Karmel, B.Z., Corning, W.C., Easton, P., Brown, D., Ahn, H., Harmony, T., Prichep, L., Toro, A., Gerson, I., Bartlett, F., Thatcher, R., Kaye, H., Valdes, P., and Schwartz, E. Neurometrics. Science, June 24, 1977, 196, 1393-1410. Topic Codes: BL18B,BN44B,CV15,DD81,DK07B, DK18,DT13,DT44,DT59B,MG,MH,MM,MR,MR07,NA07,NA07D,PI,POO7,PP,PSO7,TB35B, TB37B.

54920   Johnson, B.C., Karunas, T.M., and Epstein, F.H. Longitudinal change in blood pressure in individuals, families, and social groups. Clinical Science and Molecular Medicine, 1973, 45, 35S-45S. Topic Codes: BE,BL08, BL29B,DD28,NA44H,NH,TA80.

54930   Johnson, J.H. A cross-validation of seventeen experimental MMPI scales related to antisocial behavior. Journal of Clinical Psychology, October 1974, 30(4), 564-565. Topic Codes: CC11U,CQ59,DD02B,NE59,TA02,TA59,TB61.

54960   Johnson, M.C. Viewer aggression, self-esteem and television character preference as variables influencing social normative judgments of television violence [doctoral dissertation, University of Massachusetts, 1976]. Dissertation Abstracts International, March 1977, 37(9), 5421A. Topic Codes: CC81,CY,NA,NL,SF,TA57.

55000   Johnson, R.E. Social class and delinquent behavior: A new test. Criminology, May 1980, 18(1), 86-93. Topic Codes: BL67D,CC37Z,CC371,CE, CG11T,CQ37,NA,NL48D,SC18,SN11,SW11,SW33,SW56,TA80.

55100   Johnston, F.E., and Mack, R.W. Obesity in urban black adolescents of high and low relative weight at 1 year of age. American Journal of Diseases of Children, September 1978, 132, 862-864. Topic Codes: NA07I,NA31F,NA31R,NA44F,NC44,NC80,NJ09,NL07,PG,PK,SQ,TA52K.

55150   Johnston, J.M. Punishment of human behavior. American Psychologist, November 1972, 27(11), 1033-1054. Topic Codes: CV,PE,SI57J.

55200   Jones, K.L., Smith, D.W., Streissguth, A.P., and Myrianthopoulos, N.C. Outcome in offspring of chronic alcoholic women. Lancet, June 1, 1974, 7866, 1076-1078. Topic Codes: BB,BE,BE30C,BL05,BL06,BL11,BP,BP02,BP02B, BP03,DD02,DF48,DP22D,DP48,NA07I,NA33I,NA44D,NC44,NC59G,NJ06,NL48,PG,TA52M, TB95B.

55205   Jones, J.W., and Bogat, G.A. Air pollution and human aggression. Psychological Reports, December 1978, 43(3, part 1), 721-722. Topic Codes: BD,MC,NA,PE04,SF,SR03,TA80.

55230   Jones, R.R. The role of psychological factors in criminal behavior: A study of the convicted criminal, the hidden criminal, and the non-criminal [doctoral dissertation, Oklahoma State University, 1975]. Dissertation Abstracts International, July 1976, 37(1), 463B. Topic Codes: CC11P, CC11U,NE,TB61B.

55260   Jonssong, G. Delinquent boys, their parents and grandparents. Acta Psychiatrica Scandinavica, 1967, 43(supplement 195), 1-264. Topic Codes: BI11,BL07BD,BP02D,BP44,BP46,CC37B,CC37M,CC37N,CC37P,CC37Q,CC37Z,CQ37,CQ59, DD01,DD08KC,DF06BD,DP11D,DP44,DT44D,MG02D,MM11,NA07DF,NE37,NE59,NH59F, NH59GB,NH59GD,NH59GI,NH59PA,NH59PB,NH59PD,NH59PH,NH67B,NH67D,NL,PE01, PE64D,PM70B,PP11,SC70D,SH59JD,SH59JL,SH59RD,SH59RL,SI57D,SI59D,SR02,SW11, TA52,TA57,TA59D,TB33B,TB74B,TB78D.

55290   Jorm, A.F. Parietal lobe function in developmental dyslexia. Neuropsychologia, 1977, 15(6), 841-844. Topic Codes: BK11B,BL11,MG,ML15,NA07B, NA07I,PE10,PE64,PN,TA55,TA80.

55340   Jurkovic, G.J. The relationship of moral and cognitive development of juvenile delinquency [doctoral dissertation, University of Texas at Austin, 1975]. Dissertation Abstracts International, April 1976, 36(10), 5262B. Topic Codes: CC37B,CC37H,CC371,CQ37,MG,ML,NE37,PE10,PG,TA04, TA59D.

55360   Jurkovic, G.J., and Prentice, N.M. Dimensions of moral interaction and moral judgment in delinquent and nondelinquent families. Journal of Consulting and Clinical Psychology, 1974, 42, 256-262. Topic Codes: BL11, CC37M,CC371,CG11T,CQ37,MG,NA07DF,NA07I,NE37,NH59P,PE10,PG11,SH59,SI48, TA57,TA59,TA70,TA74,TA80,TB93,TB95.

55380   Jurkovic, G.J., and Prentice, N.M. Relation of moral and cognitive development to dimensions of juvenile delinquency. Journal of Abnormal Child Psychology, August 1977, 86(4), 414-420. Topic Codes: CC37,CC371,NE37, TA80.

55400   Justice, B., Justice, R., and Kraft, I.A. Early warning signs of violence: Is a triad enough? American Journal of Psychiatry, April 1974, 131(4), 457-458. Topic Codes: CC11C,CC11G,CC81D,CC81F,CT59B,CY,MG02D, MG18D,PE64D,SC70D.

55450   Kaada, B. Brain mechanisms related to aggressive behavior. In C.D. Clemente and D.B. Lindsley (eds.), Brain Function: Aggression and Defense: Neural Mechanisms and Social Patterns (vol. 5). Berkeley, California: University of California Press, 1967. Topic Codes: BK11B,CC11F, DK07D,DK09D.

55500   Kagan, J. Impulsive and reflective children: Significance of conceptual tempo. In J.D. Krumboltz (ed.), Learning and the Educational Process. Chicago: Rand McNally, 1965. Topic Codes: BL04,BL11,BL70,DT13,DT59,MH, MK,MR,NA07B,NA07I,NA44,NJ,PE10,PE30,PE64,PG,PI,PS,PT,SC70,SQ,TA04,TB09, TB81,TB95.

55600   Kagan, J., and Klein, R.E. Cross-cultural perspectives on early development. American Psychologist, November 1973, 28, 947-961. Topic Codes: BI,BL11,BL29,BL31,DT13,DT46,MH,MN,NA07B,NA07I,NA31D,NA31F,PE10,PE32,PG,PI, PK,PM,PQ,SF,SI48,TA59D,TB25,TB33G,TB66,TB78,TB95.

55700   Kagan, J., and Moss, H. Birth to Maturity: A Study in Psychological Development. New York: John Wiley & Sons, Inc., 1962. Topic Codes: BL11,MC,MK,MV,PC,PE04,PE10,PE48,PG,PM,PR,SI57J,SW,TB42,TB61,TB74,TB78, TB86,TB95.

55800   Kagan, J., and Moss, H.A. Parental correlates of child's IQ and height: A cross-validation of the Berkeley Growth Study results. Child Development, 1959, 30, 325-332. Topic Codes: BE,BI,BL11,BL70,DP22,NA07B,NA07I, NA44D,NH59GB,NH59PB,NH59PF,NJ06,PE10,PG,PM,SF,SH59JB,SH59RB,SH59RF,SQ, TA59D,TB78.

55900   Kahn, M.W. Superior performance IQ of murderers as a function of overt act or diagnosis. Journal of Social Psychology, 1968, 76, 113-116. Topic Codes: CC81D,CC81Y,CT57F,DT44,MK,MM,MS04B,PE30,PP,TB93D,TB96BB,TB96D.

55910   Kaiser, G. The question of the personality of lawbreakers today: On the work of Losel and Wustendorfer. Zeitschrift fur Sozialpsychologie, 1976, 7(2), 198-201 (in German). Topic Codes: CC11P,CC37W,PT11.

55915   Kalvach, Z., Neuwirth, J., and Michalova, K. Psychopathology of a case of Klinefelter's syndrome with chromosomal finding 48, XXXY. Ceskoslovenska Psychiatrie, June 1976, 72(2), 201-205. Topic Codes: BB70D,BD70B,BII1, CC11D,CC11M,DD02NF,MV11,PE66D,SR69D.

55920   Kalverboer, A.F. A Neurobehavioral Study in Pre-School Children. Philadelphia: Lippincott, 1975. Topic Codes: BK,NA07B,PE10,TA52.

55930   Kalverboer, A.F., Touwen, B.C.L., and Prechtl, H.F.R. Follow-up of infants at risk of minor brain dysfunction. New York Academy of Sciences - Annals, 1973, 205, 173-187. Topic Codes: BP,BP02B,DK48B,DP,DP11B,DT52B, MG,MG30,MG48B,NA07B,NA07D,NA33A,NA33I,PE10,SI48,TA52,TA52M.

55940   Kamin, A., Kubinger, K.D., and Schubert, M.T. Sibling constellation and intelligence in behavior disordered children. Zeitschrift fur Klinische Psychologie. Forschung und Praxis, 1981, 10(2), 98-109. Topic Codes: BP07B,MG,PM07.

55950   Kamin, L.J. Sex differences in susceptibility of IQ to environmental influence. Child Development, 1978, 49, 517-518. Topic Codes: BL11,BL70B, PG,SH59RF,SQ.

55970   Kane, B.J. The comparison of peer tutor implementors to LD teacher-implementors in implementing a computational mathematics program for incarcerated juvenile delinquents identified as learning disabled in computational mathematics ability [doctoral dissertation, University of Kansas, 1976]. Dissertation Abstracts International, February 1977, 37(8), 5037A-5038A. Topic Codes: DT44,MG,MM,NA07D,NA07I,PE10,PG,PP,SC,TA04.

55980   Karlberg, P., Taranger, J., Engstrom, I., Karlberg, J., Landstrom, T., Lichtenstein, H., Lindstrom, B., and Svennberg-Redegren, I. Physical growth from birth to 16 years and longitudinal outcome of the study during the same age period. Acta Paediatrica Scandinavica, 1976, supplement 258, 7-76. Topic Codes: BE,BE30,BL11,BL31,NA07I,NA31F,NA44F,NJ09,PG,PK.

55985   Karniski, W.M., Levine, M.D., Clarke, S., Palfrey, J.S., and Meltzer, L.J. A study of neurodevelopmental findings in early adolescent delinquents. Journal of Adolescent Health Care, December 1982, 3(3), 151-159. Topic Codes: BL11C,CC37B,CC37H,DT42D,ML03,MX11,NA07ID,PE44D,PE68D,PG11,PN11, SR02.

55987   Karr, P., Long, S.K., and Witte, A.D. Family violence: A microeconomic approach. Paper presented at the annual meeting of the American Socio- logical Association, 1981. Topic Codes: CC81N,NH11,SH11.

55990   Karshmer, J.F. The application of social learning theory to aggression. Perspectives in Psychiatric Care, September-December 1978, 16(5-6), 223- 227. Topic Codes: CV06,MC,PE04,SA07,SR03,TA80.

56000   Katz, B. The nerve impulse. Scientific American, November 1952, 187(5), 55-64. Topic Codes: BD,BK,BL25.

56060   Katz, S.H. Environmental lead and neuropsychological development. Paper of proposed research, Institute for the Continuous Study of Man, 1979. Topic Codes: BK11,BL11,DA44MB,DK,MG,NC80,PE10,PG,SF26,TA55,TA80.

56100   Katz, S.H., Hediger, M.L., Schall, J.I., Bowers, E.J., Barker, W.F., Aurand, S., Eveleth, P.B., Gruskin, A.B., and Parks, J.S. Blood pressure, growth, and maturation from childhood through adolescence: Results of a mixed longitudinal study from the Philadelphia Blood Pressure Project. Hypertension, 1980, 2(4), I55-I69. Topic Codes: BE,BL08,BL08B,BL11,BL59, BL70,DD28,DP60,NA07I,NA44F,NC70,NC80,NJ09,NL07,PG,SQ.

56200   Kaufman, A.S. Intelligence Testing with the WISC-R. New York: John Wiley & Sons, Inc., 1979. Topic Codes: DT44,MM,PE64,PI,PM,PP,SN,SQ,SW, TA04,TA59D,TB95.

56300   Kaufman, A.S. Verbal-performance IQ discrepancies on the WISC-R. Jour- nal of Consulting and Clinical Psychology, 1976, 44(5), 739-744. Topic Codes: BI07,BL04,BL67,BL70,NA07B,PE10,SN,SQ,SW56,TB95,TB96.

56400   Kawi, A.A., and Pasamanick, B. Association of factors of pregnancy with reading disorders in childhood. Journal of the American Medical Associa- tion, March 22, 1958, 166(12), 1420-1423. Topic Codes: BP02,BP22F,BP47, BP53,DP11,DP46,DP81,NA07I,TA04,TB78.

56450   Kay, D.W.K., Roth, M., Atkinson, M.W., Stephens, D.A., and Garside, R.F. Genetic hypotheses and environmental factors in the light of psychiatric morbidity in the families of schizophrenics. British Journal of Psychia- try, August 1975, 127, 109-118. Topic Codes: BI07,DD00,DF60B,DK07B,DP, DP11B,DP60,DP81,DT04EB,DT15,DT44,MG,ML15,MM,MU70,NA07D,NA33A,NH59B,PE,PP, SH59B,TB78.

56500   Kayton, L., and Borge, G.F. Birth order and the obsessive-compulsive character. Archives of General Psychiatry, December 1967, 17, 751-754. Topic Codes: BL70B,MQ,NA31A,SJ07B,SQ07.

56530   Keckich, W.A. Neuroleptics: Violence as a manifestation of akathisia. Journal of the American Medical Association, November 10, 1978, 240(20), 2185. Topic Codes: BD07,CC11D,DD00B,DT13B,DT48B,MT,PE08,PR07.

56560   Kedenburg, H.D. Androgen and aggressive behavior in man [doctoral disser- tation, Rutgers University - The State University of New Jersey (New Brun- swick), 1977]. Dissertation Abstracts International, August 1977, 38(2), 885A-886A. Topic Codes: BD30,MC,PE04,SQ.

56600   Keilitz, I., Zaremba, B.A., and Broder, P.K. The link between learning

disabilities and juvenile delinquency: Some issues and answers. Learning
Disability Quarterly, Spring 1979, 2, 2-11. Topic Codes: CC37B,CC37H,
CC37J,CC37I,CC67,CC81D,CG11CC,CG11P,CJ,CQ67,CT70,CV13,DT44D,MG,MM11,NA07D,
NE67,PE64D,PP11,SC70D,TA02,TA03,TA04,TA59D,TB09B,TB09K,TB95B.

56700   Kellaghan, T., and MacNamara, J. Family correlates of verbal reasoning
ability. Developmental Psychology, 1972, 7(1), 49-53. Topic Codes:
BL70,BP07,NA07B,PE10,PM,SI57,SJ05,SJ07,SJ22,SQ,SW,SW56,TA59D.

56800   Keller, J.F., Croake, J.W., and Riesenman, C. Relationships among handed-
ness, intelligence, sex, and reading achievement of school-age children.
Perceptual and Motor Skills, 1973, 37, 159-162. Topic Codes: BL70,BN44,
DT15,ML15,NA07B,PE10,PE64,PM,PO,SC70,SQ,TA04,TA59D.

56830   Kellerman, J. Behavioral treatment of a boy with 47, XYY karyotype.
Journal of Nervous and Mental Disease, July 1977, 165(1), 67-71. Topic
Codes: BB70B,BL11,CC37N,CV06,DK46B,MG,ML02,MV07,NA07B,NA07I,PE10,PE44B,
PE70D,SH59,SR01.

56860   Kellner, J. A model for differential treatment of the juvenile delinquent. Mental Health and Society, 1975, 2(1-2), 55-65. Topic Codes:
CC37,CQ37,CV06C,NE37.

56890   Kello, A., and Kovac, D. A probe into the relationships between emotional
lability and memory performance. Studia Psychologica, 1975, 17(4), 306-
308. Topic Codes: BL11,MN,NA07B,NA07I,PE10,TA55,TB38.

56893   Kelly, H.E. Biology and crime. In F.H. Marsh and J. Katz (eds.), Biology, Crime and Ethics. Cincinnati, Ohio: Anderson Publishing Co., 1985,
187-196. Topic Codes: BD30,BD30HD,BD52D,CC11D,CV52D,DD30D,MD11.

56896   Kelly, H.E. Biosociology and crime. In C.R. Jeffery (ed.), Biology and
Crime. Beverly Hills, California: Sage Publications, Inc., 1979, 87-99.
Topic Codes: BA,BD11,CG,DK07D,PY11,SF11,SI57PB,SU11.

56900   Kelly, S., Hook, E.B., Janerich, D.T., and Porter, I.H. Birth Defects:
Risks and Consequences. New York: Academic Press, Inc., 1976. Topic
Codes: BK11B,BL07B,BL27KL,BL33,BL52D,BN44B,BP02,BP03,BP04,BP22F,BP26GD,
BP44,BP47,BP53,DD08K,DF06B,DF34,DF60B,DF70B,DK09,DP11,DP22,DP44,DP46,
DT04E,DT15,DT44,DT46,MG,ML15,MM,MN,MR,NA07D,NA33B,PL,PM70,PO07,PP,PQ,PS,
TA02,TA04,TA59D,TB95B.

56930   Kendall, P.C., Finch, A.J., Jr., Little, V.L., Ico, B.M., and Ollendick,
T.H. Variations in a construct: Quantitative and qualitative differences
in children's locus of control. Journal of Consulting and Clinical Psychology, June 1978, 46(3), 590-592. Topic Codes: BL11,BL70,CC37W,CC371,
MG,NA07D,SQ,TA59D,TA80.

56960   Kendall, P.C., and Little, V.L. Correspondence of brief intelligence
measures to the Wechsler scales with delinquents. Journal of Consulting
and Clinical Psychology, August 1977, 45(4), 660-666. Topic Codes: BL11,
CC37Q,NA07B,NE37,PM07,TA59D,TA80,TB70B,TB93D,TB95D.

56990   Kenel, M.E. A study of the cognitive dimension of impulsivity-reflectivi-
ty and aggression in female child abusers [doctoral dissertation, Catholic
University of America, 1976]. Dissertation Abstracts International, September 1976, 37(3), 1438B. Topic Codes: CC11P,CC11S,DD10,DT13,MF11,MK11,
NL22D,PI,TA59,TA80.

57000   Kennard, M.A. The characteristics of thought disturbances as related to
electroencephalographic findings in children and adolescents. American
Journal of Psychiatry, 1959, 115, 911-921. Topic Codes: BL04B,DD08K,
DD26B,DK07B,DT15,MG,ML15,NA07D,NA44,NJ,PE64B,SC70B,TB35B.

57030   Kennedy, J.M. The dissocial type of personality and its relation to moral
development: A comparative approach [doctoral dissertation, The Wright
Institute, 1974]. Dissertation Abstracts International, July 1976, 37(1),
464B. Topic Codes: ME,N,PEC8,SR04.

57060   Kenney, J.B. Individual differences in locus of control among emotionally
disturbed adolescents [doctoral dissertation, University of Minnesota,
1974]. Dissertation Abstracts International, June 1975, 35(12, part 1),
7723A. Topic Codes: CC37,MG,MR,MR07,NA07B,NA07I,NE37,NE59,PE10,TA59,
TA80.

57100   Keogh, B.K. The Bender Gestalt with children: Research implications.
Journal of Special Education, 1969, 3(1), 15-22. Topic Codes: BL11,MG,
NA07B,NA07D,NA07I,PE10,PE64,PG,SC70,TB09,TB09K.

57200   Keogh, B.K. Hyperactivity and learning disorders: Review and specula-
tion. Exceptional Children, October 1971, 38(2), 101-109. Topic Codes:
BL48B,CV15B,DK07B,DK46,DK48B,DT44B,DT48B,MG,MG30,MG48B,MK,MM07,MO,MT48B,
NA07D,PE30,PE48B,PE64,PP07,PR07,SC70,TB66B,TB78B.

57270   Kermani, E.J. Violent psychiatric patients: A study. American Journal
of Psychotherapy, April 1981, 35(2), 215-225. Topic Codes: CC81D,CT57F,
CT57FT,MZ.

57300   Kessler, A., and Scott, R.B. Growth and development of Negro infants.
American Journal of Diseases of Children, September 1950, 80, 370-378.
Topic Codes: BL05,BL06,BL33,BL70,BP02,BP52,BP53,NA33F,NA33I,NL07,PL,SQ,
SW,TA52M.

57400   Kessler, S., and Moos, R.H. The XYY karyotype and criminality: A review.
Journal of Psychiatric Research, 1970, 7, 153-170. Topic Codes: BB70D,
CC11D,CC11M,CQ11,DD02NF,MV11,PE66D,SR69D.

57500   Kilcoyne, M.M., Richter, R.W., and Alsup, P.A. Adolescent hypertension:
I. Detection and prevalence. Circulation, October 1974, 50, 758-764.
Topic Codes: BL08B,BL11,BL67,BL70,DD28,NA07I,PG,SF,SN,SQ.

57550   Kilpatrick, D.G., Cauthen, N.R., and Roitzsch, J.C. Psychopathy, re-
pression-sensitization, and anxiety. Psychological Reports, April 1971,
28(2), 615-618. Topic Codes: CC11C,CC11U,NE59,TA80,TB61B.

57600   Kimura, D. The asymmetry of the human brain. Scientific American, March
1973, 228(3), 70-78. Topic Codes: BL48,BN44,DD81,DT42,DT48,DT59,ML,MR,
MT48,PE44,PE48,PN,PO,PR,PS,TB81.

57730   Kimura, D. Cerebral dominance and the perception of verbal stimuli.
Canadian Journal of Psychology, 1961, 15, 166-171. Topic Codes: BK11B,
BN44B,DK07,NL,PO,TA80.

57760   Kimura, D. Dual functional asymmetry of the brain in visual perception.
Neuropsychologia, 1966, 4, 275-285. Topic Codes: BK11B,BN44,DT59,NL,PO,
PS,TB81.

57765   King, G.T. A comparison of Hand Test responses of aggressive and nonag-
gressive black adolescents [doctoral dissertation, University of Oklahoma, 1973]. Dissertation Abstracts International, October 1973, 34(4),
1736A. Topic Codes: CC37,CC37W,CC371,CQ37,CQ59,MG,MS02,NA07B,NE37,NE59,
NL07D,PE10,TB49.

57766   Kinge, F.O., and Tonning, F. Hearing impairment, prevalence and relation
to school background, intellectual ability and encephalopathy: A socio-
medical study of a birth cohort from Bergen. Scandinavian Audiology,
1977, 6(4), 225-231. Topic Codes: DD,DT59,MR,NA44,NJ,PM,PS.

57767   Kinsbourne, M. Cerebral dominance, learning, and cognition. In H.R.
Myklebust (ed.), Progress in Learning Disabilities (vol. 3). New York:
Grune & Stratton, 1975. Topic Codes: BK11B,BL52D,BN44,DT13,DT42,DT44,MH,
ML,MM,PI,PN,PO,PP.

57775   Kinsbourne, M., and Warrington, E.K. Developmental factors in reading and
writing backwardness. In J. Money (ed.), The Disabled Reader: Education
of the Dyslexic Child. Baltimore: Johns Hopkins University Press, 1966.

Topic Codes: BL11,MG,ML,MM,MR,NA07B,NA07I,PE10,PG,PN,PP,SC,TA80,TB33,
TB93,TB95,TB96.

57776   Kirkegaard-Sorensen, L., and Mednick, S.A. A prospective study of predictors of criminality: 2. A description of registered criminality in the
high-risk and low-risk families. In S.A. Mednick and K.O. Christiansen
(eds.), Biosocial Bases of Criminal Behavior. New York: Gardner Press,
Inc., 1977, 229-243. Topic Codes: CC37M,NH59GD,NH59GI,NH59PB,NH59PL,
SH59JD,SH59JL,SH59RB,SH59RL.

57777   Kiyonaga, K. A follow-up study in delinquent development: I. Effects of
the home background and school life on subsequent delinquency. Reports of
the National Research Institute of Police Science, July 1983, 24(1), 1-14.
Topic Codes: CC37J,CC37M,CC37Z,PE64D,SJ09D,SW11.

57778   Klatskin, E.H., McGarry, M.E., and Steward, M.S. Variability in develop-
mental test patterns as a sequel of neonatal stress. Child Development,
December 1966, 37, 819-826. Topic Codes: BL33,BP,DF34,DP,DP11,DT42,DT48,
NA31A,NA31F,NA31R,PE32,PK,TA80,TB02.

57780   Klebba, A.J. Comparison of trends for suicide and homicide: United
States, 1900-76. Unpublished manuscript, National Center for Health
Statistics, Division of Vital Statistics, Hyattsville, Maryland, October
1978. Topic Codes: BL04D,BL67,BL67D,BL70D,CG11P,CT57F,CX,MZ,NE79,SD11,
SF11,SN,SN11,SQ11.

57782   Klein, R.P., and Durfee, J.T. Prediction of preschool social behavior
from social emotional development at one year. Child Psychiatry and Human
Development, Spring 1979, 9(3), 145-151. Topic Codes: BL31,NA31F,NH59P,
PE32,PK,SH59R,SI48,TA80,TB05.

57785   Klein-Konigsberg, E.E. Semantic integration in normal and learning dis-
abled children [doctoral dissertation, City University of New York, 1977].
Dissertation Abstracts International, January 1978, 38(7), 3804A. Topic
Codes: BL11,MG,MM,NA07B,NA07I,PE10,PG,PN,PP,TA59,TA80.

57790   Kleinpeter, U. Social integration after brain trauma during childhood.
Acta Paedopsychiatrica, 1976, 42(2), 68-75. Topic Codes: BL04B,BL11,
CC37O,DD26B,DD26D,DK07B,DK07D,DK18B,DK46,DT44,MG,MM,MO,NA07D,NA07I,PE64B,
PG,PM,PP,SC18B,SC70B.

57792   Klicpera, C., and Heyse, I. The effect of minor brain dysfunction on the
type of behavior problems in children and their prognosis. Acta Paedopsychiatrica, May 1981, 47(1), 9-18. Topic Codes: DK48B,MG.

57793   Kling, A. Frontal and temporal lobe lesions and aggressive behavior. In
W.L. Smith and A. Kling (eds.), Issues in Brain/Behavior Control. New
York: Spectrum, 1976. Topic Codes: DK07B,MC,PE04,SR03.

57796   Kloek, J. Schizophrenia and delinquency: The inadequacy of our conceptual framework. International Psychiatry Clinics, 1968, 5(3), 19-34. Topic
Codes: CC37B,MU70B.

57800   Klonoff, H., Fibiger, C.H., and Hutton, G.H. Neuropsychological patterns
in chronic schizophrenia. Journal of Nervous and Mental Disease, 1970,
150(4), 291-300. Topic Codes: CV15B,DK07B,MU70,PM07,SF07,TA02,TA80,TB46,
TB84,TB87,TB93B.

57850   Klosowska, D. Relation between ability to program actions and location of
brain damage. Polish Psychological Bulletin, 1976, 7(4), 245-255. Topic
Codes: BN44,DK07,MF,PE,PO.

57900   Kniveton, B.K. Social class and imitation of aggressive adult and peer
models. Journal of Social Psychology, 1973, 89, 311-312. Topic Codes:
MC,NA07B,PE04,PE10,SR03,SW.

57950   Knobbe, T., Meier, P., Wenar, C., and Cordero, L. Psychological development of children who received intrauterine transfusions. American Journal

of Obstetrics and Gynecology, April 15, 1979, 133(8), 877-879. Topic
Codes: BD,BL07B,BL11,BL31,BP02,BP22F,BP26GD,BP44,DP11,DP22H,DP22P,NA07B,
NA07I,PE10,PG,TA80,TB02,TB78.

58000   Knobloch, H., and Pasamanick, B. Further observations on the behavioral
development of Negro children. Journal of Genetic Psychology, 1953, 83,
137-157. Topic Codes: BE,BL06,BL11,BL31,BL48,BL67,BL70,BP02,BP52,DD,
DT42,DT48,ML,MT48,NA07B,NA07I,NA31F,NA31R,NA44,NJ,PA,PE10,PE44,PE48,PG,PK,
PM,PN,PR,PT,SC18,SF,SJ22,SN,SQ,SW,SW56,TA52K,TB42.

58050   Knobloch, H., and Pasamanick, B. Prospective studies on the epidemiology
of reproductive casualty: Methods, findings and some implications.
Merrill-Palmer Quarterly of Behavior and Development, 1966, 12, 27-43.
Topic Codes: BL07B,BL22,BL31,BL48,BL67,DF,DF06,DT42,DT48,NA31F,NL48,PE32,
PK,PN,PR,TA80,TB05,TB78.

58100   Knobloch, H., and Pasamanick, B. Syndrome of minimal cerebral damage in
infancy. Journal of the American Medical Association, July 18, 1959,
170(12), 106-109. Topic Codes: BL07B,DF06B,DF34,DF60B,DK11,DK48,DP11B,
DP60,DP81,MG,MG48,NA07D,NA31A,NA31R,NA33B,NA44,NH59P,NH59PB,NJ,SH59R,
SH59RB,TA52K,TB42.

58150   Knott, J.R. Electroencephalograms in psychopathic personality and in mur-
derers. In W.P. Wilson (ed.), Applications of Electroencephalography in
Psychiatry. Durham, North Carolina: Duke University Press, 1965. Topic
Codes: CC11F,CT57F,MS04B,TB35BB,TB35D.

58200   Kobrin, S. The conflict of values in delinquency areas. American Sociological Review, 1951, 16, 653-662. Topic Codes: CC11P,CC37L,CC37V,CC37W,
CC37Z,CG11CC,CG11P,CJ,CN,CQ37,CV13,PT11,SF11,SF26DD,SW11.

58300   Kocel, K.M. Age-related changes in cognitive abilities and hemispheric
specialization. In J. Herron (ed.), Neuropsychology of Left-Handedness.
New York: Academic Press, 1980. Topic Codes: BL04,BL11,BL70,BN44,DT13,
DT42,DT59,MH,ML,MR,NA07I,NH59,NH59B,PE44,PG,PI,PM70,PN,PO,PS,SH59,SH59B,
SQ,TA59D,TB68,TB72,TB93.

58400   Koch, H.L. The relation of "primary mental abilities" in five- and six-
year-olds to sex of child and characteristics of his sibling. Child Development, September 1954, 25(3), 209-223. Topic Codes: BL70,BP07,DT13,
DT42,DT59,MH,ML,MR,NH,PE44,PI,PM70,PN,PS,SH,SJ07,SJ09,SQ,SW,SW56,TB68.

58450   Koeningsberg, D., Balla, D.A., and Lewis, D.O. Juvenile delinquency,
adult criminality, and adult psychiatric treatment: An epidemiological
study. Child Psychiatry and Human Development, Spring 1977, 7(3), 141-
146. Topic Codes: BL11,CC37A,CC37B,CC37V,CC67,CG11P,CQ37,MF11,NE37,PE01,
PE10.

58500   Koerin, B. Violent crime: Prediction and control. Crime and Delinquency, January 1978, 24(1), 49-58. Topic Codes: CC37L,CC81D,CC81S,
CG11CC,CL,CT57,CT59,CV13,CV13D,CY,MG11.

58530   Kohlmann, T., and Joss, M. Psychological problems of laterality in
children and the young with cerebral lesions and children with neurosis.
Studia Psychologica, 1974, 16(3), 191-203 (in German). Topic Codes:
BL04,DD,NA,PA,SD,TA80.

58560   Kolar, J., Kriz, J., and Macoun, J. Our experience with the treatment of
the psychic symptomatology in epileptic children and adolescents. Acti-
vitas Nervosa Superior, 1975, 17(4), 247-248. Topic Codes: BL11,CV15B,
DK18,MG,NA07B,PE10,TA80.

58590   Kolarsky, A., Freund, K., Machek, J., and Polak, O. Male sexual devia-
tion: Association with early temporal lobe damage. Archives of General
Psychiatry, 1967, 17, 735-743. Topic Codes: BK11B,BL33,DK18SB,MV07,N,NL,
PE66B,PL,TA02,TA55,TA80.

58600   Kolata, G.B. Behavioral teratology: Birth defects of the mind. Science,

November 17, 1978, 202, 732-734. Topic Codes: BL48,BP02B,BP04,DK09B,
DT13,DT48,MG30,MH,MT48,NA07B,NA31R,NA33D,NA44D,NC44,NC59G,NC70,NJ06,PE10,
PE34,PE48,PI,PM,PR,TA52K.

58640   Kolmetz, P.F. The relation between learning disabilities and juvenile delinquency [doctoral dissertation, State University of New York at Albany,
1981]. Dissertation Abstracts International, December 1982, 43(6), 1894A.
Topic Codes: CC37H,CC37J,DT44D,PE64D.

58700   Kolvin, I., Garside, R.F., Nicol, A.R., MacMillan, A., Wolstenholme, F.,
and Leitch, I.M. Familial and sociological correlates of behavioral and
sociometric deviance in 8-year-old children. In P.J. Graham (ed.), Epidemiological Approaches in Child Psychiatry. New York: Academic Press,
1977. Topic Codes: MG,MG11,MQ,NA07D,NH59P,NH59PB,NH59PJ,NH65,PE64B,
PE64D,SC70B,SC70D,SH59R,SH59RB,SH59RJ,SI57B,SJ07B,SJ22B,SW,SW56,TA04,TA57,
TA74.

58800   Kolvin, I., Ounsted, C., Richardson, L.M., and Garside, R.F. The family
and social backgrounds in childhood psychoses. British Journal of Psychiatry, 1971, 118, 396-402. Topic Codes: BL70,DK18B,DT06,DT42B,MG,
MG04,ML02,ML04,MU70,NA07D,NH59B,NH59E,NH59P,NH59PJ,NH65B,PE44B,PN07,SH59B,
SH59F,SH59R,SH59RJ,SJ07B,SJ22B,SQ07,SW07.

58900   Kolvin, I., Ounsted, C., and Roth, M. Cerebral dysfunction and childhood
psychoses. British Journal of Psychiatry, 1971, 118, 407-414. Topic
Codes: DF34,DK07B,DK18B,DP,DP11B,DT52B,MG,MG30,MK,NA07D,NA33A,NA33B,PE30,
SF07,SW07,TA02,TA52,TB35B.

59000   Koppitz, E.M. The Bender Gestalt test for children: A normative study.
Journal of Clinical Psychology, 1960, 16, 432-435. Topic Codes: BL04,
BL11,BL70,DT44,DT59,MG,MM,MR,NA07B,NA07D,NA07I,PE10,PG,PP,PS,SQ,TB09B,
TB09K,TB95.

59100   Koppitz, E.M. Bender Gestalt test performance and school achievement: A
9-year study. Psychology in the Schools, 1973, 10, 280-284. Topic Codes:
BL11,BL48B,BL70,DT44,DT48B,DT59,MG,MM,MR,MT48B,NA07D,NA07I,PE48B,PE64,PG,
PM,PP,PRO7,PS,SC70,SQ,TA04,TA59,TA59D,TB09B,TB09K.

59200   Koppitz, E.M. Relationships between the Bender Gestalt test and the
Wechsler Intelligence test for children. Journal of Clinical Psychology,
1958, 14, 413-416. Topic Codes: BI07,DT44,DT59,MG,MM,MR,NA07B,NA07D,
PE10,PP,PS,TB09K,TB95.

59220   Koprowski, E.G. Women who kill: A study of violent behavior [doctoral
dissertation, George Washington University, 1977]. Dissertation Abstracts International, December 1977, 38(6), 2866B. Topic Codes: BL70D,
CC11S,CC81V,CQ59,CT81,CY,MK11,NE59,NL22D,SQ11,TA80,TB49D,TB61B.

59240   Korbar, K. Epilepsy and medico-legal evaluation. Neuropsihijatrija,
1972, 20(1), 93-99 (in Serbo-Croatian). Topic Codes: DK18.

59260   Koretzky, M.B., Kohn, M., and Jeger, A.M. Cross-situational consistency
among problem adolescents and application of the two-factor model. Journal of Personality and Social Psychology, September 1978, 36(9), 1054-
1059. Topic Codes: CC37B,CC37I,NE37,SF07,TA74,TA80.

59280   Korhonen, T., and Sillanpaa, M. MBD-like behavior and neuropsychological
performances. Acta Paedopsychiatrica, 1976, 42(2), 75-87. Topic Codes:
DK48B,DP11B,DT44,MG30,MG48B,MM,NA07B,PE10,PE64B,PP,SC70B,SW07,TA52,TA55,
TA74.

59290   Korn, S.J., and Gannon, S. Temperament, cultural variation and behavior
disorder in preschool children. Child Psychiatry and Human Development,
Summer 1983, 13(4), 203-212. Topic Codes: MG,PT74,SB,SW07.

59300   Korner, A.F. Methodological considerations in studying sex differences in
the behavioral functioning of newborns. In R.C. Friedman, R.M. Richart,
and R.L. Vande Wiele (eds.). Sex Differences in Behavior. New York:

John Wiley & Sons, Inc., 1974. Topic Codes: BD70,BL33,BL70,BL70B,BN68, DT69,MG,MW,NA07D,NA33D,NA33F,PE34,PL,SI57,SQ,SQ07.

59400   Korones, S.B. The newborn: Perinatal pediatrics. In J.G. Hughes (ed.), Synopsis of Pediatrics. St. Louis, Missouri: C.V. Mosby Company, 1971. Topic Codes: BA,BD30,BD30B,BD30H,BL06,BL07,BL22,BL27,BL27K,BL59,BL70,BP, BP02,BP04,BP22,BP22F,BP26,BP26G,BP47,BP52,BP53,BP61,BP70,DD02,DD05,DD08, DD08K,DD30,DF06,DF34,DF48,DF60,DF67,DF70,DP,DP11,DP22,DP22P,DP44,DP48, DP58,DP60,DP81,DT04,DT04E,DT08,NA33,NA33B,NA33I,SQ,TA52M,TB02.

59450   Kosewski, M. Theoretical problems of crime and aggression. Przeglad Penitencjarny i Kryminologiczny, 1973, 2(3), 49-64 (in Polish). Topic Codes: CG,MC,MG,PE04,SR03.

59500   Kraemer, H.C., Korner, A.F., and Thomas, E.B. Methodological consider- ations in evaluating the influence of drugs used during labor and delivery in the behavior of the newborn. Developmental Psychology, 1972, 6, 128- 134. Topic Codes: BL06,BL70,BP02,BP04,BP44,BP46,BP53,NA33D,PE34,SQ.

59530   Krauss, H. Perspectives on psychopathology. New York Academy of Sci- ences - Annals, March 18, 1977, 285, 742-745. Topic Codes: DD00,M,N.

59560   Krauss, H.H., Robinson, I., Janzen, W., and Cauthen, N. Predictions of ethical risk-taking by psychopathic and non-psychopathic criminals. Psy- chological Reports, February 1972, 30(1), 83-88. Topic Codes: CC11C, CC11U,CE,MD07,MS04B,NE59,PE08D,SR04B,TA80,TB61B.

59600   Kreuz, L., and Rose, R. Assessment of aggressive behavior and plasma testosterone in a young criminal population. Psychosomatic Medicine, July-August 1972, 34(4), 321-332. Topic Codes: BD70B,BL04D,BL11C,CC11D, CC11P,CC11U,CC37A,CC37C,CC81E,CG11CC,CG11P,CQ59,CT57,CV13,CV13DA,MC,MC11, NA07ID,NE59,PE04,PE04D,PG11,PT11,SR03,SR03B,TB19B.

59620   Krieger, D. The hypothalamus and neuroendocrinology. Hospital Practice, 1971, 6(9), 87-99. Topic Codes: BD30,BK11B,BN,DK07.

59640   Krynicki, V.E. Cerebral dysfunction in repetitively assaultive adoles- cents. Journal of Nervous and Mental Disease, January 1978, 166(1), 59- 67. Topic Codes: BK11B,BL11C,BN44D,CC37B,CC37R,CC37T,CC37I,CC81A,CC81Y, CQ37,CQ59,CQ81,DK07D,NA07B,NE37,NE59,NE81,PE01,PE10,PO11,TA55,TA80,TB09D, TB35D.

59660   Kuhn, D., Langer, J., Kohlberg, L., and Haan, N.S. The development of formal operations in logical and moral judgment. Genetic Psychology Mono- graphs, February 1977, 95(1), 97-188. Topic Codes: BL11,DT13,MH,NA07B, NA07I,NH,PE10,PG,TA80.

59680   Kulkarni, A.S., and Plotnikoff, N.P. Effects of central stimulants on aggressive behavior. Modern Problems of Pharmacopsychiatry, 1978, 13, 69-81. Topic Codes: BK11B,CV15,NL,PC,TA80.

59685   Kunce, J.T., and Hemphill, H. Delinquency and Jesness Inventory scores. Journal of Personality Assessment, December 1983, 47(6), 632-634. Topic Codes: CC37B,CC37I,TA03.

59690   Kunce, J.T., Ryan, J.J., and Eckelman, C.C. Violent behavior and differ- ential WAIS characteristics. Journal of Consulting and Clinical Psychol- ogy, February 1976, 44(1), 42-45. Topic Codes: CC11N,CC11U,CC81D,CC81Q, CC81Y,CE,CQ59,CT57,CT59,CV13DA,CY,M,NE59,PE01,PM11,TA80,TB93D.

59700   Kupfer, D.J., Detre, T.P., and Koral, J. Relationship of certain child- hood traits to adult psychiatric disorders. American Journal of Orthopsy- chiatry, January 1975, 45(1), 74-80. Topic Codes: BN68,CC37B,DK48B, DT13B,DT69,MB,MG,MG02B,MG18,MG48B,MH07,MU70,MW,NA07D,PE64B,PI07,PT,SC70B.

59730   Kupietz, S.S. Attentiveness in behaviorally deviant and nondeviant chil- dren: I. Auditory vigilance performance. Perceptual and Motor Skills,

December 1976, 43(3), 1095-1101. Topic Codes: BL11,DK48B,MG,MG48B,NA07D, PE10,TA59,TA80.

59760   Kurtines, W., and Greif, E.B. The development of moral thought: Review and evaluation of Kohlberg's approach. Psychological Bulletin, August 1974, 81(8), 453-470. Topic Codes: BL11,N,PE10,PG,TA59,TA80.

59800   Laberge-Altmejd, D. Human Aggression and Dangerousness. Montreal: Centre International de Criminologie Comparée, University of Montreal, 1978. Topic Codes: BA,BD11,BD70B,BII1,BK04D,BK11BL,BL18D,BL52DD,BN04D,BN44D, CC11C,CC11D,CC11F,CC11K,CC11M,CC11N,CC11O,CC11T,CC11U,CC67B,CC81D,CC81E, CC81G,CC81I,CC81O,CC81Q,CC81R,CC81S,CG11CC,CG11P,CQ11,CQ59,CQ67,CQ81,CT81, CV06C,CV13D,DDO2D,DD26D,DK07D,DK09D,DT13D,DT44D,MB11,MF11,MH11,MM11,NE11, NE37,NE59,NE81,NL,PC11,PEO8D,PE68D,PII1,PM11,PO11,PP11,PT74B,SI57PB,SR02, SU11,TA03,TA55,TA59D,TBO9D,TB51B,TB93D.

59820   Laborit, H. The biological and sociological mechanisms of aggression. Social Science Journal, 1978, 30(4), 727-749. Topic Codes: BD,BD70B, BK11,BK11B,BK11BL,BLO8B,CC81T,DD28,DT10,DT42,DT44,DT46,MC,MF,ML,MM,MN, MTO4,MU,MX,MZ,PE,PEO4,PE44,PE68,PN,PP,PQ,PT,PT11,SF,SI57J,SR,SR03.

59830   Lachar, D. The families of psychotic children: A review. Catalog of Se- lected Documents in Psychology, Summer 1975, 5, 286. Topic Codes: SH59B, SH59F,SI07,SI57B,SJ.

59860   Lachar, D., and Gdowski, L. Problem-behavior factor correlates of person- ality inventory for children profile scales. Journal of Consulting and Clinical Psychology, February 1979, 47(1), 39-48. Topic Codes: BL11, CC37B,DDO0,MF,MG,MGO2B,NA07B,NA07I,NL48B,PE10,PG,SI,SQ07,TA59,TA80.

59890   Lachman, J.H., and Cravens, J.M. The murderers - before and after. Psychiatric Quarterly, 1969, 43(1), 1-11. Topic Codes: CC11C,CC11G, CC11H,CC11N,CC11U,CC67B,CC81,CC81B,CC81D,CC81F,CC81G,CC81H,CC81I,CC81N, CC81O,CE,CQ59,CQ81,CV,DD26D,M,MF11,MI07,MSO4B,NE59,NE81,PC11,PEO1,SF11, SI22,SL11,TA03,TA80.

60000   Lacroix, J.M., and Comper, P. Lateralization in the electrodermal system as a function of cognitive/hemispheric manipulations. Psychophysiology, March 1979, 16(2), 116-129. Topic Codes: BK04,BL25,BL29,BNO4,BN44,DT13, DT42,MH,ML,NL22,PC,PE44,PI,PM70,PN,PO,TA55,TA80.

60090   Lahey, B.B., Hammer, D., Crumrine, P.L., and Forehand, R.L. Birth order- by-sex interactions in child behavior problems. Developmental Psychology, November 1980, 16(6), 608-615. Topic Codes: BL70,BL70B,MG,NA07D,SJ07, SJ07B.

60100   Lahey, B.B., Stempniak, M., Robinson, E.J., and Tyroler, M.J. Hyperactiv- ity and learning disabilities as independent dimensions of child behavior problems. Journal of Abnormal Psychology, 1978, 87(3), 333-340. Topic Codes: DT44B,MG,MG11,MG30,MMO7,NA07D,PE64,PPO7,SC70,TA74.

60200   Lajonc, R.B. Family configuration and intelligence. Science, 1976, 192, 227-236. Topic Codes: BL70,BPO7,NH74,PM,SH74,SI59,SJO7,SJ09,SJ22,SQ, TA04,TA59D,TB78.

60250   Lake, F. Treating psychosomatic disorders related to birth trauma. Journal of Psychosomatic Research, 1978, 22(4), 227-238. Topic Codes: BL52DB,BPO2,BPO2B,BP44,DDO8K,DF34,DP11B,DTO4E,PL.

60300   La Menza, C.A. Influences of age, race and sex on the prediction of school achievement in transitional and regular first grade students [doc- toral dissertation, University of Pittsburgh, 1977]. Dissertation Ab- stracts International, June 1978, 38(12, part 1), 7233A-7234A. Topic Codes: BL04,BL67,BL70,PE64,SC70,SN,SQ,TA04.

60400   Lampkin, A.C., and Taylor, G.G. Santa Clara County Day Care Treatment Center for Delinquents - second year evaluation report. Unpublished manuscript, American Justice Institute, August 1973. Topic Codes: CC37J, CC37I,CV06C,TB21D.

60500   Landrigan, P.J., Baloh, R.W., Barthel, W.F., Whitworth, R.H., Staehling, N.W., and Rosenbaum, B.F. Neuropsychological dysfunction in children with chronic low-level lead absorption. Lancet, March 29, 1975, 7909, 708-712. Topic Codes: BL04,BL11,BL48,DA44M,DA44MB,DT48,MG,MT48,NA07D,NA07I, PE48,PG,PR,TA52,TA57,TB09,TB95,TB96.

60580   Langevin, R., Paitich, D., Orchard, B., Handy, L., and Russon, A. Diagnosis of killers seen for psychiatric assessment: A controlled study. Acta Psychiatrica Scandinavica, September 1982, 66(3), 216-228. Topic Codes: CC11C,CC11N,CC11O,CC11P,CC11U,CT57F,DK,PT11,TA03,TA52,TA59D,TB61B.

60600   Langhorne, J.E., and Loney, J. A four-fold model for subgrouping the hyperkinetic/MBD syndrome. Child Psychiatry and Human Development, Spring 1979, 9(3), 153-159. Topic Codes: DK48B,DT52B,MC,MG11B,MG30,MG48B,NA07D, NA44,NJ,PE04,SI57B,SR03,SW07,TA02,TA59,TB09B,TB09K.

60700   Langman, J., Webster, W., and Rodier, P. Morphological and behavioral abnormalities caused by insults to the CNS in the perinatal period. In C.L. Berry and D.E. Poswillo (eds.). Teratology: Trends and Applications. New York: Springer Verlag, 1975. Topic Codes: BB,BK11B,BL22, BL48,BL52D,BL52DB,BP,BP02B,BP04,BP22F,DD02,DK07B,DK09,DT44,DT48,MM,MT48, PE48,PP,PR.

60800   Langner, T.S., McCarthy, E.D., Gersten, J.C., Simcha-Fagan, O., and Eisenberg, J.G. Factors in children's behavior and mental health over time: The family research project. Research in Community and Mental Health, 1979, 1, 127-181. Topic Codes: BL04B,BL04D,BL67B,BL67D,BL70B, BL70D,CC37A,CC37B,CC37I,CC37L,CC37X,CC37Y,CG11CC,CG11P,CL,CV13,MG11B,MX11, NA07D,NA33I,NA44,NH59B,NH59E,NH59F,NH59PB,NH59PJ,NH59PL,NJ,PE64D,PE68D, PY11,SC70D,SF07,SF11,SH59B,SH59F,SH59H,SH59RB,SH59RJ,SH59RL,SI48B,SI57B, SI57D,SI57PB,SI59B,SI59D,SJ22B,SM11,SN07,SQ07,SQ11,SR02,SU11,SW07,SW11, TA57.

60900   Lapouse, R., and Monk, M.A. An epidemiologic study of behavior characteristics in children. American Journal of Public Health, September 1958, 48(9), 1134-1144. Topic Codes: BL04B,BL67,BL67B,BL70B,MG,MG18,MP,NA07D, PE52,SN,SN07,SQ07,SW07,TA57.

61000   Larsen, V.L. Physical characteristics of disturbed adolescents. Archives of General Psychiatry, 1960, 10, 55-88. Topic Codes: BB07,BB48B,BE07, BE30,BL08BB,BL11,BL48B,BL59,BL70B,BN44B,CC37B,CV30B,DD02B,DD02KB,DD28B, DD81B,DK07B,DT48B,DT59B,MG,MR07,MT48B,NA07D,NA07I,PE48B,PO07,PR07,PS07, SL07,SQ07,TA02,TA52,TB84.

61050   Lathrop, V.E. Aggression as a response. Perspectives in Psychiatric Care, September-December 1978, 16(5-6), 202-205. Topic Codes: MC,PE04.

61100   Laufer, M.W. Cerebral dysfunction and behavior disorders in adolescents. American Journal of Orthopsychiatry, 1962, 32, 501-506. Topic Codes: BL48B,BP02B,DK46B,DP11B,DT44,DT48B,MG30,MG48B,MM,MT48B,NA07D,NA31A,PE48B, PE64B,PP,PR07,SC70B,TB09B,TB35B,TB74,TB96B.

61110   Laufer, W.S., Skoog, D.K., and Day, J.M. Personality and criminality: A review of the California Psychological Inventory. Journal of Clinical Psychology, July 1982, 38(3), 562-572. Topic Codes: CC11P,CC11U,CC37W, CC37I,TB23,TB23B.

61150   Lavigne, V.V. An investigation of the biological unity of childhood psychosis and adult schizophrenia [doctoral dissertation, University of Texas at Austin, 1975]. Dissertation Abstracts International, April 1976, 36(10), 5265B-5266B. Topic Codes: BL11,DD00,DK07,MG,NA07B,NA07I,NH59B, PE10,PG,SC18B,TA55,TA59,TA80.

61200   Lavik, N.J. Urban-rural differences in rates of disorder: A comparative psychiatric population study of Norwegian adolescents. In P.J. Graham

(ed.), Epidemiological Approaches in Child Psychiatry. New York: Academ-
ic Press, 1977. Topic Codes: BL70B,BL70D,CC37L,DA04,DA15,MD,MG11B,MI,
NA07D,NH59E,PE06,PE15,PE64B,SC70B,SF26B,SF26D,SH59F,SI57B,SJO9D,SQ07,SQ11,
SW07,SW56,TA74.

61210   Lawson, W.B., Yesavage, J.A., and Werner, P.D. Race, violence, and psychopathology. Journal of Clinical Psychiatry, July 1984, 45(7), 294-297.
Topic Codes: BL67B,BL67D,CC81D,CC81U,SN07,SN11.

61230   Laxton, G.A. 40 hz. activity in MBL, LLD, and normal children: A compar-
ative EEG study [doctoral dissertation, University of Houston, 1976].
Dissertation Abstracts International, July 1977, 38(1), 408B. Topic
Codes: BK11B,DK07,DT44,MM,NA07B,NA07I,PE10,PP,TA80,TB09B,TB95,TB98.

61260   Layman, D.E. A behavioral investigation: The effects of medication on
disruptive classroom behavior and academic performance [doctoral dissertation, Georgia State University, School of Education, 1974]. Dissertation
Abstracts International, October 1974, 35(4), 2087A-2088A. Topic Codes:
MG30B,MM07,NA07B,PE10,PP07,SC,TA80.

61290   Lazor, A., and Chandler, D. Criteria for early diagnosis of brain dysfunction. Canadian Psychiatric Association Journal, August 1978, 23(5),
317-324. Topic Codes: BL11,DK48B,DT52B,MG48B,NA07B,NA07I,PE10,PG,PP,
SC18B,TA55,TA74,TA80.

61295   Lea, B.W. Neuropsychological correlates of violent behavior in a psychi-
atric population [doctoral dissertation, Florida State University, 1982].
Dissertation Abstracts International, September 1983, 44(3), 917B. Topic
Codes: CC81D,CC81R,TA02,TA55.

61300   Le Doux, J.E., Wilson, D.H., and Gazzaniga, M.S. A divided mind: Observations on the conscious properties of the separated hemispheres. Annals
of Neurology, November 1977, 2(5), 417-421. Topic Codes: BN44,DT13,DT42,
MH,ML,NA07B,PE10,PE44,PI,PN,PO,PT74.

61330   Lee, H.K. Country group home treatment for juvenile delinquency: Minnesota experience 1971-1972. Sociological Abstracts, October 1979, 27(4),
1259 (abstract). Topic Codes: CC37A,CC37J,CC37Y,CC37Z,CG11P,CJ,CQ37,
CV13D,NE37,NL48D,PE64D,SC18D,SC70D,SN11,SW11,TA04.

61350   Lefkowitz, M.M. Effects of diphenylhydantoin on disruptive behavior:
Study of male delinquents. Archives of General Psychiatry, 1969, 20, 643-
651. Topic Codes: BL11,CC37A,CC37F,CC37L,CC371,CQ37,CV15B,DK07B,DK18D,
DK18S,DT67B,MG,NA07B,NA07I,NE37,PE10,PG,TA02,TA74,TB66B.

61500   Lefkowitz, M.M., Eron, L., Walder, L., and Huesmann, L. Growing Up to Be
Violent: A Longitudinal Study of the Development of Aggression. New
York: Pergamon Press, 1977. Topic Codes: DD26BB,DK09D,MC,NA07B,NA44S,
NJ27,NL48,PA,PE04,PE10,PG,PM,PT,SC70B,SF07B,SI22B,SI46B,SI48B,SI57BB,
SI57J,SI57P,SR03,SU.

61510   Leibowitz, A. Home investments in children. Journal of Political Economy, March 1974, 82(2, part II), S111-S131. Topic Codes: BL11,PG,PM.

61520   Lempp, R. The relationship between brain damage and reactive disturbances
in children and adolescents. Zeitschrift fur Klinische Psychologie und
Psychotherapie, 1975, 23(3), 232-246 (in German). Topic Codes: DK07,MB,
MG,NA07D.

61540   Lenz, E.J., Jr. The expression of aggression and the need for social ap-
proval in psychopathic, neurotic and subcultural delinquents [doctoral
dissertation, Loyola University of Chicago, 1973]. Dissertation Abstracts
International, July 1973, 34(1), 417B. Topic Codes: CC37B,CC37BB,CC371,
CQ37,MC11,MGO2D,NA07,NA07B,NE37,SR03B,TA59,TA80.

61560   Leonard, D.J. WISC pattern analysis: A comparison of techniques for the
diagnosis of minimal brain dysfunction in school age children [doctoral
dissertation, Montana State University, 1975]. Dissertation Abstracts

International, August 1975, 36(2), 708A.   Topic Codes: DK48B,MG48B,NA07B, TB95B.

61580   Lerner, H.D.   Hypoactivity and hyperactivity in minimal brain dysfunction children: A comparative study of psycholinguistic abilities, visual-perceptual processes and social extraversion-introversion [doctoral dissertation, Rutgers University - The State University of New Jersey, 1974].   Dissertation Abstracts International, April 1975, 35(10), 5119B-5120B.   Topic Codes: DD81B,DK48B,DT44B,DT59B,MG48B,MM07,MR07,NA07B,PE10, PP07,PS07,TA59D,TA80.

61600   Lessing, E.E., Zagorin, S.W., and Nelson, D.   WISC subtest and IQ score correlates of father absence.   Journal of Genetic Psychology, 1970, 117, 181-195.   Topic Codes: BL70,DT13B,DT42,MG,MH07,ML,NA07D,PE44,PI07,PM, PM70,PN,SI59,SI59B,SQ,SW56,TB78,TB95,TB96.

61650   Lester, D.   Firesetting.   Corrective and Social Psychiatry and Journal of Behavior Technology, Methods and Therapy, 1975, 21(2), 22-26.   Topic Codes: CC11C,CT59B,M,PE01.

61680   Levander, S.E., Schalling, D.S., Lidberg, L., Bartfai, A., and Lidberg, Y. Skin conductance recovery time and personality in a group of criminals. Psychophysiology, 1980, 17(2), 105-111.   Topic Codes: BL25D,CC11C,CC110.

61700   Levick, S.E., Voneida, T.J., Schweitzer, L., Becker, E., Welsh, H., and Gur, R.E.   Letters to the editor: Eye movements in schizophrenic vs. normal subjects.   Archives of General Psychiatry, April 1979, 36, 493-494. Topic Codes: BN44,BN44B,DT42,ML,MU70,PE44,PM70,PN,PO,PO07,TB81.

61750   Levin, B.   Psychological characteristics of firesetters.   Fire Journal, March 1976, 70(2), 36-41.   Topic Codes: CC11C,CC11P,CC37B,CC37W,CT59B.

61800   Levine, S.   Sex differences in the brain.   Scientific American, 1966, 214, 84-90.   Topic Codes: BD70,BK11B,BL52D,BL70,BP,BP02,BP04,MV,PE66,SQ,SR69.

61850   Leviton, H., and Kiraly, J.   Different views of the elephant: Conceptual models of the behavior disordered and learning disabled child.   Child Study Journal, 1976, 6(3), 127-137.   Topic Codes: CV06,DT44,MG,MM,NA07D, PP.

61900   Levy, D.M.   Maternal Overprotection.   New York: Columbia University Press, 1943.   Topic Codes: BL11,BL70,DD00B,DT59D,MC,MG18,MQ,MU,MX,PC, PE04,PE10,PG,SH59R,SH59RB.

62000   Levy, J.   Cerebral lateralization and spatial ability.   Behavior Genetics, 1976, 6(2), 171-188.   Topic Codes: BD70,BI,BN44,DT59,MR,PM70,PO,PS, TB81.

62100   Levy, J.   Possible basis for the evolution of lateral specialization of the human brain.   Nature, November 8, 1969, 224, 614-615.   Topic Codes: BN44,DT13,DT42,DT59,MH,ML,MR,PE44,PI,PN,PO,PS,TB93,TB96.

62200   Levy, J., and Gur, R.C.   Individual differences in psychoneurological organization.   In J. Herron (ed.), Neuropsychology of Left-Handedness.   New York: Academic Press, 1980.   Topic Codes: BD70,BE,BI,BL70,BN44,DD08K, DP11,DP44,DT13,DT42,MH,ML,PE44,PI,PM70,PN,PO,SF,SQ,TB81.

62250   Levy, J., and Nagylaki, T.   A model for the genetics of handedness.   Genetics, 1972, 72, 117-128.   Topic Codes: B,BI,BK11B,BN44,DK11,NL,PO,PO33, TA52.

62270   Lewandowski, D.G., and Saccuzzo, D.P.   Possible differential WISC patterns for retarded delinquents.   Psychological Reports, December 1975, 37(3, part 1), 887-894.   Topic Codes: BL11,CC37Q,CC371,CQ37,DK46D,MO11,NA07I, NE37,PE10,PG,SQ,TB95D.

62300   Lewandowski, N.G., Saccuzzo, D.P., and Lewandowski, D.G.   The WISC as a measure of personality types.   Journal of Clinical Psychology, January

1977, 33(1), 285-291. Topic Codes: BL67,BL67D,BL70D,CC37Q,CC37W,CC37Y,
CC371,CG11CC,CV13,PT11,SN,SN11,SQ11,TB95D,TB96D.

62330   Lewine, R.R., Watt, N.F., Prentky, R.A., and Fryer, J.H. Childhood behav-
ior in schizophrenia, personality disorder, depression, and neurosis.
British Journal of Psychiatry, October 1978, 133, 347-357. Topic Codes:
BL11,DD00,DD02B,MB,ME,MF,MGO2B,MS,MU,NL,PE08,PE10,PE64B,PG,PT,SR01,TA74.

62360   Lewis, A. Psychopathic personality: A most elusive category. Psychological Medicine, May 1974, 4(2), 133-140. Topic Codes: MS,PT,SR.

62400   Lewis, D.O. Delinquency, psychomotor epileptic symptoms, and paranoid
ideation: A triad. American Journal of Psychiatry, December 1976,
133(12), 1395-1398. Topic Codes: CC37B,CC37K,CC37N,CC370,CC37W,CC81M,
CG11CC,CT57,CT59,CT70,CV13,DD01,DD26D,DK09D,DK18SB,DK18SD,DP,DT10B,DT30,
MT04B,TB35D.

62430   Lewis, D.O. Diagnostic evaluation of the juvenile offender: Toward the
clarification of often overlooked psychopathology. Child Psychiatry and
Human Development, Summer 1976, 6(4), 198-213. Topic Codes: CC37B,CC37F.

62450   Lewis, D.O. Neuropsychiatric vulnerabilities and violent juvenile delinquency. Psychiatric Clinics of North America, December 1983, 6(4), 707-
714. Topic Codes: CC37B,CC37L,CC37T,CC81C,CC81R,DT13D,DT67B,MH11,PI11,
TA03,TA55.

62460   Lewis, D.O. Parental criminality and medical histories of delinquent
children. American Journal of Psychiatry, March 1979, 136(3), 288-292.
Topic Codes: BK11,BL11,CC37G,CC37M,CC37T,CG11P,CQ37,CT57BD,DD10D,DK09D,
MGO2B,MGO2D,NA07DD,NA07DF,NA07I,NE37,PE10,PG,SH59D,SH59JD,SH59RD,
SL11,TA80.

62500   Lewis, D.O. Psychobiological vulnerabilities to delinquency. Journal of
the American Academy of Child Psychiatry, 1978, 1702, 193-196. Topic
Codes: BD11,CC37B,CC37C,CC37L,CG,NH59F,SF11,SH59H,SW11.

62550   Lewis, D.O., and Balla, D. "Sociopathy" and its synonyms: Inappropriate
diagnoses in child psychiatry. American Journal of Psychiatry, July 1975,
132(7), 720-722. Topic Codes: MA07,MC,ME,MF,MG11,MS04,NA07,TA02B,TA80.

62600   Lewis, D.O., Balla, D.A., and Shanok, S.S. Delinquency and Psychopathology. New York: Grune & Stratton, 1976. Topic Codes: CC37B.

62700   Lewis, D.O., Balla, D., Shanok, S.S., and Snell, L. Delinquency, parental
psychopathology, and parental criminality: Clinical and epidemiological
findings. Journal of the American Academy of Child Psychiatry, Autumn
1976, 15(4), 665-678. Topic Codes: CC37B,CC37L,CG11CC,CG11P,CV13,NH59B,
NH59D,NH59E,NH59F,NL48,PA11,SH59B,SH59D,SH59F,SH59H,SW07.

62780   Lewis, D.O., Pincus, J.H., Shanok, S.S., and Glaser, G.H. Psychomotor
epilepsy and violence in a group of incarcerated adolescent boys. American Journal of Psychiatry, July 1982, 139(7), 882-887. Topic Codes:
CC37B,CC37H,CC37L,CC37T,CC81M,CQ59,CV13DA,DK18SB,DK18SD,DT52D,MU11

62800   Lewis, D.O., and Shanok, S.S. A comparison of the medical histories of
incarcerated delinquent children and a matched sample of non-delinquent
children. Child Psychiatry and Human Development, Summer 1979, 9(4),
210-214. Topic Codes: BP02D,CC37B,CC370,CC37P,CC37X,CG11CC,CQ59,CT57BD,
CV13,CV13DA,CV30D,DD01,DD03D,DD10D,DD26D,DK09D,MA11,MK11,NE59,PE02D,PE30D,
SI57GD,SL11.

62900   Lewis, D.O., and Shanok, S.S. Medical studies of delinquent and non-
delinquent children: An epidemiological study. American Journal of Psy-
chiatry, September 1977, 134(9), 1020-1025. Topic Codes: BL11C,BP02D,
CC37A,CC37B,CC37G,CC370,CC37P,CC37T,CC37X,CG11CC,CT57BD,CV13,CV30D,DD01,
DD03D,DD10D,DD26D,DF,DP,MA11,MK11,NA07ID,NA31C,NL48,PE02D,PE30D,PG11,
SI57D,SI57GD,SL11.

63000   Lewis, D.O., Shanok, S.S., and Balla, D. Perinatal difficulties, head and
face trauma, and child abuse in the medical histories of seriously delinquent children. American Journal of Psychiatry, April 1979, 136(4A),
419-423. Topic Codes: BP02D,CC37B,CC37O,CC37P,CC37X,CC81N,CC81O,CC81P,
CC81T,CG11CC,CQ59,CT57BD,CV13,CV13DA,DD01,DD03D,DD10D,DD26D,DF,DK09D,MA11,
MG11,NA31B,NA31C,NE59,NL48,PE02D,SI57GD.

63050   Lewis, D.O., Shanok, S.S., Balla, D.A., and Bard, B. Psychiatric correlates of severe reading disabilities in an incarcerated delinquent population. Journal of the American Academy of Child Psychiatry, Autumn 1980,
19(4), 611-622. Topic Codes: CC37B,CC37H,DT44B,DT44D,MM07,MM11,PP07,
PP11.

63080   Lewis, D.O., Shanok, S.S., Grant, M., and Ritvo, E. Homicidally aggressive young children: Neuropsychiatric and experiential correlates. American Journal of Psychiatry, February 1983, 140(2), 148-153. Topic Codes:
CC37B,CC37L,CC37M,CT57FT,DT67B,NH59GI,NH59PB,NH59PL,SH59JL,SH59RB,SH59RL,
TA03,TA55.

63090   Lewis, D.O., Shanok, S.S., Pincus, J.H., and Giammarino, M. The medical
assessment of seriously delinquent boys: A comparison of pediatric, psychiatric, neurologic, and hospital record data. Journal of Adolescent
Health Care, December 1982, 3(3), 160-164. Topic Codes: CC37B,CC37F,
CC37O,CC37P,CC37T,CC81C,CC81D,CV30D,DD01,DD26D,DT67B.

63100   Lewis, D.O., Shanok, S.S., Pincus, J.H., and Glaser, G.H. Violent juve-
nile delinquents. Journal of the American Academy of Child Psychiatry,
1979, 18(2), 307-319. Topic Codes: BE30,CC37B,CC37H,CC37J,CC37K,CC37L,
CC37Q,CC37T,CC371,CC81D,CC81J,CC81M,CC81N,CC81Q,CC81R,CC81Y,CE,CG11CC,
CQ59,CT57,CT57BD,CV13,CV13DA,CY,DD10D,DK18SD,DT44D,DT52D,MM11,NE59,NH59D,
NH59F,PE64D,PP11,SC70D,SH59D,SH59H,SI57GD,TA03,TA52,TB09D,TB35D,TB40D,
TB74B,TB95D,TB96D.

63200   Lewis, G., Jusko, W.J., Coughlin, L.L., and Hartz, S. Contribution of
cigarette smoking to cadmium accumulation in man. Lancet, February 5,
1972, 7745, 291-292. Topic Codes: BP70,DA44,SW.

63240   Lewis, M. Transitory or pseudo-organicity and borderline personality in a
7-year-old child. Journal of the American Academy of Child Psychiatry,
Winter 1976, 15(1), 131-138. Topic Codes: MG,NA07D.

63250   Lewis, R., Charles, M., and Patwary, K.M. Relationships between birth
weight and selected social, environmental and medical care factors. American Journal of Public Health, 1973, 63(11), 973-981. Topic Codes: BL06,
BL07,DF06B,NL,SF,SW,TA80.

63400   Lezak, M.D. Neuropsychological Assessment. New York: Oxford University
Press, 1976. Topic Codes: BK11BL,BL48,BL52D,DD00,DD02B,DD03B,DD26B,
DK07B,DT02,DT06,DT10,DT13B,DT15B,DT30,DT42B,DT44B,DT46,DT48,DT52B,DT59B,
DT71D,MA07,MB,MF,MH07,MK,ML02,ML04,ML15,MM07,MR07,MS,MT04,MT48,MU70,NA31R,
PE30,PE44B,PE48B,PE70,PI07,PM07,PM70,PN07,PO07,PO33,PP07,PQ,PR07,PS07,PT,
SR01,TA52K,TA55,TA80,TB78B,TB78D,TB93B.

63420   Lidberg, L., Levander, S.E., Schalling, D., and Lidberg, Y. Excretion of
adrenaline and nonadrenaline as related to real life stress and psychopathy. Reports from the Laboratory for Clinical Stress Research, September 1976, no. 50. Topic Codes: BD07,BD11,MS04.

63480   Lilenfield, B.M. Teacher identification of children with school-related
problems: Predictive validity six years later [doctoral dissertation,
Rutgers University - The State University of New Jersey, 1975]. Dissertation Abstracts International, April 1976, 36(10), 6557A. Topic Codes:
BL11,MG,NA07B,NA07I,PE10,PG,SC70,TA80.

63500   Lilienfeld, A., and Parkhurst, E. A study of the association of factors
of pregnancy and parturition with the development of cerebral palsy: A
preliminary report. American Journal of Hygienics, January 20, 1951, 53,

262-282. Topic Codes: BL07B,BL70,BP02,BP46,BP53,DF06B,DF34,DF48,DF60B, DK11,DP11,DP48,NA33B,SJ07,SQ.

63600   Lilienfeld, A., Pasamanick, B., and Rogers, M. Relationships between pregnancy experience and the development of certain neuropsychiatric disorders in childhood. American Journal of Public Health, May 1955, 45, 637-643. Topic Codes: BL07BB,BL67,BP,BP02B,DF06BB,DF34,DF60B,DK11,DK18, DK46,DP,DP11B,MG,MO,NA07D,NA33A,NA33B,SN,TB02.

63630   Lindahl, M. Emotion and cognition in vicarious instigation research. Scandinavian Journal of Psychology, 1977, 18(2), 85-91. Topic Codes: DT13,MH,NL,PI,TA80.

63660   Lindner, L.A., Goldman, H., Dinitz, S., and Allen, H.E. Antisocial personality type with cardiac lability. Archives of General Psychiatry, September 1970, 23(3), 260-270. Topic Codes: CC11C,CC11U,CQ59,DD02D,ME07, NE59,PE08D,TA59,TA80.

63695   Linn, S., Schoenbaum, S.C., Monson, R.R., Rosner, B., Stubblefield, P.G., and Ryan, K.J. No association between coffee consumption and adverse outcomes of pregnancy. New England Journal of Medicine, January 21, 1982, 306(3), 141-145. Topic Codes: BL06,BL07,BP02,BP53,BP57,BP59,BP61,BP70, DF06,DF34,DF48,NA31R,NA33I,NH59P,NL,TA52K,TA52M.

63700   Lion, J.R. Medical treatment of violent individuals. Unpublished manuscript, University of Maryland Hospital School of Medicine, n.d. Topic Codes: CC81D,CC81I,CC81M,CC81R,CV06C,CV15D,DK18D,DK48D,MC,MG48D,PE04, SR03,TB35D.

63710   Lion, J.R. Organic determinants of stress and violent behavior. In M.J. Molof (ed.), Stress and Crime: Colloquium. Arlington, Virginia, 1980, vol. 2, 123-130. Topic Codes: CC81B,CC81R,DK07D.

63730   Linnoila, M., Virkkunen, M., Scheinin, M., Nuutila, A., Rimon, R., and Goodwin, F.K. Low cerebrospinal fluid 5-hydroxyindoleacetic acid concentration differentiates impulsive from nonimpulsive violent behavior. Life Sciences, December 1983, 33(26), 2609-2614. Topic Codes: CC81R,DK09D, MK11,PE30D.

63750   Lipton, E.L., Steinschneider, A., and Richmond, J.B. Autonomic functioning in the neonate. Psychosomatic Medicine, 1961, 23, 472-484. Topic Codes: BL33,NA33D,NA33F,PL,TA80.

63810   Lira, F.T., and Fagan, T.J. The profile of mood states: Normative data on a delinquent population. Psychological Reports, April 1978, 42(2), 640-642. Topic Codes: CC11C,CC11P,CG11CC,CQ59,CT,DD01,MB11,MS02,NE11, NE59,NL48D,PT74B,SJ09D,SN11,SW11,TA03,TA04,TB15B.

63830   Lira, F.T., White, M.J., and Finch, A.J., Jr. Anxiety and mood states in delinquent adolescents. Journal of Personality Assessment, October 1977, 41(5), 532-536. Topic Codes: BL11,CC37Z,CC371,CQ37,MG,NA07B,NE37,PE10, PG,TA59,TA80.

63850   Litt, S. A study of perinatal complications as a factor in criminal behavior. Criminology, May 1974, 12(1), 125-126. Topic Codes: BP02B, BP02D,CC11C,CC11F,CC11Q,CC11T,CC81D,CC81T,CC81W,CG11CC,CG11P,CV13,CV30D, DD08KC,DD26D,DF34,DK07D,DP11D,MK11,NA33B,PE30D,SL11,SW11.

63900   Littell, W.M. The Wechsler Intelligence Scale for Children: Review of a decade of research. Psychological Bulletin, 1960, 57(2), 132-156. Topic Codes: BL04,BL67,DD81,DK07,DK46,DT44,MG,MM,MO,NA07B,NA07D,PE10,PM,PP,PV, SF,SN,SO,SW,TA59D,TB21,TB78,TB95,TB96B.

63950   Little, V.L., and Kendall, P.C. Note on locus of control and academic achievement in institutionalized juvenile delinquents. Journal of Abnormal Child Psychology, June 1978, 6(2), 281-283. Topic Codes: CC37J, CC37Q,NE37,NE59,PM11,PT,PY,SU,TA03,TA04,TA59D,TB95B,TB98D.

64000   Littlemore, D., Metcalfe, M., and Johnson, A.L. Skeletal immaturity in
psychiatrically disturbed adolescents. Journal of Child Psychology and
Psychiatry and Allied Disciplines, 1974, 15, 133-138. Topic Codes: BE,
BL04,BL11,BL70,MG,NA07D,NA07I,PG,SQ.

64030   Livingston, K.E. The frontal lobes revisited: The case for a second
look. Archives of Neurology, 1969, 20, 90-95. Topic Codes: BK11B,CV,
DK07B.

64060   Livingston, S. Epilepsy and murder. Journal of the American Medical
Association, 1964, 188, 172. Topic Codes: BA,BB11,CC11D,CC11K,CC81M,
DK18D,DK18SD.

64100   Lobl, M., Welcher, D.W., and Mellits, E.D. Maternal age and intellectual
functioning of offspring. Johns Hopkins Medical Journal, June 1971, 128,
347-361. Topic Codes: BL06,BL67,BL70,BP02,BP46,NA07B,NA44B,NC22,NC59G,
NJ03,PE10,PM,SJ07,SN,SQ,TB78.

64110   Loeb, J., and Mednick, S.A. A prospective study of predictors of crim-
inality: 3. Electrodermal response patterns. In S.A. Mednick and K.O.
Christiansen (eds.), Biosocial Bases of Criminal Behavior. New York:
Gardner Press, Inc., 1977, 245-254. Topic Codes: BL25D,CC37,CC37T,CQ37.

64115   Loeber, R., Weissman, W., and Reid, J.B. Family interactions of assaul-
tive adolescents, stealers, and nondelinquents. Journal of Abnormal Child
Psychology, March 1983, 11(1), 1-14. Topic Codes: CC11M,CT57,CT59,NH70D,
SH70D,SI11.

64130   Loftis, J.E. Anger, aggression, and attributions of arousal [doctoral
dissertation, Stanford University, 1974]. Dissertation Abstracts International, March 1975, 35(9), 4710B. Topic Codes: MC,NL,PC07B,PE04,PS11,
PY,TA52,TA59.

64160   Lombroso, C. Crime, Its Causes and Remedies (H.P. Horton, trans.).
Boston: Little, Brown, 1911. Topic Codes: BA,CC11D.

64200   Loney, J., Langhorne, J.E., and Paternite, C.E. An empirical basis for
subgrouping the hyperkinetic/minimal brain dysfunction syndrome. Journal
of Abnormal Psychology, 1978, 87(4), 431-441. Topic Codes: BL04B,BL48B,
BN68,CV15B,DK48B,DP11B,DT48B,DT69,MB,MC,MG11,MG30,MG48B,MK,MT48B,MW,NA07D,
PE04,PE30,PE48B,PE64B,PR07,SC70B,SI57B,SR03,SW07,TA02,TA52,TA57,TA74,TB02,
TB09B,TB09K,TB95B.

64230   Loney, J., Whaley-Klahn, M.A., and Kosier, T. Hyperactive boys and their
brothers at 21: Predictors of aggressive and antisocial outcomes. In K.
T. Van Dusen and S.A. Mednick (eds.), Prospective Studies of Crime and
Delinquency. Boston: Kluwer-Nijhoff Publishing, 1983, 181-207. Topic
Codes: MC,MG02,MG30,NA07DB,NA44,NH70B,NJ,PE04,PM07,SR03.

64250   Long, J.V., and Vaillant, G.E. Natural history of male psychological
health: XI. Escape from the underclass. American Journal of Psychiatry,
March 1984, 141(3), 341-346. Topic Codes: NA44,NH,SD,SD07,SF26B,SH,SW,
SW07.

64400   Looft, W.R. Egocentrism and social interaction across the life span.
Psychological Bulletin, 1972, 28(2), 73-92. Topic Codes: BL04,BL11,BL31,
BL70,DT13,DT42,MF,MH,ML,MX,NA07B,NA07I,NA31F,PE,PE10,PE44,PE68,PG,PI,PK,
PN,PT,SF,SQ,SR.

64430   Lorentz de Hass, A.M. Epilepsy and criminality. British Journal of Criminology, 1963, 3, 248-256. Topic Codes: BK11B,CC11K,DK18D,MT.

64460   Lorenz, K. On Aggression. New York: Bantam Books, 1967. Topic Codes:
MC,ME,MK,PE04,SR03,SS,SU.

64500   Lothstein, L.M., and Jones, P. Discriminating violent individuals by various psychological tests. Journal of Personality Assessment, 1978, 42(3),

237-243. Topic Codes: BL67,BL67D,CC37B,CC37W,CC37Y,CC371,CC81D,CC81S,
CC81U,CC81Y,MG11,SN,SN11,TB19B,TB61B.

64550   Louks, J., Calsyn, D., and Lindsay, F. Personality dysfunction and lat-
eralized deficits in cerebral functions as measured by the MMPI and
Reitan-Halstead battery. Perceptual and Motor Skills, October 1976,
43(2), 655-659. Topic Codes: BK11B,BN44B,DK07B,MQ,MU,NL,PO07,TA80,TB40B,
TB87,TB93.

64600   Lublin, J.S. The birthing room. The Wall Street Journal, February 15,
1979, 193(33), 1, 22. Topic Codes: BL11,BP44,NA07I,PG,PM,SI48.

64650   Lubs, H., Patil, S., Kimberling, W., Brown, J., Cohen, M., Gerald, P.,
Hecht, F., Moorhead, P., Myrianthopoulos, N., and Summitt, R. Correla-
tions between low IQ, race and variations in Q and C banding. American
Journal of Human Genetics, 1973, 25, 47A (abstract). Topic Codes: BL07B,
BL67,DF06B,MH,NC70,NL48,PI,PM,SN,TA59D,TA80.

64670   Lubs, H.A., Patil, S.R., Kimberling, W.J., Brown, J., Cohen, M., Gerald,
P., Hecht, F., Myrianthopoulos, N., and Summitt, R. Q and C banding poly-
morphisms in 7- and 8-year-old children: Racial differences and clinical
significance. In E.B. Hook and I.H. Porter (eds.), Population Cytogenetics: Studies in Humans. New York: Academic Press, 1977. Topic Codes:
BI,BL11,BL67,NA07I,NC70.

64690   Lucas, A.R. Neurological dysfunction and learning disabilities. Developmental Medicine and Child Neurology, June 1978, 20(3), 391-392. Topic
Codes: BL11,DK48,MG48,PE10,PG.

64700   Luchterhand, E., and Weller, L. Effects of class, race, sex and educational status on patterns of aggression of lower-class youth. Journal
of Youth and Adolescence, 1976, 5(1), 59-71. Topic Codes: BL04D,BL67,
BL67D,BL70,BL70D,CC37A,CC37L,CC37Y,CC37Z,CT57,CT59,CT70,MC,NA07B,PE04,
PE10,SC18D,SF26DD,SN,SN11,SQ,SQ11,SR03,SW11.

64730   Luckenbill, D.F. Criminal homicide as a situated transaction. Social
Problems, December 1977, 25(2), 176-186. Topic Codes: CC81L,CE,CQ81,
CT57F,CT81,CX,CY,CZ07,NE81,SF11.

64760   Lukianowicz, N. Battered children. Psychiatria Clinica (Basel), 1971,
4(5), 257-280. Topic Codes: CT57B,DD10,M,NE22,NH11,NH59B,NH59PA,SI57J.

64830   Lundberg, A. Gross and fine motor performance in healthy Swedish children
aged fifteen and eighteen months. Neuropaediatric, February 1979, 10(1),
35-50. Topic Codes: BL11,BL31,BL48,DT48,MT48,NA07I,NA31F,PE48,PG,PK,PR.

64850   Luria, A.R. The frontal lobes and the regulation of behavior. In K.H.
Pribram and A.R. Luria (eds.), Psychophysiology of the Frontal Lobes. New
York: Academic Press, 1973. Topic Codes: BK11B,BL18B,BL25B,BN44B,DK07B,
DT13,MF,MH,MK,PE,PE30,PI,PO07,TB37B.

64900   Luria, A.R. The Role of Speech in the Regulation of Normal and Abnormal
Behavior. New York: Liveright, 1961. Topic Codes: BK11B,DD02B,DT06,
DT42B,DT59B,ML02,ML04,MR07,PN07,PS07.

64950   Luria, A.R. Traumatic Aphasia. The Hague: Mouton, 1970. Topic Codes:
BB07,BI07,BK11B,BL48B,BN44H,BN70,DD81,DK07,DK09B,DT06,DT13,DT42,DT44,DT46,
DT48,DT71,MH,ML04,MM,MN,MT48,MY,PE44,PE48,PE70,PI,PM70,PN,PO33,PP,PQ,PR,
TA04,TA55,TA59D.

64970   Lykken, D.T. The psychopath and the lie detector. Psychophysiology,
March 1978, 15(2), 137-142. Topic Codes: BK04D,BN04D,CC11D,PC11.

64990   Lystad, M.H. Violence at home: A review of the literature. American
Journal of Orthopsychiatry, April 1975, 45(3), 328-345. Topic Codes:
DD10,SH11,SI57G.

65000   Lytton, H. Three approaches to the study of parent-child interaction:

Ethological, interview and experimental. Journal of the American Academy of Child Psychiatry, 1973, 14, 1-17. Topic Codes: NA07B,PE10,SI48,SI57, TA52.

65050   Maccoby, E.E., and Jacklin, C.N. Sex differences in aggression: A re-joinder and reprise. Child Development, December 1980, 51(4), 964-980. Topic Codes: BL70,BL70B,MC,MG,NA07B,PY.

65100   MacDonald, A.P. Manifestations of differential levels of socialization by birth order. Developmental Psychology, 1969, 1(5), 485-492. Topic Codes: BL70,PT,PY,SI57P,SJ07,SJ22,SQ,SQ70,SU.

65200   MacFarlane, J.W., Allen, L., and Honzik, M. A Developmental Study of the Behavior Problems of Normal Children Between 21 Months and 14 Years. Los Angeles: University of California Press, 1962. Topic Codes: BL11,NA07B, NA07I,PE10,PG.

65300   Mack, R.W., and Johnston, F.E. Height, skeletal maturation and adiposity in adolescents with high relative weight at one year of age. Annals of Human Biology, 1979, 6(1), 77-83. Topic Codes: BD52,BE,BL04,BL11,BL31, BL70,CV52,NA07I,NA31F,NA31R,NA44D,NA44F,NC04,NC44,NJ06,NJ09,NL07,PG,PK,SQ, TA52K.

65400   Mack, R.W., and Johnston, F.E. The relationship between growth in infancy and growth in adolescence: Report of a longitudinal study among urban black adolescents. Human Biology, December 1976, 48(4), 693-711. Topic Codes: BE,BL04,BL05,BL06,BL11,BL31,BL70,NA07I,NA31F,NA31R,NA44F,NC04, NC44,NC59G,NH59PB,NJ09,NL07,PG,PK,SQ,TA52K.

65430   Mackal, P.K. The effects of dexamethasone in suppressing the aggression hormones 17-deoxycarticosteroid and the 17-ketosteroids. Psychology, August 1976, 13(3), 3-29. Topic Codes: BD,BK11B,MC,PE04.

65460   MacLean, P.D. Alternative neural pathways to violence. In L. Ng (ed.), Alternatives to Violence. New York: Time-Life Books, 1968. Topic Codes: BK11B,CC81E,CY,MC,PE04.

65550   Makey, M.S., Jr., and Bruning, J.L. Relationship between verbal rein-forcers, source and task difficulty for youthful felons and non-felons. Psychological Reports, April 1974, 34(2), 467-470. Topic Codes: CC11C, CC11U,CQ59,MM11,NE59,NL,PP11,TA80.

65570   Malina, R.M. Adolescent growth and maturation: Selected aspects of cur-rent research. Yearbook of Physical Anthropology, 1978, 21, 63-94. Topic Codes: BE,BL,NA44,NJ.

65600   Malina, R.M. Growth and physical performance of American Negro and white children. Clinical Pediatrics, August 1969, 8(8), 476-483. Topic Codes: BE,BL11,BL31,BL48,BL67,BL70,DT48,MT48,NA07I,NA31F,PE48,PG,PK,PR,SN,SQ, TA52.

65700   Maller, J.B. Size of family and personality of offspring. Journal of So-cial Psychology, 1931, 2, 3-27. Topic Codes: NA07I,PA,PE10,PE64,PG,PM, PT,SH,SI,SJ22.

65750   Malmquist, C.P. Depressions in childhood and adolescence. New England Journal of Medicine, April 29, 1971, 284(17), 955-961. Topic Codes: MG, NA07I,PA,PE10,PG,PT.

65800   Malmquist, C. Premonitory signs of homicidal aggression in juveniles. American Journal of Psychiatry, October 1971, 128(4), 461-465. Topic Codes: CC37G,CC37I,CC37L,CC37P,CC81D,CC81H,CC81J,CC81P,CL,CX,CY,NE79, SF11.

65900   Man, E.B., and Serunian, S.A. Thyroid function in human pregnancy: IX. Development or retardation of 7-year-old progeny of hypothyroxinemic wo-men. American Journal of Obstetrics and Gynecology, August 1, 1976, 125 (7), 949-957. Topic Codes: BD,BL06,BL11,BL31,BL52D,BP02B,BP04,BP46,BP47,

BP61,DK46,MO,NA07B,NA07I,NA31F,NA31R,NA44D,NJ06,PE10,PG,PK,PM,TA52,TA52K,
TB09,TB33G,TB84,TB95,TB96.

65950   Mandelzys, N., Lane, E.P., and Marceau, R. Relationship of violence to
alpha levels in a biofeedback training paradigm. Journal of Clinical Psychology, January 1981, 37(1), 202-209. Topic Codes: CC11C,CC110,CC81D,
CC81K,TB35D.

66000   Mann, F., Friedman, C.J., and Friedman, A.S. Characteristics of self-
reported violent offenders versus court-identified violent offenders. In-
ternational Journal of Criminology and Penology, 1976, 4, 69-87. Topic
Codes: BLQ4D,BL67,CC37A,CC37B,CC37H,CC37I,CC37L,CC370,CC37U,CC37X,CC37Y,
CC371,CC81A,CC81B,CC81D,CC81H,CC81J,CC81L,CC81N,CC81P,CC81T,CC81U,CC81W,
CC81Y,CG11CC,CG11P,CL,CQ37B,CV13,CY,DA04D,DA15D,DD01,MD11,MI07,NE37D,
NH59D,NH59F,NH59PL,PE06D,PE15D,PE64D,SC18D,SC70D,SH59D,SH59H,SH59RL,SI57D,
SN,SN11,TA03,TA59,TA59D,TB76B.

66030   Mannarino, A.P., and Marsh, M.E. The relationship between sex role iden-
tification and juvenile delinquency in adolescent girls. Adolescence,
Winter 1978, 13(52), 643-652. Topic Codes: CC11G,CC11L,CC11N,CC11P,
CC11U,CC24,CC37M,CC37Q,CC37W,CC371,CQ22,CQ37,CT59,CT68,NE22,NL22,PA11,
PE08,PE66,PM,PY11,SC,SH59RH,SI22,SI48D,SI59D,SQ70D,SU11,TA59D,TA80.

66060   Manne, S.H. A communication theory of sociopathic personality. American
Journal of Psychotherapy, October 1967, 21(4), 797-801. Topic Codes: ME,
MF,MG02B,MS04,MU70,PA,PE08,PT74,SH59F,SH59J,SH59R,SI07,SI22B,SI48B,SI57BB,
SI57J,SI57P,SR04.

66100   Manne, S., Kandel, A., and Rosenthal, D. Differences between performance
IQ and verbal IQ in a severely sociopathic population. Journal of Clini-
cal Psychology, 1962, 18, 73-77. Topic Codes: CC11C,CC11N,CG11CC,CQ59,
CV13,CV13DA,MG,MS04B,NA07D,NE59,TB93D,TB96BB.

66115   Mansheim, P. Mental illness and juvenile delinquency. Psychiatric Quarterly, Winter 1982, 54(4), 247-253. Topic Codes: CC37B.

66130   Marcus, A.M., and Richmond, G. The XYY syndrome: A short review, a case
study and investigatory model. Journal of Forensic Science, April 1970,
15(2), 154-172. Topic Codes: BA,BB70B,BB70D,BD30,BE,BI,CC11D,DD02NF,
MA11,ME,MU,TA52,TA80.

66160   Marcus, A.M., and Richmond, G. The XYY syndrome: Review with a case
study. Canadian Psychiatric Association Journal, August 1970, 15(4), 389-
397. Topic Codes: BA,BB70B,BB70D,BD30,BE,BI,CC11,CC11D,CC11N,DD02NF,
MA11,ME,MU,TA52,TA80.

66200   Marecek, J., Aurand, S.K., Cardell, M.C., and Finn, S.E. Economic, social
and psychological consequences of adolescent childbearing: An analysis of
data from the Philadelphia Collaborative Perinatal Project. Unpublished
manuscript, Institute for the Continuous Study of Man, 1979. Topic Codes:
BL11,BL31,BL67,BL70,BP02,BP46,MG,NA07D,NA07I,NA31F,NA44D,NC22,NC44,NC59G,
NC70,NH59PF,NH59PH,NJ06,PG,PK,SF,SH59RF,SH59RH,SI48,SN,SQ,SW,TB09K,TB27,
TB78,TB95,TB98.

66300   Marecek, J., and Finn, S.E. Long-term neuropsychological sequelae of
lead-poisoning in children. Paper presented at the 87th annual meeting
of the American Psychological Association, New York, September 1-5, 1979.
Topic Codes: BL11,BL48,BL70B,CV30,DA44MB,DT48,MG,MT48,NA07D,NA07I,NA44D,
NC22,NC70,NJ06,PE48,PG,PR,SL,SQ07,TA52,TB09,TB27,TB44,TB78,TB95.

66400   Margen, S., and Schultz, S.R. A study of biological variables in the
etiology of aversive-violent behavior. Paper of proposed research, n.p.,
1979. Topic Codes: BD52B,BD52D,BL11,BL18D,CC11G,CC37B,CC37G,CC37P,
CC37T,CC37U,CC37V,CG11CC,CG11P,CV13,CV52B,CV52D,DD01,DK07D,NA07I,PG,TA03,
TA52,TB35D,TB37D.

66430   Marinacci, A.A. A special type of temporal lobe (psychomotor) seizures
following ingestion of alcohol. Bulletin of the Los Angeles Neurological

Society, 1963, 28, 241-250. Topic Codes: DA04B,DD02B,DK18SB,DT67,MD07,
MT,NL,PE06B.

66460   Marinello, M.J., Berkson, R.A., Edwards, J.A., and Bannerman, R.M. A
study of the XYY syndrome in tall men and juvenile delinquents. Journal
of the American Medical Association, April 14, 1969, 208(2), 321-325.
Topic Codes: BA,BB70B,BB70D,BE11,CC11D,CC11E,CC11L,CC11U,CC37C,CC37M,
CC37I,CQ37,CQ59,NE37,NE59,NL,SJ09D,SW,TA52,TA80.

66490   Marini, J.L., and Sheard, M.H. Antiaggressive effect of lithium ion in
man. Acta Psychiatrica Scandinavica, April 1977, 55(4), 269-286. Topic
Codes: BD30,BD70B,CC11D,CC11U,CC81Y,CV15D,MC11,MK11,NE59,PE04D,TA80.

66495   Marjot, D.H. Alcohol, aggression and violence. Practitioner, February
1982, 226(1364), 287-294. Topic Codes: BL04B,BL04D,CC81B,MC,PE04,SR03.

66500   Mark, V.H. Brain injury and criminality. Journal of Clinical Psychiatry,
May 1978, 39(5), 486-487. Topic Codes: BK11BL,CC81R,CG11CC,CG11P,CV13,
DK07D.

66600   Mark, V.H., and Ervin, F.R. Violence and the Brain. New York: Harper
& Row, 1970. Topic Codes: BA,BB11,BB70,BK11B,CC11F,CC11K,CC11M,CC11O,
CC81E,CC81K,CC81M,CC81O,CC81R,DD02N,DD26BB,DK07D,SB11,SF11.

66650   Markowitz, H.J. The differential diagnosis of acute schizophrenia and
organic brain damage [doctoral dissertation, West Virginia University,
1973]. Dissertation Abstracts International, October 1973, 34(4), 1754B-
1755B. Topic Codes: BK11B,DD00,DD26B,DD81,DK07B,MT,MU70,NL,TA52,TA55,
TA59,TA80,TB40B,TB49,TB61.

66680   Marsh, T.O. Roots of Crime: A Bio-Physical Approach to Crime Prevention
and Rehabilitation. Newton, N.J.: Nellen Publishing Co., Inc., 1981.
Topic Codes: BA,BD,BD30HD,BD52D,CV52D,DD30D,MC11,PE04D,SF11,SR03B.

66700   Marshall, W., Hess, A.K., and Lair, C.V. The WISC-R and WRAT as indica-
tors of arithmetic achievement in juvenile delinquents. Perceptual and
Motor Skills, 1978, 47, 408-410. Topic Codes: BL04D,BL70D,CC37A,CC37J,
CC37Q,CC37I,CG11CC,CG11P,CV13,PE64D,SC70D,SQ11,TB95D,TB98D.

66730   Martin, F. Internal-external control among pre-delinquent and delinquent
middle school pupils. Psychology, August 1975, 12(3), 24-26. Topic
Codes: CC37BB,CC37G,CC37N,CC37W,CC37I,DD03,ME,MG30BB,NA07,TA52,TA74.

66760   Martin, H.P., Beezley, P., Conway, E.F., and Kempe, C.H. The development
of abused children. Advances in Pediatrics, 1974, 21, 25-73. Topic
Codes: BE30C,BK,BL05,BL06,BL07B,BL11,BL52D,DD10,DD26,MH,MQ,NA07I,NL,PE10,
PG,PI,PT,SF,SH11,SH59D,SH59F,SI57G,SI57GB,SI57J,SI57P,SI59,SS,TA52,TA52K,
TA55,TA59,TA80.

66800   Martin, R.L., Cloninger, C.R., and Guze, S.B. The evaluation of diagnos-
tic concordance in follow-up studies: II. A blind, prospective follow-up
of female criminals. Journal of Psychiatric Research, 1979, 15, 107-125.
Topic Codes: BL67D,CC11S,CC24,CG11CC,CG11P,CQ22,CV13,DA04D,DA15D,DK46D,
MB11,MD11,MI07,MO11,MQ11,MS04B,MU70B,MV07,NA44,NE22,NJ,NL48,PE06D,PE15D,
PE66B,SC18D,SD11,SN11,SR69B,TA03,TA59.

66900   Martin, R.L., Cloninger, C.R., and Guze, S.B. Female criminality and the
prediction of recidivism. Archives of General Psychiatry, 1978, 35, 207-
214. Topic Codes: BL04D,BL67D,CC11A,CC11C,CC11G,CC11H,CC11I,CC11J,
CC11L,CC11R,CC24,CG11CC,CG11P,CQ22,CT57,CT59,CV13,DA04D,DA15D,MB11,MD11,
MG11,MI07,MQ11,MS04B,MV07,NA44,NE22,NH59F,NH59GB,NH59GI,NH59PB,NH59PJ,
NH59PL,NH67D,NJ,PE06D,PE15D,PE66B,SC18D,SD11,SH59H,SH59JB,SH59JL,SH59RB,
SH59RJ,SH59RL,SN11,SR69B.

66950   Martinez, J.A. An investigation into psychopathic aggression through behavioral conditioning [doctoral dissertation, University of Denver, 1976].
Dissertation Abstracts International, May 1976, 36(11), 5806B-5807B.

Topic Codes: BK04BB,MC,MT04,MU11,NE59,NL,PE04,PP07B,PS,PT,TA52,TA55,TA59,
TA80,TB61.

67000   Mash, E.J., and Mercer, B.J. A comparison of the behavior of deviant and
non-deviant boys while playing alone and with a sibling. Journal of Child
Psychology and Psychiatry and Allied Disciplines, 1979, 20, 197-207.
Topic Codes: MG,MX,NA07D,NH65B,PE68,SR.

67030   Massa, S. Criminological trends in the study of the relationship between
criminality and mental illness. Neuropsichiatria, July 1974, 30(3-4),
393-404. Topic Codes: CC11C.

67060   Masserman, J.H., and Borelli, N. The neuroses. Progress in Neurological
Psychiatry, 1969, 24, 436-440. Topic Codes: MQ.

67100   Matarazzo, J. Wechsler's Measurement and Appraisal of Adult Intelligence.
Baltimore: The Williams & Wilkins Company, 1975. Topic Codes: PM07,
PM70,TB93B,TB95B.

67160   Matranga, J.T. The relationship between behavioral indices of aggression
and hostile context on the TAT. Journal of Personality Assessment, April
1976, 40(2), 130-134. Topic Codes: CC37W,CC37I,NE37,PE04D,PT11,PT74B,
TA03,TA80,TB86.

67190   Matthews, C.G., Dikmen, S., and Harley, J.P. Age of onset and psychomet-
ric correlates of MMPI profiles in major motor epilepsy. Diseases of the
Nervous System, March 1977, 38(3), 173-176. Topic Codes: BK11E,DK18,NL,
TB61.

67200   Matthysse, S. Genetic detection of cerebral dysfunction. New England
Journal of Medicine, February 28, 1980, 302(9), 516-517. Topic Codes:
BD07,BI07,DK07B,DK46B,MO07,MU,MU70.

67220   Mattson, J.A. Hostility and aggression in black essential hypertensives,
diabetics and general medical patients [doctoral dissertation, University of Texas at Austin, 1975]. Dissertation Abstracts International,
November 1975, 36(5), 2477B. Topic Codes: BD07,BD30,BL08BB,DD15,DD28B,
MC,MF,NL07B,PE04,PT,TA59,TA80.

67300   Maughs, S.B. Criminal psychopathology. Progress in Neurology and Psychi-
atry, 1972, 27, 275-278. Topic Codes: BK04BB,BL04D,BL11C,BN04BB,BN68,
CC11A,CC11C,CC24,CC37B,CC37G,CC81D,CC81K,CC81M,CG11C,CQ22,CQ59,CT57,CT59,
CV13,CV13DA,DK07BB,DK18SD,DT69,MG11,MS04B,MW,NA07ID,NE22,NE59,PC07B,PG11,
TB35D.

67400   Mauser, A.J. Learning disabilities and delinquent youth. Academic
Therapy, Summer 1974, 9(6), 389-402. Topic Codes: BL04D,BL70B,BL70D,
CC37A,CC37H,CC37J,CC37Q,CC37S,CC37W,CG11P,CV06C,DK48B,DT44D,MG48B,MG48D,
MM11,PE64D,PM11,PP11,PT11,SC70D,SQ07,SQ11.

67500   Mawby, R.I. Defensible space: A theoretical and empirical appraisal.
Urban Studies, 1977, 14, 169-179. Topic Codes: CG11P,CT57,CX,NE79,SF11,
SF26DD,SW11.

67600   Mawson, A.R. Hypertension, blood pressure variability, and juvenile de-
linquency. Southern Medical Journal, 1977, 70(2), 160-164. Topic Codes:
BK04D,BL04D,BL08BB,BL08BD,BL11C,BL67,BL67D,BL70D,BNO4D,CC11A,CC11D,CC37A,
CC37D,CC37G,CC37P,CC37V,CC37Y,CC37Z,CG11P,CT59,DD01,DD28B,DD28D,MC,MG11,
MK11,MS04B,NA07ID,PC11,PE04,PE30D,PG11,SF26DD,SN,SN11,SQ11,SR03,SW11.

67700   Mawson, A.R. Stress, arousal, and juvenile delinquency: Hypothesis.
Paper presented at the annual meeting of the American Society of Crimi-
nology, Dallas, Texas, November 1978. Topic Codes: BD11,BE11,BK04D,
BL04D,BL11C,BL70D,BN04B,BN04BB,BNO4D,CC37A,CC37B,CC37C,CC37E,CC37F,CC37G,
CC37H,CC37L,CC37T,CC37V,CG11CC,CG11P,CT57,CT59,CV13,DK07D,DT13D,MH11,
NA07ID,PC07,PC07B,PC11,PG11,PI11,SF11,SQ11.

67800   May, D. Delinquent girls before the courts. Medicine, Science, and Law,

1977, 17(3), 203-212. Topic Codes: BL70D,CC37B,CC37M,CG11C,CQ22,CV13, NE22,SQ11.

67900   Mayers, K.S., Townes, B.D., and Reitan, R.M. Adaptive abilities among delinquent and non-delinquent boys. Paper of proposed research, n.p., n.d. Topic Codes: BN44D,CC37B,CC37F,CC37H,CC37J,CC37R,CC37S,CG11CC, CG11P,CV13,DK07D,DT42D,DT59D,ML03,MR11,PA11,PE44D,PN11,PO11,PS11,TB40D, TB46B,TB84,TB87C,TB95D,TB98D.

67930   McAllister, R.J. The mental health of members of religious communities. International Psychiatry Clinics, 1969, 5(4), 211-222. Topic Codes: PV07.

67960   McArthur, L.Z., and Solomon, L.K. Perceptions of an aggressive encounter as a function of the victim's salience and the perceiver's arousal. Journal of Personality and Social Psychology, November 1978, 36(11), 1278-1290. Topic Codes: DT59,MC,MR,NL,PC,PE04,PS,TA80.

68050   McBurney, A.K., and Dunn, H.G. Handedness, footedness, eyedness: A prospective study with special reference to the development of speech and language skills. In R.M. Knights and D.G. Bakker (eds.), The Neuropsychology of Learning Disorders: Theoretic Approaches. Baltimore: University Park Press, 1976. Topic Codes: BK11B,BN44H,NA44B,PE10,PG,PO11,TB95, TB96.

68100   McCall, R.B., Hogarty, P.S., and Hurlburt, N., Transitions in infant sensorimotor development and the prediction of childhood IQ. American Psychologist, August 1972, 27, 728-748. Topic Codes: BL11,BL31,BL70,NA07B, NA07I,NA31D,NA31F,NA31R,PE10,PE32,PG,PK,PM,SQ,SW,TA52K,TB05,TB25,TB42, TB68,TB78,TB95.

68130   McCandless, T.E. Perceptions of parental attitudes among children who set fires [doctoral dissertation, Boston University School of Education, 1976]. Dissertation Abstracts International, February 1977, 37(8), 4154B-4155B. Topic Codes: BL11,CC37M,CC371,CQ37,CT59B,CV,MG,NA07B,NA07ID,NE37, PE10,PG11,SH59J,TA80.

68140   McCarthy, J.J. The role of language in academic and behavioral difficulties [doctoral dissertation, Boston College, 1981]. Dissertation Abstracts International, December 1982, 43(6), 1896A. Topic Codes: DT42, MG,PE64.

68160   McClearn, G.E. Biological bases of social behavior with special reference to violent behavior. In D.J. Mulvihill, M.M. Tumin, and L.A. Curtis (eds.), Crimes of Violence; staff report to the National Commission on the Causes and Prevention of Violence (vol. 13). Washington, D.C.: U.S. Government Printing Office, 1969, 979-1016. Topic Codes: BB11,BB70D, BI11,BK04D,CC81E,CQ81,CT57,CT81,CY,DD02B,NE81.

68200   McCleary, R.D. Violent youth. International Journal of Offender Therapy and Comparative Criminology, 1975, 19, 86-87. Topic Codes: CC37B,CC37F, CC37L,CC81D,CC81L,CC81T,CQ81,CT81,CV06C,MS04B,NE81,PE04D,PT11,SF11,SR03B.

68250   McColgan, E.G. Social cognition in delinquents, pre-delinquents, and non-delinquents [doctoral dissertation, University of Minnesota, 1975]. Dissertation Abstracts International, July 1976, 37(1), 199A-200A. Topic Codes: BL11,CC37A,CC371,CQ37,MG,NE37,PE10,PG,TA59,TA80.

68280   McCord, J. A forty-year perspective on effects of child abuse and neglect. Child Abuse and Neglect, 1983, 7(3), 265-270. Topic Codes: CC37M,CC37P,CT57BD,DD10D,NH59GB,NH59GI,NH59PF,NH59PL,SH59JB,SH59JL,SH59RF, SH59RL,SI22D,SI48D,SI57GD.

68300   McCord, W. The biological basis of juvenile delinquency. In J.S. Roucek (ed.), Juvenile Delinquency. New York: Philosophical Library, Inc., 1958. Topic Codes: BE11,BI11,BL04D,BL67,BL67D,BL70D,CC37E,CC37Q,CQ59, CT57,CT59,CV13DA,DK07D,MS04B,NE59,NH67D,NH74D,PM11,SF11,SH74D,SN,SN11, SQ11,TA03,TA52,TB35B,TB35D,TB78D.

68400   McCord, W., and McCord, J. _The Psychopath_. Princeton, New Jersey: Van
        Nostrand, 1964. Topic Codes: CC37B,CC37H,CC37K,CC37M,CC37I,CG11CC,CQ37,
        CV06C,CV13DA,MB11,MC11,MF11,MG,MK11,MS04B,MX11,NA07D,NE37,NH59F,NL07D,
        PE01,PE04D,PE10,PE30D,PE68D,PT11,SF07,SI46D,SI59D,SJ09D,SR02,TA03,TA59D.

68450   McCreary, C., and Padilla, E. MMPI differences among black, Mexican-
        American, and white male offenders. _Journal of Clinical Psychology_, Janu-
        ary 1977, 33(1), 171-177. Topic Codes: BL67D,CC11C,CC11R,CC11U,CQ11,
        NE11,NL48D,SN11,TB61B.

68500   McCullough, B.C., and Zaremba, B.A. A comparative analysis of standard-
        ized achievement tests with learning disabled and non-learning disabled
        adolescent boys. Unpublished manuscript, National Center for State
        Courts, July 1979. Topic Codes: CC37H,CC37I,CG11CC,CG11P,CV13,DA44,MM,
        PP,TA02,TA04,TB09K,TB95B.

68600   McCullough, B.C., Zaremba, B.A., and Rich, W.D. The role of the juvenile
        justice system in the link between learning disabilities and delinquency.
        Unpublished manuscript, National Center for State Courts, 1979. Topic
        Codes: CC37H,CC37I,CC37J,CC81G,CG11CC,CG11P,CT57,CT59,CT70,CV13,DA04D,
        DA15D,DT44D,MD11,MI07,MM11,PE06D,PE15D,PE64D,PP11,SC,SC70D.

68650   McCullough, J.P., Huntsinger, G.M., and Nay, W.R. Self-control treatment
        of aggression in a 16-year-old male. _Journal of Consulting and Clinical_
        Psychology, April 1977, 45(2), 322-331. Topic Codes: CC37B,CV06C,DD02B,
        MG02B,NA07B,PE10,PE64B,SH11,TA57,TA74,TA80.

68700   McCurdy, J.H. A contribution to the study of mental and physical measure-
        ment in normal children. _American Physical Education Review_, 1923, 28(5),
        209-215. Topic Codes: BE,BE30C,BL04,BL11,NA07B,NA07I,PE10,PE64,PG,PM,
        SC70,TA59D.

68800   McFalls, J.A. Social science and the Collaborative Perinatal Project: An
        opportunity for research. _Public Data Use_, September 1976, 4(5), 37-47.
        Topic Codes: BL67,BP46,CG,NC,NC22,NC44,NC59,NC59G,NC70,NH59P,NH59PH,
        SH59R,SH59RH,SN.

68850   McGee, R., Williams, S., and Silva, P.A. Background characteristics of
        aggressive, hyperactive, and aggressive-hyperactive boys. _Journal of the_
        American Academy of Child Psychiatry, May 1984, 23(3), 280-284. Topic
        Codes: MC,MG,MG30,NA07D,NH,PE04,SH.

68860   McGee, R., Williams, S., and Silva, P.A. Behavioral and developmental
        characteristics of aggressive, hyperactive, and aggressive-hyperactive
        boys. _Journal of the American Academy of Child Psychiatry_, May 1984, 23
        (3), 270-279. Topic Codes: BL11,DT13,MC,MG,MG30,MH,NA07D,PI.

68900   McGrade, B.J. Newborn activity and emotional response at eight months.
        Child Development, 1968, 39, 1247-1252. Topic Codes: BL31,BP44,NA31D,
        NA31F,NA31R,NA33D,PE32,PE34,PK,TA52K,TB05.

69000   McGuinness, D., and Pribram, K.H. The origins of sensory bias in the de-
        velopment of gender differences in perception and cognition. In M.
        Bortner (ed.), _Cognitive Growth and Development: Essays in Honor of H.G._
        Birch. New York: Brunner-Mazel, 1978. Topic Codes: BD,BD70,BI,BK,BK04,
        BK11B,BK11BL,BL11,BL29,BL31,BL48,BL52D,BL70,BN04,BN44,DT13,DT42,DT46,DT48,
        DT59,MF,MH,ML,MN,MR,MT48,NA07B,NA07I,NA31D,NA31F,NA31R,PC,PE,PE10,PE32,
        PE44,PE48,PG,PI,PK,PM70,PN,PO,PR,PS,SF,SQ,TA52K,TA59D,TB93,TB95.

69100   McGurk, B.J., Bolton, N., and Smith, M. Some psychological, educational
        and criminological variables related to recidivism in delinquent boys.
        British Journal of Social and Clinical Psychology, September 1978, 17(3),
        251-254. Topic Codes: BL04D,CC37A,CC37J,CC37Q,CC37W,CC37I,CG11CC,CG11P,
        CQ59,CV13,CV13DA,MG11,NE59,PE64D,PM11,PT11,SC70D,TA03,TA04,TA59,TB72B.

69200   McInerny, T., and Chamberlin, R.W. Is it feasible to identify infants who
        are at risk for later behavioral problems? _Clinical Pediatrics_, October

1978, 17(10), 775-780. Topic Codes: BL70B,MG,NA07B,NA07D,NA31A,NA31D,
NA44,NJ,PE01,PE32,PT74,SC18,SI57B,SJ07B,SJ22B,SQ07,TA57.

69220   McIntyre, M.J. Some neuropsychological differences between left and right
temporal lobe epileptics and their implications for future research [doc-
toral dissertation, Clark University, 1975]. Dissertation Abstracts International, February 1976, 36(8), 4167B. Topic Codes: BK11B,DK18S,NL,
TB19.

69225   McKay, S.E. The neuropsychological test performance of an assaultive psychiatric population [doctoral dissertation, University of Nebraska at Lincoln, 1980]. Dissertation Abstracts International, May 1981, 41(11),
4269B. Topic Codes: MF,MS,MS04,MU11,TA02,TA02B,TA55.

69230   McKeever, W.F., Gill, K.M., and Van Deventer, A.D. Letter versus dot
stimuli as tools for "splitting the normal brain with reaction time."
Quarterly Journal of Experimental Psychology, 1975, 27, 363-373. Topic
Codes: BK11B,BN44,NL,PO,TA55.

69260   McKeever, W.F., Van Deventer, A.D., and Subery, M. Avowed, assessed and
familial handedness and differential hemispheric processing of brief sequential and non-sequential visual stimuli. Neuropsychologia, 1973, 11,
235-238. Topic Codes: BN44,NL,PO,TA80.

69270   McKerracher, D.W., Street, D.R., and Segal, L.J. A comparison of the behaviour problems presented by male and female subnormal offenders. British Journal of Psychiatry, 1966, 112(490), 891-897. Topic Codes: BL70B,
BL70D,CC11S,CQ59,CV,DD26B,M,NE59,PT74B,SF07.

69290   McKerracher, D.W., and Watson, R.A. The Eysenck Personality Inventory in
male and female subnormal psychopaths in a special security hospital.
British Journal of Social and Clinical Psychology, December 1968, 7(4),
295-302. Topic Codes: CC11C,CC11P,CG11C,CQ59,CV06C,CV13DA,CV30D,MB11,
MS02,NE59,NL22D,PT11,SL11,TB38B.

69300   McKissack, I.J. A less delinquent cohort. British Journal of Criminology, April 1974, 14(2), 158-164. Topic Codes: BL04D,CC37A,CC37I,CC37L,
CT59,SF11,SI57D,SJ07D.

69400   McMahon, R.C. Genetic etiology in the hyperactive child syndrome: A
critical review. American Journal of Orthopsychiatry, January 1980, 50
(1), 145-150. Topic Codes: BI07,DA04B,MD07,MG02B,MG30,MG30B,MS04,NH04B,
NH65B,NH74B,PE06B,SH04B,SH74B.

69470   McMichael, P. School intervention with disadvantaged children. Educational Studies, March 1980, 6(1), 65-77. Topic Codes: MG,PE64,PE64B,SC,
SW,SW07.

69500   McMillan, M., and Henao, S. (eds.). Child Psychiatry: Treatment and Re-
search. New York: Brunner-Mazel, 1977. Topic Codes: BI07,BL04B,BL04D,
BL07,BL11,BL48,BL52DB,BN44B,CC37A,CC37B,CC37I,CC37J,CG11P,CG11T,CQ37,
CT57B,CV06,DA04B,DA15D,DD10,DF34,DK07B,DK09,DT15,DT48,MD07,MF,MG,MI07,
ML15,MT48,MU70,MV07,NA07B,NA07D,NA07I,NA31D,NA33B,NA33D,NA33I,NE37,NH59PB,
NH59PJ,NL07B,NL07D,PE06B,PE15D,PE32,PE34,PE48,PE64B,PE66B,PG,PO07,PR,PT,
PT74,SC18,SC70B,SF07,SH59RB,SH59RJ,SI07,SI11,SI57,SI57G,SQ,SR69B,TA52M,
TA70,TB02.

69600   McNeil, T.F., and Wiegerink, R. Behavioral patterns and pregnancy and
birth complication histories in psychologically disturbed children.
Journal of Nervous and Mental Disease, 1971, 152(3), 315-323. Topic
Codes: BL48B,BP02B,DF34,DF60BB,DP11B,DT48B,MC,MG,MT48B,NA07D,NA33A,NA33B,
NH59GG,NH59PH,NH59PJ,PE04,PE48B,PR07,SH59JJ,SH59RH,SH59RJ,SI59B,SR03.

69650   McNeil, T.F., and Wiegerink, R. Diagnostic categories and obstetric complication histories in disturbed children. Exceptional Children, Summer
1971, 37(10), 751-752. Topic Codes: BP02B,BP44,BP53,DF06B,DP11B,DP44,
TA80.

69700   McNeil, T.F., Wiegerink, R., and Dozier, J.E. Pregnancy and birth compli-
         cation in the births of seriously, moderately and mildly behaviorally dis-
         turbed children. Journal of Nervous and Mental Disease, 1970, 151(1),
         24–34. Topic Codes: BL04B,BL05,BL06,BL27,BL70B,BP02B,BP26,DF34,DF60BB,
         DP11B,MG,NA07D,NA33A,NA33B,SQ07,SW07.

69730   McQuaid, P.E. Child criminals? Irish Medical Journal, October 31, 1978,
         71(15), 515–518. Topic Codes: BL11,CC37,CQ37,CV.

69760   Mecir, J. Mentally disturbed juvenile arsonists. Ceskoslovenska Psychia-
         trie, June 1974, 70(3), 158–166. Topic Codes: CC37B,CT59B.

69800   Mednick, B.R. Intellectual and behavioral functioning of ten- to twelve-
         year-old children who showed certain transient symptoms in the neonatal
         period. Child Development, 1977, 48, 844–853. Topic Codes: BL48B,BL70B,
         DF34,DK07B,DP11B,DT13,DT48B,MG,MG30,MH,MT48B,NA07D,NA31R,NA33A,NA33B,
         NA33I,NA44F,NJ09,PE48B,PE64B,PI,PM07,PR07,SC70B,SQ07,SW07,TA02,TA52K,
         TA52M,TA59,TA59D,TA74,TB89,TB95B,TB96B.

69830   Mednick, B.R. Neonatal neurological symptomatology predictive of the min-
         imal brain damage syndrome in preadolescence [doctoral dissertation, Co-
         lumbia University, 1976]. Dissertation Abstracts International, December
         1975, 36(6), 3008B. Topic Codes: DF34,DK48,MG,NA33I.

69850   Mednick, B.R., Baker, R., Mednick, S.A., and Gabrielli, W.F. Longitudinal
         study of social and biological factors in crime: Executive summary.
         Unpublished manuscript, University of Southern California, Los Angeles,
         1983. Topic Codes: BB48D,BN44D,CC11D,CC11L,CC11T,DD02KD,DT42D,ML03,
         NH59GD,NH59GI,NH59PL,NJ12,PE44D,PN11,PO11,SH59JD,SH59JL,SH59RL,SI11,TA03,
         TA59D,TB35D.

69890   Mednick, S.A. Autonomic nervous system recovery and psychopathology.
         Scandinavian Journal of Behaviour Therapy, 1975, 4(2), 55–68. Topic
         Codes: BK04BB,BL25BB,BL29D,MS04.

69895   Mednick, S.A. Biosocial bases of morality learning. In S.E. Martin, L.B.
         Sechrist, and R. Redner (eds.), New Directions in the Rehabilitation of
         Criminal Offenders. Washington, D.C.: National Academy Press, 1981,
         289–303. Topic Codes: BA,BK04D,CC11O,CC37T,CQ59,CV13DA,NE59,NH04D,NH74D,
         PE08D,PY11,SH04D,SH74D,SI57PB,SR04B,SU11,TB35D.

69900   Mednick, S.A. Biosocial factors and primary prevention. In S.A. Mednick
         and S.G. Shoham (eds.), New Paths in Criminology. Lexington, Massachu-
         setts: D.C. Heath and Company, 1979. Topic Codes: BI11,BK04D,BL25BB,
         BL25D,CC37M,CC37N,CC37T,CC67,CG11P,CQ67,MS04B,NA44,NE67,NH04D,NH59GD,
         NH74D,NJ,PY11,SF11,SH04D,SH59JD,SH74D,SI57PB,SU11.

70000   Mednick, S.A. Breakdown in individuals at high risk for schizophrenia:
         Possible predispositional perinatal factors. Mental Hygiene, January
         1970, 54(1), 50–63. Topic Codes: BE07,BK04B,BK11BL,BL25B,BL29B,DF60BB,
         DK07B,DP11B,DT04EB,MG,MG02B,MU70,NA07D,NA44,NH59PB,NH59PJ,NJ,PE64B,SC70B,
         SH59RB,SI46B,TA02,TA57,TA59,TA74,TB61,TB95B.

70200   Mednick, S.A., and Christiansen, K.O. (eds.). Biosocial Bases of Criminal
         Behavior. New York: Gardner Press, Inc., 1977. Topic Codes: BB70B,
         BB70D,BD70B,BD70K,BI11,BL25D,CC11A,CC11C,CC11D,CC11F,CC11L,CC11M,CC11N,
         CC11O,CC11Q,CC11U,CC24,CC37M,CC67,CC81,CQ37,CV,DA04D,DD02NF,MD11,MI,MU70B,
         NH04D,NH59B,NH59D,NH59F,NH59GD,NH59GI,NH59PB,NH59PL,NJ,PE04,PE06D,PE15,
         PM11,SH04D,SH11,SH59B,SH59D,SH59H,SH59JD,SH59JL,SH59RB,SH59RL,SH70D,SW11,
         TA80,TB35,TB61B,TB93,TB95.

70250   Mednick, S.A., and Finello, K.M. Biological factors and crime: Implica-
         tions for forensic psychiatry. International Journal of Law and Psychia-
         try, 1983, 6(1), 1–15. Topic Codes: BA,CG,PY11,SF11,SI57PB,SU11.

70255   Mednick, S.A., and Gabrielli, W.F., Jr. Gene-environment interactions and
         crime. In S. Giora Shoham (ed.), Many Faces of Crime and Deviance. White

Plains, New York: Sheridan House, 1983, 131-142. Topic Codes: BIl1,
NH04D,NH59GD,NH59GI,NH74D,SH04D,SH59JD,SH59JL,SH74D.

70260   Mednick, S.A., Gabrielli, W.F., Jr., and Hutchings, B. Genetic influences
in criminal behavior: Evidence from an adoption cohort. In K.T. Van
Dusen and S.A. Mednick (eds.), Prospective Studies in Crime and Delin-
quency. Boston: Kluwer-Nijhoff Publishing, 1983, 39-56. Topic Codes:
BIl1,BL70D,CC11L,CC11M,CC67,CQ67,NE67,NH04D,NH59D,NH59F,SH04D,SH59D,SH59H,
SQ11.

70265   Mednick, S.A., Gabrielli, W.F., Jr., and Hutchings, B. Genetic influences
in criminal convictions: Evidence from an adoption cohort. Science, May
25, 1984, 224(4651), 891-894. Topic Codes: BIl1,CC11M,CT57,CT59,NH04D,
NH59D,NH59F,NH70D,SH04D,SH59D,SH59H,SH70D.

70300   Mednick, S.A., and Hutchings, B. Genetic and psychophysiological factors
in asocial behavior. In R.D. Hare and D. Schalling (eds.), Psychopathic
Behavior: Approaches to Research. New York: John Wiley & Sons, Inc.,
1978. Topic Codes: BB70D,BI07B,BIl1,BK04D,BL25D,CC37G,CC37L,CC37M,CC37S,
CC371,CG11C,CG11P,CV13,DD02NF,MC,MF,MS04B,NA44,NH04BA,NH04D,NH59B,NH59E,
NH59GB,NH59GD,NH59GG,NH59GI,NH63B,NH67D,NJ,PE,PE04,SF11,SH04BB,SH04D,
SH59B,SH59F,SH59JB,SH59JD,SH59JJ,SH59JL,SR03,TA03,TA52,TA59,TA59D.

70350   Mednick, S.A., Kirkegaard-Sorenson, L., Hutchings, B., Knop, J., Rosenberg, R., and Schulsinger, F. An example of biosocial interaction research: The interplay of socioenvironmental and individual factors in the
etiology of criminal behavior. In S.A. Mednick and K.O. Christiansen
(eds.), Biosocial Bases of Criminal Behavior. New York: Gardner Press,
Inc., 1977, 9-23. Topic Codes: BL25D,CC11L,CC11N,CC11O,NH59F,PM11,SH59H.

70400   Mednick, S.A., Mura, E., Schulsinger, F., and Mednick, B. Perinatal con-
ditions and infant development in children with schizophrenic parents.
Social Biology, 1971, 18 (supplement), S103-S113. Topic Codes: BIO7,
BK04B,BL07BB,BL48B,BL70B,BP02B,BP46,DF06BB,DF34,DKO7B,DP,DP11B,DTO4EB,
DT48B,MG,MT48B,MU70,NAO7D,NA31B,NA31R,NA33A,NA33B,NA33I,NA44F,NH59B,NH59E,
NH59G,NH59GB,NH59GG,NH59PB,NH59PJ,NH59PP,NJ09,PE48B,PRO7,SH59B,SH59F,
SH59J,SH59JB,SH59JJ,SH59RB,SH59RJ,SH59RP,SQ07,SW07,TA52K,TA52M.

70450   Mednick, S.A., Pollock, V., Volavka, J., and Gabrielli, W.F., Jr. Biology
and violence. In M.E. Wolfgang and N.A. Weiner (eds.), Criminal Violence.
Beverly Hills, California: Sage Publications, Inc., 1982, 21-80. Topic
Codes: BB70D,BD11,BD30HD,BIl1,BK04D,BL25D,BL70D,BN44D,CC11C,CC11D,CC11H,
CC11K,CC11M,CC11S,CC11U,CC81E,CC81H,CV15D,DA04D,DA15D,DD02NF,DD26D,DD30D,
DK07D,DK18SD,MD11,MI07,MM11,NE11,NH04D,NH67D,NH74D,NL,PE06D,PE15D,PO11,
PP11,SH04D,SH74D,SQ11,SS09,TA80,TB35D.

70500   Mednick, S.A., and Volavka, J. Biology and crime. In N. Morris and M.
Tonry (eds.), Crime and Justice: An Annual Review of Research (vol. 2).
Chicago: University of Chicago Press, 1980. Topic Codes: BA,BD11,BIl1,
BK04D,TB35D.

70600   Mednick, S.A., Volavka, J., Gabrielli, W.F., and Itil, T.M. EEG as a pre-
dictor of antisocial behavior. Criminology, August 1981, 19(2), 219-229.
Topic Codes: BL11C,BL52DD,CC37F,CC37G,CC37Z,CG11P,CT59,MG11,NA07ID,NA44F,
NH59E,NH59F,NJO9,PG11,SH59F,SH59H,SW11,TB35D.

70700   Mednick, S.A., Volavka, J., Gabrielli, W.F., and Itil, T.M. EEG predicts
later delinquency. Unpublished manuscript, Social Science Research Institute, University of Southern California, n.d. Topic Codes: BKO4D,BL11C,
BN04D,CC37F,CC37G,CC37T,CG11P,MG11,NA07ID,NA44F,NJO9,PC11,PG11,TB35D.

70800   Megargee, E.I. The prediction of dangerous behavior. Criminal Justice
and Behavior, March 1976, 3(1), 3-22. Topic Codes: CC81L,CC81S,CT57,CY,
MC11,PE04D,PT11,SF11,SR03B.

70900   Megargee, E.I. The prediction of violence with psychological tests. In
C.D. Spielberger (ed.), Current Topics in Clinical and Community Psychology (vol. 2). New York: Academic Press, 1970. Topic Codes: CC11C,CC11P,

CC11U,CC37B,CC37U,CC371,CC81,CC81D,CC81T,CC81Y,CQ59,CQ81,CT57,CT59,CT81,
CV13DA,CY,MC11,MG11,MK11,MQ11,NE59,NE81,PE04D,PE30D,PT11,SR03B,TA03,TA59,
TB19B,TB23B,TB49D,TB51B,TB61B,TB74B,TB86C.

71000   Megargee, E.I., and Golden, R.E. Parental attitudes of psychopathic and
subcultural delinquents. Criminology, February 1973, 10(4), 427-439.
Topic Codes: BL67D,CC11C,CC11L,CC11P,CC11T,CC11U,CC37B,CC37L,CC37U,CC371,
CQ37B,CQ59,CV13DA,MQ11,MS04B,NE37D,NE59,NL48,PT11,SI22D,SI48D,SI57BB,SN11,
TA03,TA59.

71100   Mehler, J., and Bever, T.G. The study of competence in cognitive psychology. International Journal of Psychology, 1968, 3(4), 273-280. Topic
Codes: BL11,DT13,MH,NA07I,PG,PI.

71200   Meier, G.W., and Menzel, E.W. Prenatal oxygen deprivation and subsequent
specific behavior dysfunctions. Science, 1955, 122, 419-420. Topic
Codes: BL22,BL48,BP22F,DP11,DT04E,DT48,MT48,PE48,PR.

71300   Mellits, E.D., and Hardy, J.B. Information pertaining to birth weight,
gestational age, placental weight, and mortality. In D.M. Reed and F.J.
Stanley (eds.), The Epidemiology of Prematurity (vol. 31, no. 4). Baltimore: Urban & Schwarzenberg, 1977. Topic Codes: BL06,BL07,BL27,BL27K,
BL67,BL70,BP26,BP26G,BP61,DF06,DF48,DF60,DF70,DP22P,DP48,SN,SQ.

71350   Mendelson, J.H., and Mello, N.K. Covariance of neuroendocrine function
and behavior: A potential technique for assessing drug abuse liability.
In T. Thompson and K.R. Unna (eds.), Predicting Dependence Liability of
Stimulant and Depressant Drugs. Baltimore: University Park Press, 1977.
Topic Codes: BD07,DA15,MI,PE15.

71400   Mendelson, W., Johnson, N., and Stewart, M.A. Hyperactive children as
teenagers: A follow-up study. Journal of Nervous and Mental Disease,
1971, 153(4), 273-279. Topic Codes: BL04B,BL11,BL48B,CC37B,CG11CC,CG11P,
CT59B,CT70,CV13,DT48B,MG,MG02B,MG18,MG30,MG30D,MT48B,NA07D,NA07I,NH65B,
PE48B,PE64B,PG,PR07,SC70B,TB02.

71500   Menkes, J.H. Textbook of Child Neurology. Philadelphia: Lea & Febiger,
1974. Topic Codes: BD,BD52,BI,BL70,BN04,BN68,CV15,CV15B,CV52,DD08K,DD26,
DF,DF34,DK07,DK09,DK11,DK18B,DK18S,DK18SD,DK46,DP11,DP44,DT08,DT10,DT67,
DT69,MC,MG,MG18,MO,MT04,MW,NA31B,NA33B,NH,PC,PE04,PE64,PM,SC70,SH,SQ,SR03,
TA52,TB35,TB35B.

71600   Menkes, M.M., Rowe, J.S., and Menkes, J.H. A twenty-five year follow-up
study on the hyperkinetic child with minimal brain dysfunction. Pediatrics, March 1967, 39(3), 393-399. Topic Codes: BL04B,BL48B,CC37B,CC37S,
DK,DK46B,DK48B,DT48B,DT67,MG02B,MG30,MG30B,MG48B,MO07,MT48B,MU,PE48B,PM07,
PR07,SD07,SJ22B,SW07,SW56,TA02,TA04,TA52,TA59,TB09B,TB78B.

71700   Mensh, I.N., Kantor, M.B., Domke, H.R., Gildea, M.C.L., and Glidewell,
J.C. Children's behavior symptoms and their relationships to school ad-
justment, sex, and social class. Journal of Social Issues, 1959, 15, 815.
Topic Codes: BL70B,BN68,DT69,MG18,MG21,MW,NA07B,NA07D,PE10,PE22,PE64B,
SC70B,SQ07,SW07,TA57,TA74,TB02.

71703   Menuck, M., and Voineskos, G. The etiology of violent behavior: An overview. General Hospital Psychiatry, March 1981, 3(1), 37-47. Topic Codes:
CC81,CC81D,CC81E,CQ81,CT81,NE81.

71705   Mercy, J.A., and Steelman, L.C. Familial influence on the intellectual
attainment of children. American Sociological Review, August 1982, 47(4),
532-542. Topic Codes: BL11,DT42,NA07I,NH,PG,PM,SH,SW.

71710   Mesinger, J.F. Juvenile delinquents: A relatively untapped population
for special education professionals. Behavioral Disorders, August 1976,
2(1), 22-28. Topic Codes: CC37B,CC37J,CQ37,CV06,SC18D,SC70D.

71720   Mesnikoff, A.M., and Lauterbach, C.G. The association of violent dangerous behavior with psychiatric disorders: A review of the research litera-

ture. Journal of Psychiatry and Law, Winter 1976, 3(4), 415-445. Topic
Codes: CC11C,CC11D,CC81D,CC81E,CG11CC,CQ59,CQ81,CT81,CV06C,CV30D,CY,MF11,
NE59,NE81,PE01.

71730   Messent, P.R. Female hormones and behavior. In B.B. Lloyd and J. Archer
(eds.), Exploring Sex Differences. New York: Academic Press, 1976.
Topic Codes: BD52,BD70,BD70B,BK04,BK11,BL52D,MC,PE04,PE48,PG11,PO,PT,PY,
SB,SC,SI57B,SQ70,SR03,SU.

71750   Meyer, M.B. Effects of maternal smoking and altitude on birth weight and
gestation. In D.M. Reed and F.J. Stanley (eds.), The Epidemiology of
Prematurity (vol. 31, no. 4). Baltimore: Urban & Schwarzenberg, 1977.
Topic Codes: BL06,BL22,BL27,BP22F,BP26,BP70,DF06,DF60,DP,DP46.

71760   Meyer-Bahlburg, H.F.L. Aggression, androgens, and the XYY syndrome. In
R.C. Friedman, R.M. Richart, and R.L. Vande Wiele (eds.), Sex Differences
in Behavior. New York: John Wiley & Sons, Inc., 1974, 433-453. Topic
Codes: BB70D,BD70B,BE11,BI11,BL70D,CC11D,CC11E,CC11M,CC11N,CC37E,CC37H,
CC37N,CC81E,CC81G,CC81Q,CC81V,CG11CC,CQ59,DD02NF,DT44D,MM11,MV11,NE59,NL,
PE66D,PM70B,PP11,SQ11,SW11.

71770   Meyer-Bahlburg, H.F.L., and Ehrhardt, A.A. Effects of prenatal hormone
treatment on mental abilities. In R. Gemme and C.C. Wheeler (eds.), Progress in Sexology. New York: Plenum Press, 1977. Topic Codes: BD70,
BK11B,BL11,BL22,BL52D,BP02,BP04,DP11,DP60,DT42,NC04,NC59G,NC70,PM70,TB95.

71800   Meyer-Bahlburg, H.F.L., Grisanti, G.C., and Ehrhardt, A.A. Prenatal effects of sex hormones on human male behavior: Medroxyprogesterone ace-
tate. Psychoneuroendocrinology, 1977, 2, 383-390. Topic Codes: BD70,
BL06,BL22,BP02,BP63,MV,NA44F,NC22,NC44,NC70,NJ09,SW,TB95.

71900   Michaels, J.J. Eneuresis in murderous aggressive children and adolescents. Archives of General Psychiatry, 1961, 5, 94-97. Topic Codes:
CC37BB,CT57F,MG18D,MS04B.

72000   Michelsson, K., Ylinen, A., Saarnivaara, A., and Donner, M. Occurrence of
risk factors in newborn infants: A study of 22,359 consecutive cases.
Annals of Clinical Research, December 1978, 10(6), 334-336. Topic Codes:
BD30H,BL07B,BL27K,BL31,BL52,BP47,DD30,DF06,DF34,DK,DP22P,DP46,DT08,NA31C,
NA33B,PK,TB02.

72050   Milich, R.H. A study of the effects of symbiotic-gratification stimuli
and aggressive fantasizing on the psychopathology of chronic hospitalized
schizophrenics [doctoral dissertation, Columbia University, 1976]. Dissertation Abstracts International, December 1976, 37(6), 3086B-3087B.
Topic Codes: CV06,MU70.

72060   Milich, R.H., and Loney, J. The role of hyperactive and aggressive symp-
tomatology in predicting adolescent outcome among hyperactive children.
Annual Progress in Child Psychiatry and Child Development, 1980, 336-356.
Topic Codes: BL11,MC,MG,MG30,NA07D.

72070   Milich, R.H., Loney, J., and Landau, S. Independent dimensions of hyper-
activity and aggression: A validation with playroom observation data.
Journal of Abnormal Psychology, June 1982, 91(3), 183-198. Topic Codes:
MG,MG30.

72150   Miller, E. Handedness and the pattern of human ability. British Journal
of Psychology, 1971, 62, 111-112. Topic Codes: BK11B,BN44,DT42,PM70.

72170   Miller, R.T. Childhood schizophrenia: A review of selected literature.
International Journal of Mental Health, Spring 1974, 3(1), 3-46. Topic
Codes: MG,MU70.

72200   Milner, B. Brain mechanisms suggested by studies of temporal lobes. In
F.L. Darley (ed.), Brain Mechanisms Underlying Speech and Language. New
York: Grune & Stratton, 1967. Topic Codes: BK11B,BN44,BN70,DT06,DT42,
DT46,ML,PM70.

72300   Milner, B. Effects of different brain lesions on card sorting: The role of the frontal lobes. Archives of Neurology, July 1963, 9, 90-100. Topic Codes: BK11B,BL70,BN44,DK07B,DT44,MH,MM,PI,PO,PP,SQ,TA55,TA80.

72400   Milner, B. Interhemispheric differences in the localization of psychological process in man. British Medical Bulletin, 1971, 27(3), 273-277. Topic Codes: BN44,DT13,DT42,DT44B,DT46,DT59,MH,ML,MM07,MN,MR,PE44,PI,PN, PO07,PP07,PQ,PS,TA55,TB81.

72500   Milner, B. Visually-guided maze learning in man: Effects of bilateral hippocampal, bilateral frontal, and unilateral cerebral lesions. Neuropsychologia, 1965, 3, 317-338. Topic Codes: DK07B,DT44,MM,TB66B.

72600   Minde, K., Webb, G., and Sykes, D. Studies on the hyperactive child: VI. Prenatal and paranatal factors associated with hyperactivity. Developmental Medicine and Child Neurology, 1968, 10(3), 355-363. Topic Codes: BP02B,DK07B,DP11B,DP60,DP81,DT04EB,MG30.

72630   Minor, J.A. Elementary vs. special education teachers' perceptions of handling learning, behavior, and neurological problems [doctoral dissertation, University of South Dakota, 1976]. Dissertation Abstracts International, December 1976, 37(6), 3398A-3399A. Topic Codes: DT44,MG,SC.

72660   Mises, R. Psychogenic factors in the psychoses: Contributions of child psychopathology. Annales Medico-Psychologiques, June 1975, 2(1), 124-128 (in French). Topic Codes: MG02B,MU.

72690   Mitchell, S., and Jackson, D. The feasibility of tracing a sample of school-boys after a lapse of fifteen years. Psychological Medicine, August 1978, 8(3), 509-513. Topic Codes: MF,MG02B,NA07B,NA44,NJ.

72700   Moffitt, T.E., Gabrielli, W.F., Mednick, S.A., and Schulsinger, F. Socioeconomic status, IQ, and delinquency. Journal of Abnormal Psychology, April 1981, 90(2), 152-156. Topic Codes: CC37Q,CC37Z,NA44,NJ,PM11,SW11.

72800   Monahan, J. The prediction of violence. In D. Chappell and J. Monahan (eds.), Violence and Criminal Justice. Lexington, Massachusetts: D.C. Heath and Company, 1975. Topic Codes: CC11U,CC67B,CC81D,CC81L,CC81S, CE81,CQ81,CT81,CV06,CY,MC11,PE04D.

72810   Monahan, J. The prediction of violent behavior: Toward a second generation of theory and policy. American Journal of Psychiatry, January 1984, 141(1), 10-15. Topic Codes: CG,CY.

72820   Money, J. Child abuse: Growth failure, IQ deficit, and learning disability. Journal of Learning Disabilities, December 1982, 15(10), 579-582. Topic Codes: CT57BB,DD10B,DT44,MM,PM,PP,SI57GB.

72830   Money, J. Use of an androgen depleting hormone in the treatment of male sex offenders. Journal of Sex Research, 1970, 6, 165-172. Topic Codes: BD70B,CC11D,CC11S,CT68,CV15D,MV11,PE66D,SR69D.

72860   Money, J., Wiedeking, C., Walker, P., Migeon, C., Meyer, W., and Borgaonkar, D. 47, XYY and 46, XY males with antisocial and/or sex-offending behavior: Antiandrogen therapy plus counseling. Psychoneuroendocrinology, October 1975, 1(2), 165-178. Topic Codes: BB70D,CC11C, CC11M,CT59,CT68,CV06C,CV15B,CV15D,ME07,MS04B.

72880   Monroe, R.R. Brain dysfunction in prisoners. In J.R. Hays, T.K. Roberts, and K.S. Solway (eds.), Violence and the Violent Individual. Jamaica, New York: Spectrum Publications, 1981, 75-86. Topic Codes: CC11B,CC11F, CC81C,CC81I,CC81R,CQ59,CV13DA,DK07D,DT67B,NE59,TB35D.

72900   Monroe, R.R., Hulfish, B., Balis, G., Lion, J., Rubin, J., McDonald, M., and Barcik, J.D. Neurologic findings in recidivist aggressors. In C. Shagass, S. Gershon, and A.J. Friedhoff (eds.), Psychopathology and Brain Dysfunction. New York: Raven Press, 1977. Topic Codes: CC11F,CC67, CQ67,DK09D,NE67.

72950   Monroe, R.R. Episodic dyscontrol in criminals. Unpublished manuscript, Institute of Psychiatry and Human Behavior, University of Maryland School of Medicine, 1978. Topic Codes: BK11BL,BN44BB,CC81B,CC81C,CC81I,CC81K, CC81M,CC81S,DD26D,DK07D,DK09D,DK18SD,DK48B,DK48D,DT46,DT52B,DT52D,MB11, MC,MC11,MG11,MG48B,MG48D,MK11,MN,MS04B,PE04,PE04D,PE30D,PO07B,PQ,SR03, SR03B,TA03,TA52,TA59,TB35BB,TB35D,TB51B,TB61B,TB66D,TB96BB.

72960   Montemayor, R. Men and their bodies: The relationship between body types and behavior. In F.H. Marsh and J. Katz (eds.), Biology, Crime and Ethics. Cincinnati, Ohio: Anderson Publishing Co., 1985, 176-186. Topic Codes: BE11,CC11E,S.

72970   Monti, P.M., Crown, W.A., and Conivean, D.P. Testosterone and components of aggressive and sexual behavior in man. American Journal of Psychiatry, June 1977, 134(6), 692-694. Topic Codes: BD70B,MC,MV,PE66.

72990   Mooney, C., and Algozzine, B. A comparison of the disturbingness of behaviors related to learning disability and emotional disturbance. Journal of Abnormal Child Psychology, September 1978, 6(3), 401-406. Topic Codes: DT44,MG,PE64B,TA74.

73000   Moore, D.R. Determinants of deviancy: A behavioral comparison of normal and deviant children in multiple settings. Doctoral dissertation, University of Tennessee, 1975. Topic Codes: MG,MX,NA07D,SF07,TA02,TA74.

73100   Moore, M., and Welcher, D.W. A descriptive analysis of the seven year psychological data. Johns Hopkins Medical Journal, June 1971, 128, 332-346. Topic Codes: BL11,BL67,BL70,NA44,NC70,TB09K,TB33G,TB53,TB95B.

73200   Morgan, D. A mixed message on education from the home of the "bomb." The Washington Post, October 19, 1980, A1. Topic Codes: PE64,SC18.

73250   Morgan, J.W. The differences between underachieving institutionalized male delinquents and nondelinquents as measured by psychological tests, scales and inventories [doctoral dissertation, Duke University, 1973]. Dissertation Abstracts International, January 1974, 34(7), 3471B. Topic Codes: CC37J,CC37M,CC37W,CC37I,PE64D,PM11,TB95D.

73300   Morgan, M.J., and Corballis, M.C. On the biological basis of human laterality: II. The mechanisms of inheritance. Behavioral and Brain Sciences, 1978, 2, 261-269. Topic Codes: BI,BN44,NH,NH59,NH74,PO,SH,SH59, SH74.

73400   Morrison, J.R., and Stewart, M.A. Evidence for polygenetic inheritance in hyperactive child syndrome. American Journal of Psychiatry, July 1973, 130(7), 791-792. Topic Codes: BI07,DA04,DK48B,DT42,MD,MG,MG30,MG48B,ML, NA07D,NH04B,NH65B,PE06,PE44,PN,SH04B.

73500   Morrison, J.R., and Stewart, M.A. A family study of the hyperactive child syndrome. Biological Psychiatry, 1971, 3, 189-195. Topic Codes: CC37B, DA04,MG02B,MG30,MS04,NH59B,NH59E,NH65B.

73600   Moscovitch, M., and Smith, L.C. Differences in neural organization between individuals with inverted and noninverted handwriting postures. Science, August 1979, 205(17), 710-712. Topic Codes: BN44,PO.

73700   Moss, H.A. Sex, age, and state as determinants of mother-infant interaction. Merrill-Palmer Quarterly of Behavior and Development, January 1967, 13(1), 19-36. Topic Codes: BL04,BL70,NA31D,PE32,SI48,SQ.

73800   Moyer, K.E. Kinds of aggression and their physiological basis. Communications in Behavioral Biology, August 1968, 2(2), 65-87. Topic Codes: BD,BD70B,BK11B,BL70,DK07,MC,PE04,SQ,SR03.

73900   Moyer, K.E. Physiological determinants of human aggression. Unpublished manuscript, Carnegie-Mellon University, 1978. Topic Codes: BK11B,DK07B, MC,MF,PE04,PM,SR03.

73930   Moyer, K.E. A preliminary model of aggressive behavior. In J.P. Scott and B.E. Eleftheriou (eds.), The Physiology of Fighting and Defeat. Chicago: University of Chicago Press, 1969. Topic Codes: B,MC,PE04,SR03.

73940   Moyer, K.E. What is the potential for biological violence control? In C.R. Jeffery (ed.), Biology and Crime. Beverly Hills, California: Sage Publications, Inc., 1979, 19-46. Topic Codes: CV15D,DK09D,DK18SD,MC11, PE04D,SR03B.

73960   Mueller, G.O. Seduction and the law. Medical Aspects of Human Sexuality, January 1972, 6(1), 14-27. Topic Codes: CT68.

73980   Mugishma, F. A cohort study on delinquent differentiation among girls: II. From the viewpoint of their attitude toward educational attainment at the 3rd grade in junior high schools. Reports of the National Research Institute of Police Science, July 1983, 24(1), 99-105. Topic Codes: CC24,CC37J,PE64D.

74000   Mullen, J.M., and Dudley, H.K. Development of an actuarial model for predicting dangerousness of maximum security mental patients. Paper presented at the 12th annual symposium sponsored by Texas Research Institute of Mental Sciences: Violence and the Violent Individual, n.p., November 1978. Topic Codes: BL04D,CC81D,CC81F,CC81N,CC81Y,CY,MU,TA03,TA59D,TB19B, TB51B,TB61B,TB93D,TB98D.

74005   Muller-Kuppers, M. Criminal aggression and neurotic ideology. Praxis der Kinderpsychologie und Kinderpsychiatrie, January 1971, 20(1), 3-8. Topic Codes: CC11B,CC37B,MC,MQ11,PE04,SR03.

74010   Mulligan, G., Douglas, J.W.B., Hammond, W.A., and Tizard, J. Delinquency symptoms of maladjustment: The findings of a longitudinal study. Proceedings from the Royal Society of Medicine, 1963, 56(12), 1083-1086. Topic Codes: CC37B,NA44,NJ.

74020   Mulligan, W. Dyslexia, specific learning disability and delinquency. Juvenile Justice, 1972, 23, 20-25. Topic Codes: CC37B,CC37H,CC37J,DT15, DT44D,PE64D.

74025   Mungas, D. An empirical analysis of specific syndromes of violent behavior. Journal of Nervous and Mental Disease, June 1983, 171(6), 354-361. Topic Codes: CC81D,CC81I,CC81R,TA03,TA52.

74030   Munkvad, I. The mechanism of action of psychopharmacological agents on behavior. Acta Pharmacologica et Toxicologica, 1975, 36(supplement 2), 21-30. Topic Codes: CV15B,MF.

74040   Munnich, I. Psychological examination of a murderer guilty twice of infanticide. Magyar Psichologiai Szemle, 1971, 28(2), 213-220. Topic Codes: CC81D,CG11CC,CQ81,CT57F,CT81,CV06,MF11,NE81,TA59.

74050   Mura, E.L. Perinatal differences: A comparison of child psychiatric patients and their siblings. Psychiatric Quarterly, 1974, 48(2), 239-255. Topic Codes: BP02B,DP11B,MG,NH65B,NH70B.

74100   Murray, C.A., Schubert, J.G., Gunn, A.E., Casserly, M.D., Scott, A.B., Harper, P.P., Bektemirian, M., and Hines, S.L. The Link Between Learning Disabilities and Juvenile Delinquency: Current Theory and Knowledge. Washington, D.C.: U.S. Government Printing Office, April 1976. Topic Codes: CC37B,CC37H,CC37J,CC371,CG,DT44D,DT59D,MM11,PE64D,PP11.

74150   Musaph, H. On the relationship of aggression to illness. Biological Psychiatry, 1979, 159, 107-113. Topic Codes: CC11C,DD02B,MC,MX07,PE04,SR03.

74200   Myers, R.E. Two patterns of perinatal brain damage and their conditions of occurrence. American Journal of Obstetrics and Gynecology, 1972, 112, 246-276. Topic Codes: BK11B,BL22,BL29,BP22F,BP47,BP61,DP46,DP48,DP58,NL, TA80.

74250   Myrianthopoulos, N.C. An approach to the investigation of maternal fac-
tors in congenital malformations. In N.E. Morton and C.S. Chung (eds.),
Genetic Epidemiology. New York: Academic Press, 1978. Topic Codes:
BL22,BL33,BP02,BP22F,BP47,BP53,BP59,BP63,DD08K,DF34,DK07,DP11,DP22,DP46,
DT04,NC59G,PL.

74300   Myrianthopoulos, N.C. Concepts, definitions and classification of con-
genital and developmental malformations of the central nervous system and
related structures. In P.J. Vinken and G.W. Bruyn (eds.), Handbook of
Clinical Neurology, vol. 30: Congenital Malformations of the Brain and
Skull. New York: Elsevier, 1977. Topic Codes: BB,BB70,BI,DD02,
DD02N,DK09,NC,NC80.

74400   Myrianthopoulos, N.C. Epidemiology of central nervous system malformations. In P.J. Vinken and G.N. Bruyn (eds.), Handbook of Clinical Neurology, vol. 30: Congenital Malformations of the Brain and Skull. New
York: Elsevier, 1977. Topic Codes: BB,BI,BL67,BL70,DD02,DK09,DK46,MO,
NA33D,NC44,NC80,PE34,SF,SN,SQ.

74450   Myrianthopoulos, N.C. Maternal factors influencing risk of epilepsy. In
M. Alter and W.A. Hauser (eds.), The Epidemiology of Epilepsy: A Workshop
(NINDS monograph no. 14). Washington, D.C.: U.S. Government Printing Of-
fice, 1972. Topic Codes: BP02,DK18,NH59P,SH59R.

74500   Myrianthopoulos, N.C., and French, K.S. An application of the U.S. Bureau
of the Census Socioeconomic Index to a large, diversified patient population. Social Science and Medicine, 1968, 2, 283-299. Topic Codes: BL67,
NC59,NC80,NH59PF,NH59PH,SF,SH59RF,SH59RH,SN,SW,SW33,SW56.

74600   Myrianthopoulos, N.C., and Melnick, M. Malformations in monozygotic
twins: A possible example of environmental influence on the developmental
genetic clock. In E. Inouye and H. Nishimura (eds.), Gene-Environment Interaction in Common Diseases. Baltimore: University Park Press, 1977.
Topic Codes: BB,BI,BP,BP61,DD02,DP,NC44,NH74,SH74.

74660   Nachshon, I., Denno, D., and Aurand, S. Lateral preferences of hand, eye
and foot: Relation to cerebral dominance. International Journal of
Neuroscience, 1983, 18, 1-10. Topic Codes: BK11B,BL52D,BL67,BL70,BN44,
DD08K,DP44,NA07I,NA44D,NC70,NJ06,NL07,NL22,NL48,PO,SN,SQ,TA52.

74700   Naeye, R.L. Amniotic fluid infections, neonatal hyperbilirubinemia, and
psychomotor impairment. Pediatrics, October 1978, 62(4), 497-503. Topic
Codes: BD30B,BL48,DF34,DK,DP,DP46,DT42,DT48,DT59,MG,ML,MR,MT48,NA07D,
NA31,NA31D,NA33B,NA33D,NA44D,NC22,NC44,NC70,NJ06,PE32,PE34,PE44,PE48,PN,
PR,PS,TB05,TB66,TB78.

74800   Naeye, R.L. Causes and consequences of placental growth retardation.
Journal of the American Medical Association, March 20, 1978, 239(12),
1145-1147. Topic Codes: BL27,BP26,BP46,BP52,DF48,DP48,DP58,DP60,NC44,
NC59G,SW33.

74900   Naeye, R.L. Causes of perinatal mortality in the U.S. Collaborative
Perinatal Project. Journal of the American Medical Association, July 18,
1977, 238(3), 228-229. Topic Codes: BA,BP47,BP61,DD02,DF48,DP22H,DP44,
DP48.

75000   Naeye, R.L. Effects of maternal cigarette smoking on the fetus and placenta. British Journal of Obstetrics and Gynaecology, October 1978, 85,
732-737. Topic Codes: BD30,BL06,BL27K,BP26G,BP47,BP61,BP70,DF70,DP,
DP22H,DP22P,DT04,NC44,NC59G,SJ07.

75040   Naeye, R.L. Fetal hypoxia: A prospective study. Pediatric Research,
1975, 9, 298 (abstract no. 249). Topic Codes: BP22,DF48,DP58,DT04E,NC.

75070   Naeye, R.L. Neonatal apnea: Underlying disorders. Pediatrics, 1979, 63,
8-12. Topic Codes: DF34,DP58,DT04,DT08E,NA33B,NC44.

75100   Naeye, R.L. Placenta previa: Predisposing factors and effects on the fetus and surviving infants. Obstetrics and Gynecology, November 1978, 52(5), 521-525. Topic Codes: BL27K,BP26G,BP53,BP61,DF48,DF70,DK,DP22P, DP48,NC44,NC59G,NH59PP,SH59RP.

75200   Naeye, R.L. Relationship of cigarette smoking to congenital anomalies and perinatal death. American Journal of Pathology, February 1978, 90(2), 289-293. Topic Codes: BB,BL70,BP46,BP70,DD02,DF48,DP48,NC44,NC59G,SQ,SW.

75230   Naeye, R.L., and Friedman, E.A. Causes of perinatal death associated with gestational hypertension and proteinuria. American Journal of Obstetrics and Gynecology, 1979, 133, 8-10. Topic Codes: BL08B,BL22,BP02,BP22F, BP47,BP59,BP61,BP63,DD28,DF48,DP11,DP46,DP48,DP58,NC59G,NC80,NL48.

75240   Nagaraja, J. The hyperactive child. Child Psychiatry Quarterly, April 1976, 9(2), 1-4. Topic Codes: MG30.

75270   Nahas, A.D., and Krynicki, V. Discriminant analysis of EEG in children with situational, learning and impulse disorders. Neuropsychobiology, 1978, 4(2), 74-85 (in French). Topic Codes: DT44,MG,MK,MM,NA07D,PE30,PP, TB35B.

75300   Nakamura, C.Y., and Rogers, M.M. Parents' expectations of autonomous behavior and children's autonomy. Developmental Psychology, 1969, 1, 613-617. Topic Codes: BL11,NA07B,NH59,SI57.

75400   Nassi, A.J., and Abramowitz, S.I. From phrenology to psychosurgery and back again: Biological studies of criminality. American Journal of Orthopsychiatry, 1976, 46(4), 591-607. Topic Codes: BB70D,BD11,BD70B,BEI1, BI11,BK11BL,CC81M,CG,CV06,DD02NF,DK07D,DK18SD,DT10B,MT04B,NH67D,NH74D, PM11,SH74D,TB35B,TB35BB,TB35D,TB78D.

75500   National Institute of Law Enforcement and Criminal Justice, Law Enforcement Assistance Administration. Correlates of Crime and Determinants of Criminal Behavior. Colloquium proceedings (part 1), Arlington, Virginia, March 30, 1978. Topic Codes: BB11,BD11,BI11,BK04D,BK11B,BL67D,BN04D, BN44D,CC11C,CC11D,CC11F,CC11G,CC11H,CC11I,CC11L,CC11M,CC11N,CC11S,CC11T, CC11U,CG11CC,CG11P,CV06C,DA04D,DA15D,DD02D,DK07D,DK09D,NL48.

75600   National Institute of Law Enforcement and Criminal Justice, Law Enforcement Assistance Administration. Correlates of Crime and Determinants of Criminal Behavior. Colloquium proceedings (part 2), Arlington, Virginia, March 31, 1978. Topic Codes: CC11,CQ11,NE11.

75650   National Institute of Mental Health. Report on the XYY Chromosomal Abnormality. Washington, D.C.: U.S. Government Printing Office, 1970. Topic Codes: BB70B,DD02ND.

75700   Nauta, W.J.H. Neural associations of the frontal cortex. Acta Neurobiologiae Experimentalis, 1972, 32, 125-140. Topic Codes: BK11B,DT59,MR,PS.

75800   Nauta, W.J.H. The problem of the frontal lobe: A reinterpretation. Journal of Psychiatric Research, 1971, 8, 167-187. Topic Codes: BK11B, DK07,DT13,MF,MH,MS,PE,PI,TA59D.

75900   Nebes, R.D. Handedness and the perception of part-whole relationship. Cortex, 1971, 7, 350-356. Topic Codes: BN44,DT13,MH,PI,PO.

76000   Needleman, H.L., Davidson, I., Sewell, E.M., and Shapiro, I.M. Subclinical lead exposure in Philadelphia school children: Identification by dentine lead analysis. New England Journal of Medicine, January 31, 1974, 290(5), 245-248. Topic Codes: BL11,DA44,NL07.

76050   Neki, J.S. Personality disorders: Some problems of nosology and classification. Australian Journal of Psychiatry, June 1973, 7(2), 78-83. Topic Codes: CC11P,MS,PT,TA59.

76100   Nelson, G.K. Neuropsychological research approaches in the epilepsies.

South African Medical Journal, March 30, 1974, 48, 657-660. Topic Codes: DA04,DK18B,DK18D,DK18SB,DK18SD,MD,MS04,PE06,TA59D,TB35,TB35BB,TB35D.

76130   Nelson, J.G. Creativity and delinquency as a function of physiological arousal and the stimulation-seeking motive: Test of a theory [doctoral dissertation, University of Wisconsin - Madison, 1976]. Dissertation Abstracts International, April 1977, 37(10), 6374A. Topic Codes: BN04D, CC37T,CC37W.

76150   Nelson, K.B. The "continuum of reproductive causality." In R. MacKeith and M. Bax (eds.), Clinics in Developmental Medicine, No. 27, Studies in Infancy. Suffolk, England: Spastics International Medical Publications in association with William Heinemann Medical Books, Ltd., 1968. Topic Codes: BP02,DF,DP11,NA31C.

76200   Nelson, K.B., and Broman, S.H. Perinatal risk factors in children with serious motor and mental handicaps. Annals of Neurology, November 1977, 2(5), 371-377. Topic Codes: BL06,BL27,BL48,BP26,DK,DK11,DK46,DP,DT04, DT08,DT48,MO,MT48,NA44D,NC44,NC59G,NJ06,PE48,PR,TB02.   .

76300   Nelson, K.B., and Deutschberger, J. Head size at one year as a predictor of four year IQ. Developmental Medicine and Child Neurology, 1970, 12, 487-495. Topic Codes: BE30C,BL11,BL67,BL70,DK46,MO,NA07I,NA44D,NC22, NC44,NC59G,NH59PJ,NJ06,PG,PM,SH59RJ,SN,SQ,TB78.

76400   Nelson, K.B., and Ellenberg, J.H. Neonatal signs as predictors of cere- bral palsy. Pediatrics, August 1979, 64(2), 225-232. Topic Codes: BD30, BD30B,BE30,BL07B,DF06B,DF34,DK07,DK11,DT08E,NA33,NA33B,NA33I,NA44D,NC44, NC70,NJ06,TA52M,TB02.

76500   Newcombe, F., and Ratcliff, G. Handedness, speech lateralization and ability. Neuropsychologia, 1973, 11, 399-407. Topic Codes: BL70,BN44, DK07B,DT06,DT42,ML,ML04,PE44,PN,PO,SQ,TB96.

76600   Nichols, P.L. Minimal brain dysfunction: Associations with behavior in infancy. Paper presented at the 85th annual convention of the American Psychological Association, San Francisco, California, August 26-30, 1977. Topic Codes: DK48,MG48,NA31A,NA31D,PE32.

76700   Nichols, P.L., and Anderson, V.E. Intellectual performance, race, and so- cioeconomic status. Social Biology, 1973, 20(4), 367-374. Topic Codes: BL67,NA44D,NC22,NC59,NC70,NJ06,PM,SN,SW,TB78,TB95,TB96.

76750   Nichols, P.L., and Broman, S.H. Familial resemblance in infant mental de- velopment. Developmental Psychology, 1974, 10, 442-446. Topic Codes: BI,BL31,BL67,BL70,NA31F,NC44,NC80,NH70,NH74,PK,PM,SH70,SH74,SN,SQ,TB05.

76790   Nichols, P.L., and Chen, T.C. Minimal Brain Dysfunction: A Prospective Study. Hillsdale, New Jersey: Lawrence Erlbaum Associates, 1981. Topic Codes: BI07,BK11B,BL07,BL11,BL22,BL27,BL52DB,BL67,BL67B,BL70,BL70B,BP02, BP02B,BP22F,BP44,BP47,BP48,BP52,BP61,BP63,BP70,DD02B,DD26,DD26B,DF,DF34, DF48,DK07B,DK46,DK46B,DK48,DK48B,DP,DP44,DP46,DP48,DP58,DP60,DT08,DT08E, DT44,DT44B,DT48,DT48B,MG,MG48,MG48B,MM,MM07,MT,N,NC,NC70,PE10,PE48,PE48B, PE64,PE64B,PG,PP,PP07,PR,PR07,SC,SC70,SC70B,SH04B,SH59B,SH59J,SH59JB, SH59R,SH59RA,SH59RB,SH59RF,SH59RH,SH70,SI48,SI48B,SN,SN07,SQ,SQ07,SW,SW07, SW16,TB02,TB05,TB09,TB35,TB44,TB66B,TB84,TB98B.

76800   Nichols, P.L., Chen, T.C., and Pomeroy, J.D. Minimal brain dysfunction: The association among symptoms. Paper presented at the 84th annual con- vention of the American Psychological Association, Washington, D.C., Sep- tember 3-7, 1976. Topic Codes: BL48B,BL67B,DK48,DP11B,DT44B,DT52B,MG, NA44D,NC70,TB09B,TB27,TB33B,TB42,TB53,TB84,TB95B.

76820   Nield, J.B. A study of birth order and family constellation among high school and delinquent students [doctoral dissertation, Idaho State Univer- sity, 1976]. Dissertation Abstracts International, December 1976, 37(6), 3527A. Topic Codes: CC37J,CC37M,CQ37,NE37,NH59F,PE64D,SC70D,SH59H,SI11, SI57D,SJ07D,SJ09D.

76840   Nielsen, J. Criminality among patients with Klinefelter's syndrome and the XYY syndrome. British Journal of Psychiatry, 1970, 117, 365-369. Topic Codes: BB70B,BB70D,BI,CC11C,CC11M,MS04,PM,TB35.

76860   Nielsen, J. The XYY syndrome in a mental hospital. British Journal of Criminology, 1968, 8(2), 186-203. Topic Codes: BB70B,BB70D,BI07,CC11C, CC11M.

76880   Nielsen, J., and Friedrich, U. Length of the Y chromosome in criminal males. Clinical Genetics, 1972, 3(4), 281-285. Topic Codes: BB70D,BI11, CC11M,CQ59,DD02NF,NE59,NL,TA80.

76890   Nielsen, J., and Henriksen, F. Incidence of chromosome aberrations among males in a Danish youth prison. Acta Psychiatrica Scandinavica, 1972, 48(2), 87-102. Topic Codes: BB70B,BB70D,BI11,CC11C,CC11M,CC37B,CC37M, CC37N,NH59GD,NH59GI,NH59PF,NH59PL,NH67D,NH70D.

76900   Nielsen, J., and Tsuboi, T. Correlation between stature, character disorder and criminality. British Journal of Psychiatry, 1970, 116, 145-150. Topic Codes: BB70B,BB70D,BE11,BI07B,BI11,BL04D,CC11C,CC11D,CC11M,CC37BB, CC37N,MS04B.

76920   Nielsen, J., Tsuboi, T., Sturup, G., and Romano, D. XYY chromosomal constitution in criminal psychopaths. Lancet, September 7, 1968, 567, 276. Topic Codes: BB70D,BI11,CC11M,CQ11,CQ59,DD02NF,NE11,NE59.

76930   Nielsen, J., Tsuboi, T., Tuver, B., Jensen, J.T., and Sachs, J. Prevalence and incidence of the XYY syndrome and Klinefelter's syndrome in an institution for criminal psychopaths. Acta Psychiatrica Scandinavica, 1969, 45(4), 402-424. Topic Codes: BB70B,BB70D,BE11,CC11C,CC11M,MS04B.

76950   Niswander, K.R. Obstetric factors related to prematurity. In D.M. Reed and F.J. Stanley (eds.), The Epidemiology of Prematurity (vol. 31, no. 4). Baltimore: Urban & Schwarzenberg, 1977. Topic Codes: BL07,BL22,BL27, BP02,BP22F,BP44,BP46,BP47,BP53,BP57,BP59,BP70,DD08,DF06,DF60,DP,DP44,DP46, DP81,NC59G,TA52.

76970   Niswander, K.R., and Drage, J.S. Environment and reproduction: The American study; proceedings of the VIII World Congress of Gynecology and Obstetrics. In L. Castelazo-Ayala and C. MacGregor (eds.), Excerpta Medica International Congress Series No. 412, Gynecology and Obstetrics. New York: Elsevier, 1977. Topic Codes: BP44,SF.

76990   Niswander, K.R., Friedman, E.A., and Berendes, H. Do placenta previa, abruptio placentae and prolapsed cord cause neurologic damage to the infant who survives? In R. MacKeith and M. Bax (eds.), Clinics in Developmental Medicine, No. 27, Studies in Infancy. Suffolk, England: Spastics International Medical Publications in association with William Heinemann Medical Books, Ltd., 1968. Topic Codes: DF,DK09,DP11,DP44,DP58,NA31C.

77000   Niswander, K.R., and Gordon, M. The Women and Their Pregnancies: The Collaborative Perinatal Study of the National Institute of Neurological Diseases and Stroke (DHEW publication no. NIH 73-379). Washington, D.C.: U.S. Government Printing Office, 1972. Topic Codes: BD30BA,BK11,BL04, BL05,BL06,BL07B,BL22,BL27KL,BP07,BP22,BP26GD,BP44,BP46,BP47,BP48,BP53, BP57,BP59,DD05,DD08,DF06B,DF48,DF60B,DF67B,DF70B,DK07,DK09,DK11,DP11,DP44, DP46,DP48,DP60,DP81,NA33B,NA33F,NA33I,NC44,NC59,NH59PA,NH59PH,NH59PP,NH70, NH74,NL,PE34,PL,SF26,SH59J,SH59RA,SH59RF,SH59RH,SH59RP,SH70,SH74,SJ07,SN, SQ,SW,TA52,TA52M,TA80.

77100   Niswander, K.R., Gordon, M., and Drage, J.S. The effect of intrauterine hypoxia on the child surviving to 4 years. American Journal of Obstetrics and Gynecology, April 1, 1975, 121(7), 892-899. Topic Codes: BL07B,BL48, BP61,DF06B,DK07,DK11,DK48,DP,DP44,DP58,DT04,DT48,MG48,MT48,NA44,NC22,NC44, NJ,PE48,PR,TB02,TB05,TB78.

77200   Niswander, K., and Jackson, E.C. Physical characteristics of the gravida and their association with birth weight and perinatal death. American

Journal of Obstetrics and Gynecology, June 1, 1974, 119(3), 306-313.
Topic Codes: BL06,BL07,BP02,BP59,DF48,NA44,NC44,NC59G.NH59PP.

77220   Nordund, O. Behavior problems of pre-school children. *Skolepsykologi*,
1976, 13(1), 43-50 (in Swedish). Topic Codes: CC37B,CC37M,CQ37,MG11,MK,
NA07D,NE37,PE10,PE30,SR01.

77240   Norland, S., and Shaver, N. Gender roles and female criminality: Some
critical comments. *Criminology*, May 1977, 15(1), 87-104. Topic Codes:
BL70D,CC11S,CC24,SQ70D.

77260   Norton, A. The concept of dangerousness. *Journal of Medical Ethics*, December 1976, 2(4), 160-162. Topic Codes: CC81,CQ81,CT81,CY,NE81.

77280   Norwood, D.J. An experimental study of the comparative effects of aggressive film and television content on physiological arousal and psychological mood [doctoral dissertation, Southern Illinois University, 1976].
Dissertation Abstracts International, March 1977, 37(9), 5406A. Topic
Codes: BN04,MC,PT74,SF.

77300   Nye, F.I. *Family Relationships and Delinquent Behavior*. New York: John
Wiley & Sons, Inc., 1958. Topic Codes: BL70D,CC37BB,CC37G,CC37K,CC37M,
CC37W,CC37Z,CC371,CJ,CQ37,CV,N,SF26D,SF26DD,SH11,SH59,SH59D,SH59J,SH59RF,
SH59RP,SI11,SI22D,SI48D,SI57D,SI57J,SI57PB,SJ07D,SJ09D,SJ22D,SQ11,SS09,
SU11,SW11.

77302   Nygard, N.K. A test of Hare's temporal conflict model of psychopathy
[doctoral dissertation, University of Iowa, 1974]. *Dissertation Abstracts International*, January 1975, 35(7), 3590B-3591B. Topic Codes:
CC11C,CQ59,DT44BB,MS04B,PY,SI57J.

77305   Nyhan, W.L. Behavior in the Lesch-Nyhan Syndrome. *Journal of Autism and
Childhood Schizophrenia*, September 1976, 6(3), 235-252. Topic Codes:
BB70B,BI07,CV06C,CV15B,CV30B,DD02ND,DK46B,DT44B,MC,MM07,MO07,PE04,PP07,
SL07,SR03,TA02.

77310   O'Banion, D., Armstrong, B., Cummings, R.A., and Stange, J. Disruptive
behavior: A dietary approach. *Journal of Autism and Childhood Schizophrenia*, September 1978, 8(3), 325-337. Topic Codes: BD52B,CV52B,MG30.

77315   O'Callaghan, C.A. A general systems theory approach to the diagnosis of
emotional, behavioral, and learning disorders of childhood [doctoral dissertation, Boston University School of Education, 1976]. *Dissertation
Abstracts International*, February 1976, 36(8), 5199A-5200A. Topic Codes:
DT44,MG.

77318   Ochitill, H.N., and Krieger, M. Violent behavior among hospitalized medical and surgical patients. *Southern Medical Journal*, February 1982, 75
(2), 151-155. Topic Codes: CC81D,CC81P,CC81R,CV30D,DD01,DK07,SL11.

77320   O'Conner, M., Dollinger, S., Kennedy, S., and Polletiersmetko, P. Proso-
cial behavior and psychopathology in emotionally disturbed boys. *American
Journal of Orthopsychiatry*, April 1979, 49(2), 301-310. Topic Codes: MC,
MG11,MX07,NA07D,NL48B,PE04,PE10,PT74,SR02,TA02,TA57,TA74.

77325   O'Connor, B.E. A comparison of children labeled learning disabled and
children labeled behavioral disordered on a set of measures of cognitive,
academic, and visual-motor behaviors [doctoral dissertation, Purdue University, 1976]. *Dissertation Abstracts International*, February 1977, 37
(8), 5042A. Topic Codes: BL48B,DT13B,DT44,MG,TB09B,TB09K,TB33B,TB33G,
TB74,TB95B,TB98B.

77328   Odell, L.M. Maternal intellectual functioning. *Johns Hopkins Medical
Journal*, June 1971, 128, 362-368. Topic Codes: BL11,BL67,NC59G,NC70,
NH59P,PM,TB76,TB95.

77330   Oettinger, L., Jr., Majovski, L.V., and Gauch, R.R. Coding A and coding B of the WISC are not equivalent tasks. Perceptual and Motor Skills, December 1978, 47(3, part 1), 987-991. Topic Codes: DK48,TB95.

77335   Offer, D. Rebellion and anti-social behavior. American Journal of Psychoanalysis, 1971, 31(1), 13-19. Topic Codes: BL11,MC,ME,NA07B.

77400   Offer, D., Marohn, R., and Ostrov, E. Delinquent and normal adolescents. Comprehensive Psychiatry, July/August 1972, 13(4), 347-355. Topic Codes: CC37B,CC37I,CC37J,CC37W,DA04D,MG,PM11,TA03,TA59.

77500   Offer, D., Marohn, R.C., and Ostrov, E. The Psychological World of the Juvenile Delinquent. New York: Basic Books, Inc., 1979. Topic Codes: BL48D,CC37B,CC37H,CC37T,CC37W,DK07D,DT44D,TA03,TA59.

77600   Offer, D., Marohn, R.C., and Ostrov, E. Violence among hospitalized delinquents. Archives of General Psychiatry, 1975, 32, 1180-1186. Topic Codes: CC37B,CC37T,CC81D,MK11,PM11,SB11.

77700   Offord, D.R. The natural histories of schizophrenia, depression, disorder and psychopathy: Current status. Psychosomatics, 1971, 12, 179-185. Topic Codes: MB,MG02B,MS04,MU70,PM07.

77800   Offord, D.R., Abrams, N., Allen, N., and Poushinsky, M. Broken homes, parental psychiatric illness, and female delinquency. American Journal of Orthopsychiatry, April 1979, 49(2), 253-264. Topic Codes: CC24,CC37BB, CC37M,CC37Z,NH59B,NH59F,SH59B,SH59H,SJ09D,SJ22D,SW11.

77900   Offord, D.R., Allen, N., and Abrams, N. Parental psychiatric illness, broken homes, and delinquency. Journal of the American Academy of Child Psychiatry, 1978, 17(2), 224-237. Topic Codes: CC37BB,CC37M,CC37Z,NH59B, NH59F,SJ09D,SJ22D,SW11.

78000   Offord, D.R., and Poushinsky, M.F. School performance, IQ and delinquency. British Journal of Criminology, April 1978, 18(2), 110-126. Topic Codes: CC37BB,CC37J,CC37Q,CC37Z,MG,NH59B,NH59F,PE64D,PM11.

78100   Offord, D.R., and Poushinsky, M.F. School performance, IQ and female delinquency. International Journal of Social Psychiatry, 1981, 27(1), 53-62. Topic Codes: CC37B,CC37H,CC37J,CC37M,CC37Q,CG11C,CQ22,MM11,NE22, NH59F,NH70D,NL22D,PE64D,PM11,PP11,SC70D,SH59H,SH70D,SJ09D,SJ22D,TA03,TA04, TA57,TA59D,TA74.

78150   Ohman, A., and Hygge, S. When apple definitions become orange realities in banana theories: Epistemological and psychophysiological considerations on Lindahl's analysis of vicarious instigation research. Scandinavian Journal of Psychology, 1977, 18(2), 92-102. Topic Codes: CG.

78200   Okasha, A., Sadek, A., and Moneim, A. Psychosocial and electroencephalographic studies of Egyptian murderers. British Journal of Psychiatry, 1975, 126, 34-40. Topic Codes: CC11C,CC11O,CC11U,CC81D,CC81R,CC81Y, CT57F,DK18D,MB11,MS04B,MU70B,TB35D,TB86C.

78300   O'Keefe, E.J. Porteus Maze Q-score as a measure of impulsivity. Perceptual and Motor Skills, 1975, 41, 675-678. Topic Codes: CC37B,CC371,MK11, TB66D.

78400   O'Leary, K.D., O'Leary, S., and Becker, W.C. Modification of a deviant sibling interaction pattern in the home. Behavior Research and Therapy, 1967, 5, 113-120. Topic Codes: CV06,MG,SI07.

78430   Oliva, C.F. A study of the relationship between age, cortical integrity, and reading level [doctoral dissertation, George Peabody College for Teachers, 1977]. Dissertation Abstracts International, November 1977, 38(5), 2379B. Topic Codes: BK11B,BL04,BN44H,DK07,DK09,DT44,MM,NA07D,PM, PO33,PP,TA55,TA59D.

78500   Olton, D.S. Spatial memory. Scientific American, June 1977, 236(6), 82-98. Topic Codes: DT13,DT46,MH,MN,PI,PQ.

78600   Olweus, D. Antisocial behavior in the school setting. In R.D. Hare and
         D. Schalling (eds.), Psychopathic Behavior: Approaches to Research. New
         York: John Wiley & Sons, Inc., 1978. Topic Codes: ME,MG11,MS04,NA07B,
         PE08,PE64,SC70,SR04.

78610   Olweus, D. Testosterone in the development of aggressive antisocial be-
         havior in adolescents. In K.T. Van Dusen and S.A. Mednick (eds.), Pro-
         spective Studies of Crime and Delinquency. Boston: Kluwer-Nijhoff Pub-
         lishing, 1983, 237-247. Topic Codes: BD70B,MC,NA07B,PE04,PE10,SR03.

78615   Olweus, D., Mattsson, A., Schalling, D., and Low, H. Testosterone, ag-
         gression, physical, and personality dimensions in normal adolescent males.
         Psychosomatic Medicine, March 1980, 42(2), 253-269. Topic Codes: BD70B,
         BE,MC,ME,NA07B.

78650   O'Malley, J.E., and Eisenberg, L. The hyperkinetic syndrome. Seminars
         in Psychiatry, 1973, 5, 95-103. Topic Codes: DK48B,DT13,DT44,MG30,MK.

78700   O'Neal, P., Robins, L.N., King, L.J., and Schaefer, J. Parental deviance
         and the genesis of sociopathic personality. American Journal of Psychia-
         try, June 1962, 118, 1114-1124. Topic Codes: MS04,NA44,NH59B,NH59E,
         NH59GB,NH59GG,NH59PB,NH59PJ,NJ,SH59B,SH59F,SH59JB,SH59JJ,SH59RB,SH59RJ,
         SI22B,SI48B,SI57BB,SW07B.

78800   Ontario Perinatal Mortality Study Committee. Second Report of the Peri-
         natal Mortality Study, with a Supplement. Toronto, Ontario: Ontario De-
         partment of Health, 1967. Topic Codes: DF48,DP48.

78900   Orme, J.E. Left-handedness, ability and emotional instability. British
         Journal of Social and Clinical Psychology, 1970, 9, 87-88. Topic Codes:
         BL11,BN44,DT42,PE64,TA04,TA59D.

79000   Osborn, S.G., and West, D.J. Conviction records of fathers and sons com-
         pared. British Journal of Criminology, April 1979, 19(2), 120-133. Topic
         Codes: CC11L,CC37L,NH59GD,NH59GI,SH59JD,SH59JL.

79100   Oshea, H.E., Oshea, E.H., and Higbe, R.V. Studies of B vitamins in the
         human subject: IV. Mental changes in experimental deficiency. American
         Journal of Medical Sciences, 1942, 1203, 388-397. Topic Codes: BD52,
         CV52.

79180   Ostroff, R., and Novelly, R.A. Adult minimal brain dysfunction and anti-
         social personality disorder. Journal of Psychiatric Treatment and Evalua-
         tion, 1982, 4(2), 147-148. Topic Codes: DK48B,MS04.

79200   Ostrov, E., Offer, D., Marohn, R.C., and Rosenwein, T. The "impulsivity
         index": Its application to juvenile delinquency. Journal of Youth and
         Adolescence, 1972, 1(2), 179-196. Topic Codes: CC37W,CC371,CG11T,MK11,
         PE30D,TB64B,TB96D.

79205   Ottenberg, P. Violence in the family: Abused wives and children. Bul-
         letin of the American Academy of Psychiatry and Law, 1977, 5(4), 380-390.
         Topic Codes: CT57B,DD10,MH11,NH11,SH11,SI57G.

79207   Otto, U. Male youths: A sociopsychiatric study of a total annual popula-
         tion of Swedish adolescent boys. Acta Psychiatrica Scandinavica, 1976,
         supplement 264, 5-312. Topic Codes: BE07,DD81B,DK18B,DT13B,DT44B,MG18,
         MH07,MM07,MP07,MQ,MS,PE52B,PE64B,PE68B,PM07,PP07,PT,SC70B,TA52,TA59D.

79210   Ounsted, C. Aggression and epilepsy rage in children with temporal lobe
         epilepsy. Journal of Psychosomatic Research, 1969, 13, 237-242. Topic
         Codes: BL70,DK09B,DK18D,MC,MG,PM07.

79212   Ouston, J. Delinquency, family background and educational attainment.
         British Journal of Criminology, January 1984, 24(1), 2-26. Topic Codes:
         CC37J,CC37M,NH,PE64D,SC70D,SH,SI11.

79215   Owen, D.R.   The 47, XYY male: A review.   Psychological Bulletin, September 1972, 78(3), 209-233.   Topic Codes: BB70B,BB70D,BE,CC11M,CC37N,MF,PM.

79217   Owen, G.M., and Lubin, A.H.   Anthropometric differences between black and
white preschool children.   American Journal of Diseases of Children,
August 1973, 126, 168-169.   Topic Codes: BE,BL04,BL11,BL67,BL70.

79220   Pacht, A.R., and Cowden, J.E.   An exploratory study of five hundred sex
offenders.   Criminal Justice and Behavior, March 1974, 1(1), 13-20.   Topic
Codes: BD70B,CC11C,CC11D,CT68,MV11,PE66D,SR69D.

79225   Pagelow, M.D.   Violence in families: Is there an intergenerational trans-
mission?   Paper presented at the annual meeting of the Society for the
Study of Social Problems, 1982.   Topic Codes: CC81F,CC81N,NH11,NH59GD,
NH59GI,NH59PD,NH59PL.

79227   Paget, K.D.   Intellectual patterns of conduct problem children on the
WISC-R.   Psychology in the Schools, October 1982, 19(4), 439-445.   Topic
Codes: MG11,PM07,TB96B.

79230   Palmer, L.L.   Inability to wink an eye and eye dominance.   Perceptual and
Motor Skills, June 1976, 42(3, part 1), 825-826.   Topic Codes: BL48,BN44,
DD81,DT48,NA07,PE48,PO,TA52.

79240   Palmer, L.L.   Unilateral ocular suppression and tests of eye dominance.
Perceptual and Motor Skills, June 1976, 42(3, part 2), 1089-1090.   Topic
Codes: BN44,PO.

79245   Palmour, R.M.   Genetic models for the study of aggressive behavior.   Progress in Neuro-psychopharmacology and Biological Psychiatry, 1983, 7(4-6),
513-517.   Topic Codes: BI07,MC,PE04,SR03.

79260   Panton, J.H.   Significant increase in MMPI MF scores within a state prison
population.   Journal of Clinical Psychology, July 1976, 32(3), 604-606.
Topic Codes: CC11C,CC11P,CC11U,PT11,TB61B.

79270   Papatheophilou, R., and Turland, D.N.   The electroencephalogram of normal
adolescent males: Visual assessment and relationship with other variables.   Developmental Medicine and Child Neurology, October 1976, 18(5),
603-619.   Topic Codes: BL11,DK07,DT67,MG,NA07I,PG,SW,TB35.

79280   Papen, J.H.   The differential effects of field orientation and maturity of
moral judgment of preferred delinquent style in a seriously delinquent
population [doctoral dissertation, Rosemead Graduate School of Psychology,
1976].   Dissertation Abstracts International, December 1976, 37(6),
3527A-3528A.   Topic Codes: CC37B,CC37H,CC37W,CC37Z,CE,CQ59,MS02,MX11,
NE59,PT11,PY11,SQ11,SR02,SU11,SW11,TA03,TA59,TB23B.

79300   Papousek, H., and Papousek, M.   Cognitive aspects of preverbal social in-
teraction between human infants and adults.   CIBA Symposium on Parent-
Child Interaction.   Amsterdam: North Holland, 1975.   Topic Codes: BK04,
BL31,BL48,DT13,DT48,MH,MT48,MV,NA31D,NA31F,PE32,PE48,PE66,PI,PK,PR,SI48,
SR69.

79330   Parashar, O.D.   Investigation of the academically relevant disturbed
classroom behaviors of the clinically diagnosed mentally retarded, learn-
ing disabled and emotionally disturbed children as measured by the
Devereux Elementary School Behavior Rating Scale [doctoral dissertation,
University of Cincinnati, 1973].   Dissertation Abstracts International,
March 1974, 34(9, part 2), 5758A-5759A.   Topic Codes: DK46B,DT44B,MG,
MM07,MO07,PE64,PP07,SC70,TA02.

79360   Parashar, O.D.   Psycho-Educational Diagnosis.   New York: Carlton, 1976.
Topic Codes: MG,NA07D,PE64,SC70.

79390   Park, G.E., and Schneider, K.A.   Thyroid function in relation to dyslexia.
Journal of Reading Behavior, Summer 1975, 7(2), 197-199.   Topic Codes:
DD00,DT15,ML15.

79400   Park, J., Johnson, R.C., Defries, J.C., McClearn, G.E., Mi, M.P., Rashad, M.N., Vandenberg, S.G., and Wilson, J.R. Parent-offspring resemblance for specific cognitive abilities in Korea. Behavior Genetics, 1978, 8(1), 43-52. Topic Codes: BI,BL11,DT13,MH,NH59,PI,SH59.

79460   Parmelee, A.H., Kopp, C.B., and Sigman, M. Selection of developmental assessment techniques for infants at risk. Merrill-Palmer Quarterly of Behavior and Development, July 1976, 22(3), 177-199. Topic Codes: BL07B, DF06B,DF34,DP11,DP44,NA31C,NA31D,NA31R,NA33A,NA33B,NA33I,PE32,TA52K,TA52M.

79490   Parr, V.E. Auditory word discrimination in male children diagnosed as having minimal brain dysfunction. Journal of Clinical Psychology, October 1977, 33(4), 1064-1069. Topic Codes: DK48B,DT42,MG48B,ML,PE44,PN.

79495   Parrott, C.A., and Strongman, K.T. Locus of control and delinquency. Adolescence, Summer 1984, 19(74), 459-471. Topic Codes: CC37,CC37J, CC37M,CC37W,CQ37,PE64D,SC70D,SJ07D.

79500   Pasamanick, B. Epidemiologic studies on the complications of pregnancy and the birth process. In G. Caplan (ed.), Prevention of Mental Disorders in Children. New York: Basic Books, 1961. Topic Codes: BL07BB, BL11,BL27KL,BL31,BL67B,BP,DD02B,DF06BB,DF70B,DP,NA31A,NA31F,PK,SF07,TA80.

79600   Pasamanick, B., and Knobloch, H. Brain and behavior: Session II symposium, 1959, brain damage and reproductive casualty. American Journal of Orthopsychiatry, 1960, 30, 298-305. Topic Codes: BL67,BP02B,BP52,DK07B, DP11B,MG30,SW07.

79650   Pasamanick, B., and Knobloch, H. Retrospective studies on the epidemiology of reproductive casualty: Old and new. Merrill-Palmer Quarterly of Behavior and Development, 1966, 12, 1-26. Topic Codes: BP02B,BP59,DF48, DK09B,DP11B,DP44,SW07.

79700   Pasamanick, B., Knobloch, H., and Lilienfeld, A.M. Socioeconomic status and some precursors of neuropsychiatric disorder. American Journal of Orthopsychiatry, 1956, 26, 594-601. Topic Codes: BL06,BL31,BL67,BP02B, DF60B,DK07B,DP11B,DP44,DP60,DP81,MF,NA31D,PE,PM,SW07,TB42.

79800   Pasamanick, B., and Lilienfeld, A.M. Association of maternal and fetal factors with development of mental deficiency: 1. Abnormalities in the prenatal and paranatal periods. Journal of the American Medical Association, September 1955, 159(3), 155-160. Topic Codes: BL07BB,BL70,DF06BB, DF60B,DK07B,DK46,DP11B,DT04EB,MO,NA33A,SQ.

79900   Pasamanick, B., Rogers, M.E., and Lilienfeld, A.M. Pregnancy experience and the development of behavior disorder in children. American Journal of Psychiatry, February 1956, 112, 613-618. Topic Codes: BP02B,DP11B,MG.

80000   Passingham, R.E. Brain size and intelligence in man. Brain Behavior and Evolution, 1979, 16, 253-270. Topic Codes: BE30C,BK11B,BL70,PM,SQ,SW, TB93,TB96.

80020   Pasternack, S.A. Evaluation of dangerous behavior of active duty servicemen. Military Medicine, February 1971, 136(2), 110-113. Topic Codes: CC11F,CC11S,CC81,MG02B,MG02D.

80030   Pastor, D.L., and Swap, S.M. An ecological study of emotionally disturbed preschoolers in special and regular classes. Exceptional Children, November 1978, 45(3), 213-215. Topic Codes: CV06,MG,NA07D,PE64,SC59.

80040   Patalano, F. Comments on criminal offenders and the WAIS picture arrangement "hold-up" item. Psychological Reports, December 1976, 39(3, part 2), 1148-1150. Topic Codes: CC11U,CV06,MG,NA07D,SC59,TB93D.

80050   Patil, S.R., Lubs, H.A., Kimberling, W.J., Brown, J., Cohen, M., Gerald, P., Hecht, F., Moorhead, P., Myrianthopoulos, N.C., and Summitt, R.L. Chromosomal abnormalities ascertained in a collaborative survey of 4,342 seven- and eight-year-old children: Frequency, phenotype and epidemiolo-

gy; proceedings of a symposium on human population cytogenetics. In E.B.
Hook and I.H. Porter (eds.), Population Cytogenetics: Studies in Humans.
New York: Academic Press, 1977. Topic Codes: BB70,BI,BL11,DD02N,NA07I,
NA44D,NC70,NJ06,PG.

80060   Paty, J., and Benezech, M. EEG studies in male polygonosomic psychopaths
(47, XYY and 47, XXY). British Journal of Psychiatry, September 1978,
133, 285-286. Topic Codes: BB70B,MS04,TB35BB.

80080   Pauleikhoff, B., and Hoffmann, D. Thefts without motive of gain as a psy-
chopathologic syndrome. Fortschritte der Neurologie, Psychiatrie und
Ihrer Grenzgebiete, May 1974, 43(5), 254-271 (in German). Topic Codes:
CT59,MS04B.

80090   Paulsen, K., and O'Donnell, J.P. Construct validation of children's behavior problem dimensions: Relationship to activity level, impulsivity,
and soft neurological signs. Journal of Psychology, March 1979, 101(second half), 273-278. Topic Codes: DT52B,MG,MK,NA07B.

80100   Paulson, M.J., Stone, D., and Sposto, R. Suicide potential and behavior
in children ages 4-12. Suicide and Life Threatening Behavior, Winter
1978, 8(4), 225-242. Topic Codes: MB,MZ,NA07B,NA07D,NH11.

80130   Payne, C., McCabe, S., and Walker, N. Predicting offender-patients' re-
convictions. British Journal of Psychiatry, July 1974, 125, 60-64.
Topic Codes: CC11C,CC67,MB11,MS04B,MU70B.

80160   Pazzaglia, P., and Frank-Pazzaglia, L. Record in grade school of pupils
with epilepsy: An epidemiological study. Epilepsia, December 1976,
17(4), 361-366. Topic Codes: BL11,DK18,MG,PE64,TA74.

80200   Pearce, J.W. Relationship of socioeconomic status and aggression in preschool children. Psychological Reports, 1978, 43(2), 379-382. Topic
Codes: MC,NA07B,SW.

80300   Pearson, V.L. A study of relationships between the Porteus Maze tests and
recidivism rates of female correctional institution inmates [doctoral
dissertation, Texas Women's University, 1972]. Dissertation Abstracts
International, 1973. Topic Codes: CC11U,CC24,CC67,CQ22,CQ67,NE22,NE67,
TB66D.

80350   Pederson, F.A., Rubenstein, J.L., and Yarrow, L.J. Infant development in
father-absent families. Journal of Genetic Psychology, 1979, 135, 51-61.
Topic Codes: BL31,NL07,SI59,SJ09,TB05.

80400   Penchaszadeh, V.B., Hardy, J.B., Mellits, E.D., Cohen, B.H., and McKusick,
V.A. Growth and development in an "inner city" population: An assessment
of possible biological and environmental influences: I. Intra-uterine
growth. Johns Hopkins Medical Journal, June 1972, 130, 384-397. Topic
Codes: BL06,BL22,BL27,BL67,BP22F,BP26,BP46,BP70,DF48,DK,DP48,SN.

80500   Penchaszadeh, V.B., Hardy, J.B., Mellits, E.D., Cohen, B.H., and McKusick,
V.A. Growth and development in an "inner city" population: An assessment
of possible biological and environmental influences: II. The effect of
certain maternal characteristics on birth weight, gestational age and
intra-uterine growth. Johns Hopkins Medical Journal, July 1972, 131,
11-23. Topic Codes: BL06,BL22,BL25,BL27,BL67,BP22F,BP46,BP70,NC44,NC59G,
SN.

80550   Penner, M.J. Role of selected health problems in the causation of juvenile delinquency. Adolescence, Summer 1982, 17(66), 347-368. Topic
Codes: CC37P,CC37T,DD01.

80600   Pepitone, A. The social psychology of violence. International Journal
of Group Tensions, 1972, 2(2), 19-32. Topic Codes: CC81.

80700   Pepitone, A., and Dinubile, M. Contrast effects in judgment of crime severity and the punishment of criminal violators. Journal of Personality

and Social Psychology, April 1976, 33(4), 448-459. Topic Codes: CE, CV13D.

80750   Perry, L., Harburg, E., and Crowley, J.E. Urban families and assault: A framework for research focused on black families. Unpublished manuscript, University of Michigan, 1978. Topic Codes: CC11,CC11L,CC37K,CC37M,CG, CQ11,CT57,NE11,NH11,NL07D,SF26DD,SH11,SI11,SW11.

80760   Perry, R.W. Social status and the black violence hypothesis. Journal of Social Psychology, June 1980, 111(1), 131-137. Topic Codes: BL04D,BL67D, CC11A,CC11R,CC11T,CC81A,CC81U,CC81W,SW11.

80800   Persky, H., Smith, K.D., and Basu, G.K. Relation of psychologic measures of aggression and hostility to testosterone production in man. Psychosomatic Medicine, May-June 1971, 33(3), 265-277. Topic Codes: BD70B,BL04, MB,MC,TB19.

80830   Persons, R.W. Psychometric evaluation of sociological factors in a boys' reformatory. Psychological Reports, October 1970, 27(2), 407-413. Topic Codes: CC37K,CC37W,CG11CC,CQ59,CV06C,CV13DA,MS02,NE59,PT11,SF11,SS09, TA59,TA70.

80860   Persons, R.W., and Marks, P.A. The violent 4-3 MMPI personality type. Journal of Consulting and Clinical Psychology, April 1971, 36(2), 189-196. Topic Codes: CC11P,CC81S,CC81Y,PT11,TB61B.

80890   Persson, T. An XYY man and his relatives. Journal of Mental Deficiency Research, December 1967, 11(4), 239-245. Topic Codes: BB70B,BB70D,BE07, CC11M,ME,NH59E,NH70B,PM.

80900   Peter, B.M., and Spreen, O. Behavior rating and personal adjustment scales of neurologically and learning handicapped children during adolescence and early adulthood: Results of a follow-up study. Journal of Clinical Neuropsychology, 1979, 1(1), 75-92. Topic Codes: DK07B,DK48B, DT44B,MG,PA.

80950   Peterfy, G., Solyom, L., Kendall, A., and Turcan, M. The relationship between ABO blood groups and schizophrenia: A report of negative findings. Canadian Psychiatric Association Journal, August 1976, 21(5), 303-307. Topic Codes: BD30,MU70.

80980   Petersen, K.G., Matousek, M., Mednick, S.A., Volavka, J., and Pollock, V. EEG antecedents of thievery. Acta Psychiatrica Scandinavica, May 1982, 65(5), 331-338. Topic Codes: CC37F,CC371,CT59,TB35D.

81000   Peterson, L.R. Short-term memory. Scientific American, July 1966, 215(1), 90-95. Topic Codes: DT44,DT46,MM,MN,PP,PQ.

81100   Petrauskas, R., and Rourke, B. Identification of subtypes of retarded readers: A neuropsychological, multivariate approach. Journal of Clinical Neuropsychology, 1979, 1(1), 17-37. Topic Codes: BL04B,BL48B,BL70B, DT15,DT42,DT44,DT59,MG,ML15,NA07D,TB98B.

81200   Pfeffer, C.R. Psychiatric hospital treatment of assaultive homicidal children. American Journal of Psychotherapy, April 1980, 34(2), 197-207. Topic Codes: CC37B,CT57F,CV06C,CV30B,CV30D.

81210   Pfeffer, C.R., Plutchik, R., and Mizruchi, M.S. Predictors of assaultiveness in latency age children. American Journal of Psychiatry, January 1983, 140(1),31-35. Topic Codes: CC37G,CC37H,CC37Q,CT59B,MG,MG11B,NA07D.

81220   Pfeffer, C.R., Plutchik, R., and Mizruchi, M.S. Suicidal and assaultive behavior in children: Classification, measurement and interrelations. American Journal of Psychiatry, February 1983, 140(2), 154-157. Topic Codes: MG,MZ,NA07D,NH59B,NH59E,SH59B,SH59F.

81300   Phillips, I. Annual progress in child psychiatry and child development:

Book review. <u>Journal of the American Academy of Child Psychiatry</u>, October 1975, 14(4), 737-738. Topic Codes: BL11C,CV06,MG,NA07D,NA07ID,PG11.

81400   Piddington, M., and Piddington, R. Report of fieldwork in northwestern Australia. <u>Oceania</u>, 1932, 2, 342-358. Topic Codes: BL67,TA59D.

81500   Pihl, R.O., and Parkes, M. Hair element content in learning disabled children. <u>Science</u>, October 14, 1977, 198, 204-206. Topic Codes: DA44M, DT44,MM,PP,TA59D.

81600   Pikler, E. The competence of the infant. <u>Acta Paediatrica Academiae Scientarum Hungaricae</u>, 1979, 20(2-3), 185-192. Topic Codes: BL31,NA31D, NA31F,PE32,PK,SI48,TB57.

81630   Pilling, E.K. A comparison of visual discrimination ability between non-defective, brain-injured children and normals [doctoral dissertation, Brigham Young University, 1974]. <u>Dissertation Abstracts International</u>, July 1974, 35(1), 521B. Topic Codes: DK07,DK48.

81660   Pincus, J.H., and Glaser, G.H. The syndrome of "minimal brain damage" in childhood. <u>New England Journal of Medicine</u>, 1966, 275, 27-35. Topic Codes: DD00B,DK18SB,DK48,MG30,PM,TB35B.

81700   Pincus, J.H., and Tucker, G.J. Violence in children and adults. <u>Journal of the American Academy of Child Psychiatry</u>, Spring 1978, 17(2), 277-288. Topic Codes: BI11,BK11BL,CC37K,CC81B,CC81I,CC81M,CC81R,DA04D,DD26D,DK07D, DK18SD,DT10B,MD11,ME07,MK11,MS04,MT04B,MU70,NI59F,PE06D,PE08D,PE30D,SH59H, SR04B,TB35B,TB35D.

81750   Pishkin, V., and Thorne, F.C. Factored scales for the personal health survey with schizophrenics, alcoholics, felons, unmarried mothers, and college students. <u>Journal of Clinical Psychology</u>, April 1978, 34(2), 269-275. Topic Codes: CC11,CQ59,CV13DA,DA04,DD00,DD01,MU70,NE59,TA02,TA03, TA52.

81800   Piotrowski, R.J. Abnormality of subset score differences on the WISC-R. <u>Journal of Consulting and Clinical Psychology</u>, 1978, 46(3), 569-570. Topic Codes: TB95.

81830   Pitcher, D.R. The XYY syndrome. <u>British Journal of Psychiatry</u>, 1975, 9(special no.), 316-325. Topic Codes: BB70D,BI11,CC11D,CC11M,DD02NF, MV11,PE66D,SR69D.

81860   Pivato, E., and Das, J.P. Malnutrition and mental development. <u>Mental Retardation Bulletin</u>, 1973-1974, 2(3), 100-104. Topic Codes: BD52B, CV52B,DT13,MH,PI.

81900   Platt, T., and Takagi, P. Biosocial criminology: A critique. <u>Crime and Social Justice</u>, Spring/Summer 1979, 11, 5-13. Topic Codes: BD11,BI11,CG, DK07D,SF11,SW11.

81930   Plomin, R., and Foch, T.T. Hyperactivity and pediatrician diagnoses, parental ratings, specific cognitive abilities, and laboratory measures. <u>Journal of Abnormal Child Psychology</u>, March 1981, 9(1), 55-64. Topic Codes: CV06,DT13,DT13B,MG,MG30,NH59E.

81950   Plovnick, N. Autonomic nervous system functioning as a predisposing influence on personality, psychopathy and schizophrenia [doctoral dissertation, New School for Social Research, 1977]. <u>Dissertation Abstracts International</u>, December 1977, 36(6), 2926B-2927B. Topic Codes: BK04BB, BL25BB,BN04BB,MG,MS04,MU70.

82000   Plutchik, R., Climent, C., and Ervin, F. Research strategies for the study of human violence. In W.L. Smith and A. Kling (eds.), <u>Issues in Brain/Behavior Control</u>. New York: Spectrum, 1976. Topic Codes: CC11F, CC81D,CC81I,CC81M,CC81R,CC81Y,CG,CQ81,CT81,DK07D,DK18D,DT67B,MB11,MC11, NE81.

82020   Podolsky, E. The epileptic murderer. _Medico-Legal Journal_, 1962, 38,
         176-179. Topic Codes: CC11K,CC37L,CC81M,CT57F,DK18D.

82040   Pogul, L.J. The effects of reduced linguistic complexity on intelligence
         test performance in children with minimal brain dysfunction and associated
         disorders [doctoral dissertation, Columbia University, 1974]. _Disserta-
         tion Abstracts International_, January 1977, 37(7), 3584B. Topic Codes:
         DK48B,DT42,MG,TA02,TA59D.

82060   Polk, K. Schools and the delinquency experience. _Criminal Justice and
         Behavior_, December 1975, 2(4), 315-338. Topic Codes: CC37H,CC37J,CQ37,
         MM11,MX11,NE37,PE64D,PP11,SC18D,SC70D,SR02,TA03.

82080   Polk, W.M. Perceptual orientation, empathy, and the inhibition of aggres-
         sion [doctoral dissertation, North Carolina State University at Raleigh,
         1976]. _Dissertation Abstracts International_, February 1977, 37(8), 4225B.
         Topic Codes: MC,PE04,SR03,TA59.

82090   Pollack, M. Mental subnormality and "childhood schizophrenia." _Proceed-
         ings of the American Psychopathological Association_, 1967, 56, 460-471.
         Topic Codes: DK46,MG,MO,MU70,NA07D.

82100   Ponitus, A.A., and Ruttiger, K.F. Frontal lobe system maturational lag in
         juvenile delinquents shown in narratives test. _Adolescence_, Winter 1976,
         11(44), 509-518. Topic Codes: BL11,CC37F,DK07D.

82150   Poole, F.R. Reading comprehension gain and factors of personality in the
         male juvenile felon in Oklahoma [doctoral dissertation, University of
         Oklahoma, 1975]. _Dissertation Abstracts International_, October 1975,
         36(4), 2110A. Topic Codes: CC37J,CC37W,PE64D,PT11.

82200   Pope, C.E. Race and crime revisited. _Crime and Delinquency_, July 1979,
         25(3), 347-357. Topic Codes: BL67D,CC11R,CC37Y,CG11T.

82250   Poremba, C.D. Learning disabilities, youth and delinquency: Programs for
         intervention. In H.R. Myklebust (ed.), _Progress in Learning Disabili-
         ties_ (vol. 3). New York: Grune & Stratton, 1975. Topic Codes: CC37A,
         CC37H,CC37J,CQ37,CV06C,DT44D,MM11,NE37,PE64D,PP11,SC70D,TA59D.

82300   Porteus, S.D. _The Maze Test and Clinical Psychology_. Palo Alto, Cali-
         fornia: Pacific Books, 1959. Topic Codes: MG,NA07D,TB66B.

82400   Porteus, S.D. _The Maze Test and Mental Differences_. Vineland, New Jer-
         sey: Smith Printing House, 1933. Topic Codes: BL11,NA07I,PG,TB66.

82500   Porteus, S.D. _The Maze Test: Recent Advances_. Palo Alto, California:
         Pacific Books, 1955. Topic Codes: TB66.

82600   Porteus, S.D. Mental tests with delinquents and Australian aboriginal
         children. _Psychological Review_, 1917, 24, 32-42. Topic Codes: CC37H,
         CC37I,TB66D.

82700   Porteus, S.D. Namatjira: Famous Australian artist. _Perception and Motor
         Skills_, 1963, 17, 13-14. Topic Codes: CC11,SB11.

82800   Porteus, S.D. _The Porteus Maze Test and Intelligence_. Palo Alto, Cali-
         fornia: Pacific Books, 1950. Topic Codes: BL11,NA07I,PG,PM,TB66.

82900   Porteus, S.D. _Porteus Maze Tests: Fifty Years' Application_. Palo Alto,
         California: Pacific Books, 1965. Topic Codes: BL67,BL70,DD00,N,P,SQ,
         TA59,TA59D,TB09,TB33G,TB66,TB66B,TB66D,TB74,TB78,TB93.

83000   Porteus, S.D. _The Porteus Mazes: The Supplement Series of Mazes_. New
         York: Psychological Corporation, 1959. Topic Codes: TB66.

83100   Porteus, S.D. _Porteus' Tests: The Vineland Revision_ (research publica-
         tion, vol. 16). Vineland, New Jersey, 1919. Topic Codes: TB66.

83400   Porteus, S.D.   Q-scores, temperament and delinquency.   Journal of Social Psychology, 1945, 21, 81-103.   Topic Codes: CC37W,CC371,PT74B,TB66D.

83530   Power, J.H.   A comparison of the characteristics of a clinical population of learning disabled adolescents and preadolescents [doctoral dissertation, University of Cincinnati, 1975].   Dissertation Abstracts International, January 1976, 36(7), 4405A-4406A.   Topic Codes: BL04B,DT44,MG.

83560   Poznanski, E.O., Krahenbuhl, V., and Zrull, J.P.   Childhood depression: A longitudinal perspective.   Journal of the American Academy of Child Psychiatry, Summer 1976, 15(3), 491-501.   Topic Codes: MB,MGO2,MS,NA44V, NJ30,PE10,PE68B,PT.

83600   Prechtl, H., and Beintema, D.   The Neurological Examination of the Full-Term Newborn Infant; Little Club Clinics in Developmental Medicine no. 12.   London: Spastics International Medical Publications in association with Heinemann Medical Books, Ltd., 1964.   Topic Codes: NA33I,TA52,TA52M.

83700   Prentice, N.M., and Kelly, F.J.   Intelligence and delinquency: A reconstruction.   Journal of Social Psychology, 1963, 60, 327-337.   Topic Codes: CC37BB,CC37Q,CC371,MS04B,PM11,TB95D,TB96BB,TB96D.

83750   Prentky, R.A.   Effects of introversion/extraversion, caffeine, and provocation on affective aggressive behavior [doctoral dissertation, Northwestern University, 1975].   Dissertation Abstracts International, May 1976, 36(11), 5769B.   Topic Codes: BD52,BL59,MC,PT.

83800   Prescott, J.W.   Body pleasure and the origins of violence.   The Futurist, April 1975, 9, 64-74.   Topic Codes: BL52DD,CC67,CC81,CC81B,CC81F,CC81H, CC81L,CQ67,CQ81,CT57,CT57BD,CT59,CT81,CV13D,DA04D,DA15D,DD10D,DK07D,MD11, MI07,MV07,NE67,NE81,PEO6D,PE15D,PE66B,SF11,SI57D,SI57GD,SI57J,SR69B.

83900   Prescott, J.W., and Wallace, D.   Role of pain and pleasure in the development of destructive behaviors: A psychometric study of parenting, sexuality, substance abuse and criminality.   Paper presented at the Colloquium on the Correlates of Crime and Determinants of Criminal Behavior, March 30-31, 1978, Washington, D.C.   Topic Codes: CC11H,CC11L,DA04D, DA15D,MD11,MI07,MV11,NH59F,PEO6D,PE15D,PE66D,SH59H,SI57D,SR69D.

83930   Price, W.H.   Sex determination, mental subnormality, crime and delinquency in males.   Journal of Mental Subnormality, 1969, 15(1), 37-44.   Topic Codes: BB70D,BNO4B,CC11C,CC11D,CC11M,CC11N,CC11S,CC37N,CC37Q,DDO2NF, DK46D,MO11.

83960   Price, W.H., and Jacobs, P.A.   The 47, XYY male with special reference to behavior.   Seminar in Psychiatry, February 1970, 2(1), 30-39.   Topic Codes: BB70B,CC11L,CC11M,CQ59,DK46,MF,NH67D,NH70D.

83990   Price, W.H., and Whatmore, P.B.   Behavior disorders and pattern of crime among XYY males identified at a maximum security hospital.   British Medical Journal, March 4, 1967, 1(5539), 533-536.   Topic Codes: BB70B,BB70D, BL04D,CC11C,CC11L,CC11M,CC37M.CC37N,CC67,CQ59,NH59D,NH59F,NH70D.

84000   Pringle, M.L.K., Butler, N.R., and Davie, R.   Eleven Thousand Seven-Year-Olds: First Report of the National Child Development Study (1958 Cohort). London: Longmans, Green, and Company, Ltd., 1966.   Topic Codes: BE, BL07B,BL11,BPO2,BP26,BP46,BP57,BP59,BP70,DFO6B,DF48,DF60B,DP48,NAO7I, NA31F,NA33F,NA44D,NH59PA,NH59PP,NJ06,PG,PK,SJ07,SJ22,SW,TA52.

84030   Prinz, R.J.   Hyperkinetic boys at adolescence: Changes over time, a comparison to peers and predictors of achievement, behavior, and intelligence [doctoral dissertation, University of Iowa, 1981].   Dissertation Abstracts International, May 1982, 42(11), 4774A.   Topic Codes: MG,MG30, PE64B,PM07.

84040   Prinz, R.J., Connor, P.A., and Wilson, C.C.   Hyperactive and aggressive behaviors in childhood: Intertwined dimensions.   Journal of Abnormal Child Psychology, June 1981, 9(2), 191-202.   Topic Codes: MC,MG,MG30.

84045   Prinz, R.J., Myers, D., Holden, E.W., Tarnowski, K.J., and Roberts, W.A.
         Marital disturbance and child problems: A cautionary note regarding
         hyperactive children. Journal of Abnormal Child Psychology, September
         1983, 11(3), 393-399. Topic Codes: MG30,SI07.

84060   Psarska, A.D. Some aspects of delinquency in the mentally retarded. Psy-
         chiatria Polska, March 1972, 6(2), 151-157. Topic Codes: CC37B,CC37Q,
         DK46D,MO07.

84080   Psatta, D.M., Apostol, V., Florescu, D., and Ioan, N. Late survey of
         cerebral birth injury by quantitative analysis of EEG and clinical assess-
         ment. Neurological Psychiatry, April-June 1978, 16(2), 107-116. Topic
         Codes: BK11B,BP02,DD08K,DK07,TA59,TB35B.

84090   Psatta, D.M., Florescu, D., Apostol, V., and Ioan, N. Deviations from
         normal limits of EEG variation in school-age children born at risk.
         Neurological Psychiatry, April-June 1978, 16(2), 97-106. Topic Codes:
         DP11,TB35.

84095   Quadagno, D.M., Briscoe, R., and Quadagno, J.S. Effect of perinatal go-
         nadal hormones on selected nonsexual behavior patterns: A critical as-
         sessment of the nonhuman and human literature. Psychological Bulletin,
         January 1977, 84(1), 62-80. Topic Codes: BD70,BP02,BP04,MF,PM.

84100   Quay, H.C. Juvenile Delinquency: Research and Theory. Princeton, N.J.:
         Van Nostrand Company, Inc., 1965. Topic Codes: CC37G,CC37J,CC37K,CC37M,
         CC37Q,CC37W,CC37Z,CC371,CG11CC,CJ,CL,CQ37B,CQ59,CV06C,CV13DA,ME07,MS04B,
         NE37D,NE59,PG11,PM11,PM70B,PT11,PY11,SC18D,SC59,SC70B,SC70D,SF26D,SH59D,
         SI11,SI57,SU,TA04,TB61B,TB66D,TB95D.

84200   Quay, H.C., and Quay, L.C. Behavior problems in early adolescence. Child
         Development, 1965, 36, 215-220. Topic Codes: MG11,TA02,TA74.

84300   Quay, H.C., and Werry, J.S. Psychopathological Disorders of Childhood.
         New York: John Wiley & Sons, Inc.,1972. Topic Codes: BK11B,BL11,BL70B,
         BP63,CV,DD26B,DF60,DK18,MG11,MG30B,MS,NA07B,PE10,SI,SJ07B.

84400   Querec, L.J. Apgar score in the United States, 1978. Monthly Vital Sta-
         tistics Report, May 6, 1981, 30(1, supplement), 1-15. Topic Codes:
         NA33I,TB02.

84430   Quereshi, M.Y. The internal consistency of the WISC scores for ages 5 to
         16. Journal of Clinical Psychology, 1968, 24, 192-195. Topic Codes:
         BL04,PM,TB95.

84470   Quinton, D., and Rutter, M. Early hospital admissions and later distur-
         bances of behaviour: An attempted replication of Douglas' findings. De-
         velopmental Medicine and Child Neurology, August 1976, 18(4), 447-459.
         Topic Codes: CC37M,CC37P,CC37Z,CV30B,CV30D,MG11,SW07,SW11.

84500   Quitkin, F., Rifkin, A., and Klein, D.F. Neurologic soft signs in schizo-
         phrenia and character disorders. Archives of General Psychiatry, 1976,
         33(7), 845-853. Topic Codes: DK07BB,DT52B,MS04,MU70,PM07,TA02B,TA52.

84520   Rabkin, J.G. Criminal behavior of discharged mental patients: A critical
         appraisal of the research. Psychological Bulletin, January 1979, 86(1),
         1-27. Topic Codes: CC11C,CC11H,DA04D,DA15D,MQ11,MS02,MS04B,MU11,MU70B.

84540   Rada, R.T., Kellner, R., Kellner, W., and Walter, W. Plasma testosterone
         and aggressive behavior. Psychosomatics, 1976, 17(3), 138-147. Topic
         Codes: BD70B,CC81E,MC.

84560   Rada, R.T., Laws, D.R., and Kellner, R. Plasma testosterone levels in the
         rapist. Psychosomatic Medicine, July-August 1976, 38(4), 257-268. Topic
         Codes: BD70B,CC11D,CC11H,CC81E,CT68,DA04D,TB19B.

84565   Rada, R.T., Laws, D.R., Kellner, R., Stivastava, L., and Peake, G. Plasma
         androgens in violent and nonviolent sex offenders. Bulletin of the Ameri-

can Academy of Psychiatry and the Law, 1983, 11(2), 149-158. Topic Codes: BD70B,CC81E,CT68.

84580   Rader, C.M. MMPI profile types of exposers, rapists, and assaulters in a court services population. Journal of Consulting and Clinical Psychology, February 1977, 45(1), 61-69. Topic Codes: CC11C,CC11P,CC11U,CG11CC,CT57, CT68,CV13,PT11,TB61B.

84590   Ragins, N., Schachter, J., Elmer, E., Preisman, R., Bowes, A.E., and Harway, V. Infants and children at risk for schizophrenia: Environmental and developmental observations. Journal of the American Academy of Child Psychiatry, Winter 1975, 14(1), 150-177. Topic Codes: DF,MG,MU70,NA07D, NA31A,NA31C,SF07.

84595   Rahav, G. Family size and delinquency. Sociology and Social Research, October 1981, 66(1), 42-51. Topic Codes: CC37M,SJ22D.

84600   Raim, J.F. Effect of lateral dominance on cognitive functioning and edu-cational achievement of seven- and ten-year-old children [doctoral disser-tation, Fordham University, 1976]. Dissertation Abstracts International, August 1976, 37(2), 893A. Topic Codes: BL04,BN44H,DT13,MH,NA07D,PE64,PI, PM,PO33,SC70,TA04,TA55,TB76,TB95.

84680   Raine, A., and Venables, P.H. Classical conditioning and socialization: A biosocial interaction. Personality and Individual Differences, 1981, 2 (4), 273-283. Topic Codes: B,ME,MG,MS04,PY11,SW07B,SW11.

84700   Rainer, J.D., Abdullah, S., and Jarvik, L.F. XYY karyotype in a pair of monozygotic twins: A 17-year life history study. British Journal of Psy-chiatry, 1972, 120, 543-548. Topic Codes: BB70B,BE07,BL11,BL33,DD02ND, DT67,ME,MG,NA07D,NA07I,NA33F,PE08,PG,PL,PM,SR04.

84750   Raloff, J. Locks: A key to violence? Science News, August 20,1983, 124, 122-125. Topic Codes: BD11,BD52B,CC37C,CC37U,CC81E,CV52D,DA44MB.

84800   Ramney, C.T., Campbell, F.A., and Nicholson, J.E. The predictive power of the Bayley Scales of Infant Development and the Stanford-Binet Intelli-gence Test in a relatively constant environment. Child Development, 1973, 44, 790-795. Topic Codes: BI,BL11,BL31,NA07I,NA31F,PG,PM,PR,SF,TB05, TB53,TB78.

84805   Rasayon, N.K.B. Mental retardation and black offenders: A look at psy-chosocial factors and diet. In A.R. Harvey and T. Carr (eds.), Black Men-tally Retarded Offender: A Holistic Approach to Prevention and Habilita-tion. New York: United Church of Christ, Commission of Racial Justice, 1982, 109-123. Topic Codes: BD52B,BL11,BL67B,CV52B,DT44,MM,MX,NA07I, PE68,PG,PP,SN07,SR.

84810   Raskin, D.C. Scientific assessment of the accuracy of detection of decep-tion: A reply to Lykken. Psychophysiology, March 1978, 15(2), 143-147. Topic Codes: BK04BB,BL25BB,BL29B,BL59,BN04BB,MS04.

84820   Raskin, D.C., and Hare, R.D. Psychopathy and detection of deception in a prison population. Psychophysiology, March 1978, 15(2), 126-136. Topic Codes: BK04BB,BK04D,BL25BB,BL25D,BL29B,BL29D,BN04BB,BN04D,CC11C,CC11U, CQ59,MS04B.

84830   Raskin, D.C., and Podlesny, J.A. Truth and deception: A reply to Lykken. Psychological Bulletin, January 1979, 86(1), 54-59. Topic Codes: BL25D, BL29D,CC11,CG.

84840   Ratcliffe, S.G., Stewart, A.L., Melville, M.M., Jacobs, P.A., and Keay, A.J. Chromosome studies on 3500 newborn male infants. Lancet, January 17, 1970, 7638, 121-122. Topic Codes: BB70,DD02N,NA31.

84850   Ream, J.H., III. Evaluation of intelligence in youthful offenders: The Kahn intelligence tests. Perceptual and Motor Skills, June 1978, 46(3, part 1), 835-838. Topic Codes: CC37Q,CC37I,TA03,TA59D,TB93.

84860   Reckless, J.B. Enforced outpatient treatment of advantaged pseudosocio-
         pathic neurotically disturbed young women. Canadian Psychiatric Associa-
         tion Journal, August 1970, 15(4), 335-345. Topic Codes: CV06C,MQ,MS04,
         NL22B,NL22D,SW07.

84865   Reed, D.M., and Stanley, F.J. (eds.). The Epidemiology of Prematurity
         (vol. 31, no. 4). Baltimore: Urban & Schwarzenberg, 1977. Topic Codes:
         BL06,BL07,BL22,BL27,BL27K,BL67,BL70,BP02,BP22F,BP26,BP26G,BP44,BP46,BP47,
         BP53,BP59,BP61,BP70,DD08,DF06,DF48,DF60,DF70,DP22P,DP44,DP46,DP48,DP81,
         NC59G,SN,SQ,TA52.

84870   Reeves, A.G., and Plum, F. Hyperphagia, rage, and dementia accompanying a
         ventromedial hypothalamic neoplasm. Archives of Neurology, 1969, 20,
         616-624. Topic Codes: DK07B,MF.

84880   Regard, M., and Perret, E. Neuropsychological diagnosis and localization
         of brain lesions: Their agreement with other examination visits. Fort-
         schritte der Neurologie, Psychiatrie und Ihrer Grenzgebiete, October 1977,
         45(10), 517-528 (in German). Topic Codes: DK07B,TA52,TA55.

84890   Reid, W.H. The sadness of the psychopath. American Journal of Psycho-
         therapy, October 1978, 32(4), 496-509. Topic Codes: CV06C,MS04,SI07.

84895   Reidy, T.J., Jr. The social, emotional, and cognitive functioning of phy-
         sically abused and neglected children [doctoral dissertation, De Paul Uni-
         versity, 1976]. Dissertation Abstracts International, July 1976, 37(1),
         476B-477B. Topic Codes: BL11,CT57B,CT57BB,DT13,MC,MG.

84900   Reinisch, J.M. Prenatal exposure to synthesized progestins increases
         potential for aggression in humans. Science, March 13, 1981, 211, 1171-
         1173. Topic Codes: BD70,BL04,BL22,BL70,BP04,BP22F,MC,PE04,PM,SJ07,SQ,
         SR03,TA59,TB93,TB95.

84950   Reiss, D.J. The relationship between brain norepinephrine and aggressive
         behavior. Research Publications of the Association for Research in Ner-
         vous and Mental Disease, 1972, 50, 266-296. Topic Codes: BD07,BK11B,MC,
         PE04,SR03.

85000   Reitan, R.M., and Boll, T.J. Neuropsychological correlates of minimal
         brain dysfunction. New York Academy of Sciences - Annals, 1973, 205, 65-
         88. Topic Codes: BL48B,BL70B,BN44B,DK07B,DK48,DT42,DT44,DT48B,DT52B,MG,
         MG48,ML,MM,MT48B,NA07DB,PE44,PE48B,PM70,PN,PO07,PP,PR07,SQ07,TA02,TA52,
         TA59D,TB40B,TB46,TB84,TB95B,TB98B.

85100   Reitan, R.M., and Davison, L.A. Clinical Neuropsychology: Current Status
         and Applications. New York: John Wiley & Sons, Inc., 1974. Topic Codes:
         BK11B,BL04,BL48,BN44H,DD26,DK07,DK09,DK18,DK46,DK48,DT06,DT13,DT42,DT44,
         MH,ML,MM,NL,PE44,PE64,PI,PM,PO33,PP,SC70,SQ,SW,TA04,TA55,TA59D,TB09,TB12,
         TB33,TB35,TB40,TB46,TB51,TB61,TB66,TB74,TB78,TB84,TB87,TB93,TB95,TB96,
         TB98.

85200   Remschmidt, H., Hohner, G., Merschmann, W., and Walter, R. Epidemiology
         of delinquent behavior in children. In P.J. Graham (ed.), Epidemiologi-
         cal Approaches in Child Psychiatry. New York: Academic Press, 1977.
         Topic Codes: BL70D,CC37,CC37J,CC37W,CC37Z,CC371,CC67,CE,CG11P,CG11T,CJ,
         CQ37,CQ67,MC11,MS02,NE37,NE67,PE04D,SQ11,SR03B,SW11,SW56,TA03,TA59,TA70.

85300   Report of the Fourth Workshop of the Interdisciplinary Group on Criminol-
         ogy. Saleem A. Shah, Chairman. N.p., December 1979. Topic Codes: BA,
         BD11,BD70B,BK04D,BL18D,BL25D,CC11,CC37,CC37T,CC67,CC81,CC81D,CC81E,CC81K,
         CC81R,CC81Y,CE,CG,CG11P,CQ11,CQ37,CQ59,CQ67,CQ81,CT81,CV13DA,MGO2D,MK11,
         MS04B,NA44,NC,NE11,NE37,NE59,NE67,NE81,NJ,PE30D,SF11,TB35D,TB37D,TB72B,
         TB86C.

85400   Report of the Interdisciplinary Group on Criminology. Saleem A. Shah,
         Chairman. Leiden: Beugelsdijk Leiden, 1977. Topic Codes: BA,BD11,BI11,
         BK04D,CC11,CC37,CC67,CC81,CG,CQ11,CQ37,CQ59,CQ67,CQ81,CT81,CV13DA,NA44,
         NE11,NE37,NE59,NE67,NE81,NJ,PT11,SF11,TA03,TA55,TA59.

85450   Restak, R. The origins of violence. Saturday Review, May 12, 1979, 16-
         19. Topic Codes: BK11BL,BL31,CC81,CC81R,CQ81,CT57BD,CT81,DD10D,DKO7D,
         NA31B,NA31F,NE81,PK,SI48D,SI57GD.

85500   Rheingold, H.L. The development of social behavior in the human infant.
         In H.W. Stevenson (ed.), Concept of Development: A Report of a Conference
         Commemorating the 40th Anniversary of the Institute of Child Development.
         Monographs of the Society for Research in Child Development, 1966, 31(1,
         serial no. 103). Topic Codes: BL31,MX,NA31D,NA31F,PE32,PE68,PK,SI48,SR.

85560   Ricciuti, H.N. Malnutrition and psychological development. Research
         Publications of the Association for Research in Nervous and Mental Dis-
         ease, 1973, 51(10), 63–78. Topic Codes: BD52B,BL52D,CV52B.

85600   Richardson, H.M., and Surko, E.F. WISC scores and status in reading and
         arithmetic of delinquent children. Journal of Genetic Psychology, 1956,
         89, 251–262. Topic Codes: CC37J,CC37Q,CC37I,PE64D,SC70D,TA03,TA04,TB95D,
         TB96D.

85625   Richman, N. Behavior problems in pre-school children: Family and social
         factors. British Journal of Psychiatry, November 1977, 131, 523–527.
         Topic Codes: MG,MX07,NA07D,NH59,PE10,PE68B,PY,SI57B,SI57P,SJ,SR01,SU,
         TA02.

85650   Richman, N., Stevenson, J.E., and Graham, P.J. Prevalence of behavior
         problems in 3-year-old children: An epidemiological study in a London
         borough. Journal of Child Psychology and Psychiatry and Allied Disci-
         plines, October 1975, 16(4), 277–287. Topic Codes: BL70B,BN68,MG18,MX,
         NA07D,SQ07,SW07,SW56,TA02,TA59.

85680   Rie, E.D., Rie, H.E., Stewart, S., and Rettemnier, S.C. An analysis of
         neurological soft signs in children with learning problems. Brain and
         Language, 1978, 6, 32–46. Topic Codes: BL04,BL48B,BL70B,DK48,DT13,DT44,
         DT48B,DT52B,MG,MG48,MH,MM,MT48B,NA07D,PE48B,PI,PP,PR07,SQ07,TA02,TA52,
         TB09B,TB12,TB53,TB55,TB86,TB95B.

85700   Rie, H., and Rie, E. (eds.). Handbook of Minimal Brain Dysfunctions:
         A Critical View. New York: John Wiley & Sons, Inc., 1980. Topic Codes:
         BI07,BK11B,BL04,BL52DB,BN44B,BP02B,DD02B,DK09B,DK48B,DT44B,MG30,MG48B,
         MM07,MX07,NL,PE10,PE64B,PE68B,PO07,PP07,SC70,TA02,TA59D.

85850   Rieder, R.O., Broman, S.H., and Rosenthal, D. The offspring of schizo-
         phrenics: II. Perinatal factors and IQ. Archives of General Psychia-
         try, July 1977, 34, 789–799. Topic Codes: BL07BB,BL70,DF06BB,DP11B,DP60,
         DP81,MG,MU70,NA07D,NA44D,NC59,NC70,NH59B,NH59E,NJ06,PM07,SH59B,SH59F,SQ,
         SW,TB02,TB95B.

85900   Rigg, L.I., and Scott, T.F.M. Childhood behavioral deviations in an inner
         city population: I. Prevalence at ages 4 and 7 years. Unpublished manu-
         script, Children's Hospital of Philadelphia and the Department of Pedia-
         trics, School of Medicine, University of Pennsylvania, n.d. Topic Codes:
         BL11,BL67B,BL70B,BN68,BN70,DT69,DT71,MG,MG11,MG18,MG21,MP,MW,MX,MY,NA07D,
         NA07I,NA44D,NC22,NC70,NJ06,PE22,PE52,PE68,PE70,PG,SN07,SQ07,SR,TA57.

85930   Riley, J.M. An analysis of the relationship between qualitative cognitive
         abilities and juvenile delinquency [doctoral dissertation, Boston College,
         1976]. Dissertation Abstracts International, August 1976, 37(2), 893A–
         894A. Topic Codes: CC37H,CC37I,DT13D,TA03,TA59D.

85960   Rime, B., Bouvy, H., Leborgne, B., and Rouillon, F. Psychopathy and non-
         verbal behavior in an interpersonal situation. Journal of Abnormal Psy-
         chology, December 1978, 87(6), 636–643. Topic Codes: CC37BB,CC37I,CQ59,
         CV13DA,MF11,MS04,MX07,NE59,PE68,SR01.

85970   Rimland, B., and Larson, G.E. Hair mineral analysis and behavior: An
         analysis of 51 studies. Journal of Learning Disabilities, May 1983, 16
         (5), 279–285. Topic Codes: BD,BD07,DK46,DT44,MF,PM.

85975   Rimland, B., and Larson, G.E.   Nutritional and ecological approaches to the reduction of criminality, delinquency and violence.   Journal of Applied Nutrition, 1981, 33(2), 116-137.   Topic Codes: BD52D,BP70,CC37U, CC81E,CV52D,DA44MB,DK07D.

85980   Rimmer, J., and Jacobsen, B.   Antisocial personality in the biological relatives of schizophrenics.   Comprehensive Psychiatry, July-August 1980, 21(4), 258-262.   Topic Codes: MS04,MU70,NH04B,NH65,NH65B.

86000   Risse, G.L., and Gazzaniga, M.S.   Well-kept secrets of the right hemisphere: A carotid amytal study of restricted memory transfer.   Neurology, September 1978, 28, 950-953.   Topic Codes: BN44,DT42,DT46,ML,MN,PE44,PN, PO,PQ.

86050   Rizzo, N.D.   Dyslexia and delinquency: A new dyslexia screening test.   International Journal of Offender Therapy and Comparative Criminology, 1975, 19(2), 164-177.   Topic Codes: CC37H,CC37J,DT15B.

86100   Robbins, D.M., Pries, R., Jacobs, D., Beck, J., and Smith, C.   A preliminary report on the neuropsychological development of a group of clinic-referred juvenile delinquents.   Paper presented at the 86th annual convention of the American Psychological Association, Toronto, Canada, August 1978.   Topic Codes: BL48D,BN44D,CC37H,CC37I,CC37J,CC37L,CC37P,CC37Q, CC37R,CC37T,CC37I,CG11C,CT57,CT59,DK09D,DT44D,DT48D,MM11,MT48D,NL48D, PE48D,PO11,PP11,PR11,SJ09D,TA03,TA52,TB09D,TB09K,TB93D,TB95D,TB96D,TB98D.

86150   Robbins, P.G., Gorbach, A.G., and Reid, D.E.   Neurologic abnormalities at one year in infants delivered after late-pregnancy hemorrhage.   Obstetrics and Gynecology, March 1967, 29, 358-361.   Topic Codes: BL06,BP02,BP44, BP46,BP57,DF,DK,DP11,DP44,DP58,DP81.

86200   Roberts, C.J.   Manifestations of cerebral dysfunction in infancy and their association with toxemia and antepartum hemorrhage: A cohort study.   British Journal of Preventive and Social Medicine, 1971, 25, 135-139.   Baltimore: The Williams & Wilkins Company, 1966.   Topic Codes: DF,DK07, DP11B,DP60,DP81.

86450   Robins, L.N.   Discussion of genetic studies of criminality and psychopathy.   Proceedings of the American Psychopathological Association, 1975, 63, 117-122.   Topic Codes: BI11,CC11M,MS04B.

86500   Robins, L.N.   Sturdy childhood predictors of adult antisocial behavior: Replications from longitudinal studies.   Psychological Medicine, November 1978, 8(4), 611-622.   Topic Codes: CC11G,CC37V,ME,MG02B,MG02D,MS04B,NA44, NH59E,NJ,PE08,SH59F,SR04,SW07B.

86600   Robins, L.N., Hesselbrock, M., Wish, E.D., and Helzer, J.E.   Alcohol and crime in veterans.   Paper presented at the National Institute of Law Enforcement and Criminal Justice Colloquium, n.p., March 30, 1978.   Topic Codes: CC11H,CC37V,CC81,CG11T,CQ81,CT59,CT81,DA04D,DA15D,MD11,MI07,NE81, PE06D,PE15D,TA70.

86700   Robins, L.N., and Lewis, R.G.   The role of the antisocial family in school completion and delinquency: A three generation study.   Sociological Quarterly, 1966, 7, 500-514.   Topic Codes: CC37J,CC37L,CC37Z,NH59D,NH59G, NH59GI,NH59E,NH59PF,NH59PL,NH67D,SC18B,SH59D,SH59F,SH59J,SH59JL,SH59RF, SH59RL,SW11.

86800   Robins, L.N., West, P.A., and Herjanic, B.L.   Arrests and delinquency in two generations: A study of black urban families and their children.   Journal of Child Psychology and Psychiatry and Allied Disciplines, 1975, 16, 125-140.   Topic Codes: BL70D,CC37A,CC37L,CC37Z,CC67,CG11P,CQ67,CT57, CT59,CT70,NE67,NH59D,NH59F,NH59G,NH59GD,NH59GI,NH59PD,NH59PL,NH67D,NH70D, NL07D,PE64D,SC70D,SH59D,SH59H,SH59J,SH59JD,SH59JL,SH59RD,SH59RL,SH70D, SJ09D,SJ22D,SQ11.

86900   Robins, L.N., and Wish, E.   Development of childhood deviance: A study of 223 urban black men from birth to 18.   In M. McMillan and S. Henao (eds.),

Child Psychiatry: Treatment and Research. New York: Brunner-Mazel,
1977. Topic Codes: BL04B,BL04D,BL11C,CC37,CC37A,CC37B,CC37I,CC37J,CG11P,
CG11T,CQ37,DA04B,DA15,DA15D,MD07,MG,MI,MI07,MV07,NA07D,NA07ID,NE37,NLO7B,
NLO7D,PE06B,PE15,PE15D,PE64B,PE66B,PG11,SC18,SC70B,SI07,SI11,SR69B,TA70.

86950   Robinson, R.G. Differential behavioral and biochemical effects of right
and left hemispheric cerebral infarction in the rat. Science, August 17,
1979, 205, 707-710. Topic Codes: BD,BN44,MF,PE,PO.

86960   Rochford, J.M., Swartzburg, M., Chowdhrey, S.M., and Goldstein, L. Some
quantitative EEG correlates of psychopathology. Research Communications
in Psychology, Psychiatry and Behavior, 1976, 1(2), 211-226. Topic Codes:
TB35B.

87000   Rodin, E.A. Psychomotor epilepsy and aggressive behavior. Archives of
General Psychiatry, February 1973, 28, 210-213. Topic Codes: DK07B,
DK18D,DT10,MC,MT04,PE04,PE64B,SC70B,SR03,TB35B.

87100   Roe, A.V., Howell, R.J., and Payne, I.R. Comparison of prison inmates
with and without juvenile records. Psychological Reports, 1974, 34, 1315-
1319. Topic Codes: BE11,CC11G,CC11P,CC11U,CC37B,CC37V,CG11CC,CQ59,CT57,
CT57F,CT59,CV13,CV13DA,NE59.

87130   Roff, J.D. Adolescent development and family characteristics associated
with a diagnosis of schizophrenia. Journal of Consulting and Clinical
Psychology, December 1976, 44(6), 933-939. Topic Codes: BL11,CT57BB,MB,
MG02B,MU70,NA07DD,NH59B,NH59E,NH70B,SH59B,SH59F,SH70B,SI07,SI09B.

87160   Roff, J.D., Knight, R., and Wertheim, E. A factor-analytic study of
childhood symptoms antecedent to schizophrenia. Journal of Abnormal Psychology, December 1976, 85(6), 543-549. Topic Codes: MC,MG02B,MQ,MU70,
PE64B,PM07,PY.

87200   Rogers, M.E. Prenatal and paranatal factors in the development of childhood behavior disorders. Acta Psychiatrica et Neurologica Scandinavica,
1955, supplement 102. Topic Codes: BP02B,DP11B,MG,NA07D.

87250   Rollin, H.R. Deviant behavior in relation to mental disorder. Proceedings of the Royal Society of Medicine, January 1973, 66(1), 99-103. Topic
Codes: MF,MQ,MS,MU,PE.

87300   Rosanoff, A.J., Handy, L.M., and Plesset, I.R. The etiology of child behavior difficulties, juvenile delinquency and adult criminality with special reference to their occurrence in twins. State of California Department of Institutions Psychiatric Monograph, No. 1, January 1941. Topic
Codes: BL04D,CC11A,CC11L,CC11M,CC11Q,CC11S,CC37A,CC37L,CC37N,CC37X,CC67,
CQ67,DD08KC,DP11B,DP11D,MG,NA07D,NE67,NH74B,NH74D,SH74B,SH74D.

87400   Rosen, E.J. Behavioral and emotional disturbances associated with cere-
bral dysfunction. Applied Therapeutics, 1969, 11(10), 531-543. Topic
Codes: BL48B,DK48B,DK48D,DT44,DT48B,MG,MG48B,MG48D,MM,MQ,MT48B,NA07D,
PE48B,PP,PR07.

87450   Rosenblith, J.F. Prognostic value of neonatal behavioral tests. Early
Child Development and Care, 1973, 3, 31-50. Topic Codes: BL31,DF34,
NA33D,NA33I,NA44B,NC22,NC44.

87500   Rosenblith, J.F. Relations between neonatal behaviors and those at eight
months. Developmental Psychology, 1974, 10(6), 779-792. Topic Codes:
BL27,BL31,BL67,BL70,BP26,DF,DF34,DF60B,NA31C,NA31D,NA31F,NA31R,NA33B,
NA33D,NA33I,NA44,NC44,NJ,PE32,PE34,PK,SN,SQ,TA52K,TA52M,TB05.

87600   Rosenblith, J., and Anderson-Huntington, R.B. Relations between newborn
and 4-year behavior. Abstract Guide of XXth International Congress of
Psychology, 1972, 511. Topic Codes: DF,MG,NA07D,NA31C,NA31D,NA44B,NC22,
NC44,NJ03,PE32,TB05,TB27,TB44.

87700   Rosenthal, D. Genetic Theory and Abnormal Behavior. New York: McGraw-

Hill, 1970. Topic Codes: BB07,BB70,BI,BK11B,BL70,DA04B,DD00,DD02B,DD15,
MD07,MU70,NH74,NH74B,SF,TA80,TB35.

87800   Rosenthal, M.K. The study of infant—environment interaction: Some com-
         ments on trends and methodologies. Journal of Child Psychology and Psy-
         chiatry and Allied Disciplines, 1973, 14, 301-317. Topic Codes: CG,NA31,
         SF.

87830   Roslund, B., and Larson, C.A. Mentally disturbed violent offenders in
         Sweden. Neuropsychobiology, 1976, 2(4), 221-232. Topic Codes: CC11C,
         CC81D.

87850   Rosser, P.L. Minimal brain dysfunction in children. Comprehensive Thera-
         py, September 1978, 4(9), 22-28. Topic Codes: CV06,DK48,DK48B,MG48,
         MG48B.

87860   Ross, E. The development of moral judgment in children [doctoral disser-
         tation, University of New South Wales (Australia), 1975]. Disserta-
         tion Abstracts International, March 1976, 36(9), 4670B-4671B. (Copies
         available from Librarian, University of New South Wales, P.O. Box 1, Ken-
         sington, Australia 2033.) Topic Codes: BL11,DT13.

87890   Ross, R.R. Reading disability and crime: In search of a link. Crime
         and Justice, May 1977, 5(1), 10-22. Topic Codes: CC11I,CC11N,DT44D,MM11,
         PE64D,PP11,SC70D.

87895   Rossi, G.F., and Rosadini, G., Experimental analysis of cerebral dominance
         in man. In F.L. Darley and C.H. Millikan (eds.), Brain Mechanisms Under-
         lying Speech and Language. New York: Grune & Stratton, 1967, 167-175.
         Topic Codes: BN44,BN70,DT13,DT71,MH,MY,PE70,PI,PO,PT74.

87900   Rossi, P.H., Waite, E., Bose, C.E., and Berk, R.E. The seriousness of
         crimes: Normative structure and individual differences. American Socio-
         logical Review, April 1974, 39, 224-237. Topic Codes: BL04,BL67,BL70,
         CE,CT57,CT57F,CT59,CT68,CT70,SC18,SN,SQ.

87910   Rossman, P.G., and Knesper, D.J. The early phase of hospital treatment
         for disruptive adolescents: The integration of behavioral and dynamic
         techniques. Journal of the American Academy of Child Psychiatry, August
         1976, 15(4), 693-708. Topic Codes: CV06,MG,NA07D.

87915   Roszkowski, M.J. The relationship between the performance greater than
         verbal (P greater than V) sign and violent behavior in a sample of mental-
         ly retarded subjects. Journal of Genetic Psychology, December 1983, 143
         (second half), 279-280. Topic Codes: CC81Q,CC81Y,DK46D,MO11,TB96D.

87920   Rotenberg, M. Psychopathy, insensitivity and sensitization. Professional
         Psychology, August 1975, 6(3), 283-292. Topic Codes: CV06C,MS04.

87940   Roth, M. Cerebral disease and mental disorders of old age as causes of
         antisocial behavior. International Psychiatry Clinics, 1968, 5(3), 35-
         58. Topic Codes: BL04B,BL04D,BL70D,CC11A,CC11C,CC11F,CC81A,CT57,CT59,
         CT68,DD26B,DK07B,DK18D,SQ11.

87950   Roth, M. Human violence as viewed from the psychiatric clinic. American
         Journal of Psychiatry, March 1972, 128(9), 1043-1056. Topic Codes:
         CC81D,CC81F,CC81L,CC81M,CC81S,MS04B,PT11.

87960   Roth, M.R. A comparison of the three methods for producing the reduction
         of annoyance and aggressive behavior [doctoral dissertation, Washington
         University, 1976]. Dissertation Abstracts International, October 1976,
         37(4), 1927B-1928B. Topic Codes: CV06,MC,MF.

87970   Rothballer, A. Aggression, defense and neurohumors. In C.D. Clemente and
         D.B. Lindsley (eds.), Brain Function: Aggression and Defense (vol. 5).
         Berkeley, California: University of California Press, 1967. Topic Codes:
         BK11B,DK07B,MC,MF,PE04,SR03.

87980   Rothenberg, M.B. Violence and children. <u>Mental Hygiene</u>, October 1969, 53(4), 539-544. Topic Codes: CC81F,CC81J,CQ81,CT81,CY,NA07DB,NE81,PE15D, PY11,SC18D,SI57PB,SR02,SU11.

87990   Rotheram, M.J. Patterns of aggressive behavior in delinquents [doctoral dissertation, University of Southern California, 1977]. <u>Dissertation Abstracts International</u>, February 1978, 38(8), 3904B-3905B. (Copies available from Micrographics Department, Doheny Library, USC, Los Angeles, California 90007.) Topic Codes: BE11,CC37E,CC37H,CG11CC,CQ59,DT42D,ML03, NE59,PE44D,PN11,TA02,TA59D.

88000   Routtenberg, A. The reward system of the brain. <u>Scientific American</u>, November 1978, 239(5), 154-164. Topic Codes: BK11B,CV15,DT44,DT46,MM,MN, MV,PE66,PP,PQ,SR69.

88100   Rovet, J., and Netley, C. Phenotypic vs. genotypic sex and cognitive abilities. <u>Behavior Genetics</u>, 1979, 9(4), 317-322. Topic Codes: BB70, BD70,BI,BL70,DD02N,PM,SQ,TB93,TB95,TB96.

88150   Rowe, D.C. Temperament, school adjustment and peers: A study of self-reported delinquency in high school students [doctoral thesis, University of Colorado, 1977]. Topic Codes: BI11,CC37B,CC37H,CC37I,CC37J,CC37Q,CC37Z, CG11T,DT13D,MH11,PE64D,PI11,PT74B,SC70D,SI11,TA03,TA04,TA59D,TA70.

88200   Royce, J.R., Yeudall, L.T., and Bock, C. Factor analytic studies of human brain damage: 1. First- and second-order factors and their brain correlates. <u>Multivariate Behavioral Research</u>, 1976, 4, 381-418. Topic Codes: BN44B,DK07B,DT13,DT42,DT46,DT59,MH,ML,MN,MR,PE44,PI,PM70,PN,PO07,PQ,PS, TA02,TA52,TB40B,TB87,TB93B.

88300   Rubel, R.J. Dealing with rotten kids in schools: An examination of options. Paper presented at the annual meeting of the American Society of Criminology, San Francisco, November, 1980. Topic Codes: CC37,CG11,CQ37, CT57,CT59,NE37,PE64D,SC,SC70D,SF26D,SF26DD.

88400   Rubin, B. Prediction of dangerousness in mentally ill criminals. In S. Pasternack (ed.), <u>Violence and Victims</u>. New York: SP Books, 1973. Topic Codes: CC81D,CG11CC,CQ59,CT57,CV13,CV13DA,CY,MU11,NE59.

88430   Rubin, R.A., Balow, B., and Fisch, R.O. Neonatal serum bilirubin levels related to cognitive development at ages 4 through 7 years. <u>Journal of Pediatrics</u>, April 1979, 94(4), 601-604. Topic Codes: BD30BA,BL11,DF34, DT13,NA33I,NC22,NC44,NC70.

88440   Rubin, R.T. Conference support: Fifth annual workshop of the Interdisciplinary Group on Criminology; final report. Washington, D.C.: U.S. Department of Justice, National Institute of Justice, 1980. Topic Codes: BA,CC11D,CC11Q,CC37K,CC37X,CC81E,CC81L,CC81R,CQ59,CV13DA,NA44F,NC,NE59, NJ09,SF26D.

88460   Rubino, C.A. Rapid visual identification and unilateral temporal lobe damage [doctoral dissertation, York University (Canada), 1969]. <u>Dissertation Abstracts International</u>, April 1976, 36(10), 5316B. (Copies available from National Library of Canada at Ottawa.) Topic Codes: BN44B, DK07B,DK18SB,DT13.

88490   Rudolph, G.C. The effects of forced aggression on subsequent aggressive behavior under conditions of threat and no threat of retaliation [doctoral dissertation, University of Illinois at Chicago Circle, 1973]. <u>Dissertation Abstracts International</u>, March 1974, 34(9), 4674B. Topic Codes: MC, NA07B.

88500   Rugel, R.P., and Mitchell, A. Characteristics of familial and nonfamilial disabled readers. <u>Journal of Learning Disabilities</u>, May 1977, 10(5), 54-59. Topic Codes: BL25B,DK48B,DT15,DT44,MG,MG48B,ML15,MM,NA07D,NH65B,PP, TA02,TA52,TA57,TA74.

88530   Rule, B.G., and Nesdale, A.R. Emotional arousal and aggressive behavior.

Psychological Bulletin, September 1976, 83(5), 851-863. Topic Codes:
BN04,MC.

88600   Russell, D.H. Juvenile murderers. International Journal of Offender
Therapy and Comparative Criminology, 1973, 17, 235-239. Topic Codes:
CC37B,CC37K,CT57F.

88700   Russell, D.H. A study of juvenile murderers. International Journal of
Offender Therapy, 1965, 9(3), 55-86. Topic Codes: CC37,CC37B,CC37L,
CC67B,CG11CC,CQ37,CT57F,CV13,NE37,NH11,SH11,SI57D.

88800   Rutter, M.L. Psycho-social disorders in childhood, and their outcome in
adult life. Journal of the Royal College of Physicians of London, April
1970, 4(3), 211-218. Topic Codes: BL11,DT15,MG02B,MG04GB,MG11,ML15,MQ,
NA07DD,NA07I,NH59B,NH59E,PG,SH59B,SH59F,SI57B,SW07.

88900   Rutter, M.L. School influences on children's behavior and development.
Pediatrics, February 1980, 65(2), 208-220. Topic Codes: BL11,CC37J,MF,
MG,NA07D,NA07I,NA44,NJ,PE,PE64,PG,PM,SC,SC70.

89000   Rutter, M., and Bartak, L. Causes of infantile autism: Some considerations from recent research. Journal of Autism and Childhood Schizophrenia, 1971, 1(1), 20-32. Topic Codes: BI07,BL70B,BN04B,DK07B,DK46B,DT42B,
MG04,ML02,MO07,MX07,NA31A,PC07,PE44B,PE68B,PN07,SF07,SQ07,SR01,TA02,TA52.

89050   Rutter, M., Graham, P., and Birch, H.G. Interrelations between the
choreiform syndrome, reading disability and psychiatric disorder in children of 8-11 years. Developmental Medicine and Child Neurology, April
1966, 8(2), 149-159. Topic Codes: DT44B,MG,MM07,NA07D,PP07,SR01,TA02.

89100   Rutter, M., and Yule, W. The concept of specific reading retardation.
Journal of Child Psychology and Psychiatry and Allied Disciplines, 1975,
16, 181-197. Topic Codes: BI07,BL48B,BL70,BN70,DK07B,DT15,DT42,DT48B,
DT71,MG,ML,ML15,MT48B,MY,NA07D,NH59E,NH70B,PE44,PE48B,PE64,PE70,PM,PN,
PR07,SC70,SH59F,SH70B,SQ,SW07B.

89120   Rymer, R.A. An examination of intellectual functioning, school achievement, and personality characteristics of male juvenile delinquents [doc-
toral dissertation, Virginia Commonwealth University, 1979]. Dissertation
Abstracts International, March 1980, 40(9), 4505B. Topic Codes: CC37H,
CC37J,CC37Q,CC37W,DT44D,PE64D,PM11,PT11,SC70D.

89150   Sabatino, D., and Becker, J.T. Relationship between lateral preference
and selected behavioral variables for children failing academically.
Child Development, 1971, 42, 2055-2060. Topic Codes: BN44B,MM,NA07B,
PO07,PO33,PP,TA03,TA52,TB09,TB53,TB95.

89175   Sabatino, D.A., Heald, J.E., Rothman, S.G., and Miller, T.L. Destructive
norm-violating school behavior among adolescents: A review of protective
and preventive efforts. Adolescence, Winter 1978, 13(52), 675-686. Topic
Codes: CC37J,CQ37,CT59,CV06,NE37,PE64B,SC70B,SF11.

89200   Saccuzzo, D.P., and Lewandowski, D.G. The WISC as a diagnostic tool.
Journal of Clinical Psychology, January 1976, 32(1), 115-124. Topic
Codes: BL67,BL70,CC371,SN,SQ,TB95B,TB95D,TB96D.

89300   Sadoff, R.L. Violence in families: An overview. Bulletin of the American Academy of Psychiatry and the Law, 1976, 4(4), 192-296. Topic Codes:
CC81N,CT57B,DD10,NH11,SH11,SI57G.

89320   Safer, D.J. A familial factor in minimal brain dysfunction. Behavioral
Genetics, June 1973, 3(2), 175-186. Topic Codes: BI07,DK48,MG48,NH59E,
SH59F.

89340   Saklofske, D.H. Antisocial behavior and psychoticism in adolescent
schoolboys. Psychological Reports, October 1977, 41(2), 425-426. Topic
Codes: ME,MG,MU,NA07D,PE08,PE64,TA02B,TA70,TA74,TB38.

89360   Saklofske, D.H., McKerracher, D.W., and Eysenck, S.B.G. Eysenck's theory
         of criminality: A scale of criminal propensity as a measure of antisocial
         behavior. Psychological Reports, December 1978, 43(3, part 1), 683-686.
         Topic Codes: ME,MG,MU,NA07D,NE59,PE02,PE08,TA02B,TA70,TA74.

89400   Sandberg, S.T. Psychiatric disorders in children with birth anomalies.
         Acta Psychiatrica Scandinavica, 1976, 54, 1-16. Topic Codes: BB07,BL11,
         DD02B,DK,ME,MG,NA07D,NA07I,NH59GB,NH59PB,PE08,PG,PM,SH59JB,SH59RB,SR04,SW,
         SW07,TB09B,TB95B.

89410   Sandberg, S.T., Wieselberg, M., and Shaffer, D. Hyperkinetic and conduct
         problem children in a primary school population: Some epidemiological
         considerations. Journal of Child Psychology and Psychiatry and Allied
         Disciplines, October 1980, 21(4), 293-311. Topic Codes: BB48,BB48B,BL11,
         BN44B,DD02K,DD02KB,DK,DK07B,MG,MG11,MG30,NA07D,TA02,TA57,TA74.

89420   Sandel, A., and Alcorn, J.D. Individual hemisphericity and maladaptive
         behaviors. Journal of Abnormal Psychology, June 1980, 89(3), 514-517.
         Topic Codes: BN44B,BN44BB,DA04,MB,MD,MS04,MU70,PE06,P007,P007B.

89450   Sandler, M., Ruthven, C.R.J., and Goodwin, B.L. Phenylethylamine overpro-
         duction in aggressive psychopaths. Lancet, December 16, 1978, 8103,
         1269-1270. Topic Codes: BA,BB11,BD11,BD30,CC81E,MC,NE59,NE81,PE04,TB.

89500   Sankar, D.V.S. Plasma levels of folates, riboflavin, vitamin B6, and
         ascorbate in severely disturbed children. Journal of Autism and Develop-
         mental Disorders, 1979, 9(1), 73-82. Topic Codes: BD07,BD30,BD52B,BL04,
         BL67,CV52B,MG,NA07D,NL48B,SN,TB95.

89550   Sano, K., Mayanagi, Y., Sekino, H., Ogashiwa, M., and Ishijima, B. Re-
         sults of Stimulation and Destruction of the Posterior Hypothalamus in Man.
         Journal of Neurosurgery, 1970, 33, 689-707. Topic Codes: BK11BL,DK18B,
         M,N,TA55,TA80.

89600   Santostefano, S. Psychologic testing in evaluating and understanding or-
         ganic brain damage and the effects of drugs in children. Medical Prog-
         ress, May 1963, 62(5), 766-781. Topic Codes: DK07B,TB09B,TB72,TB74,
         TB86,TB95B.

89700   Sarason, I.G. A cognitive social learning approach to juvenile delin-
         quency. In R. Hare and D. Schalling (eds.), Psychopathic Behavior: Ap-
         proaches to Research. New York: John Wiley & Sons, Inc., 1978. Topic
         Codes: CC37,CG11C,CL,CQ37,CV06C,DT13D,MH11,NE37,PI11.

89800   Satterfield, J.H. The hyperactive child syndrome: A precursor of adult
         psychopathy? In R. Hare and D. Schalling (eds.), Psychopathic Behaviour:
         Approaches to Research. Chichester: John Wiley & Sons, Inc., 1978.
         Topic Codes: BL18B,BL52DB,BN04B,CC37B,CG11C,CG11P,CL,CV15B,MG30D,
         MS04,PC07,TB37B.

89810   Satterfield, J.H., and Schell, A.M. Childhood brain function differences
         in delinquent and non-delinquent hyperactive boys. Electroencephalography
         and Clinical Neurophysiology, March 1984, 57(3), 199-207. Topic Codes:
         BK11B,CC37,CC37B,CC37F,CQ37,DK07B,DK07D,MG,MG30,NA07D.

89900   Satterfield, J.H., and Cantwell, D.P. Psychopharmacology in the preven-
         tion of antisocial and delinquent behavior. International Journal of Men-
         tal Health, Spring-Summer 1975, 4(1-2), 227-237. Topic Codes: BN04D,
         CC37B,CC37S,CC37I,CV15D,ME,MG30D,PC11,PE08,SR04.

90000   Satterfield, J.H., Cantwell, D.P., Lesser, L.I., and Podosin, R.L. Phys-
         iological studies of the hyperkinetic child. American Journal of Psychi-
         atry, May 1972, 128(11), 1418-1424. Topic Codes: BL04B,BL18B,BN04B,
         CV15B,DK09B,MG30,PC07,TA74,TB35B,TB37B,TB95B.

90100   Satterfield, J.H., Cantwell, D.P., and Satterfield, B.T. Pathophysiology
         of the hyperactive child syndrome. Archives of General Psychiatry, De-

cember 1974, 31(6), 839-844. Topic Codes: BL18B,BL25B,BN04B,CV15B,DK09B, DK48B,MG30,MG48B,PC07,TA74,TB35B,TB37B.

90200   Satterfield, J.H., Cantwell, D.P., Saul, R.E., and Yusin, A. Intelli-
gence, academic achievement and EEG abnormalities in hyperactive children.
American Journal of Psychiatry, April 1974, 131(4), 391-395. Topic Codes:
DK48B,DT13B,DT44B,DT52B,MG30,MG48B,MH07,MM07,PI07,PP07,SW07,SW56,TA02,
TA52,TA57,TA74,TB09B,TB33G,TB35B,TB53,TB57B,TB66B,TB95B,TB98B.

90300   Satterfield, J.H., and Dawson, M.E. Electrodermal correlates of hyperactivity in children. Psychophysiology, March 1971, 8(2), 191-197. Topic
Codes: BL25B,BN04B,CV15B,DK48,MG30,MG48,PC07.

90350   Satz, P. Laterality effects in dichotic listening. Nature, 1968, 218,
277-278. Topic Codes: BK11B,BL18,BN44,PO,PS,TA52,TB37.

90400   Satz, P. Left-handedness and early brain insult: An explanation. Neuropsychologia, 1973, 11, 115-117. Topic Codes: BN44,DK07,PO,SJ07.

90500   Satz, P. Pathological left-handedness: An explanatory model. Cortex,
1972, 8, 121-135. Topic Codes: BN44,DD08K,DF,DF34,DK07,DK18,DK46,MO,
NA31C,NA33B,PO.

90550   Satz, P., Achenbach, K., Pattishall, E., and Fennell, E. Order of report,
for asymmetry and handedness in dichotic listening. Cortex, 1965, 1, 377-
396. Topic Codes: BK11B,BL18,BN44,NL,PO,PS,TA52,TB37.

90600   Satz, P., and Morris, R. Learning disability subtypes: A review. In F.
Pirozzolo and J. Wittrock (eds.), Neuropsychological and Cognitive Pro-
cesses in Reading. New York: Academic Press, 1981. Topic Codes: DK07B,
DT15,DT44,ML15,MM,PP.

90700   Satz, P., and Morris, R. Classification of learning disabled children.
In R.E. Tarter (ed.), The Child at Psychiatric Risk. New York: Oxford
University Press, 1983. Topic Codes: DT15,DT44,DT52B,MG,ML15,MM,NA07D,
NA44,NH59E,NJ,PP,SH59F,SW07,TA02,TA04,TA52,TA55,TA59,TA59D,TB98B.

90800   Satz, P., and Todd, J. WAIS performance in brain-damaged left- and right-
handers. Annals of Neurology, 1977, 2, 422-424. Topic Codes: BK11B,
BN44H,DD26,DK07,PM,PO33,TB93.

90900   Saul, L.J. Personal and social psychopathology and the primary prevention
of violence. American Journal of Psychiatry, June 1972, 128(12), 128-131.
Topic Codes: CC81F,CC81N,SI57B,SI57D.

90920   Savitsky, J.C., and Czyzewski, D. The reaction of adolescent offenders
and nonoffenders to nonverbal emotion displays. Journal of Abnormal Child
Psychology, March 1978, 6(1), 89-96. Topic Codes: CC11N,CC37Q,ML03,MY11,
NE37,NE59,PA,PE44D,PE70D,PM,PN11,PT.

90940   Saxe, D.B. Psychiatry, sociopathy and the XYY chromosome syndrome. Journal of Forensic Medicine, July-September 1971, 18(3), 84-95. Topic Codes:
BB70B,BB70D,BI07B,BI11,CC11D,CC11M,MS02,MS04B,PE30D.

90960   Say, B., Carpenter, N.J., Lanier, P.R., Banez, C., Jones, K., and
Coldwell, J.G. Chromosome variants in children with psychiatric disor-
ders. American Journal of Psychiatry, April 1977, 134(4), 424-426. Topic
Codes: BI07,DD02B,MG,NA07D,PE10,TA80.

90980   Sayed, Z.A., Lewis, S.A., and Brittain, R.P. An electroencephalographic
and psychiatric study of thirty-two insane murderers. British Journal of
Psychiatry, 1969, 115, 1115-1124. Topic Codes: BK11B,CC81D,CC81K,CT57F,
CT81,DK07D,MU70B,NE59,NE81,TA52,TB35D.

91000   Scanlon, J.W., Brown, W.U., Weiss, J.B., and Alper, M.H. Neurobehavioral
response of newborn infants after maternal epidural anesthesia. Anes-
thesiology, 1974, 40, 121-128. Topic Codes: BL06,BL27,BP02,BP04,BP26,
BP44,BP46,BP57,NA33D,NA33I,PE34,TA52M,TB02.

91050   Schachter, F.F., and Apgar, V. Perinatal asphyxia and psychologic signs of brain damage in childhood. Pediatrics, December 1959, 24, 1016-1025. Topic Codes: BL67,BL70,DF34,DF60BB,DK07,DP11B,DT04EB,MG,NA07D,NA33B, NL48B,SN,SQ,TA02,TA57,TA59,TB09B,TB74,TB95.

91100   Schachter, S. Birth order, eminence and higher education. American Sociological Review, 1963, 28, 757-768. Topic Codes: NA33I,PE64,SC18, SC70,SJ07,SJ22,TA52M.

91200   Schachter, S. Birth order and sociometric choice. Journal of Abnormal and Social Psychology, 1964, 68, 453-456. Topic Codes: PT,SJ07.

91300   Schachter, S., and Latané, B. Crime, cognition, and the autonomic nervous system. In D. Levine (ed.), Nebraska Symposium on Motivation (vol. 12). Lincoln, Nebraska: University of Nebraska Press, 1964. Topic Codes: BK04D,BN04D,CC11C,CC11D,DT13D,MH11,PC11,PI11,TA59.

91350   Schalling, D., Lidberg, L., Levander, S.E., and Dahlin, Y. Spontaneous autonomic activity as related to psychopathy. Biological Psychology, 1973, 1(2), 83-97. Topic Codes: BL,CC11U,NE59,TA80.

91400   Schalling, D., and Rosen, A.S. Porteus Maze differences between psychopathic and non-psychopathic criminals. British Journal of Social and Clinical Psychology, 1968, 7, 224-228. Topic Codes: CC11C,CC11D,CC11N, CG11CC,CQ11,DA04D,DT13D,MD11,MH11,NE11,PE06D,PI11,TB66D,TB93D.

91500   Scharf, P., and Lininger, R., Moral reasoning and judgment in hypothetical and actual dilemmas involving the police officer's use of deadly force in the line of duty. Unpublished paper, n.p., n.d. Topic Codes: BL11,CC81, CG11P,CQ81,CT57F,CT81,DT13,MF,MH,NA07I,NE81,PE,PG,PI,SC.

91580   Schauss, A.G. Diet, Crime and Delinquency. Berkeley, California: Parker House, 1980. Topic Codes: BD52D,CC37C,CC37K,CC37P,CC37V,CV52D,DD01.

91590   Schauss, A.G. Effects of environmental and nutritional factors on potential and actual batterers. In M. Roy (ed.), Abusive Battering. New York: Van Nostrand Reinhold, 1982, 76-90. Topic Codes: BD11,BD52D, CC11D,CV52D,NH11,SH11.

91600   Schauss, A.G. Tranquilizing effect of color reduces aggressive behavior and potential violence. Orthomolecular Psychiatry, 1979, 8(4), 218-221. Topic Codes: BD,CC11,CC37K,CC81L,CQ11,CQ59,CV13DA,MC,NE11,NE59,PE04,SF11, SR03.

91700   Schauss, A.G., Bland, J., and Simonsen, C.E. A critical analysis of the diets of chronic juvenile offenders. Orthomolecular Psychiatry, 1979, 8(3), 149-157. Topic Codes: BD11,BD52B,BD52D,BL04B,BL04BB,BL70,CC37A, CC37U,CC67,CG11C,CQ67,CV52B,CV52D,MG,NA07D,NE67,SJ09B,SJ09D,SQ.

91800   Scheerer, M. Problem-solving. Scientific American, April 1963, 208(4), 118-128. Topic Codes: DT44,MM,PM,PP.

91850   Scheidt, P.C., Mellits, E.D., Hardy, J.B., Drage, J.S., and Boggs, T.R. Toxicity to bilirubin in neonates: Infant development during first year in relation to maximum neonatal serum bilirubin concentration. Journal of Pediatrics, 1977, 91, 292-297. Topic Codes: BD30BA,BL07B,BL27KL,DF, MT48,NC44,PL,TA52K,TA80,TB05.

91900   Schevill, H.S. Tactile learning, handedness, and reading disability. In J. Herron (ed.), Neuropsychology of Left-Handedness. New York: Academic Press, 1980. Topic Codes: BN44B,DT15,DT44,DT46,DT59,MG,ML15,MM,MN,MR, NA07D,PM70,PO07,PP,PQ,PS,TA02,TA04,TA59D,TB95B.

91930   Schipkowensky, N. Affective disorders: Cyclophrenia and murder. International Psychiatry Clinics, 1968, 5(3), 59-75. Topic Codes: CC11C, CC81D,MB11,MU70B.

91960   Schlebusch, L. The diagnosis and treatment of conduct disorders in young people. <u>South African Medical Journal</u>, February 1979, 55(5), 163-165. Topic Codes: MG02B,NA07D,NL22B,PE10,TA59.

91990   Schlegel, H.J., Schonwetter, H.P., and Langenbeck, U. Clinical symptoms and psychopathology of the XYY chromosomal configuration. <u>Fortschritte der Neurologie, Psychiatrie und Ihrer Grenzgebiete</u>, June 1975, 43(6), 305-312 (in German). Topic Codes: BB70B,BI07,DD02NF,SF07.

92000   Schlesinger, S.E. The prediction of dangerousness in juveniles: A replication. <u>Crime and Delinquency</u>, January 1978, 24(1), 40-48. Topic Codes: BL11,CC37B,CC37L,CC371,CC67,CC81D,CC81N,CG11C,CG11CC,CL,CQ37,CQ67,CV13, CV13D,CY,MG,NA07ID,NE37,NE67,NH59F,PE10,SH59H,SJ09D,TA80.

92040   Schmauk, F.J. Punishment, arousal, and avoidance learning in sociopaths. <u>Journal of Abnormal Psychology</u>, December 1970, 76(3), 325-335. Topic Codes: ME,MS04,NE,PE08,TA02,TA59,TA80.

92080   Schmitt, B.D., Martin, H.P., Nellhaus, G., Cravens, J., Camp, B.W., and Jordan, K. The hyperactive child. <u>Clinical Pediatrics</u> (Philadelphia), March 1973, 12(3), 154-169. Topic Codes: BB07,BL25B,BL31,BP02B,DK07B, DK48B,DT52B,MF,MG30B,MG48B,MT,NA07,PE10,SF07,SI59B.

92084   Schoenthaler, S.J. Alabama diet-behavior program: An empirical evaluation at the Coosa Valley Regional Detention Center. <u>International Journal of Biosocial Research</u>, 1983, 5(2), 79-87. Topic Codes: BD52D,CC37C, CV52D,ME,PE08,SR04.

92086   Schoenthaler, S.J. Effects of citrus on the treatment and control of antisocial behavior: A double-blind study of an incarcerated juvenile population. <u>International Journal of Biosocial Research</u>, 1983, 5(1), 107-117. Topic Codes: BD52D,CC37C,CV52D,ME,PE08,SR04.

92088   Schoenthaler, S.J. Northern California diet-behavior program – an empirical examination of three thousand incarcerated juveniles in Stanislaus County Juvenile Hall. <u>International Journal of Biosocial Research</u>, 1983, 5(1), 99-106. Topic Codes: BD52D,CC37C,CQ59,CV13DA,CV52D,ME,NE59,PE08, SR04.

92090   Schooler, N.R., Collins, P.J., and Sakalis, G. Statistical strategies for prediction of clinical response performance tests as predictors of reduction in psychopathology. <u>Psychopharmacology Bulletin</u>, October 1978, 14(4), 86-88. Topic Codes: MU70,PI,TA02,TA59,TB93B.

92100   Schreiber, D.J., Goldman, H., Kleinman, K.M., Goldfader, P.G., and Snow, M.Y. The relationship between independent neuropsychological and neurological detection and localization of cerebral impairment. <u>Journal of Nervous and Mental Disease</u>, 1976, 162(5), 360-365. Topic Codes: BN44, DK07,PO,TB46.

92200   Schroder, J., de la Chapelle, A., Hakola, P., and Virkkunen, M. The frequency of XYY and XXY men among criminal offenders. <u>Acta Psychiatrica Scandinavica</u>, 1981, 63, 272-276. Topic Codes: BB70B,BB70D,CG11C,CT57, CT59,CT59B,CT68,DD02ND,DD02NF,DK09D,PM11.

92250   Schroeder, N.H. The relationship between the conjugate lateral eye-shift and internal-external locus of control, creativity, and language use in elementary school children [doctoral dissertation, University of Maryland, 1977]. <u>Dissertation Abstracts International</u>, February 1978, 38(8), 3949B. Topic Codes: BN44H,NA07B,PG,PI,PM70,PO,TA04,TA52,TA59D,TA74.

92300   Schuck, S., Dubeck, J.A., Cymbalisty, S.Y., and Green, C. Delinquency, personality tests, and relationships to measures of guilt and adjustment. <u>Psychological Reports</u>, 1972, 31, 219-229. Topic Codes: BL67D,CC37J, CC37W,PA11,PT11,PY11,SI57PB,SN11,SU11,TA03,TA59,TB38B.

92320   Schuckit, M.A., and Chiles, J.T. Family history as a diagnostic aid in two samples of adolescents. <u>Journal of Nervous and Mental Disease</u>, March 1978, 166(3), 165-176. Topic Codes: MB,MD,MG,MI04,MS04,MU,NA07B,NA07D,

NE37,NH11,NH59B,NH59D,NH59E,NH59GB,NH59GD,NH59GG,NH59PB,NH59PJ,PE06,PE08,
PE15B,SJ09,SR01,SR04,SW.

92330   Schuckit, M.A., Howard, H.L., and Swanson, V.A. Genetic Aspects of Psychiatric Syndrome Relating to Antisocial Problems in Youth. Seattle,
Washington: University of Washington Center for the Assessment of Delinquent Behavior and Its Prevention, 1979. Topic Codes: BI07,BI11,CC37B,
CC37N,MB11,ME07,MG30D,MU70B,PE08D,SR04B.

92340   Schuckit, M.A., Petrich, J., and Chiles, J. Hyperactivity: Diagnostic
confusion. Journal of Nervous and Mental Disease, February 1978, 166(2),
79-87. Topic Codes: BK11B,DK48B,MG48B,NA07D,PE10,TA02.

92360   Schulsinger, F. Psychopathy: Heredity and environment. International
Journal of Mental Health, 1972, 1, 190-206. Topic Codes: BI07,BP02B,M,
NH04B,SH04B,TA80.

92380   Schulte, F.J. Current concepts in minimal brain dysfunction. Journal of
the American Medical Association, 1971, 217, 1237-1238. Topic Codes:
DK48,MG48.

92390   Schultz, C.G. Sociopathic and non-sociopathic female felons [doctoral
dissertation, Ohio State University, 1973]. Dissertation Abstracts
International, May 1974, 34(11), 7357A. Topic Codes: CC24B,CQ59,ME07,
NE22,NE59,NL22B,NL22D,PE08D,TA80.

92400   Schultz, S.R. Study of biologically oriented evaluations (medical-neuro-
logical-perceptual-nutritional) performed on juveniles under the authority
of juvenile courts. Unpublished manuscript, University of California,
Berkeley, n.d. Topic Codes: BA,BD30HD,BD52D,CC37U,CG,CG11CC,CV06,CV13,
CV52D,DD30D.

92450   Schuster, R., and Guggenheim, P.D. An investigation of the intellectual
capabilities of juvenile offenders. Journal of Forensic Sciences, April
1982, 27(2), 393-400. Topic Codes: CC37B,CC37H,CC37Q,CC37S,CC371,DK46D,
DK48D,MG48D,MO11,TB09D,TB95D,TB98D.

92500   Schweizer, I.T. Orton revisited. Reading Teacher, December 1974, 28(3),
295-297. Topic Codes: DT15,DT42,DT44,ML,MM,PN,PP.

92530   Schwitzgebel, R.K. Learning theory approaches to the treatment of criminal behavior. Seminars in Psychiatry, August 1971, 3(3), 328-344. Topic
Codes: CC11,CV06,MD,MM,PE06,PP,SI57J.

92600   Scott, D.F. Psychiatric aspects of epilepsy. Postgraduate Medical Journal, April 1968, 44(510), 319-326. Topic Codes: BK11B,CC11B,CC11F,CC11K,
DK07D,DK18D,DK18SD.

92610   Scott, E.M. The act of murder. International Journal of Offender Therapy
and Comparative Criminology, 1975, 19(2), 154-163. Topic Codes: CC11H,
CC11J,CC11P,CC81L,CC81S,CV06,MC11,MD11,MF,MH11,NE59,PE04D,PE15B,PE30D,
SF11.

92620   Scott, J.P. Biology and human aggression. American Journal of Orthopsychiatry, 1970, 40, 568-576. Topic Codes: BI07,BL,MC,PA,PE04,SA07,SB,
SF07.

92630   Scott, M.V. Death, anxiety, and attitudes toward violence and aggression
[doctoral dissertation, United States International University, 1976].
Dissertation Abstracts International, August 1976, 37(2), 989B. Topic
Codes: CC11A,MC,NL,PE04,PT74,SQ07B,TA59,TB.

92650   Scott, P.D. Medical aspects of delinquency. British Journal of Psychiatry, 1975, 9(special no.), 287-295. Topic Codes: BB11,BB70D,CC37,CC37F,
CC37P,CC37X,CQ37,DD01,DD02D,DD02NF,DK07D,DK18D,MS02,NE37.

92670   Scott, P.D. Non-accidental injury in children: Memorandum of evidence to
the Parliamentary Select Committee on Violence in the Family. British

Journal of Psychiatry, October 1977, 131, 366-380. Topic Codes: BL31,DD10,NA07I,NA31F,PG,PK,PL,SH11,SI22,SI57G,TA52.

92680   Scripp, M.W. The neuropsychological differentiation of delinquents at two intelligence levels [doctoral dissertation, Illinois Institute of Technology, 1979]. *Dissertation Abstracts International*, February 1980, 40(8), 3967B-3968B. Topic Codes: CC37F,CC37H,CC37J,CC37Q,CC37I,DK07D,DT44D, PM11,TA03,TB59B.

92690   Scurry, A. The interrelationships among disruptive student behavior and student perceptions of alienation, and internal-external control in black high school seniors [doctoral dissertation, Florida State University, 1976]. *Dissertation Abstracts International*, December 1976, 37(6), 3541A-3542A. Topic Codes: NA,PA,PE64,PE68,PT11,SC18,SC70,SS,TB.

92700   Scutt, J.A. Toward the liberation of the female law-breaker. *International Journal of Criminology and Penology*, February 1978, 6(1), 5-18. Topic Codes: BL70D,CC24,CC37,CG,CQ22,CQ37,CT68,NE22,NE37,SQ11,SQ70D.

92800   Sealy, A.P., and Banks, C. Social maturity, training, experience, and recidivism among British borstal boys. *British Journal of Criminology*, 1971, 11, 245-264. Topic Codes: BL11C,CC37G,CC37W,CC67,CQ59,CQ67,CV13DA, MX11,NA07ID,NE59,NE67,PE68D,PG11,PT11,SR02,TA03,TA59,TB66D.

92900   Sears, R.R. Ordinal position in the family as a psychological variable. *American Sociological Review*, 1950, 15, 397-401. Topic Codes: BL11, NA07B,NL,PE10,PG,PK,PT,SI48,SI57P,SJ07,SW18,TA57,TA74.

93000   Segal, S.S. Retarded readers and antisocial young people: An English study. *International Journal of Offender Therapy and Comparative Criminology*, 1973, 17, 297-302. Topic Codes: CC37I,ME,PE08,PE64B,PE64D,SC, SC70B,SC70D,SR04.

93100   Senate of Canada. *Proceedings of the Subcommittee on Childhood Experiences as Causes of Criminal Behaviour*. Thirtieth Parliament, 1977-78, February 16, 1978, issue no. 9, 36-47. Topic Codes: CC11G,CC11L,CT57BD, DD10D,NH59F,SH59H,SI57GD.

93200   Sendi, I., and Blomgren, P.G. A comparative study of predictive criteria of homicidal adolescents. *American Journal of Psychiatry*, 1975, 132, 423-427. Topic Codes: CC37B,CC37J,CC37L,CC37Q,CC81D,CC81I,CC81N,CQ59,CT57BD, CT57F,CT57B,CV13DA,CX,CZ07,DD10D,MG18D,MS02,MU70B,MV11,NE59,NE79,NH11, PE64D,PE66D,PM11,SC70D,SH11,SI57D,SI57GD,SR69D,SY11,TB35D.

93300   Sepsi, V.J. Girl recidivists. *Journal of Research in Crime and Delinquency*, January 1974, 11(1), 70-79. Topic Codes: BB11,BL04D,CC24,CC37, CC37A,CC37E,CC37J,CC37L,CC37P,CC37Q,CC67,CG11C,CG11CC,CQ22,CQ37,CQ67,CT59, CT70,CV13,DD02D,NE22,NE37,NE67,NH59GI,PE64D,SC18D,SC70D,SH59JL,SI57J.

93400   Serpell, R. How specific are perceptual skills? A crosscultural study of pattern reproduction. *British Journal of Psychology*, 1979, 70, 365-380. Topic Codes: NA07I,PI,PM,PS,SB,SC59,SF26,SN,TA59,TB33,TB49.

93500   Serunian, S.A. Relationship of Apgar scores and Bayley mental and motor scores. *Child Development*, 1975, 46, 696-700. Topic Codes: BL31,BL67, DF,DF48,DP48,NA31C,NA31F,NA33,NC44,NL48,PK,SN, TB02,TB05.

93550   Sever, J.L. Perinatal infections affecting the developing fetus and newborn. *Conference on the Prevention of Mental Retardation through the Control of Infectious Diseases* (U.S. Public Health Service publication no. 1692). Washington, D.C.: U.S. Government Printing Office, 1968. Topic Codes: BL22,BP02,BP22F,BP47,DF34,NA33,NA33B.

93600   Sever, J.L., Fuccillo, D.A., Ellenberg, J., and Gilkeson, M.R. Infection and low birth weight in an industrialized society. *American Journal of Diseases of Children*, May 1975, 129(5), 557-558. Topic Codes: BB,BL07, BP47,DD02,DF06,DF34,NA33B,NC44,NC59G.

93650   Sever, J.L., and Terasaki, P.I. Maternal-fetal incompatibility: III.
         Central nervous system and cardiac anomalies. In P.I. Terasaki (ed.),
         Histocompatibility Testing. Copenhagen: Munksgaard, 1970. Topic Codes:
         BB,BD30,BP02,BP47,BP53,DD02,DF34,DK09,NA33B,NC44,NC59G.

93660   Sex chromosomes and crime. Annals of Internal Medicine, August 1968,
         69(2), 399-401. Topic Codes: BB70D,CC11M.

93670   Shaffer, D. Psychiatric aspects of brain injury in childhood: A review.
         Developmental Medicine and Child Neurology, April 1973, 15(2), 211-220.
         Topic Codes: BK11B,BP02B,DK07B,DK18B,DT67,MG,PE10.

93680   Shaffer, D., Meyer-Bahlburg, H.F.L., and Stokman, C.L. The development of
         aggression. In M. Rutter (ed.), Scientific Foundations of Developmental
         Psychiatry. London: Heineman, 1980. Topic Codes: BB70,BD70,BK11B,
         BK11BL,BL04,BL11,BL70,CC81,CQ37B,CQ81,CT81,DD02N,DK07,MC,NA07B,NA07I,
         NE37D,NE81,PE04,PE10,PG,SF,SI57,SI57J,SQ,SR03.

93700   Shagass, C., Gershon, S., and Friedhoff, A.J., (eds). Psychopathology
         and Brain Dysfunction. New York: Raven Press, 1977. Topic Codes:
         BD07,BI07,BK11BL,BL04B,BL11,BL25B,BL29B,BL70B,BN44B,CC11F,CC67,CQ67,DK07B,
         DK09D,DK18SB,DP11B,DT13B,DT15,DT44BB,DT59B,DT67,MB,MG18B,MH07,ML15,MM07B,
         MP07,MR07,MS04,MU70,NA07D,NA07I,NE67,PE52B,PG,PI07,PN07,PO07,PP07B,PS07,
         PT74,SQ07,TA02,TA52,TA59,TA80,TB35B,TB81,TB95B,TB96B,TB98B.

93760   Shah, S.A. The 47, XYY chromosomal abnormality: A critical appraisal
         with respect to antisocial and violent behavior. In W.L. Smith and A.
         Kling (eds.), Issues in Brain/Behavior Control. New York: Spectrum,
         1976. Topic Codes: BB70D,CC81E,DD02NF,DT04ED.

93800   Shanker, A. The nonsense of attacking education tests. The Washington
         Post, October 19, 1980, C1. Topic Codes: PE64,SC,SC70,TA59D.

93900   Shannon, L.W. Assessing the relationship of juvenile careers to adult ca-
         reers. Paper presented at the annual meeting of the American Society of
         Criminology, San Francisco, California, November 1980. Topic Codes:
         BL70D,CC11A,CC11S,CC37A,CC67,CE,CG11P,CG11T,CL,CQ67,CT57,CT59,NA44B,NE67,
         NJ03,SQ11,TA70.

93990   Shanok, S.S., and Lewis, D.O. Medical histories of abused delinquents.
         Child Psychiatry and Human Development, Summer 1981, 11(4), 222-231.
         Topic Codes: CC37M,CC37O,CC37P,CT57BB,CT57BD,CV30B,DD01,DD03D,DD10B.

94000   Shanok, S.S., and Lewis, D.O. Medical histories of female delinquents:
         Clinical and epidemiologic findings. Archives of General Psychiatry, Feb-
         ruary 1981, 38(2), 211-213. Topic Codes: CC11,CC11O,CC24,CC37P,CC37T,
         CG11CC,CQ11,CQ22,CT57BD,CT59,CV13,CV30D,DD01,DD10D,DD26D,DK,DK09D,DP11D,
         NE11,NE22,SI57GD,SL11,TA03,TA52.

94010   Shanok, S.S., Malani, S.C., Ninan, O.P., Guggenheim, P., Weinstein, H.,
         and Lewis, D.O. A comparison of delinquent and nondelinquent adolescent
         psychiatric inpatients. American Journal of Psychiatry, May 1983, 140(5),
         582-585. Topic Codes: CC11M,CC37B,CC37H,CC37M,CC37T,CV06C,CV30D,NH59PL,
         SH59RL,SL11.

94050   Shapiro, A. Delinquent and disturbed behaviour within the field of mental
         deficiency. International Psychiatry Clinics, 1968, 5(3), 76-90. Topic
         Codes: BB70D,BK11B,BL11,CT59,CT68,CT70,DD26,DK18,PE10,SI.

94100   Shapiro, S., Hartz, S.C., Siskind, V., Mitchell, A.A., Slone, D.,
         Rosenberg, L., Monson, R.R., and Heinonen, O.P. Anticonvulsants and pa-
         rental epilepsy in the development of birth defects. Lancet, February 7,
         1976, 7954, 272-275. Topic Codes: BB,BL11,BL31,BL48,BP02,BP04,BP47,
         CV15,DD02,DF48,DK18,DP48,DT48,MT48,NA07I,NA31F,NA44B,NC22,NC44,NC59,NC59G,
         NJ03,NL48,PE48,PK,PM,PR,TB05.

94200   Shapiro, S., Monson, R.R., Kaufman, D.W., Siskind, V., Heinonen, O.P., and
         Slone, D. Perinatal mortality and birth-weight in relation to aspirin

taken during pregnancy. Lancet, June 26, 1976, 7974, 1375-1376. Topic Codes: BL06,BL07,BL67,BP02,BP04,DF06,DF48,DP48,NC44,NC59G,SN.

94230   Sheard, M.H., Marini, J.L., Bridges, C.I., and Wagner, E. The effect of lithium on impulsive aggressive behavior in man. American Journal of Psychiatry, December 1976, 133(12), 1409-1413. Topic Codes: CC81Y,CT81, CV15D,NE59,NE81,TA80,TB19B,TB38B,TB61B.

94260   Sheard, M.H., Marini, J.L., and Giddings, S.S. The effect of lithium on luteinizing hormone and testosterone in man. Diseases of the Nervous System, October 1977, 38(10), 765-769. Topic Codes: CC81Y,CT81,CV15D,NE59, NE81,TA80.

94290   Shein, J.H. The concurrent validity of Bender Gestalt recall for differential assessment of organicity in children [doctoral dissertation, Fordham University, 1975]. Dissertation Abstracts International, February 1976, 36(8), 5162A. Topic Codes: BK11B,BL11,DK07,MG,NA07D,NA07I,PE10,PG, TB09.

94300   Sherman, J.A. Field articulation, sex, spatial visualization, dependency, practice, laterality of the brain and birth order. Perceptual and Motor Skills, 1974, 38, 1223-1235. Topic Codes: BL70,BN44,DT44,MM,PM70,PO,PP, PT,SJ07,SQ,TA59D,TB33.

94400   Sherman, J.A. Problem of sex differences in space perception and aspects of intellectual functioning. Psychological Review, 1967, 74, 290-299. Topic Codes: BL70,DT13,DT44,MH,MM,PI,PM,PM70,PP,SQ,SQ70,TA59D.

94500   Shore, M.F. Psychological theories of the causes of antisocial behavior. Crime and Delinquency, 1971, 17, 456-468. Topic Codes: BA,CC11,CC11P, CC37,CC37G,CC37L,CG,CQ11,CQ37,NE11,NE37,PT11,PV11,SI57D,SI57J,SI57PB, SJ09D,SS09,SU11.

94550   Shostak, D.A., and McIntyre, C.W. Stimulus-seeking behavior in three delinquent personality types. Journal of Consulting and Clinical Psychology, June 1978, 46(3), 582. Topic Codes: CC37BB,CC37W,CC371,CQ37,MG, NA07DF,NE37,PE10,TA03,TA59,TA80.

94600   Shover, N., Norland, S., James, J., and Thornton, W.E. Gender roles and delinquency. Social Forces, September 1979, 58(1), 162-175. Topic Codes: CC24,CC37,CC37W,CG11T,CQ22,CQ37,CT57,CT59,NE22,NE37,PT11,SQ70D,TA70.

94620   Siddle, D.A.T., Mednick, S.A., Nicol, A.R., and Foggitt, R.H. Skin conductance recovery in anti-social adolescents. In S.A. Mednick and K.O. Christiansen (eds.), Biosocial Bases of Criminal Behavior. New York: Gardner Press, Inc., 1977, 213-216. Topic Codes: BL25D,CC37,CC37T,CQ37.

94640   Siegel, R.A. Probability of punishment and suppression of behavior in psychopathic and nonpsychopathic offenders. Journal of Abnormal Psychology, October 1978, 87(5), 514-522. Topic Codes: CC11C,CC11U,CQ59,CT68, CV13D,CV13DA,DT13D,MH11,MS04B,NE59,PI11,SI57J.

94660   Siegel, R.K. Phencyclidine, criminal behavior, and the defense of diminished capacity. National Institute on Drug Abuse Research Monograph Series, August 1978, 21, 272-288. Topic Codes: CC11H,CG,DA15B,DA15D,MI04, MI07,PE15B,PE15D.

94670   Sigman, M., Ungerer, J.A., and Russell, A. Moral judgment in reaction to behavioral and cognitive disorders in adolescents. Journal of Abnormal Child Psychology, December 1983, 11(4), 503-511. Topic Codes: DT13,MG.

94675   Sigvardsson, S., Cloninger, C.R., Bohman, M, and von Knorring, A.L. Predisposition to petty criminality in Swedish adoptees: III. Sex differences and validation of the male typology. Archives of General Psychiatry, November 1982, 39(11), 1248-1253. Topic Codes: BI07B,BL70D,CC11M, CC11S,NH04D,SH04D,SQ11.

94680   Silver, M.B. The effect of minor hemisphere brain damage on auditory processing [doctoral dissertation, City University of New York, 1977]. Dissertation Abstracts International, April 1977, 37(10), 4974B. Topic Codes: BK11B,BN44,DK07,NL,TA55,TA80.

94690   Silverman, A.J., Adevai, G., and McGough, E.W. Some relationships between handedness and perception. Journal of Psychosomatic Research, 1966, 10, 151-158. Topic Codes: BN44,DT59,MR,NL,PO,PS,TA59,TA80.

94700   Silverman, D. Clinical and electroencephalographic studies on criminal psychopaths. Archives of Neurology and Psychiatry, 1943, 50, 18-33. Topic Codes: CC11,CC11C,CC11F,CC11U,CC37BB,CC37F,CC371,CQ11,CQ59,CT57, CT59,CT68,CV13DA,DD08KC,DD26BB,DK07BB,MS04,NE11,NE59,SI57BB,SJ09D,TA02B, TA03,TA52,TB35BB,TB78B.

94750   Silverman, I., Raskin, L.M., Davidson, J.L., and Bloom, A.S. Relationships among token test, age and WISC scores for children with learning problems. Journal of Learning Disabilities, February 1977, 10(2), 104-107. Topic Codes: BL11,DT44,MM,NA07B,NA07I,PE10,PG,PM,PP,TA59,TA80,TB95.

94800   Silverstein, A.B. The internal consistency of the Stanford-Binet. American Journal of Mental Deficiency, 1969, 73, 753-754. Topic Codes: DK46, MQ,TB78.

94850   Silverstein, A.B., The measurement of intelligence. International Review of Research in Mental Retardation, 1970, 4, 193-227. Topic Codes: BL04, BL70,DK46,MO,PM,SQ,TB78,TB93,TB95.

94900   Silverstein, A.B. Validity of WISC short forms at three age levels. Journal of Consulting Psychology, 1967, 31(6), 635-636. Topic Codes: BL04,TB95.

94920   Simeon, J., and Itil, T.M. Computerized electroencephalogram: A model of understanding the brain function in childhood psychosis and its treatment. Journal of Autism and Childhood Schizophrenia, September 1975, 5(3), 247-265. Topic Codes: BK11B,BL11,CV15B,DK07B,MG02B,MG04,MU70,NA07D,NA07I, PE10,PG,SH59B,SH59RP,TB35B.

94940   Simmons, J.Q., III, and Tymchuk, A. The learning deficits in childhood psychosis. Pediatric Clinics of North America, August 1973, 20(3), 665-679. Topic Codes: BL11,DT44B,MG04GB,MM07,PE10,PP07.

94960   Simon, N. Echolalic speech in childhood autism: Consideration of possible underlying loci of brain damage. Archives of General Psychiatry, November 1975, 32(11), 1439-1446. Topic Codes: BL11,BN70,DD02B,DK07B, DT42B,DT71,MG02B,NL,PE10,PG,PP.

94980   Simon, N.M., and Senturia, A.G. Adoption and psychiatric illness. American Journal of Psychiatry, February 1966, 122(8), 858-868. Topic Codes: BL11,NH04B,PG,SH04B.

94990   Simons, J.M. Observations on compulsive behavior in autism. Journal of Autism and Childhood Schizophrenia, January-March 1974, 4(1), 1-10. Topic Codes: BL11,DD00,MG04G,NA07D,PE10,PG.

95000   Simons, R.L., Miller, M.G., and Aigner, S.M. Contemporary theories of deviance and female delinquency: An empirical test. Journal of Research in Crime and Delinquency, January 1980, 17(1), 42-53. Topic Codes: BL11,BL70D,CC37,CC37J,CC37K,CC37L,CG11T,CQ37,NA07I,NE37,PE10,PG,SI57D, SQ11,SS09,TA70,TA80.

95100   Simonsen, S.E. Prognostic value of ERG (oscillatory potential) in juvenile diabetics. Acta Opthalmologica, 1974, supplement no. 123, 223-224. Topic Codes: BL11,DD15,DD81,NA07I,PG.

95200   Sinclair, I., and Chapman, B. A typological and dimensional study of a sample of prisoners. British Journal of Criminology, 1973, 13, 341-354. Topic Codes: CC11A,CC11C,CC11H,CC11I,CC11J,CC11L,CC11P,CC11U,CC67,CC81,

CQ59,CQ67,CQ81,CT59,CT81,CV13DA,DA04D,MD11,MQ11,MX11,NE59,NE67,NE81,PE06D,
PE68D,PT11,PV11,SC18D,SD11,SO11,SR02,SW56,TB59B,TB72B.

95300   Sinclair, I.A.C., Shaw, M.J., and Troop, J. The relationship between in-
troversion and response to casework in a prison setting. British Journal
of Social and Clinical Psychology, 1974, 13, 51-60. Topic Codes: CC11C,
CC11N,CC11P,CC67,CC67B,CQ59,CQ67,CV06C,CV13DA,MQ11,MS04B,NE59,NE67,PM11,
PT11,SB11.

95350   Singer, J.E., Westphal, M., and Niswander, K.R. Sex differences in the
incidence of neonatal abnormalities and abnormal performance in early
childhood. Child Development, March 1968, 39, 103-112. Topic Codes:
BL11,BL31,BL70,DP44,NA44B,NC44,NJ03,TA52K,TA80,TB02,TB05,TB78.

95400   Singer, J.L. (ed.). The Control of Aggression and Violence. New York:
Academic Press, 1971. Topic Codes: B,BD30HD,BD70B,BK11B,BK11BL,BL11,
BL70,CC11C,CC11U,CC37B,CC371,CC81,CC81Y,CG11T,CQ81,CT57,CT59,CT81,CV06C,
CV15B,CX,DD30D,DK07,DT44,MC,MM,NA07B,NA07I,NE79,NE81,NH11,PE04,PE10,PG,PP,
PY,SB,SB11,SF11,SH11,SI57,SI57J,SI57P,SQ,SR03,SS09,SU,TA03,TA59,TA70,
TB23B,TB51B,TB61B,TB74B,TB86C.

95430   Skelton, W.D. Alcohol, violent behavior and the electroencephalogram.
Southern Medical Journal, 1970, 63, 465-466. Topic Codes: CC81B,CQ81,
CT57F,CT81,DA04D,MD11,NL,PE06D,TB35D.

95460   Skrzypek, G.J. Effect of perceptual isolation and arousal on anxiety,
complexity preference, and novelty preference in psychopathic and neurotic
delinquents. Journal of Abnormal Psychology, June 1969, 74(3), 321-329.
Topic Codes: CC37B,CC37BB,CC371,MQ11,MS04B.

95500   Sletto, R.F. Sibling position and juvenile delinquency. American Journal
of Sociology, 1934, 39, 657-669. Topic Codes: BL70D,CC37,CC37L,CQ37,
NE37,NH70D,SH70D,SJ07D,SQ11.

95600   Slone, D., Heinonen, O.P., Kaufman, D.W., Siskind, V., Monson, R.R., and
Shapiro, S. Aspirin and congenital malformations. Lancet, June 26, 1976,
7974, 1373-1375. Topic Codes: BB,BP02,BP04,DD02,NC44,NC59G.

95700   Slone, D., Heinonen, O.P., Monson, R.R., Shapiro, S., Hartz, S.C., and
Rosenberg, L. Maternal drug exposure and fetal abnormalities. Clinical
Pharmacology and Therapeutics, 1973, 14(4, part 2), 648-653. Topic Codes:
BB,BL07B,BP02,BP04,DD02,DF06B,DF48,DP48,DP58,DP81,NC44,NC59G.

95750   Slone, D., Shapiro, S., Heinonen, O.P., Monson, R.R., Hartz, S.C.,
Siskind, V., Rosenberg, L., and Mitchell, A.A. Maternal drug exposure and
birth defects. In S. Kelly, E.B. Hook, D.T. Janerich and I.H. Porter
(eds.), Birth Defects: Risks and Consequences. New York: Academic
Press, 1976. Topic Codes: BB,BP02,BP04,DD02,NC44,NC59G,NH70,SH70.

95770   Slone, D., Siskind, V., Heinonen, O.P., Monson, R.R., Kaufman, D.W., and
Shapiro, S. Antenatal exposure to the phenothiazines in relation to con-
genital malformations, perinatal mortality rate, birth weight, and intel-
ligence quotient score. American Journal of Obstetrics and Gynecology,
July 1, 1977, 128(5), 486-488. Topic Codes: BL06,BP02,BP04,DF34,DF48,
DP48,NA33A,NA44B,NC22,NC44,NJ03,PM07,TB78B.

95800   Small, J.G. The organic dimension of crime. Archives of General Psychi-
atry, July 1966, 15, 82-89. Topic Codes: BL04D,BL67D,BL70D,CC11A,
CC11C,CC11H,CC11O,CC11R,CC11S,CC11U,CC37F,CQ59,CT57,CT59,CT68,CV13DA,
DA04D,DD26D,DK09D,DT67B,MD11,NE59,PE06D,SN11,SQ11,TA03,TA59,TB09D,TB12B,
TB35D,TB93D.

95900   Smart, R.G. Alcoholism, birth order, and family size. Journal of Abnormal and Social Psychology, 1963, 66(1), 17-23. Topic Codes: DA04,MD,
PE06,PV07,SF26B,SJ07B,SJ22B,SO07.

96000   Smith, A.C., Flick, G.L., Ferriss, G.S., and Sellmann, A.H. Prediction of
developmental outcome at seven years from prenatal, perinatal, and post-

natal events. Child Development, 1972, 43, 495-507. Topic Codes: BL11,
BP02,DF,DF34,DP11,NA07I,NA31C,NA33B,NA44D,NC70,NJ06,PG,TB09K,TB33G,TB53,
TB84,TB95,TB98.

96100   Smith, A.L., Hays, J.R., and Solway, K.S. Comparison of the WISC-R and
culture fair intelligence test in a juvenile delinquent population. Journal of Psychology, November 1977, 97, 179-182. Topic Codes: BL67,CC371,
CQ59,CV13DA,NE59,PM,SN,TA59D,TB95.

96300   Smith, D.A., and Visher, C.A. Sex and involvement in deviance/crime: A
quantitative review of the empirical literature. American Sociological
Review, August 1980, 45, 691-701. Topic Codes: BL04D,BL67D,BL70D,CC11S,
CC37,CC81V,CG11C,CG11P,CG11T,CQ37,CT57,CT59,CT70,NE37,SF26D,SJ09D,SN11,
SQ11,SW11,TA70.

96350   Smith, J.P. Psychopathic criminals in Denmark. Nursing Mirror, July 19,
1968, 127(3), 40. Topic Codes: CG11CC,CQ59,CV06C,CV13DA,NE59.

96400   Smith, N.C., Jr. A comparison of short-form estimation methods in the
WISC in juvenile public offenders. Journal of Clinical Psychology, 1971,
27, 77-79. Topic Codes: BL70,CC37Q,CC371,SQ,TB95.

96500   Smith, S. The adolescent murderer. Archives of General Psychiatry, 1965,
13(4), 310-319. Topic Codes: CC11C,CC11G,CC37B,CC37G,CC37L,CC81D,CT57F,
CV06C,SI57D,SJ09D.

96525   Smith, S.M., Honigsberger, L., and Smith, C.A. EEG and personality factors in baby batterers. British Medical Journal, July 7, 1973, 3(870),
20-22. Topic Codes: CC81K,CC81Q,CC81S,CG11CC,CQ81,CT57B,CT81,MS02,NE81,
PM11,PT11,TB35D,TB93D.

96600   Snyder, R.F., and Kalil, J. Item analysis, interexaminer reliability and
scoring problems for Koppitz scoring on the Bender Gestalt for six-year-
olds. Perceptual and Motor Skills, 1968, 27, 1351-1358. Topic Codes:
BL11,NA07I,PG,TB09K.

96700   Sobel, D. Schizophrenia: Vast effort focuses on four areas. New York
Times, November 13, 1979, C-1. Topic Codes: BD07,BI07,CV15B,DK07B,MU70,
NH04B,NH65B,NH74B,SH04B,SH74B.

96800   Sobotka, K.R., Black, F.W., Hill, S.D., and Porter, R.J. Some psychological correlates of developmental dyslexia. Journal of Learning Disabilities, June/July 1977, 10(6), 42-48. Topic Codes: BL04B,BL11,DT15,DT42,
DT59,MG,ML,ML15,MR,NA07D,NA07I,PE44,PG,PN,PS,TA02,TA59D,TB09B,TB09K,TB95B,
TB98B.

96850   Sobotka, K.R., and May, J.G. Visual evoked potentials and reaction time
in normal and dyslexic children. Psychophysiology, January 1977, 14(1),
18-24. Topic Codes: BL18,DD81,DT15,DT44,MM,MR,PP,PS,TB09,TB35,TB95,TB98.

96900   Solomons, G., Holden, R.H., and Denhoff, E. The changing picture of cerebral dysfunction in early childhood. Journal of Pediatrics, July 1963,
63, 113-120. Topic Codes: BK11B,BL31,BP02,DD08K,DF34,DK07,DP11,NA31A,
NA33A,NA44B,NC44,NJ03,NL48B,PK,PL.

96920   Solway, K.S., Cook, T.H., and Hays, J.R. WISC subtest patterns of delinquent female retardates. Psychological Reports, February 1976, 38(1), 42.
Topic Codes: CC37H,CC37Q,CQ37,M011,NE37,NL48D,PM70B,SQ11,TB95D.

96940   Solway, K.S., Hays, J.R., Roberts, T.K., and Cody, J.A. Comparison of
WISC profiles of alleged juvenile delinquents living at home versus those
incarcerated. Psychological Reports, October 1975, 37(2), 403-407. Topic
Codes: CC37B,CC37BB,CC37H,CC37L,CC37Q,CC371,CC81D,CG11C,CT57F,CX,CZ07,
DT44D,MM11,MS04B,NE79,NH11,NL48D,PM11,PP11,SH11,SI22D,SI48D,SJ09D,SY11,
TA03,TA59D,TB09D,TB61B,TB74B,TB95D,TB98D.

96970   Sommer, B. The troubled teen: Suicide, drug use, and running away. Wom-

en and Health, Summer-Fall 1984, 9(2-3), 117-141. Topic Codes: CT70,
DA15,MG,MI,MZ,NA07D,PE15.

96980   Sommers, R.K., Moore, W.H., Brady, W., and Jackson, P. Performances of
articulatory defective, minimal brain dysfunctioning, and normal children
on dichotic ear preference, laterality, and fine-motor skills tasks.
Journal of Special Education, Spring 1976, 10(1), 5-14. Topic Codes:
BN44,BN70,DD81,DK48,DT44,DT71,MG30,MG48,MM,MY,NA07,PE70,PO,PP,TA55,TA59D,
TB35.

97000   Sorrells, J.M. Kids who kill. Crime and Delinquency, July 1977, 23(3),
312-320. Topic Codes: BL67D,BL70D,CC37B,CC37E,CC37I,CC37L,CC37P,CC37Y,
CC67,CC81,CQ67,CQ81,CT57F,CT59,CT81,NE67,NE81,NH59B,NH59D,NH59F,SH59B,
SH59D,SH59H,SJ09D,SN11,SQ11.

97030   Sosa-Soto, J.N. Vascular effects of frustration and aggression-anxiety on
members of a clinical population [doctoral dissertation, Florida State
University, 1974]. Dissertation Abstracts International, January 1975,
35(7), 3600B. Topic Codes:BK04D,BL08BD,BN04D,CC11D,CG11CC,CQ59,CQ67,
DD28D,MX11,NE59,NE67,PC11,PE04D,PE68D,SR02,TA52.

97060   Soulairac, A., Lambinet, H., and Aymaro, N. Action of the serotonin precursor 5-hydroxytryptophan on aggressive symptomatology. Annales Medico-
psychologiques, October 1976, 2(3), 459-463 (in French). Topic Codes:
CV15B,CV15D,MC,PE04,SR03.

97100   Sparling, M.E. Intelligence of Indian children: The relationship between
Binet and Porteus scores. American Journal of Mental Deficiency, 1941,
46, 60-62. Topic Codes: NA07,NL,PM,TB66,TB78.

97200   Spaulding, E.R., and Healy, W. Inheritance as a factor in criminality.
Journal of Criminal Law, 1913-14, 4, 837-858. Topic Codes: BI11,CC11,
CC11L,CC11M,CC37K,CC37L,CC37N,CG,CQ11,NE11,NH67B, NH67D,SF11.

97300   Spellacy, F. Neuropsychological differences between violent and nonvio-
lent adolescents. Journal of Clinical Psychology, October 1977, 33(4),
966-969. Topic Codes: BN44D,CC37F,CC37H,CC37J,CC37R,CC81G,CC81R,CC81Y,
DK07D,MK11,NL48D,PE30D,PO11,TA03,TA55,TB61B,TB95D.

97400   Spellacy, F. Neuropsychological discrimination between violent and non-
violent men. Journal of Clinical Psychology, January 1978, 34(1), 49-52.
Topic Codes: BL48D,CC11,CC11C,CC11O,CC11U,CC81G,CC81R,CC81Y,CQ11,DK07D,
DT13D,DT42D,DT48D,DT59D,MH11,MK11,ML03,MR11,MT48D,NE11,PE30D,PE44D,PE48D,
PI11,PN11,PR11,PS11,TA03,TA55,TB61B,TB93D.

97480   Spera, S.P. An investigation of the relationship of developmental changes
in aggressive behaviors and social cognitive skills [doctoral dissertation, Tulane University, 1981]. Dissertation Abstracts International,
December 1982, 43(6), 2046B. Topic Codes: BL11,DT13,MC,MX.

97500   Sperry, R.W., and Gazzaniga, M.S. Language following surgical disconnec-
tion of the hemispheres. In F.L. Darley (ed.), Brain Mechanisms Underlying Speech and Language. New York: Grune & Stratton, 1967. Topic
Codes: BN44,DT13,DT42,MH,ML,PE44,PI,PN,PO.

97600   Spong, P., Halder, M., and Lindsley, D.B. Selective attentiveness and
cortical evoked responses to visual and auditory stimuli. Science, April
16, 1965, 145, 395-397. Topic Codes: BL18,DT13,MH,PI,TB37.

97680   Spreen, O. The relationship between learning disability, neurological impairment, and delinquency: Results of a follow-up study. Journal of Nervous and Mental Disease, December 1981, 169(12), 791-799. Topic Codes:
CC37F,CC37H,CC37T,CE,DK,DK07D,TA02,TA03,TA52.

97700   Springer, S.P., and Searleman, A. Left handedness in twins: Implications
for the mechanisms underlying cerebral asymmetry of function. In J.
Herron (ed.), Neuropsychology of Left Handedness. New York: Academic

Press, 1980. Topic Codes: BI,BL22,BN44,BP22F,DK07,DT42,ML,NH74,PE44,
PM70,PN,PO,SB,SH74,TA59D,TB68.

97800   Sroufe, L.A., Sonies, B.C., West, W.D., and Wright, F.S. Anticipatory
heart rate deceleration and reaction time in children with and without re-
ferral for learning disability. Child Development, 1973, 44, 267-273.
Topic Codes: BL04,BL29B,CV15B,DK48,MG,MG48,NA07D.

97850   Stafford, F.P. Comment on "Home investments in children" by A. Leibowitz.
Journal of Political Economy, March 1974, 82(2, part II), S132-S135.
Topic Codes: NH59PF,PM,SC18,SC70,SD,SH59RF,SI22,SI46,SI48,SI57P,SI59,
SW16,SW18,SW33,SW56.

97900   Stafford-Clark, D., and Taylor, F.H. Clinical and EEG studies of prisoners charged with murder. Journal of Neurology, Neurosurgery and Psychiatry, 1949, 12, 325-330. Topic Codes: CC11,CC11L,CC110,CC37,CC37K,CG11C,
CG11CC,CQ11,CQ37,CQ59,CT57F,CV13,CV13DA,DK18D,NE11,NE37,NE59,NH67,NH67B,
TB35D.

97950   Stamm, J.S., and Kreder, S.V., Minimal brain dysfunction: Psychological
and neurophysiological disorders in hyperkinetic children. In M.S.
Gazzaniga (ed.), Handbook of Behavioral Neurobiology, vol. 2. New York:
Plenum Press, 1979. Topic Codes: BK04B,BL18B,BL25B,BL29B,BL48B,BN04B,
CV15B,DK07B,DK48B,DT13,DT48B,DT52B,MG,MG30,MG48B,MH,MK,MT48B,NA07D,PC07,
PE30,PE48B,PI,PR07,TA02,TA57,TA59D,TA74,TB09B,TB33,TB33G,TB35B,TB37B,
TB57B,TB95B.

98000   Standley, K., and Nicholson, J. Observing the childbirth environment: A
research model. Birth and the Family Journal, Spring 1980, 7(1), 15-20.
Topic Codes: BP44,BP48.

98100   Standley, K., Soule, A.B., Copans, S.A., and Duchowny, M.S. Local-re-
gional anesthesia during childbirth: Effect on newborn behaviors. Science, November 1974, 186, 634-635. Topic Codes: BP02,BP04,NA33D,NA33I,
NA44,NJ,PE34,TA52M.

98150   Stang, H.J. A diagnostic and prognostic study of a material comprising
abnormal Norwegian delinquents. Acta Psychiatrica Scandinavica, 1967,
43(2), 113-120. Topic Codes: CC11C,CC11D,CC11H,CC11N,CC67B,CG11CC,CQ67,
CT57,CT59,CT68,DA04D,DK07D,DK46D,MD11,MQ11,MU11,NE67,PM70B,TA03,TA59D.

98200   Steelman, L.C., and Mercy, J.A. Unconfounding the confluence model: A
test of sibship size and birth-order effects on intelligence. American
Sociological Review, August 1980, 45(4), 571-582. Topic Codes: BP07,PM,
SJ05,SJ07,SJ22,SW33,TB95.

98250   Stefanowicz, J.P., and Hannum, T.E. Ethical risk-taking and sociopathy in
incarcerated females. Correctional Psychologist, January 1971, 4(4), 138-
152. Topic Codes: CC11C,CC24,CQ22,CQ59,CV13DA,MS04B,NE22,NE59.

98300   Steffensmeier, D.J. Crime and the contemporary woman: An analysis of
changing levels of female property crime, 1960-75. Social Forces, December 1978, 57(2), 566-584. Topic Codes: BL70D,CC11S,CC24,CC81V,CG11,CQ22,
CT59,NE22,SQ11,SQ70D.

98400   Steffensmeier, D.J. Sex differences in patterns of adult crime, 1965-77:
A review and assessment. Social Forces, June 1980, 58(4), 1080-1102.
Topic Codes: BL70D,CC11S,CC24,CC81V,CE,CG11,CG11C,CG11P,CQ22,CT57,CT59,
CT68,DA04D,DA15D,MD11,MI07,NE22,PE06D,PE15D,SQ11,SQ70D.

98500   Steffensmeier, D.J., and Steffensmeier, R.H. Trends in female delinquency: An examination of arrest, juvenile court, self-report, and field
data. Criminology, May 1980, 18(1), 62-85. Topic Codes: BL70D,CC24,
CC37,CC81V,CE,CG11,CG11C,CG11T,CQ22,CQ37,CQ37B,CT57,CT57F,CT59,CT59B,CT68,
CT70,DA04D,DA15D,MD11,MI07,NE22,NE37,NE37D,PE06D,PE15D,SQ11,SQ70D,TA70.

98530   Steigerwald, F., and Schmidt, L.R. On the diagnosis of juvenile delinquency with the Saarbrucken MMPI. *Psychologie und Praxis*, April–June 1974, 18(2), 49–60 (in German). Topic Codes: CC37B,CC371,TB61B.

98560   Stein, J.R. Effects of feedback on performance of introverted and extroverted delinquents and non-delinquents. *Criminal Justice and Behavior*, December 1976, 3(4), 371–378. Topic Codes: CC37W,CQ37,CV06,MS02,NE22, PT11,TA03.

98590   Steinberg, E.P., and Schwartz, G.E. Biofeedback and electrodermal self-regulation in psychopathy. *Journal of Abnormal Psychology*, August 1976, 85(4), 408–415. Topic Codes: BL25BB,BL29B,MS04,TB61.

98600   Steinberg, H. Selective effects of an anaesthetic drug on cognitive behavior. *Quarterly Journal of Experimental Psychology*, 1954, 6, 170–180. Topic Codes: BL48,CV15,DT13,DT42,DT48,MH,ML,MT48,PE44,PE48,PI,PN,PR, TA59D.

98610   Stellern, J., Marlowe, M., and Cossairt, A. Cognitive mode and classroom behavior. *Psychology in the Schools*, January 1984, 21(1), 103–111. Topic Codes: BN44D,MH,NA07B,NA07D,PE64,PE64B,PI,PO07.

98625   Stevenson, J., and Richman, N. Behavior, language and development in three-year-old children. *Journal of Autism and Childhood Schizophrenia*, September 1978, 8(3), 299–313. Topic Codes: BL11,DT42B,MG11,MG30B,MK, ML02,NA07D,PE44B,PN07,SR01,TA02,TA55,TA59D,TB53.

98635   Stewart, D.J. Dependency correlates of psychopathic, neurotic and subcultural delinquents [doctoral dissertation, Temple University, 1972]. *Dissertation Abstracts International*, July 1972, 33(1), 453B–454B. Topic Codes: CC37W,TA80.

98637   Stewart, D.J. Effects of social reinforcement on dependency and aggressive responses of psychopathic, neurotic, and subcultural delinquents. *Journal of Abnormal Psychology*, February 1972, 79(1), 76–83. Topic Codes: CC37B,CC37W,CG11CC,CJ,CQ37,CQ59,CV06C,MS02,MX07,NE37,NE59,PE68B,PT11,PV11, SR02,SU11,TA59,TA70.

98640   Stewart, D.W., and Deiker, T. An item factor analysis of the Mooney problem check list. *Educational and Psychological Measurement*, Summer 1976, 36(2), 509–513. Topic Codes: CC37B,CL,MF11,NL,PE01,SR01,TA03.

98641   Stewart, M.A., and Behar, D. Subtypes of aggressive conduct disorder. *Acta Psychiatrica Scandinavica*, September 1983, 68(3), 178–185. Topic Codes: CV06,DT42B,ME,MG11,MG30B,ML02,PE08,PE44B,PN07,SR04.

98642   Stewart, M.A., Cummings, C., Singer, S, and DeBlois, C.S. The overlap between hyperactive and unsocialized aggressive children. *Journal of Child Psychology and Psychiatry and Allied Disciplines*, January 1981, 22(1), 35–45. Topic Codes: MC,MG,MG30,NA07D,PE04,PY,SI57B,SU.

98643   Stewart, M.A., de Blois, C.S., and Cummings, C. Psychiatric disorder in the parents of hyperactive boys and those with conduct disorders. *Journal of Child Psychology and Psychiatry and Allied Disciplines*, October 1980, 21(4), 283–292. Topic Codes: DA04,MD,MG11,MG30,MS04,NH59B,NH59E,PE06, SH59B,SH59F.

98644   Stewart, M.A., de Blois, C.S., Meardon, J., and Cummings, C. Aggressive conduct disorder of children: The clinical picture. *Journal of Nervous and Mental Disease*, October 1980, 168(10), 604–610. Topic Codes: BL70B,ME,MG11,MV07,SQ07.

98645   Stewart, M.A., and Leone, L. A family study of unsocialized aggressive boys. *Biological Psychiatry*, February 1978, 13(1), 107–117. Topic Codes: BI11,CC37M,CC37N,CQ37,MG,NA07B,PE10,PG,SH59B.

98650   Stokman, C.L.J., and Heiber, P.G., Incidents in hospitalized forensic patients. *Victimology*, 1980, 5(2), 175–192. Topic Codes: BL67B,BL67D, BL70B,BL70D,CC11C,CC11R,CC11S,CC67B,CC81D,CQ59,CT57,CT57F,CT59,CT59B,

CV06C,CV13DA,CY,DA04D,DA15D,DK46D,MD11,MI07,MO11,MS02,MU70B,NE59,PE06D,
PE15D,SF07,SF11,SN07,SN11,SQ07,SQ11.

98655   Stokman, C.L.J., and Heiber, P.G., Neuropsychological correlates of ag-
gression and violence. Proceedings of the North Atlantic Treaty Organiza-
tion Advanced Study Institute on Neuropsychology and Cognition, vol. 2.
Rockville, Maryland: Sijthoff and Nordhoff International, 1981. Topic
Codes: BA,BB70D,BD70B,BI11,BK11BL,CC81D,CC81E,CC81L,CC81R,CC81W,CC81Y,CG,
CY,DD02NF,DK07D,MC,PE04,SF11,SR03,SS09,TA03,TA55,TA59,TB61B.

98660   Stone, D.A. A study to determine group differences between truant and
non-truant students in a selected secondary school [doctoral dissertation,
University of Michigan, 1974]. Dissertation Abstracts International,
May 1975, 35(11), 7070A-7071A. Topic Codes: BL11,CC37K,CC371,CQ37,MG11,
NA07B,PG,TA80.

98665   Stoops, J.W. The effects of response modality and situational variation
on the measurement of children's aggression [doctoral dissertation, Kent
State University, 1975]. Dissertation Abstracts International, July
1976, 37(1), 480B. Topic Codes: BL11,MC,NA07B,PE04,PE10,SW,TA80.

98670   Stoops, J.W., and Graham, J.R. The Missouri Children Picture Series:
Correlates of the aggression scale in normal fourth-grade males. Journal
of Research in Personality, June 1976, 10(2), 223-227. Topic Codes: MC,
NA07B,PE04,PE10,TB86.

98675   Stores, G. School-children with epilepsy at risk for learning and behaviour problems. Developmental Medicine and Child Neurology, August 1978,
20(4), 502-508. Topic Codes: BK11B,BL11,DK18,MG,PE10,PG.

98680   Stott, D.H. Evidence for a congenital factor in maladjustment and delin-
quency. American Journal of Psychiatry, March 1962, 118, 781-794. Topic
Codes: BB11,BE11,BP02B,BP02D,CC37,CC37B,CC37E,CC37G,CC37P,CC37X,CG11CC,
CQ37,CV13,DD01,DD02D,DD81D,DF48,DP48,MG02D,NE37.

98685   Stott, D.H. Follow-up study from birth of the effects of prenatal
stresses. Developmental Medicine and Child Neurology, 1973, 15, 770-787.
Topic Codes: BB,BL11,BL48,BP02,BP47,BP48,DD,DD02,DF60B,DK,DP44,DP60,DT48,
MG,MT48,NA07D,NA07I,NA44B,NJ03,PE48,PG,PR,SF,SI46B,SM,SW56.

98690   Stott, D.H. Physical and mental handicaps, following a disturbed pregnan-
cy. Lancet, May 18, 1957, 227, 1006-1012. Topic Codes: BB07,BL07BB,
BP02B,BP47,BP48,DD00,DD02B,DF,DF06BB,DK46,DP11B,DP60,MG,MO,NA07D,NA31A,
NA31C.

98695   Stott, D.H. Studies of Troublesome Children. New York: Humanities
Press, 1966. Topic Codes: BA,BB11,BB48,BP02,CC37C,CC37G,CC37M,CC37T,
DD02K,MA,MB,MC,ME07,MG11,MH,MQ,MS,NA07B,NA07I,PA,PC07B,PE04,PE08,PE10,
PG,SC70B,SI57,SQ70,SU.

98700   Stott, D.H., and Latchford, S.A. Prenatal antecedents of child health,
development, and behavior: An epidemiological report of incidence and association. Journal of the American Academy of Child Psychiatry, Winter
1976, 15(1), 161-191. Topic Codes: BB,BL11,BL31,BP02,BP47,BP48,BP53,
BP70,DD,DD02,DD05,DF,DP11,DP81,MG,MG18,NA07D,NA07I,NA31C,NA31F,PG,PK,SM,
SW16.

98705   Stott, D.H., and Wilson, D.M. The adult criminal as juvenile. British
Journal of Criminology, 1977, 17, 47-57. Topic Codes: CC11,CC11C,CC11G,
CC11S,CC11U,CC37B,CC67,CG11C,CQ11,CQ67,CT57,CT59,CT68,MG02D,NE11,NE67,
TA03,TA59.

98710   Strang, J.S. A comparative study of full term and prematurely born children, aged 10-13, on factors of intelligence, personality, and perceptual-
motor development [doctoral dissertation, University of Alabama, 1974].
Dissertation Abstracts International, August 1975, 36(2), 798A-799A.
Topic Codes: BL11,DF60B,NA07I,PE10,PG,TA80.

98715   Stratton, A.J. Validity of the SRA non-verbal form for adults. Psycho-
         logical Reports, 1968, 22, 163-167. Topic Codes: BL04,PM,TB76,TB93.

98720   Strother, C.R. Minimal cerebral dysfunction: A historical overview. New
         York Academy of Sciences - Annals, 1973, 205, 6-17. Topic Codes: DK07B,
         DK48B,DT06,DT15,DT42,MG,MG48B,ML,ML04,ML15,NA07D,PE44,PN.

98725   Sturup, G.K. Treatment of sexual offenders in Herstedvester, Denmark:
         The rapists. Acta Psychiatrica Scandinavica, 1968, supplement 204, 5-62.
         Topic Codes: BD70B,CC81D,CC81E,CC81Y,CQ81,CT68,CV,DD01,MV11,NE81,PE68D,
         TA02,TA03,TA80.

98730   Suchman, E.A. Accidents and social deviance. Journal of Health and So-
         cial Behavior, 1970, 11, 4-15. Topic Codes: BL70B,DD03B,DD03D,MA07,MA11,
         MF,MX,PE,PE02B,PE02D,PE68,PT,SQ07,SR,SW07,TA59.

98732   Surwillo, W.W. The electroencephalogram and childhood aggression. Ag-
         gressive Behavior, 1980, 6(1), 9-18. Topic Codes: BL04,BL04B,BL11,DK07,
         DK07B,MC,MG,NA07B,TB35,TB35B.

98735   Sutker, P.B. Personality differences and sociopathy in heroin addicts and
         nonaddict prisoners. Journal of Abnormal Psychology, December 1971,
         78(3), 247-251. Topic Codes: CC11H,CC11P,CQ11,DA15D,MS02,NE11,PE15D,
         PT11.

98740   Sutker, P.B., Allain, A.N., and Geyer, S. Female criminal violence and
         differential MMPI characteristics. Journal of Consulting and Clinical
         Psychology, October 1978, 46(5), 1141-1143. Topic Codes: CC11C,CC11U,
         CC81D,CC81Y,CQ59,CT57F,CV13DA,NE59,NL22D,TB61B.

98745   Sutker, P.B., and Moan, C.E. A psychosocial description of penitentiary
         inmates. Archives of General Psychiatry, November 1973, 29, 663-667.
         Topic Codes: BL67D,BL70D,CC11A,CC11C,CC11I,CC11N,CC11R,CC11S,CC11T,CC11U,
         CG11CC,CQ59,CT57,CT57F,CT59,CT68,CV13,CV13DA,DA15D,MI07,MQ11,MS02,MU11,
         NE59,NL48D,PE15D,PM11,PV11,SJ07D,SJ09D,SN11,SO11,SQ11,TA03,TA59D,TB61B.

98750   Sutker, P.B., Moan, C.E., and Swanson, W.C. Porteus Maze Test qualitative
         performance in pure sociopaths, prison normals and antisocial psychotics.
         Journal of Clinical Psychology, 1972, 28(3), 349-353. Topic Codes:
         CC11C,CC11N,CC11U,CQ59,CV13DA,MS04B,MU11,NE59,PA,TB61B,TB66B,TB66D.

98755   Sutorova, D., and Travnikova, M. The effect of concussion on some person-
         ality characteristics and behavior of the child. Psychologia a Patopsy-
         chologia Dietata, 1976, 11(2), 143-150 (in Slovak). Topic Codes: BD11,
         CC11C,CC11D,DD26,NA07B,PE10.

98760   Swadlow, H.A., Geschwind, N., and Waxman, S.G. Commissural transmission
         in humans. Science, May 4, 1979, 204, 530-531. Topic Codes: BK11B,BL18,
         BN44,DK07,PO,TB37.

98765   Swaiman, K.F. Brain development in the middle childhood years. Journal
         of School Health, May 1978, 48(5), 288-292. Topic Codes: BK11B,DD26B,
         DK48B,MG48B,PR.

98775   Swanson, L. Free recall of phonemically varied lists by normal and read-
         ing disabled children. Psychological Reports, December 1977, 41(3, part
         2), 1130. Topic Codes: BL11,DT44B,MG,MH07,ML02,MM07,NA07B,NA07I,PE10,PG,
         TA59D,TA80.

98780   Swartz, V.D. The effects of aggression and awareness on Rorschach perfor-
         mance [doctoral dissertation, University of Nebraska - Lincoln, 1973].
         Dissertation Abstracts International, November 1973, 34(5), 2319B-2320B.
         Topic Codes: MC,NL,PE04,TA80,TB74.

98785   Sweet, W.H., Ervin, F.R., and Mark, V.H. The relationship of violent be-
         havior to focal cerebral disease. In S. Garattini and E.B. Sigg (eds.),
         Aggressive Behavior. New York: John Wiley & Sons, Inc., 1969. Topic
         Codes: CC11F,CC81I,CC81R,DK07D.

98790   Syndulko, K., and Parker, D.A. Psychophysiology of sociopathy: Electro-
cortical measures. Biological Psychology, November 1975, 3(3), 185-200.
Topic Codes: BL18B,ME,NL,PE08,TA59,TA80,TB37,TB61.

98792   Szegal, B. Development of aggressive behavior in early childhood.
Magyar Pszichologiai Szemle, 1981, 38(1), 30-42. Topic Codes: BL11,MC,
MG,MX.

98795   Taffel, S. Factors Associated with Low Birth Weight. DHEW publication
no. (PHS) 80-1915. Hyattsville, Maryland: National Center for Health
Statistics, 1980. Topic Codes: BL07,BL67,BP02,BP07,BP46,DF06,DF60,
NH59PF,SH59RF,SJ05,SJ07,SN,SW.

98798   Takahashi, Y., Nishimura, H., and Suzuki, S. A study of violence among
pupils in junior high schools: III. Social psychological traits of violent pupils. Reports of the National Research Institute of Police Science, July 1983, 24(1), 30-43. Topic Codes: BL11,CC81J,CC81N,CC81S,PT.

98800   Tamayo, A., and Raymond, F. Self-concept of psychopaths. Journal of Psychology, September 1977, 97(first half), 71-77. Topic Codes: MS04,PA,
TA02,TA59.

98805   Tandon, A.K. Psychosocial variables in a delinquent group. Indian Journal of Pediatrics, September 1977, 44(356), 245-252. Topic Codes: CC37B,
CC37BB,CC37K,CC37M,CC37Z.

98810   Tandon, A.K., Bajpai, M., Tandon, R.K., and Shukla, R. Aggressive behavior disorders of juvenile delinquents. Journal of the Association of Physicians in India, September 1978, 26(9), 787-792. Topic Codes: CC37B,
MC11,MG11B,PE04D,SR03B.

98815   Tarleton, G.J., Jr., Crump, E.P., and Horton, C.P. Growth and development. Radiology, 1960, 75, 932-941. Topic Codes: BL05,BL06,BL27,BL33,
BL67,BL70,BP26,BP46,BP52,BP57,BP59,NA33F,NA33I,NL07,PL,SN,SQ,SW,TA52M.

98820   Tarnopol, L. Delinquency and learning disabilities. In L. Tarnopol
(ed.), Learning Disabilities. Springfield, Illinois: C.C. Thomas, 1969.
Topic Codes: BL48D,BL67,BL67B,BN44B,CC11F,CC11N,CC11U,CC37H,CC37J,CC37L,
CC37Q,CC37S,CC37I,CG11C,CG11P,DD01,DF48,DF60BB,DF60BD,DK48B,DK48D,DP11B,
DP48,DT15,DT44D,DT48D,MG48B,MG48D,ML15,MM11,MT48D,NL48D,PE48D,PE64D,PM07,
PO07,PP11,PR11,SC18,SC70D,SJ09D,SN,SN07,TA03,TA55,TB09D,TB35D,TB96D.

98825   Tarnopol, L. Delinquency in minimal brain dysfunction. Journal of Learn-
ing Disabilities, April 1970, 3(4), 22-28. Topic Codes: BL48D,CC11F,
CC11I,CC11N,CC37H,CC37J,CC37Q,CC37S,CG11C,CG11P,DD01,DT44D,DT48D,DT59D,
MM11,MR11,MT48D,NL48D,PE48D,PE64D,PM11,PP11,PR11,PS11,SC18D,SC70D,TA03,
TA55,TB93D,TB96D.

98830   Taub, B.R. Differences in heart rate and galvanic skin response reactivity in primary and secondary psychopaths and nonpsychopathic controls [doc-
toral dissertation, University of Waterloo (Canada), 1972]. Dissertation
Abstracts International, November 1973, 34(5), 2320B. (Available for con-
sultation at the University of Waterloo Library.) Topic Codes: BL25D,
BL29D,BN04D,CC11D,CG11CC,CQ59,CV06C,NE59,PC11,PY11,SU11,TA52,TA59.

98840   Taylor, D.C. Aggression and epilepsy. Journal of Psychosomatic Research,
1969, 13, 229-236. Topic Codes: BK11BL,BL70,BL70B,BN44B,CV06C,CV30B,DF,
DK07B,DK18D,DK18SB,DT10,MC,ME,MS04,MT04,MX07,NA31C,NH65B,PE04,PE08,PE68B,
PM07,PO07,PY,SI07,SI57P,SJ09B,SL07,SQ,SQ07,SR01,SR03,SR04,SU,SW07,TB35B,
TB35BB.

98843   Taylor, P.J., and Gunn, J. Violence and psychosis: I. Risk of violence
among psychotic men. British Medical Journal, June 30, 1984, 288(6435),
1945-1949. Topic Codes: CC11C,CC81D,CQ59,CT57,CT59,MB11,MQ11,MU11,MU70B.

98845   Taylor, T., and Watt, D.C. The relation of deviant symptoms and behavior
in a normal population to subsequent delinquency and maladjustment. Psy-

chological Medicine, February 1977, 7(1), 163-169. Topic Codes: BN68B, CC37B,CC37H,CC37P,DD01,MG18D.

98850   Teichman, M. Ego defense, self-concept and image of self ascribed to parents by delinquent boys. Perceptual and Motor Skills, June 1971, 32(3), 819-823. Topic Codes: CC37B,CC37M,CC37W,CC37I,TA02,TA59.

98855   Telegdy, G.A. The relationship between socioeconomic status and patterns of WISC scores in children with learning disabilities. Psychology in Schools, 1973, 10(4), 426-430. Topic Codes: DT44,MG,MM,NA07D,PE64B,PP, SC70B,SW07,SW56,TB95B,TB96B.

98860   Telfer, M.A. Are some criminals born that way? Think, November-December 1968, 34, 24-28. Topic Codes: CC11M,CC37B,CC37K,CC37W,SF11,SS09,SW11.

98865   Tennenbaum, D.J. Personality and criminality: A summary and implications of the literature. Journal of Criminal Justice, Fall 1977, 5(3), 225-235. Topic Codes: CC11P,CC11U,PT11,TA03,TA59.

98875   Terestman, N. Mood quality and intensity in nursery school children as predictors of behavior disorder. American Journal of Orthopsychiatry, January 1980, 8(1), 125-138. Topic Codes: MG,NA07B,NA07D,NA44,NJ,PE10, PT74,TA57,TA74.

98880   Terry, G. A five-year-old boy's aggressive and compensatory behavior in response to immobilization. Maternal-Child Nursing Journal, Spring 1979, 8(1), 29-38. Topic Codes: CC37B,MG11,NA07D,PE04,PE10.

98885   Thatcher, A.A. Personality correlates of abuse and neglect in children [doctoral dissertation, Michigan State University, 1976]. Dissertation Abstracts International, March 1977, 37(9), 4657B-4658B. Topic Codes: CT57BB,DD10B,MG,PT11,TB86.

98890   Thayer, W.H. The relationship between learning disabilities and interpersonal maturity [doctoral dissertation, University of Northern Colorado, 1976]. Dissertation Abstracts International, January 1977, 37(7), 4248A. Topic Codes: CC37A,CC37H,CC37W,CG11CC,CQ59,DT44B,MM07,NE59,PP07,TA02, TA59D.

98895   Thomas, A., and Chess, S. Development in middle childhood. Seminars in Psychiatry, November 1972, 4(4), 331-341. Topic Codes: BL04B,BL11, BL70B,MG,MX,NA07B,NA07D,NA07I,NA44F,NJ09,PE10,PE68,PG,PT,SQ07,SR.

98900   Thomas, A., and Chess, S. Evolution of behavior disorders into adolescence. American Journal of Psychiatry, May 1976, 133(5), 539-542. Topic Codes: BL04B,BL11,MG,MQ,NA07D,NA07I,NA44F,NJ09,PG,PT74,SI57B.

98905   Thomas, A., and Chess, S. A longitudinal study of three brain-damaged children. Archives of General Psychiatry, April 1975, 32, 457-462. Topic Codes: BL11,BL31,BL48B,BN70,DK07B,DK46,DK48B,DT15,DT48B,DT71,MG,MG48B, ML15,MO,MT48B,MX,MY,NA07D,NA07I,NA31F,NA44F,NJ09,PE48B,PE68,PE70,PG,PK, PR07,PT74,SI57B,SR,TB78B,TB95B.

98910   Thomas, A., Chess, S., and Birch, H.G. Temperament and Behavior Disorders in Children. New York: New York University Press, 1968. Topic Codes: BB07,BE07,BK11B,BL11,DD00,DD02B,DD26B,DK07B,DT42B,DT44B,DT48B,MF,MG30B,ML, MM,N,NJ,PE10,PG,PN,PP,PR,SF07,SH59J,SI22B,TB78B,TB95.

98915   Thomas, A., Chess, S., Birch, H.G., Hertzig, M.E., and Korn, S. Behavioral Individuality in Early Childhood. New York: New York University Press, 1971. Topic Codes: BK,BL11,BL31,BL33,BN04,BN68,BP,NA31D,NA31F, NA31R,NA33D,NA33F,NA44,NH59,NH70,NJ,PA,PC,PE32,PE34,PK,PL,SB,SH59,SH70, SI57,TA52K,TA52M,TA57.

98920   Thompson, A.L. Cultural hemisphericity: Evidence from cognitive tests. International Journal of Neuroscience, 1979, 9, 37-43. Topic Codes: BL67,BL70,BN44,DT13,MH,PI,PM,PO,SB,SF26,SN,SQ,TA59D,TB93.

98930   Thompson, E.W., and Dodder, R.V. Containment theory reevaluated: A factor analysis of inner and outer containment variables as they relate to
juvenile delinquency by race and sex. Sociological Abstracts, 1979,
27(supplement 91), 1755. Topic Codes: BL67D,BL70D,CC37,CC37Y,CG11T,CQ37,
NE37,SN11,SQ11,TA70.

98935   Thompson, V.D. Family size: Implicit policies and assumed psychological
outcomes. Journal of Social Issues, 1974, 30(4), 93-124. Topic Codes:
BP07,PE64,PM,PT,PY,SB,SC18,SC70,SI57,SI57P,SJ05,SJ07,SJ22,SU.

98940   Thomson, M. Laterality and reading attainment. British Journal of Educational Psychology, November 1975, 45(3), 317-321. Topic Codes: BN44B,
DT44,MG.

98945   Thorne, F.C. The etiology of sociopathic reactions. American Journal of
Psychotherapy, 1959, 13, 319-330. Topic Codes: CV06C,MS04.

98950   Thurston, J.R., Benning, J.J., and Feldhusen, J.F. Problems of prediction
of delinquency and related conditions over a seven year period. Criminology, August-November 1971, 9, 154-164. Topic Codes: CG,CJ,CL,NA44,NJ.

98955   Tiber, N., and Kennedy, W.A. The effects of incentives on the intelligence test performance of different social groups. Journal of Consulting
Psychology, 1964, 28(2), 187-194. Topic Codes: BL67,SN,SW,TB78.

98960   Tieger, T. On the biological basis of sex differences. Child Development, December 1980, 51(4), 943-963. Topic Codes: BD70,BL11,BL70,MC.

98965   Ting, R.Y., Wang, M.H., and Scott, T.F.M. The dysmature infant: Associ-
ated factors and outcome at 7 years of age. Journal of Pediatrics, June
1977, 90(6), 943-948. Topic Codes: BD30,BD30B,BL05,BL06,BL11,BL27,
BL27KL,BL31,BL67,BP02,BP26,BP26GD,BP46,BP53,BP61,DF48,DF70B,DP22H,DP48,
NA07I,NA31F,NA31R,NA44D,NC22,NC59,NC70,NJ06,NL07,PG,PK,SN,SW,TA52K,TB02,
TB09,TB27,TB33G,TB78,TB95,TB98.

98970   Tittle, C.R., and Villemez, W.J. Social class and criminality. Social
Forces, December 1977, 56(4), 474-502. Topic Codes: BL04D,BL67D,BL70D,
CC11A,CC11R,CC11S,CC11T,CC37,CC37Y,CC37Z,CE,CG,CG11,CG11C,CG11P,CG11T,
CQ37,CT57,CT59,NE37,SA11,SN11,SQ11,SW11.

98975   Tittle, C.R., Villemez, W.J., and Smith, D.A. The myth of social class
and criminality: An empirical assessment of the empirical evidence.
American Sociological Review, October 1978, 43, 643-656. Topic Codes:
BL04D,BL67D,BL70D,CC11R,CC11S,CC11T,CC37,CC37Y,CC37Z,CC81,CG,CG11,CG11T,
CQ37,CT57,CT59,CT70,CT81,NE37,NE81,SN11,SQ11,SW11,TA70.

98980   Tjossem, T.D. (ed.). Intervention Strategies for High Risk Infants and
Young Children. Baltimore: University Park Press, 1976. Topic Codes:
BL07B,BL11,BL27KL,BL31,BL33,BL52,BP02,BP26GD,BP44,BP47,CV,DD00,DD08K,
DF06B,DF34,DF60B,DF70B,DP11,DP44,MG,NA07D,NA31A,NA33A,NL,PG,PK,PL,TA02,
TA52,TA59D.

98985   Toby, J. The differential impact of family disorganization. American So-
ciological Review, October 1957, 22(5), 505-512. Topic Codes: BL04D,
BL67D,BL70D,CC37,CC37A,CC37K,CC37L,CC37Y,CG11C,CG11CC,CQ37,CV13,NE37,
SF26D,SF26DD,SI11,SJ09D,SN11,SQ11.

98990   Toch, H. (ed.). Psychology of Crime and Criminal Justice. New York:
Holt, Rinehart and Winston, 1979. Topic Codes: CC11C,CC37B,CC37L,CC37S,
CC37V,CG11CC,CG11P,CQ37B,CT70,CV06C,CV13D,MQ11,MS02,NE37D,SD11.

98995   Todd, J., and Satz, P. WAIS performance in brain-damaged left- and right-
handers. Annals of Neurology, 1977, 2, 422-424. Topic Codes: BN44B,
DK07,DK09,DT42,ML,PE44,PM70,PN,PO,TB93B.

98998   Tonge, B.J., Lipton, G.L., and Crawford, G. Psychological and educational
correlates of strabismus in school children. Australian and New Zealand

Journal of Psychiatry, March 1984, 18(1), 71-77. Topic Codes: DK,DT44, DT59,MG,MM,MR,NA07D,PP,PS.

99000   Tooley, K. The small assassins: Clinical notes on a subgroup of murderous children. Journal of the American Academy of Child Psychiatry, Spring 1975, 14(2), 306-318. Topic Codes: MC,MG,NA07D,NH70B,PE04,SH70B,SI22B, SI48B,SJ09B,SR03.

99005   Tooth, G. The aggressive psychopathic offender. Lancet, January 4, 1969, 584, 42-45. Topic Codes: CC11C,CQ59,MC,MS04B.

99010   Torrey, E.F., Hersh, S.P., and McCabe, K.D. Early childhood psychosis and bleeding during pregnancy: A prospective study of gravid women and their offspring. Journal of Autism and Childhood Schizophrenia, 1975, 5, 287-297. Topic Codes: BL67B,BL70B,BP,BP02B,DK07B,DP,DP11B,DP81,MG,MG04,MU70, NA07D,NA44D,NC22,NC44,NC59G,NC70,NJ06,PM,SN07,SQ07,TA02,TA52.

99012   Touliatos, J., and Lindholm, B.W. Birth order, family size, and behavior problems in children. Child Psychiatry Quarterly, January-March 1980, 13 (1), 1-8. Topic Codes: MG,SJ07B,SJ22B.

99013   Touliatos, J., and Lindholm, B.W. Birth order, family size, and children's mental health. Psychological Reports, June 1980, 46(3, pt. 2), 1097-1098. Topic Codes: BL11C,CC37M,MG,MX,MX11,PY,PY11,SJ07,SJ07B,SJ07D, SJ22,SJ22B,SJ22D.

99015   Towbin, A. Central nervous system damage in the human fetus and newborn infant. American Journal of Diseases of Children, June 1970, 119, 529-542. Topic Codes: BL27,BP22,BP26,DD08K,DF34,DF48,DF60B,DK09,DK11,DP11, DP44,DP48,DP58,DT04E,NA33B,NC44,NC59G,TB02.

99020   Towbin, A. Cerebral dysfunctions related to perinatal organic damage: Clinical-neuropathologic correlations. Journal of Abnormal Psychology, 1978, 87(6), 617-635. Topic Codes: BL22,BL27,BL27KL,BP22,BP22F,BP26, BP26GD,DD08K,DF34,DF48,DF60B,DF70B,DK07B,DK11,DK18,DK46,DK48B,DP11,DP22, DP44,DP48,DP58,DT04E,DT04EB,MG48B,MO,NA33B,NC44,NC59G.

99025   Towbin, A. Latent spinal cord and brain stem injury in newborn infants. Developmental Medicine and Child Neurology, February 1969, 11, 54-68. Topic Codes: DD08,DF34,DK07,DK09.

99030   Towbin, A. Organic causes of minimal brain dysfunction: Perinatal origin of minimal cerebral lesions. Journal of the American Medical Association, August 30, 1971, 217(9), 1207-1214. Topic Codes: BP22,DD08K,DF34,DF60B, DF60BB,DK09,DK09B,DK11,DK46,DK48,DP11B,DT04EB,MG48,MO,NA33B,NC44.

99035   Towbin, A. Spinal cord and brain stem injury at birth. Archives of Pathology, June 1964, 77, 620-632. Topic Codes: DD08,DF34,DK09.

99040   Trasler, G. Crime, conscience and electrodermal recovery. Paper presented at the annual meeting of the American Society of Criminology, San Francisco, California, November 1980. Topic Codes: BL25,BL25D,CC11,CC37T, DT44,MF,MM,MS04B,PE,PP,SI57J.

99045   Trupin, E.W., and Townes, B.D. Neuropsychological evaluation as an adjunct to behavioral interventions with children. Professional Psychology, May 1976, 7(2), 153-160. Topic Codes: CV06,DK07B,MG,NA07B,TA02,TA52.

99050   Tryphonas, H., and Trites, R. Food allergy in children with hyperactivity, learning disabilities and/or minimal brain dysfunction. Annals of Allergy, January 1979, 42(1), 22-27. Topic Codes: BD52B,BI07,CV52B,DD00, DK48B,DT44,MG,MG30,MG30B,MG48B,MM,NA07D,NH65,PP,TA02,TA55,TA57,TA74.

99055   Tsuboi, T. Crimino-biologic study of patients with the XYY syndrome and Klinefelter's syndrome. Humangenetik, 1970, 10, 68-84. Topic Codes: BB70D,CC11C,CC11D,CC11M,CC11N,CG11CC,CQ59,DD02NF,MU11,NE59,NE67,NH70D, PM11,SH70D,TA52,TA59D.

99060   Tunks, E.R., and Dermer, S.W. Carbamazepine in the dyscontrol syndrome
         associated with limbic system dysfunction. Journal of Nervous and Mental
         Disease, January 1977, 164(1), 56-63. Topic Codes: BK11BL,CC11F,CC81I,
         CV15D,DK07D,TB35B,TB35D.

99065   Tutone, R.M. Correlates of illness susceptibility. British Journal of
         Medical Psychology, March 1977, 50(1), 79-86. Topic Codes: BL25,BL59,DD,
         SF.

99075   Ulatowska, H.K., and Baker, W.D. A linguistic study of processing strate-
         gies in right and left brain-damaged patients. International Journal of
         Psycholinguistics, 1976, 6, 35-63. Topic Codes: BN44B,DK07B,DT06,DT42,
         ML04,PE44,PN,POO7.

99080   Ullman, C.A. Identification of Maladjusted School Children (Public Health
         monograph no. 7, Public Health Service publication no. 211). Washington,
         D.C.: U.S. Government Printing Office, 1957. Topic Codes: BL04D,BL70B,
         BL70D,CC37,CC37A,CG11CC,CQ37,CV13,DD02ND,MG,MX,NA07D,NE37,PA,PE64B,PE68,
         SC70B,SQ11,SR,TA02,TA59,TA74.

99085   Ullman, D.G., Barkley, R.A., and Brown, H.W. The behavioral symptoms of
         hyperkinetic children who successfully responded to stimulant drug treat-
         ment. American Journal of Orthopsychiatry, July 1978, 48(3), 425-437.
         Topic Codes: CV15B,MG30,NA07D,TA02,TA59.

99090   Unikel, I., and Blanchard, E.B. Psychopathy, race, and delay of gratifi-
         cation by adolescent delinquents. Journal of Nervous and Mental Disease,
         1973, 156(1), 57-60. Topic Codes: BL67BB,CC37BB,CC37J,CQ59,CV13DA,MK11,
         MS04B,NE59,PE30D,SN07B,TB61B.

99095   Uyeno, E.T., Chang, D., and Folkers, K. Substance P found to lower body
         temperature and aggression. Biochemical and Biophysical Research Communi-
         cations, February 14, 1979, 86(3), 837-842. Topic Codes: BL48,CV15B,
         DT48,MC,MF,MT48,PE04,PE48,PR,SR03.

99100   Vaillant, C.M. Crime and mental illness in a group of psychopathic per-
         sonalities. Medicine, Science and the Law, January 1969, 9(1), 11-18.
         Topic Codes: CC11C,CC11N,MS04B,PM11.

99105   Vaillant, G.E. Sociopathy as a human process: A viewpoint. Archives of
         General Psychiatry, February 1975, 32(2), 178-183. Topic Codes: CC11C,
         CC11H,CV06C,DA15B,DA15D,MI04,MI07,MS04B.

99110   Valenstein, E.S. Brain stimulation and behavior control. Nebraska Sympo-
         sium on Motivation, 1975, 22, 251-292. Topic Codes: BK11B,CV06,MF.

99115   Valentine, G.H. The YY chromosome complement: What does it mean? Clini-
         cal Pediatrics (Philadelphia), June 1969, 8(6), 350-355. Topic Codes:
         BB70B,BB70D,CC37N,DD02ND,DD02NF,TB35.

99120   Valzelli, L. Drugs and aggressiveness. Advances in Pharmacology, 1967,
         5, 79-108. Topic Codes: BD07,BK11B,CV15B,DA15B,MC,PE04,SR03.

99123   Vance, B., Fuller, G.B., and Ellis, R. Discriminant function analysis of
         LD/BD children scores on the WISC-R. Journal of Clinical Psychology,
         September 1983, 39(5), 749-753. Topic Codes: DT44,MG,TB95B,

99125   Vance, H.B., and Wallbrown, F.H. The structure of intelligence for
         black children: A hierarchical approach. Psychological Record, 1978, 28,
         31-39. Topic Codes: BL11,NA07I,NL07,PG,PM,TB95.

99130   Vandenberg, S.G. Possible hereditary factors in minimal brain dysfunc-
         tion. New York Academy of Sciences - Annals, 1973, 205, 223. Topic
         Codes: BB07,BB70B,BI07,BL11,BL70B,BN44B,BN70,DD02B,DD02ND,DK11,DK46,
         DK48B,DP11B,DT15,DT71,MG48B,ML15,MO,MY,NA07I,PE70,PG,PM,POO7,SQ07.

99135   Van Den Berghe, P.L. Bringing beasts back in: Toward a biosocial theory

of aggression. American Sociological Review, December 1974, 39, 777-788.
Topic Codes: B,MC,PE04,SA,SF,SR03.

99140   Van Des Vlugt, H. Aspects of normal and abnormal neuropsychological de-
velopment. In M.S. Gazzaniga (ed.), Neuropsychology. New York: Plenum
Press, 1979. Topic Codes: BK11BL,BL04B,BL11,BL48,BL52D,BN44,BN44B,DK07,
DT13,DT15,DT42,DT48,DT59,MG,MH,ML,ML15,MR,MT48,NA07D,NA07I,PE44,PE48,PG,
PI,PM70,PN,PO,PO07,PR,PS.

99142   Van Dusen, K.T., Mednick, S.A., Gabrielli, W.F., Jr., and Hutchings, B.
Social class and crime in an adoption cohort. Journal of Criminal Law
and Criminology, Spring 1983, 74(1), 249-269. Topic Codes: BI11,BL70D,
CG11C,NH04D,NH59D,NH59F,SH04D,SH59D,SH59H,SQ11,SW11.

99145   Van Hagen, J. Content analysis of language behavior in childhood psychoses [doctoral dissertation, Adelphi University, 1974]. Dissertation Abstracts International, November 1974, 35(5), 2452B. Topic Codes: DT42B,
MG,ML02,MU.

99150   Varga, J.R. More on long-term sequelae of exposure to lead. Journal of
Pediatrics, April 1979, 94(4), 680-681. (Letter) Topic Codes: DA44M,
DT44,MG.

99152   Vaux, A., and Ruggiero, M. Stressful life change and delinquent behavior.
American Journal of Community Psychology, April 1983, 11(2), 169-183.
Topic Codes: CC11A,CC37,CC37Z,CG11T,CQ37,CT57,CT59,DA15,MI,NE37,PE15,
TA70.

99153   Venables, P.H. Outcome at age nine of psychophysiological selection at
age three for risk of schizophrenia: A Mauritian study. British Journal
of Developmental Psychology, March 1983, 1(1), 21-30. Topic Codes:
BL25B,MC,MG,MU11,NA44,PM.

99155   Ventura, S.J. Trends and Differentials in Births to Unmarried Women:
United States, 1970-1976. DHHS publication no. (PHS) 80-1914. Hyatts-
ville, Maryland: National Center for Health Statistics, 1980. Topic
Codes: BL07,BL67,BP44,BP53,BP63,DF06,DF48,DP48,MG,NA07D,NH59PA,NH59PF,
NH59PH,SF26,SH59RA,SH59RF,SH59RH,SI07,SN,SW16.

99160   Vernon, P.E. Environmental handicaps and intellectual development: Parts
I and II. British Journal of Educational Psychology, 1965, 35, 9-20, 117-
126. Topic Codes: BL67B,DT44B,MM07,NA07D,PP07,SI22B,SI46B,SI48B,SI57B,
SI59B,SJ09B,SN07,SU,SW07,SW16,TA02,TA59D,TB33,TB66,TB95.

99165   Vicary, T.C. An investigation into the use of non-verbal tests of intelligence in India. Unpublished master's thesis, University of London,
1938. Topic Codes: PM,TA59D.

99170   Vinson, T., and Homel, R. Crime and disadvantage: The coincidence of
medical and social problems in an Australian city. British Journal of
Criminology, January 1975, 15(1), 21-31. Topic Codes: CC37B,CC37J,CC37M,
CC37P,CC37X,CC37Z,DD01,DP11D,PE64D,SD11,SF26D,SJ09D,SW11.

99175   Violent crime and the EEG. British Medical Journal, April 25, 1970, 2,
193. Topic Codes: CC81K,TB35D.

99180   Virkkunen, M. Alcohol as a factor precipitating aggression and conflict
behaviour leading to homicide. British Journal of Addiction to Alcohol
and Other Drugs, 1974, 69, 149-154. Topic Codes: BL70D,CC11H,CG11P,
CT57F,CX,DA04D,MC11,MD11,NE79,PE04D,PE06D,SQ11,SR03B.

99185   Virkkunen, M. Alcoholism and antisocial personality. Acta Psychiatrica
Scandinavica, 1979, 59, 493-501. Topic Codes: BL04B,BL04D,CC11A,CC11H,
CC11I,CC11L,CC11N,CC37A,CC37BB,CC37I,CC37L,CC37Q,CC81A,CQ59,CT59,CV13DA,
DA04BB,DA04D,MD07B,MD11,MS04,MS04B,NE59,NH11,NH59GB,NH59GI,PE06BB,PE06D,
SC18D,SH11,SH59JB,SH59JL.

99190   Virkkunen, M. Arrests for drunkenness and recidivism in juvenile delinquents. British Journal of Addiction, 1977, 72, 201-204. Topic Codes: CC11H,CC37,CC37I,CC67,CC81B,CQ37,CT59,DA04D,MD11,NE37,NE67,PE06D.

99195   Virkkunen, M. The child as participating victim. In M. Cook and K. Howells (eds.), Adult Sexual Interest in Children. London: Academic Press, 1981. Topic Codes: CC11A,CC11C,CT68,CX,MS04B,NA07B,NE79,NH11, PE10,SH11,SI11.

99200   Virkkunen, M. Incest offences and alcoholism. Medicine, Science, and the Law, April 1974, 14(2), 124-128. Topic Codes: BL04B,BL04D,CC11A,CC11H, CC11L,CC67B,CT68,CX,DA04D,MD11,NE79,NH11,NH59GB,NH59GD,PE06D,SH11,SH59JB, SH59JD,SI11.

99205   Virkkunen, M. Observations on violence in schizophrenia. Acta Psychia-trica Scandinavica, 1974, 50, 145-151. Topic Codes: BL70D,CC11C,CC11S, CC81D,CQ59,CT57F,CV13DA,CX,MU70B,NE59,NE79,SQ11.

99210   Virkkunen, M. On arson committed by schizophrenics. Acta Psychiatrica Scandinavica, 1974, 50, 152-160. Topic Codes: CC11C,CC11H,CC11S,CN,CQ59, CT59B,CV13DA,DA04D,MD11,MU70B,MV11,NE59,PE06D,PE66D,SI11,SR69D.

99215   Virkkunen, M. Parental deprivation and recidivism in juvenile delin-quents. British Journal of Criminology, January 1976, 16(4), 378-384. Topic Codes: BL11C,BL70D,CC11L,CC37L,CC37V,CC67,CQ59,CQ67,CV13DA,NA07ID, NE59,NE67,PG11,SI46D,SI57J,SI59D,SJ09D,SQ11.

99220   Virkkunen, M. The pedophilic offender with antisocial character. Acta Psychiatrica Scandinavica, 1976, 53, 401-405. Topic Codes: CC11C,CC11N, CT68,MG02D,MG30,MS04B,PM11.

99222   Virkkunen, M. Reactive hypoglycemic tendency among habitually violent of-fenders: A further study by means of the glucose tolerance test. Neuro-psychobiology, 1982, 8(1), 35-40. Topic Codes: BD30HD,CC11D,CC81B,CC81E, CC81P,CQ59,CV13DA,DA04D,DD30D,MD11,NE59,PE06D.

99225   Virkkunen, M. Self-mutilation in antisocial personality disorder. Acta Psychiatrica Scandinavica, 1976, 54, 347-352. Topic Codes: CC11C,CQ59, CV13DA,MS04B,MZ,NE59,SF07,SI22B,SJ09B.

99230   Virkkunen, M. Serum cholesterol in antisocial personality. Neuropsycho-biology, 1979, 5, 27-30. Topic Codes: BD07,BK04BB,BL04,BL04BB,BN04BB, CC11C,CC11H,CC11I,CC11N,CC81D,CQ59,CT59,CT68,CV13DA,DA04BB,DA15B,MD07B, MI04,MS02,MS04B,NE59,PC07B,PE06BB,PE15B,PM07,SC18B.

99232   Virkkunen, M. Serum cholesterol levels in homicidal offenders: A low cholesterol level is connected with a habitually violent tendency under the influence of alcohol. Neuropsychobiology, 1983, 10(2-3), 65-69. Topic Codes: BD11,CC81E,CT57F.

99235   Virkkunen, M. Studies about criminal violence. Correspondence to Marvin E. Wolfgang from Matti Virkkunen, Helsinki, Finland, March 10, 1981. Topic Codes: CC81,CQ81,CT81,NE81.

99240   Virkkunen, M. Suicide linked to homicide. Psychiatric Quarterly, 1974, 48(2), 276-282. Topic Codes: BL04D,CC11,CC11C,CG11,CQ11,CT57FT,CV30D, CZ07,MU11,MU70B,MZ,NE11,NH11,SF26D,SH11,SL11,SY11.

99245   Virkkunen, M. Victim-precipitated pedophilia offences. British Journal of Criminology, April 1975, 5(2), 175-180. Topic Codes: BL04D,BL70D, CC11C,CC11N,CT68,CX,MU70B,NE79,PM11,SQ11.

99248   Virkkunen, M., and Huttunen, M.O. Evidence for abnormal glucose tolerance test among violent offenders. Neuropsychobiology, 1982, 8(1), 30-34. Topic Codes: BD30HD,CC81E,CC81P,DD30D.

99250   Virkkunen, M., and Luukkonen, P. WAIS performance in antisocial person-ality disorder. Acta Psychiatrica Scandinavica, 1977, 55, 220-224. Topic Codes: BL04BB,CC11C,CC11U,CQ59,CV13DA,MS04B,NE59,PM07,TB93BB.

99255   Virkkunen, M., Luukkonen, P., and Ecrikainen, K. On personality devia-
         tions among violent offenders. Psychiatria Fennica, 1978, 73-78. Topic
         Codes: BL04D,CC11A,CC11C,CC11H,CC11I,CC11N,CC11U,CC37BB,CC37I,CC37J,
         CC81B,CC81D,CC81H,CC81J,CC81Q,CC81Y,CT57,CT57F,CT59,CT59B,CT68,DA04D,
         DA15D,MD11,MIO7,MK11,MS02,MS04B,PE06D,PE15D,PE30D,SC18D,TB61B,TB93BB,
         TB93D.

99260   Virkkunen, M., and Nuutila, A. Specific reading retardation, hyperactive
         child syndrome, and juvenile delinquency. Acta Psychiatrica Scandinavica,
         1976, 54, 25-28. Topic Codes: CC11C,CC11G,CC37B,CC37H,CG11C,DT15B,MG30D,
         ML15B.

99265   Virkkunen, M., Nuutila, A., and Huusko, S. Brain injury and criminality:
         A retrospective study. Diseases of the Nervous System, November 1977,
         38(11), 907-908. Topic Codes: CC11F,CC11H,CC810,CC81R,DA04D,DK07D,MD11,
         PE06D.

99270   Virkkunen, M., Nuutila, A., and Huusko, S. Effect of brain injury on so-
         cial adaptability. Acta Psychiatrica Scandinavica, 1976, 53, 168-172.
         Topic Codes: BN44D,CC11F,CC810,CC81R,CG11C,CG11CC,CV13,DK07D,PA11,PO11.

99275   Vogel, M.P. The relationship of socioeconomic status, child/parent rela-
         tionships, and gender to juvenile delinquency [doctoral dissertation, Duke
         University, 1977]. Dissertation Abstracts International, July 1978,
         39(1), 206A. Topic Codes: BL70D,CC37,CC37L,CC37Z,CG11T,CQ37,NE37,SI57D,
         SQ11,TA03,TA57,TA70.

99280   Vogt, A., and Heaton, R.K. Comparison of Wechsler Adult Intelligence
         Scale indices of cerebral dysfunction. Perceptual and Motor Skills, Octo-
         ber 1977, 45(2), 607-615. Topic Codes: DK07,TB93B.

99285   Volavka, J., Mednick, S.A., Rasmussen, L., and Sergeant, J. EEG spectra
         in XYY and XXY men. Electroencephalography and Clinical Neurophysiology,
         December 1977, 43(6), 798-801. Topic Codes: BB70,DD02N,TB35B.

99290   Volavka, J., Mednick, S.A., Sergeant, J., and Rasmussen, L. Electroen-
         cephalograms of XYY and XXY men. British Journal of Psychiatry, January
         1977, 130, 43-47. Topic Codes: BB70,DD02N,TB35B.

99295   Von Hilsheimer, G. A psychobiological study of delinquents. Orthomolec-
         ular Psychiatry, 1978, 7(4), 286-291. Topic Codes: BD07,BD11,CC37B,
         CC37C,CC37H,DT44D,MM11,PP11.

99300   Von Hilsheimer, G., Levy, A., Tucker, J.T., and Moore, L.S. HOD-MMPI: A
         comparison. Orthomolecular Psychiatry, 1977, 6(1), 8-17. Topic Codes:
         CC37B,CC371,MG,NA07D,TA02,TA03,TA59,TB61,TB61B.

99305   Von Hilsheimer, G., Philpott, W., Buckley, W., and Klotz, S.D. Correcting
         the incorrigible: A report on 229 "incorrigible" adolescents. American
         Laboratory, September 1977, 9(9), 107-118. Topic Codes: BB48D,BD11,BD30,
         BD30HD,BD52D,BL25D,BN04D,CC37,CC37B,CC37C,CC37P,CC37T,CC37U,CQ37,CV52D,
         DA44MB,DD01,DD02KD,DD30D,DT44D,MG,MG04,MM11,NA07D,NE37,PC11,PP11,SI57J.

99308   Voorhees, J. Neuropsychological differences between juvenile delinquents
         and functional adolescents: A preliminary study. Adolescence, Spring
         1981, 16(61), 57-66. Topic Codes: BL48D,CC37B,CC37H,CC37I,CC37T,CC371,
         DT46,DT48D,MN,MT48D,PE48D,PQ,PR11,TA03,TA55,TBO9D.

99310   Vorhees, C.V., and Brunner, R.L. Psychotropic drugs as behavioral terato-
         gens. Science, September 21, 1979, 205, 1220-1225. Topic Codes: BP02,
         BP02B,BP04,MF,PE.

99315   Vreeland, R.G., and Waller, M.B. The Psychology of Firesetting: A Review
         and Appraisal. Washington, D.C.: U.S. Department of Commerce, Bureau of
         Standards, 1979. Topic Codes: CC11C,CC37B,CT59B.

99320   Vrtunski, P.B., Mack, J.L., Boller, F., and Kim, Y. Response to delayed auditory feedback in patients with hemispheric lesions. Cortex, December 1976, 12(4), 395-409. Topic Codes: BN44B,BN70,DK07B,DT59,MR,PO07.

99325   Waber, D.P. Sex differences in cognition: A function of maturation rate? Science, May 1976, 192(4239), 572-573. Topic Codes: BK11B,BL11,BL70,MH, NA07I,PE10,PG,PO,SQ,TA55,TA80,TB09,TB95.

99330   Wadsworth, M.E.J. Delinquency in a national sample of children. British Journal of Criminology, April 1975, 15(2), 167-174. Topic Codes: BL04D, CC11A,CC37A,CC37Z,CC67,CC81,CG11C,CG11CC,CQ67,CQ81,CT57,CT59,CT68,CT81, CV13,NA44H,NE67,NE81,NJ12,SW11,SW56.

99335   Wadsworth, M.E.J. Delinquency, pulse rates and early emotional deprivation. British Journal of Criminology, July 1976, 16(3), 245-256. Topic Codes: BE,BK04D,BL29D,BL59,BL59D,BL70,CC37L,CC37T,CC37Z,CC81,CE,CQ81, CT57,CT59,CT68,CT81,NA44H,NE81,NJ12,SJ07D,SJ09,SJ09D,SJ22,SQ,SW,TA59, TA74,TB59.

99340   Wagner, E.E., and Klein, I. WAIS differences between murderers and attackers referred for evaluation. Perceptual and Motor Skills, February 1977, 44(1), 125-126. Topic Codes: CC81Q,CC81U,CG11C,CQ81,CT57,CT81, NE81,NL48D,PM70B,SN11,TB93D.

99345   Waid, W.M. Skin conductance response to both signaled and unsignaled noxious stimulation predicts level of socialization. Journal of Personality and Social Psychology, November 1976, 34(5), 923-929. Topic Codes: BL25, BN04,CV,MB,PC,PY,SI57J,SI57P,SU,TA52,TB38,TB93.

99350   Waid, W.M. Skin conductance responses to punishment as a predictor and correlate of learning to avoid two classes of punishment. Journal of Abnormal Psychology, 1976, 85(5), 498-504. Topic Codes: BK04,BK04BB,BL25, BL25BB,DT44,DT44BB,MM,MM07B,MS04,PP,PP07B,PY,SI57J,SI57P,SU.

99360   Waldron, J.A. A study of consistently violent criminals [doctoral dissertation, Ohio State University, 1975]. Dissertation Abstracts International, May 1976, 36(11), 5775B. Topic Codes: CC81D,CC81S,CG11CC,CQ67, CQ81,CT81,CY,MB11,NE81,PE01,SR02,TB61B.

99365   Waldron, S. The significance of childhood neurosis for adult mental health: A follow-up study. American Journal of Psychiatry, May 1976, 133(5), 532-538. Topic Codes: CV06,MB,ME,MG02B,MQ,MS,MU,MV07,MX07,PE08, PE66B,PE68B,SR01,SR04,SR69B,TA02,TA59.

99370   Waldrop, M.F., Bell, R.Q., and Goering, J.D. Minor physical anomalies and inhibited behavior in elementary school girls. Journal of Child Psychology and Psychiatry and Allied Disciplines, 1976, 17, 113-122. Topic Codes: BB48B,BL11,BL48B,BL70B,DD02KB,DP11B,DP81,DT48B,MG,MT48B,MX07,NA07D,NA07I, NH59PF,NL22B,NL48B,PE48B,PE64,PE68B,PG,PM07,PR07,SC70,SH59RF,SQ07,SR01, TA04,TA59D,TA74.

99375   Walker, H.A., and Birch, H.G. Intellectual patterning in schizophrenic children. Journal of Autism and Childhood Schizophrenia, March 1974, 4(2), 143-161. Topic Codes: BK11,DK09B,DT13B,MH07,MU70,NA07D,PE10,PI07, PM07,TB95B.

99380   Walker, H.A., and Bortner, M. Concept usage in schizophrenic children. Journal of Autism and Childhood Schizophrenia, June 1975, 5(2), 155-167. Topic Codes: BL04,DK09,DT13B,MH07,MU70,NA07D,PI07,TB78B,TB95B.

99385   Walker, H.A., Danielson, E., and Levitt, M. Catechol-o-methyltransferase activity in psychotic children. Journal of Autism and Childhood Schizophrenia, September 1976, 6(3), 263-268. Topic Codes: BL04,DT13B,MH07, MU70,NA07D,PI07,TA80.

99390   Walkey, F.H., and Boshier, R. Semantic differential response bias in psychopathic, delinquent, and normal boys. Psychological Reports, February 1969, 24(1), 91-94. Topic Codes: CC37H,CQ37,DT59D,MR11,PS11,TA59D.

99395   Wallston, B. The effects of maternal employment on children. Journal of Child Psychology and Psychiatry and Allied Disciplines, 1973, 14, 81-95. Topic Codes: BL11,CC37L,NA07I,NH59P,NH59PL,PE64,PG,SC70,SD,SH59R,SH59RL, SI46,SI48,SI48B.

99400   Walnum, A.R. The diagnosis of brain damage in children: Criterion considerations [doctoral dissertation, Brigham Young University, 1976]. Dissertation Abstracts International, March 1977, 37(9), 5720A-5721A. Topic Codes: DK07B,MB,MG,MX07,TB59B.

99405   Walsh, T.H. Anhedonia as a symptom of minimal brain dysfunction in children [doctoral dissertation, University of Rhode Island, 1975]. Dissertation Abstracts International, March 1976, 36(9), 4714B. Topic Codes: DK48,MB,MG48,NA07D,SR01.

99410   Walsh-Brennan, K.S. An analysis of homicide by young persons in England and Wales. Acta Psychiatrica Scandinavica, August 1976, 54(2), 90-98. Topic Codes: BL04,CC81E,CC81L,CC81M,CC81N,CC81Q,CC81S,CC81W,CG11CC,CQ81, CT57F,CT81,CY,MS02,NA07D,NE81,NH59GB,NH59GD,NH59GI,NH59PB,NH59PD,NH59PL, PT11,SH59JB,SH59JD,SH59JL,SH59RB,SH59RD,SH59RL,SI22D,SI46D,SI48D,SI59D, SJ09D,SW11,TA03,TA52,TA59D,TB95D.

99415   Walsh-Brennan, K.S. Children who have murdered. Medicolegal Journal, 1975, 43, 20-24. Topic Codes: CC37B,CC37F,CC37K,CC37L,CC37Z,CC37I, CG11CC,CT57F,CV13,NH59F,SH59H,SJ07D,TB25,TB35D,TB95D.

99420   Walsh-Brennan, K.S. Psychopathology of homicidal children. Royal Society of Health, 1974, 94, 274-277. Topic Codes: BL04D,BL70D,CC37A,CC37B, CC37K,CC37L,CC37Q,CC37W,CC37Z,CC37I,CT57F,NH59F,NH59PL,PM11,PT11,SD11, SF26D,SH59H,SH59RL,SI22D,SI48D,SJ07D,SJ09D,SQ11,SW11,TB25,TB95D.

99425   Walsh-Brennan, K.S. A socio-psychological investigation of young murderers. British Journal of Criminology, January 1977, 17(1), 58-63. Topic Codes: BL70D,CC37B,CC37L,CC37W,CC37Z,CC37I,CT57F,CV06C,NH59F,NH59PL, SH59H,SH59RL,SI48D,SI57D,SJ07D,SQ11,SW11,TA03,TA52.

99430   Walters, R.H., and Parke, R.D. The influence of punishment and related disciplinary techniques on the social behavior of children: Theory and empirical findings. Progress in Experimental Personality Research, 1976, 4, 179-228. Topic Codes: CV,MX07,NA07D,PE10,PE68B,PY,SI57J,SI57P,SR01, SU,TA02.

99435   Walzer, S., Gerald, P.S., and Shah, S.A. The XYY genotype. Annual Review of Medicine, 1978, 29, 563-570. Topic Codes: BB70,BB70B,BB70D,BE,CQ59, CV13DA,DD02N,DD02ND,DD02NF,MC,NE59,PE04,PM,SR03.

99440   Walzer, S., and Richmond, J.B. Minimal brain dysfunction: Introduction. Seminars in Psychiatry, February 1973, 5(1), 1-3. Topic Codes: BK11B, DK48,MG48.

99445   Walzer, S., Wolff, P.H., Bowen, D., Silbert, A.R., Bashir, A.S., Gerald, P.S., and Richmond, J.B. A method for the longitudinal study of behavioral development in infants and children: The early development of XXY children. Journal of Child Psychology and Psychiatry and Allied Disciplines, 1978, 19, 213-229. Topic Codes: BB70B,BL11,BL31,BL48,BN70, DD02ND,DT42,DT44,DT48,DT71,MC,ML,MM,MT48,MX,MY,NA07B,NA07I,NA31D,NA31F, NA44,NJ,PA,PE04,PE10,PE32,PE44,PE48,PE68,PE70,PG,PK,PM70,PN,PP,PR,PT74,SR, SR03,TA57,TB05,TB95,TB96.

99448   Warren, J.Q. A multiple regression approach to the study of the influence of psychotropic medication on the Halstead-Reitan Neuropsychology Battery in a neuropsychiatric setting [doctoral dissertation, University of Kansas, 1976]. Dissertation Abstracts International, August 1977, 38(2), 922B. Topic Codes: BK11B,BL04,CV15B,DK07,PM07,SC18B,SL07,TB46,TB61.

99450   Warren, J.R. Birth order and social behaviour. Psychological Bulletin, 1966, 65, 38-49. Topic Codes: BL70,BN04,CC37L,DA04,MD,MU70,MX,PC,PE06, PE68,PM,PT,SC18,SJ07,SJ07B,SJ07D,SJ22B,SQ,SR,TB86.

99460   Warren, M.Q. "The impossible child," the difficult child, and other as-
sorted delinquents: Etiology, characteristics and incidence. Canadian
Psychiatric Association Journal, December 1978, 23(special supplement),
SS41-SS60. Topic Codes: BL11,CC37G,CJ,CL,CQ37,CV,MG,PE10,PG,SF.

99465   Washington, E.D., and Teska, J.A. Correlations between the Wide Range
Achievement Test, the California Achievement Tests, the Stanford-Binet,
and the Illinois Test of Psycholinquistic Abilities. Psychological Reports, 1970, 26, 291-294. Topic Codes: TB21,TB53,TB78,TB98.

99470   Watson, C.G., Davis, W.E., and McDermott, M.T. MMPI-WAIS relationships in
organic and schizophrenic patients. Journal of Clinical Psychology, July
1976, 32(3), 539-540. Topic Codes: BK11B,DK07,MU70,NL,TB61,TB93.

99475   Wattenberg, W.W. The juvenile delinquent. In H. Toch (ed.), Psychology
of Crime and Criminal Justice. New York: Holt, Rinehart, and Winston,
1979. Topic Codes: CC37B,CC37L,CC37S,CC37V,CG11P,CQ37B,CT70,CV06,MQ11,
MS02,NE37D,SD11.

99480   Waugh, R.P. The ITPA: Ballast or bonanza for the school psychologist.
Journal of School Psychology, 1975, 13(3), 201-208. Topic Codes: DT42,
ML,PE44,PN,TB53,TB78,TB95.

99485   Wechsler, D. Measurement and Appraisal of Adult Intelligence (J.
Matarazzo, ed.). Baltimore: The Williams & Wilkins Co., 1972. (Origi-
nally published, 1944.) Topic Codes: BK11B,BL11,BL67,BL70,DK07,DK09,DK46,
DK48,DT13,DT15,DT42,DT44,DT52,MG48,MH,ML,MM,MO,NA44,NJ,NL,PE64,PI,PM,PN,
PP,SC,SJ,SN,SQ,SR,SW,TA02,TA04,TA55,TA59D,TB93,TB95,TB96.

99490   Weiner, I.B. Symposium on behavioral pediatrics: Juvenile delinquency.
Pediatric Clinics of North America, August 1975, 22(3), 673-684. Topic
Codes: BL11,CC37B,CC37G,CC37K,MG,PE10,PG.

99495   Weinschenk, C. Definition, symptomatology, diagnosis and therapy of congenital legasthenia. Acta Paedopsychiatrica, April 1971, 38(4), 111-118.
Topic Codes: MH,ML,MM,PI,PN,PP.

99500   Weinschenk, C. Pseudo-brain damage during early childhood. Praxis der
Kinderpsychologie und Kinderpsychiatrie, August 1969, 18(6), 194-202.
Topic Codes: DK07.

99505   Weintraub, P. The brain: His and hers. Discover, April 1981, 15-20.
Topic Codes: BD70,BK11B,BL22,BL70,BN44,BP22F,MV,PE66,PM70,PO,SQ,SR69.

99507   Weintraub, S., and Mesulam, M.M. Developmental learning disabilities of
the right hemisphere: Emotional, interpersonal, and cognitive components.
Archives of Neurology, August 1983, 40(8), 463-468. Topic Codes: BN44B,
DK07B,DT42,MB,ML,PE44,PM70,PN,POO7.

99510   Weir, K., Stevenson, J., and Graham, P. Behavioral deviance and teacher
ratings of prosocial behavior. Journal of the American Academy of Child
Psychiatry, 1980, 19, 68-77. Topic Codes: BL70,MG,MG11,MQ,MX,NA07B,
NA07D,PE10,PE68,SQ,SR,TA74.

99515   Weiss, G., and Hechtman, L. The hyperactive child syndrome. Science,
September 28, 1979, 205, 1348-1354. Topic Codes: B,BL70B,CV15B,DF,MG30,
MG30D,MK,NA31A,NA31C,PE30,PE64,SC70,SF07,SF26B,SQ07,TB35B.

99520   Weiss, G., Minde, K., Werry, J.S., Douglas, V., and Nemeth, E. Studies on
the hyperactive child: VIII. Five year follow-up. Archives of General
Psychiatry, 1971, 24, 409-414. Topic Codes: BL11,MG30,NA07I,NA44,PE10,
PG,TB09,TB33G,TB35B,TB57B,TB95B.

99525   Weiss, W., and Jackson, E.C. Maternal factors affecting birth weight.
Perinatal Factors Affecting Human Development; proceedings of the special session held during the eighth meeting of the PAHO (Pan American
Health Organization) Advisory Committee on Medical Research, 1969, scientific publication no. 185, 54-59. Topic Codes: BL06,BL07,BP02,DF06,DP11.

99530   Welcher, D.W., Mellits, E.D., and Hardy, J.B. A multivariate analysis of factors affecting psychological performance. Johns Hopkins Medical Journal, July 1971, 129, 19-35. Topic Codes: BL11,BL31,BL48,BL70,DT48,MT48, NA07I,NA31F,NA44D,NC22,NC44,NC70,NJ06,NL07,PE48,PG,PK,PM,PR,SQ,TB05,TB09K, TB33G,TB53,TB78,TB84,TB95.

99535   Welcher, D.W., Wessel, K.W., Mellits, E.D., and Hardy, J.B. The Bender Gestalt Test as an indicator of neurological impairment in young inner-city children. Perceptual and Motor Skills, 1974, 38, 899-910. Topic Codes: BL11,BL48,BL67,BL70,DK07,DT48,MT48,NA07I,NC70,NL48,PE48,PG,PR, SF26,SN,SQ,TA04,TA52,TB09K,TB95,TB98.

99540   Welner, Z., Welner, A., McCrary, M.D., and Leonard, M.A. Psychopathology in children of inpatients with depression: A controlled study. Journal of Nervous and Mental Disease, June 1977, 164(6), 408-413. Topic Codes: BL11,MB,MG,NA07D,TA74,TA80.

99545   Welner, Z., Welner, A., Stewart, M., Palkes, H., and Wish, E. A controlled study of siblings of hyperactive children. Journal of Nervous and Mental Disease, August 1977, 165(2), 110-117. Topic Codes: BL11, MG30B,NA07D,NH70B,PE10,PG,TB95B.

99550   Wender, P.H. Minimal Brain Dysfunction in Children. New York: John Wiley & Sons, Inc., 1971. Topic Codes: BI07,BK11BL,BL11,BL22,BL31,BL33, BN04B,BP22F,CV06,CV15B,DD26B,DF06BB,DF60BB,DK07B,DK48B,DT44B,DT48B,ME, MG18,MG48B,MH07,MK,MM07,MT48B,PE10,PE30,PE48B,PG,PI,PP07,SR01,TA80.

99555   Wender, P.H. Minimal brain dysfunction in children: Diagnosis and management. Pediatric Clinics of North America, February 1973, 20(1), 187-202. Topic Codes: BK11B,BL11,DK07B,MG48B,PE10,PG.

99560   Wender, P.H. The minimal brain dysfunction syndrome in children. Journal of Nervous and Mental Disease, July 1972, 155(1), 55-71. Topic Codes: BB07,BD07,BI07,BN04B,CV15B,DD02B,DK48B,DT44,DT52B,MB,MG02B,MG30,MG48B,MM, MS04,MU70,NA44,NJ,PC07,PP.

99565   Wender, P.H. Speculations concerning a possible biochemical basis of minimal brain dysfunction. International Journal of Mental Health, 1974, 4, 11-28. Topic Codes: BD07,BI07,BK04B,BN04B,DK48B,DT44,MG30,MG48B,MM, NH04B,PC07,PP,SH04B,TB35B.

99570   Wener, B.D., and Pisano, R.L. Relationship between altruism and aggression using behavioral measures. Psychological Reports, April 1977, 40(2), 673-674. Topic Codes: MC,NA07B,PE04,TA80.

99575   Wener, B.D., and Templer, D.I. Relationship between WISC verbal-performance discrepancies and motor and psychomotor abilities of children with learning disabilities. Perceptual and Motor Skills, 1976, 42, 125-126. Topic Codes: BL48,DT44,DT48,MG,MM,MT48,NA07D,PE48,PP,PR,TA02,TA55,TB96B.

99580   Wenger, M.A. Studies of autonomic balance: A summary. Psychophysiology, January 1966, 2(3), 173-186. Topic Codes: BK04,BK04B,BL08B,DD,DD15,DD28, MQ,MU70.

99585   Wenk, E.A., and Emrich, R.L. Assaultive youth: An exploratory study of the assaultive experience and assaultive potential of California Youth Authority wards. Journal of Research in Crime and Delinquency, July 1972, 9(2), 171-196. Topic Codes: CC81A,CC81Y,CQ37,CQ81,CT81,CY,NE37,NE81, TB23B,TB61B.

99590   Wenk, E.A., Halatyn, T.V., and Harlow, N. An analysis of classification factors for young adult offenders. Unpublished manuscript, National Council on Crime and Delinquency, 1974. Topic Codes: BL67,BL67D,CC11C, CC11F,CC11H,CC11I,CC11J,CC11N,CC11P,CC11U,CC37,CC67,CC81,CG11CC,CQ37,CQ67, CQ81,CT57,CT59,CT68,CT81,CV13,CZ07,DA04D,DA15D,DK07D,MD11,MI07,MQ11,MS02, MS04B,MU11,NE37,NE67,NE81,PE06D,PE15D,PE64D,PM11,PT11,SC18D,SC70D,SD11,SN, SN11,SY11,TA03,TA59,TA59D,TB15B,TB21D,TB23B,TB61B,TB72B,TB86C,TB93D.

99595   Werner, E.E. From birth to latency: Behavioral differences in a multi-
         racial group of twins. Child Development, 1973, 44(3), 438-444. Topic
         Codes: BL07,BL11,BL31,BL70,BP57,DD,DF06,DF34,DK46,DP11,MG,MO,MX,NA07D,
         NA07I,NA31D,NA31F,NA33B,NA44D,NH74,NJ06,NL48,PE64,PE68,PG,PK,PM,PT74,SC70,
         SH74,SQ,SR,SW,TA57,TA74,TB09,TB25,TB68,TB89,TB95.

99600   Werner, E.E., Bierman, J.M., French, F.E., Simonian, K., Conner, A.,
         Smith, R.S., and Campbell, M. Reproductive and environmental casualties:
         A report on the 10 year follow-up of the children of the Kauai pregnancy
         study. Journal of Pediatrics, July 1968, 42(1), 112-127. Topic Codes:
         BL11,BL70B,DA,DD,DD02,DK46,DP11B,DT13,DT42,DT59,MG,MG30,MH,ML,MO,MR,NA07D,
         NA07I,NA44D,NJ06,PE44,PE64,PG,PI,PM,PN,PS,SC70,SF07,SI57B,SQ07,SW07,SW16,
         TB09K,TB33,TB68,TB74,TB86,TB95.

99605   Werner, E.E., Honzik, M.P., and Smith, R.S. Prediction of intelligence
         and achievement at ten years from twenty-month pediatric and psychologic
         examinations. Child Development, 1968, 39(4), 1063-1075. Topic Codes:
         BL11,BL31,BL70,BL70B,DF34,DK46,DP11,MG,MO,NA07D,NA07I,NA31F,NA31R,NA33B,
         NA44D,NH59PF,NJ06,PE64,PG,PK,PM,SC70,SH59RF,SQ,SQ07,SW,SW16,TA52K,TB25,
         TB42,TB68,TB89,TB95.

99610   Werner, E.E., Simonian, K., Bierman, J.M., and French, F.E. Cumulative
         effect of perinatal complications and deprived environment on physical,
         intellectual, and social development of preschool children. Journal of
         Pediatrics, April 1967, 39(4), 490-505. Topic Codes: BL07BB,BL11,BL31,
         BL67,BL70,BP02,BP46,DD,DF06BB,DF34,DF60BB,DK07B,DK46,DP11,DP11B,DT04E,
         DT08E,MG,MO,NA07B,NA07D,NA07I,NA31F,NA31R,NA33B,NA44,NH,NH59PF,NH59PJ,NJ,
         NL48B,PE10,PG,PK,PM,SF07,SH,SH59RF,SH59RJ,SN,SQ,SW,SW07,TA52K,TB05,TB25,
         TB42,TB78,TB89.

99615   Werry, J.S. Developmental hyperactivity. Pediatric Clinics of North
         America, August 1968, 15(3), 581-599. Topic Codes: BL11,MG30,PE10,PG.

99620   Werry, J.S., and Aman, M.G. The reliability and diagnostic validity of
         the Physical and Neurological Examination for Soft Signs (PANESS). Jour-
         nal of Autism and Childhood Schizophrenia, September 1976, 6(3), 253-262.
         Topic Codes: BK11B,BL11,DK07B,MG30,NA07D,PE10,TA52,TA80.

99625   Werry, J.S., and Sprague, R.L. Hyperactivity. In C. Costello (ed.),
         Symptoms of Psychopathology. New York: John Wiley & Sons, Inc., 1970.
         Topic Codes: BL48,CV06,CV15B,DK07B,DK48B,DT44B,DT48,MG,MG02B,MG30,MG30B,
         MG48B,MM07,MT48,NA07D,PE48,PP07,PR,TA02,TA57,TA74.

99630   Wetzel, K.H., Welcher, D.W., and Mellits, E.D. The possibility of over-
         diagnosing brain dysfunction from a single administration of Bender
         Gestalt Test. Johns Hopkins Medical Journal, July 1971, 129, 6-53. Topic
         Codes: BL04,BL11,BL67,NA07I,NC70,PG,SN,TB09K.

99635   Whaley-Klahn, M., and Loney, J. A multivariate study of the relationship
         of parental management to self-esteem and initial drug response in hyper-
         kinetic/MBD boys. Psychology in the Schools, October 1977, 14(4), 485-
         492. Topic Codes: BL11,MG30B,NA07D,PE10,PG,SI07,TA80.

99640   Wheaton, B. The sociogenesis of psychological disorder: Examining the
         causal issues with longitudinal data. American Sociological Review, 1978,
         43(3), 383-403. Topic Codes: MB,NL,SF07,SF26B,TA80.

99645   Wheeler, C.A. The relationship between psychopathy and the weak automati-
         zation cognitive style [doctoral dissertation, Florida State University,
         1973]. Dissertation Abstracts International, April 1974, 34(10), 5214B-
         5215B. Topic Codes: CC11N,CG11CC,CQ59,DT13D,MH11,NE59,PI11,TA55,TA59D,
         TB95D.

99650   White, L. Diagnostic classification and equivocal neurological signs in
         childhood schizophrenia and minimal brain dysfunction: A factorial study
         of GSR conditioning [doctoral dissertation, New School for Social Re-
         search, 1973]. Dissertation Abstracts International, January 1974, 34(7),

3512B.   Topic Codes: BL25B,DK48B,DT52B,MG48B,MU70,NA07D,PE10,SR01,TA52,
TA59D.

99655   White, L. Organic factors and psychophysiology in childhood schizophrenia. Psychological Bulletin, April 1974, 81(4), 238-255. Topic Codes:
BK11B,BL11,DK07B,DK18B,MG,MU70,PE10,PG,TB35B.

99660   White, M.J., Snyder, J., and Lira, F.T. Some sociocultural determinants
of academic performance among behaviorally disturbed adolescents. Journal
of Genetic Psychology, September 1978, 133(first half), 145-146. Topic
Codes: BL11,BL67B,BL70B,MG11,NA07B,PE10,PG,SC70B,SI07,SN07,SQ07,TA74,
TA80.

99665   White, R.G. Children's cognitive spatial development and facilitative
environmental design [doctoral dissertation, York University (Canada),
1975]. Dissertation Abstracts International, April 1976, 36(10), 5241B.
(Copies available from National Library of Canada at Ottawa) Topic Codes:
BL11,MC,NA07B,PE10,PG,PM70,SF07,TA80.

99675   Whitehouse, D. Behavior and learning problems in epileptic children. Behavioral Neuropsychiatry, April-March 1975-1976, 7(1-12), 23-29. Topic
Codes: DK18B,DT44B,MM07,NA07D,PP07,SR01,TA52,TA59D.

99680   Whiteley, J.S. The psychopath and his treatment. British Journal of Psychiatry, 1975, 9(special no.), 159-169. Topic Codes: CC11C,CV06C,CV13D,
SI57J.

99685   Whitsell, L.J. Learning disorders as a school health problem: Neurological and psychiatric aspects. California Medicine, December 1969, 111(6),
433-445. Topic Codes: CV06,CV15B,DT44B,MM07,NA07D,PE64B,PP07,SC70B.

99690   Widom, C.S. A methodology for studying noninstitutionalized psychopaths.
Journal of Consulting and Clinical Psychology, August 1977, 45(4), 674-
683. Topic Codes: DD00B,ME,MS04B,NL,TA02B,TA59,TA80,TB23,TB61,TB66B.

99695   Widom, C.S. Toward an understanding of female criminality. Progress in
Experimental Personality Research, 1978, 8, 245-308. Topic Codes: BB48D,
BB70D,BD70B,CC11C,CC11E,CC11M,CC11S,CC24B,CQ22,DD01,ME07,MF,NE22,PE08D,
PM11,SF11,SH11,SQ70D,TB23B,TB38B,TB61B.

99700   Wiener, G. The relationship of birth weight and length of gestation to
intellectual development at ages 8 to 10 years. Journal of Pediatrics,
May 1970, 76(5), 694-699. Topic Codes: BL06,BL07B,BL11,BL27,BL27KL,BL67,
BP26,BP26GD,DF06B,DF60B,DF70B,DP11,DP81,NA07I,NA44D,NJ06,PG,PM,SN.

99705   Wiener, G. Varying psychological sequelae of lead ingestion in children.
Public Health Reports, January 1970, 85(1), 19-24. Topic Codes: BL11,
DA44MB,MG,PE10,PG.

99710   Wiens, A.N., Matarazzo, J.D., and Gaver, K.D. Performance and verbal IQ
in a group of sociopaths. Journal of Clinical Psychology, 1959, 15, 191-
193. Topic Codes: CC11,CC11C,CC11N,CC11U,CG11C,CQ11,CT68,MS04,NE11,
TB93BB,TB93D,TB96BB,TB96D.

99715   Wiig, E.H. Language disabilities of adolescents: Implications for diagnosis and remediation. British Journal of Disorders of Communication,
April 1976, 11(1), 3-17. Topic Codes: DT42,MG,ML,NA07D,PE44,PN.

99720   Wikler, A., Dixon, J.F., and Parker, J.B. Brain function in problem
children and controls: Psychometric, neurological and EEG comparisons.
American Journal of Psychiatry, November 1970, 127(5), 634-645. Topic
Codes: BL48B,DK48B,DT48B,DT52B,DT59,MG,MG30,MG48B,MR,MT48B,NA07D,PR07,PS,
TA52,TA59D,TB33,TB35B,TB95B,TB96B,TB98B.

99725   Wilder, J. Problems of criminal psychology related to hypoglycemic
states. Journal of Criminal Psychopathology, 1940, 1, 219-320. Topic
Codes: BD30HD,BD52D,CC11D,DD30D,SR03B.

99730   Wilder, J. Sugar metabolism in its relation to criminology. In R.M. Lindner and R.V. Seliger (eds.), Handbook of Correctional Psychology. New York: Philosophical Library, 1947. Topic Codes: BD30HD,BD52D,CC11D, DD30D,SR03B.

99735   Wilkinson, K., Stitt, B.G., and Erickson, M.L. Siblings and delinquent behavior: An exploratory study of a neglected family variable. Criminology, August 1982, 20(2), 223-239. Topic Codes: BL70D,CC37J,CC37M, NH70D,SH70,SH70D,SJ07D,SJ22,SJ22D.

99740   Willerman, L. Biosocial influences on human development. American Journal of Orthopsychiatry, 1972, 42, 452-462. Topic Codes: BL07B,BL27KL, BL67B,BL70B,BP02,BP26GD,BP46,BP47,DD08K,DF06B,DF60B,DP11,DP44,DP46,NA44B, NC22,NC59,NJ03,NL48B,PM,SJ05,SN07,SW07,TB78.

99745   Willerman, L. Social aspects of minimal brain dysfunction. New York Academy of Sciences - Annals, February 28, 1973, 205, 164-172. Topic Codes: DK48,MG48,PE10,PG.

99750   Willerman, L., and Broman, S.H. Infant development, preschool IQ, and social class. Child Development, 1970, 41, 69-77. Topic Codes: BL11, BL31,BL48,BL70,DK46,DT48,MO,MT48,NA07I,NA31F,NA44B,NC22,NC44,NJ03,PE48,PG, PK,PM,PR,SQ,SW,TB05,TB78.

99755   Willerman, L., and Fiedler, M.F. Infant performance and intellectual precocity. Child Development, 1974, 45, 483-486. Topic Codes: BI,BL06, BL11,BL31,BL70,NA07I,NA31F,NA44B,NC22,NC44,NH59PF,NJ03,PG,PK,PM,SF,SH59RF, SJ07,SQ,SW16,TB05,TB78.

99760   Willerman, L., Naylor, A.F., and Myrianthopoulos, N.C. Intellectual development of children from interracial matings. Science, December 18, 1970, 170, 1329-1331. Topic Codes: BL05,BL06,BL27,BL67,BL70,BP26,NA44B, NH59P,NH59PF,NH59PH,NJ03,PM,SH59R,SH59RF,SH59RH,SN,SQ,SW16,TB78.

99765   Willerman, L., Naylor, A.F., and Myrianthopoulos, N.C. Intellectual development of children from interracial matings: Performance in infancy and at 4 years. Behavior Genetics, 1974, 4, 83-90. Topic Codes: BI07, BL67,NA07D,NA31A,NA44B,NC22,NC44,NC59,NJ03,NL48B,PM,SN07,TB05,TB78.

99770   Williams, D. Neural factors related to habitual aggression: Consideration of differences between those habitual aggressives and others who have committed crimes of violence. Brain, 1969, 92(3), 503-520. Topic Codes: CC11C,CC11F,CC11H,CC11K,CC37B,CC37F,CC37K,CC67,CC81A,CC81B,CC81D,CC81K, CC81M,CC81N,CC81O,CQ11,CQ37,CQ67,CT57F,CT68,DK18D,MC11,NE11,NE37,NE67, PE04D,SR03,TB35D.

99775   Wilson, E.O. Biology and the social sciences. Daedalus, 1977, 106, 127-140. Topic Codes: B,BI,CG,MF,PE,SF.

99780   Wingerd, J., Schoen, E.J., and Solomon, I.L. Growth standards in the first two years of life based on measurements of white and black children in a prepaid health care program. Pediatrics, May 1971, 47(5), 818-825. Topic Codes: BE,BE30,BL31,BL67,BL70,NA31F,PK,SN,SQ,SW.

99785   Winick, M. Malnutrition and Brain Development. New York: Oxford University Press, 1976. Topic Codes: BD52B,BK11B,BL22,BL52D,BP02,BP22F,BP52, DF06B,DF34,DK07,DK09,DK46,DP11,DP22,NA31A,NA33A,PK,PL,PM.

99790   Witelson, S.F. Neural and cognitive correlates of developmental dyslexia: Age and sex differences. In C. Shagass, S. Gershon and A.J. Friedhoff (eds.), Psychopathology and Brain Dysfunction. New York: Raven Press, 1977. Topic Codes: BI07,BL04B,BL11,BL70B,BN44B,DK07B,DP11B,DT15,DT59B, MG,ML15,MR07,NA07D,NA07I,PG,PM70,PO07,PS07,SQ07,TA02,TA52,TA59,TA80,TB81, TB95B,TB96B,TB98B.

99795   Witkin, H.A., Mednick, S.A., Schulsinger, F., Bakkestrom, E., Christiansen, K.O., Goodenough, D.R., Hirschhorn, K., Lundsteen, C., Owen, D.R., Philip, J., Rubin, D.B., and Stocking, M. Criminality in XYY and

XXY men: The elevated crime rate of XYY males is not related to aggression; it may be related to low intelligence. Science, August 13, 1976, 193(4253), 547-555. Topic Codes: BB70D,BE11,CC11D,CC11E,CC11N,CC11T, CG11C,CQ11,DD02NF,DT13D,MH11,MO11,NE11,PM11,SC18D,SR02,SW11,TA59D.

99800   Witkin-Lanoil, G.H. Psychopathy, autonomic hyporeactivity, and social class [doctoral dissertation, New School for Social Research, 1977]. Dissertation Abstracts International, January 1978, 38(7), 3376B. Topic Codes: BI11,BKO4D,BL25D,BNO4D,CC37B,CC37M,CC37N,CC37W,CC37Z,MB11,MSO4B, MU70B,NH59F,NH59GD,NH59GI,NH59PB,NH59PD,PC11,PT74B,SH59JD,SH59JL,SH59RD, SH59RL,SU11,SW11,TA03,TA52.

99805   Wolff, C.M. The effects of aggressive toys on aggressive behavior in children [doctoral dissertation, University of Montana, 1976]. Dissertation Abstracts International, November 1976, 37(5), 2487B. Topic Codes: CV06,MC,MG11,NAO7D,PEO4,PE10,SRO3,SU,TA02.

99808   Wolff, P.H. Maturational factors in behavioral development. In M. McMillan and S. Henao (eds.), Child Psychiatry: Treatment and Research. New York: Brunner-Mazel, 1977. Topic Codes: B,BL07,BL11,BL48,BL52D, BL52DB,BN44,BN44B,DKO7B,DT15,DT48,MF,MG,ML15,MT48,NAO7B,NAO7I,PE,PE48,PG, PO,POO7,PR,SQ.

99809   Wolff, P.H., Waber, D., Bauermeister, M., Cohen, C., and Ferber, R. The neuropsychological status of adolescent delinquent boys. Journal of Child Psychology and Psychiatry, July 1982, 23(3), 267-279. Topic Codes: CC37B,CC37H,CC37T,CC37I,DT44D,MM11,PP11,TA03,TA52.

99810   Wolff, S. The contribution of obstetric complications to the etiology of behavior disorders in childhood. Journal of Child Psychology and Psychiatry and Allied Disciplines, May 1967, 8(1), 57-66. Topic Codes: BI07, BL07BD,BL11,BL22,BPO2B,BP22F,BP44,BP46,BP53,DF60BB,DP11B,MG,NAO7D,PE10,PG, TA02,TA74,TA80.

99813   Wolfgang, M.E. From boy to man: From delinquency to crime. Paper presented at the National Symposium on the Serious Juvenile Offender, Minneapolis, Minnesota, 1977. Topic Codes: BL04,CC11A,CC11R,CC37A,CC37Y,CC67B, CC81A,CC81U,CG11P,CQ37,CQ67,NE37,NE67,NE81,NL48D,SN11,SW11.

99817   Wolfgang, M.E., and Ferracuti, F. The Subculture of Violence. Beverly Hills: Sage Publications, 1982 (reprint of 1967 ed.). Topic Codes: BA, CC11,CC11A,CC11R,CC11S,CC11T,CC11U,CC81A,CC81D,CC81E,CC81F,CC81L,CC81U, CC81V,CC81W,CC81Y,CE81,CG,CT57F,CT81,CY,MC11,NE81,SB11,SF11,SQ70D,SRO3B, SU11,SW11,TA59D,TB74B.

99821   Wolfgang, M.E. Figlio, R.M., and Sellin, T. Delinquency in a Birth Cohort. Chicago: University of Chicago Press, 1972. Topic Codes: CC11A, CC11R,CC11S,CC11T,CC37A,CC37Y,CC37Z,CC67,CE,CG11C,CG11CC,CG11P,CQ37,CV13, NA44,NE37,NJ,SC18,SF26D,SN11,SS,SW11.

99823   Wolfgang, M.E., Weiner, N.A., and Pointer, W.D. (eds.). Criminal Violence: Biological Correlates and Determinants: A Selected Bibliography. Washington, D.C.: U.S. Department of Justice, National Institute of Justice, 1981. Topic Codes: BA,CC81E,CG.

99825   Wolfgarth, A. Perceptual and cognitive factors in therapy with antisocial individuals. Ontario Psychologist, April 1976, 8(1), 26-35. Topic Codes: DT13B,DT59B,DT59D,ME,MHO7,MRO7,MR11,MSO4,PEO8D,PIO7,PSO7,PS11,SRO4B.

99829   Wolkind, S., Hall, F., and Pawlby, S. Individual differences in mothering behavior: A combined epidemiological and observational approach. In P.J. Graham (ed.), Epidemiological Approaches in Child Psychiatry. New York: Academic Press, 1977. Topic Codes: NA31,NH59P,NH59PH,SH59R,SH59RH,SI48, SJ09.

99833   Wood, D.R., Reimherr, F.W., Wender, P.H., and Johnson, G.E. Diagnosis and treatment of minimal brain dysfunction in adults: A preliminary report.

Archives of General Psychiatry, December 1976, 33(12), 1453-1460. Topic Codes: CV15B,DK48,MG48,MK,NL,TA80.

99837   Woodman, D.D., Hinton, J.W., and O'Neill, M.T. Abnormality of catechole-mines balance relating to social deviance. *Perceptual and Motor Skills*, October 1977, 45(2), 593-594. Topic Codes: CC81Y,CQ59,NE59,TA80.

99841   Woodman, D.D., Hinton, J.W., and O'Neill, M.T. Plasma catecholamines, stress, and aggression in maximum security patients. *Biological Psychol-ogy*, 1978, 6, 147-154. Topic Codes: BD07,CC11D,CC11P,CC81E,CC81S,CQ59, CV13DA,CX,MC,NE59,NE79, PE04,PT74,SR03.

99845   Woodruff, R.A., Jr., Guze, S.B., and Clayton, P.J. The medical and psy-chiatric implications of anti-social personality (sociopathy). *Diseases of the Nervous System*, October 1971, 32(10), 712-714. Topic Codes: BL04BB,BL67BB,BL70BB,CV30B,DA04BB,DD00B,MB,MD07B,MS04B,PE06BB,SL07,SN07B, SQ07B.

99849   Woods, B.T. The restricted effects of right-hemisphere lesions after age one: Wechsler test data. *Neuropsychologia*, 1980, 18, 65-70. Topic Codes: BN44B,DD08K,DF34,DK07B,DP11,DP44,NA33B,NH70B,PO07,SH70B,TB95,TB96.

99851   Woods, B.T., and Eby, M.D. Excessive mirror movements and aggression. *Biological Psychiatry*, January 1982, 17(1), 23-32. Topic Codes: MC,MG, NA07D,PE04,SR03,TA02,TA52,TB35B.

99853   Wool, R., and Clements, C.B. Adolescent verbal behavior: An investiga-tion of noncontent styles as related to race and delinquency status. *Journal of Abnormal Child Psychology*, 1975, 3(3), 245-254. Topic Codes: BL67D,BN70D,CC37,CC37H,CC37Y,CG11C,CQ37,DT42D,DT71D,MF11,ML03,MY11,NE37, PE01,PE44D,PE70D,PN11,SN11.

99857   Worrall, E.P., Moody, J.P., and Naylor, G.J. Lithium in non-manic depres-sives: Anti-aggressive effect and red blood cell lithium values. *British Journal of Psychiatry*, May 1975, 126, 464-468. Topic Codes: CV15B,MC,NL, PE04,TA80.

99861   Wright, C. The qualitative performance of delinquent boys on the Porteus Maze Test. *Journal of Consulting Psychology*, 1944, 8, 24-26. Topic Codes: CC371,PE10,TB66D,TB78D.

99865   Wright, W.H., and Michael, W.B. The development and validation of a scale for school observation of characteristics associated with learning disa-bilities and minimal brain dysfunction in elementary school boys. *Educa-tional and Psychological Measurement*, Winter 1977, 37(4), 917-928. Topic Codes: DK48,DT44,MG48,NA07B,NA07I,PE10,PG,PP,SC70,TA74,TA80.

99869   Wyers, E.J., Adler, H.E., Carpen, K., Chiszar, D., Demarest, J., Flanagan, O.J., Jr., Von Glasersfeld, E., Glickman, S.E., Mason, W.A., Menzel, E.W., and Tobach, E. The sociobiological challenge to psychology: On the pro-posal to "cannibalize" comparative psychology. *American Psychologist*, November 1980, 35(11), 955-979. Topic Codes: B,DT13,MF,MH,PE,PI,SF.

99873   Wysocki, A.C., and Wysocki, B.A. Human figure drawings of sex offenders. *Journal of Clinical Psychology*, January 1977, 33(1), 278-284. Topic Codes: CC81Y,CQ59,CT68,CV06,TA80.

99877   Yamatani, H. Antisocial mentally retarded individuals [doctoral disserta-tion, University of Pittsburgh, 1976]. *Dissertation Abstracts Interna-tional*, February 1977, 37(8), 5362A. Topic Codes: DK46B,ME,MO07,NL,PM07, TA80.

99881   Yang, D.C., Ting, R.Y., and Kennedy, C. The predictive value of the neurologic examination in infancy for mental status at four years of age. In R. MacKeith and M. Bax (eds.), *Clinics in Developmental Medicine, No. 27, Studies in Infancy*. Suffolk, England: Spastics International Medi-cal Publications in association with William Heinemann Medical Books, Ltd., 1968. Topic Codes: DF34,NA44B,NC22,NC44,NJ03,PK,PM,TA52,TB78.

99885   Yarden, P.E., and Nevo, B.F. The differential effect of the schizophrenic mother's stages of illness on her children. British Journal of Psychiatry, 1968, 114, 1089-1096. Topic Codes: BL22,BL52DB,BP02B,BP22F,BP48, MG,MU,MU70,NA07D,NH59PB,NH59PJ,NH70B,SH59RB,SH59RJ,SH70B,SI46B.

99889   Yarden, P.E., and Suranyi, I. The early development of institutional children of schizophrenic mothers. Diseases of the Nervous System, June 1968, 29(6), 380-384. Topic Codes: BL06,BL31,BL70,BP02,BP02B,BP48,BP57, DF,MU70,NA31C,NA31F,NH59PB,NH59PJ,PK,SH59RB,SH59RJ,SQ.

99893   Yarrow, L.J. Maternal deprivation: Toward an empirical and conceptual re-evaluation. Psychological Bulletin, 1961, 58(6), 459-490. Topic Codes: BL11,BL31,BL48,CV30B,DT13,DT42,DT48,MG,MH,ML,MS,MT48,MX,NA07D, NA07I,NA31F,PE44,PE48,PE68,PG,PI,PK,PN,PR,SF,SI46,SI48B,SL07,SR.

99897   Yarrow, L.J. Research in dimensions of early maternal care. Merrill-Palmer Quarterly of Behavior and Development, 1963, 9(2), 101-114. Topic Codes: BL11,BL31,MX,NA07I,NA31D,NA31F,NH04,PE32,PE68,PG,PK,PM,SF, SH04,SI48,SR.

99901   Yarvis, R.M. Psychiatric pathology and social deviance in 25 incarcerated offenders. Archives of General Psychiatry, January 1972, 26(1), 79-84. Topic Codes: CC11C,CC11H,CC11I,CC11J,CC67,CQ59,CQ67,CT59,CT68,CV13DA, CV30D,DA15D,MC11,MI07,MV11,NE59,NE67,PE04D,PE15D,PE66D,SC18B,SD11,SL11, SR03B,SR69D.

99905   Yaryura-Tobias, J.A., and Nezirogh, F.A. Violent behavior, brain dysrhythmia, and glucose dysfunction: A new syndrome. Journal of Orthomolecular Psychiatry, 1975, 4(3), 182-188. Topic Codes: BD30HB,BD52B, CV15B,CV52B,DD30B,DK07B,MC,PE04,SR03,TB35B.

99907   Yates, A., Beutler, L.E., and Crago, M. Characteristics of young violent offenders. Journal of Psychiatry and Law, Summer 1983, 11(2), 137-149. Topic Codes: BL67D,CC37,CC37M,CC37W,CC37Y,CC81N,CC81S,CC81U,CQ37,NH,PM11, SH.

99909   Yekell, H.S. Distractibility and attention in MBD and normal children [doctoral dissertation, Hofstra University, 1974]. Dissertation Abstracts International, July 1974, 35(1), 530B. Topic Codes: DK48,MG48,TA80.

99913   Yepes, Y.E., Balka, E.B., Winsberg, B.G., and Bialer, I.W. Amitriptyline and methylphenidate treatment of behaviorally disordered children. Journal of Child Psychology and Psychiatry and Allied Disciplines, January 1977, 18(1), 39-52. Topic Codes: BL11,CV15B,MG,NA07D,PE10,PG,TA80,TB95.

99914   Yesavage, J.A. Inpatient violence and the schizophrenic patient: A study of Brief Psychiatric Rating Scale scores and inpatient behavior. Acta Psychiatrica Scandinavica, May 1983, 67(5), 353-357. Topic Codes: CC81D,MU70,TA02,TA59.

99915   Yesavage, J.A., Becker, J.M., Werner, P.D., Patton, M.J., Seeman, K., Brunsting, D.W., and Mills, M.J. Family conflict, psychopathology, and dangerous behavior by schizophrenic in-patients. Psychiatry Research, April 1983, 8(4), 271-280. Topic Codes: CC81D,CC81F,CC81N,MU11,SI11, SI57B.

99916   Yeudall, L.T. Neuropsychology of aggression. Unpublished manuscript, National Institute of Justice, Washington, D.C., 1978. Topic Codes: BN44D,CC81I,CC81K,CC81M,CC81R,CQ59,CV13DA,DK07D,DK18D,NE59,PO11,TB35D.

99917   Yeudall, L.T. Neuropsychosocial perspective of persistent juvenile delinquency and criminal behavior. New York Academy of Sciences - Annals, 1980, 347, 349-355. Topic Codes: BL70D,BN44D,CC11C,CC11F,CC37,CC37B, CC37F,CC37H,CC37O,CC37X,CC37Z,CQ37,DK07B,DK07D,DT42D,MB11,ML03, MS04B,NE37,PE44D,PN11,PO11,SQ11,SW11,TA03,TA55,TB35D.

99921   Yeudall, L.T., Neuropsychological assessment of forensic disorders. Canadian Mental Health, 1977, 25, 7-16. Topic Codes: BN44B,BN44D,CC11C,

CC11F,CC11U,CC37R,CT57,CT57F,CT68,DD26D,DK07B,DK07D,MB,MS04B,P007,P011,
TA02,TA03,TA52,TA55,TB46,TB93B,TB93D,TB96B,TB96D.

99925   Yeudall, L.T., Fedora, D., Fedora, S., and Wardell, D., Neurosocial perspective on the assessment and etiology of persistent criminality. Australian Journal of Forensic Sciences, 1980, 13(4), 131-159; 1981, 14(1),
20-44. Topic Codes: BI11,BK04D,BK11BL,BL70B,BN04D,BN44D,CC11C,CC11F,
CC11M,CC11O,CC11P,CC11T,CC11U,CC67B,CC81I,CC81K,CT57,CT57F,CT68,DD26B,
DD26D,DK07D,MB11,MK11,MS02,MS04B,PC11,PE30D,P011,SQ07,SW11,TA03,TA52,TA55,
TA59,TB35B,TB35D,TB38B,TB61B,TB93D,TB96BB.

99927   Yeudall, L.T., Fromm-Auch, D., and Davies, P. Neuropsychological impair-
ment of persistent delinquency. Journal of Nervous and Mental Disease,
May 1982, 170(5), 257-265. Topic Codes: BN44D,CC37B,CC37R,CC37T,CC371,
P011,TA03,TA55,TB95D.

99929   Yochelson, S., and Samenow, S.E. The Criminal Personality: 1. A Profile
for Change. New York: Jason Aronson, 1976. Topic Codes: CC11C,CC11G,
CC11I,CC11N,CC11P,DD01,MF,MS02,MS04,PA11,PE01,PE64,PM,PT11,PV07,PV11,PY11,
SC70B,SC70D,SF07B,SH59,SH70,SI11,SO11,SR04.

99933   Young, F.A., and Lindsley, D. (eds.). Early Experience and Visual Information Processing in Perceptual and Reading Disorders. Washington: National Academy of Sciences, 1970. Topic Codes: BK11BL,BL18,BN44,BP04,
DD81,DF06B,DT06,DT15,DT44,DT59,ML15,MM,MR,PM,PO,PP,PS,SC59,SC70,SF.

99937   Young, V.D. Women, race, and crime. Criminology, May 1980, 18(1), 26-34.
Topic Codes: BL04D,BL67D,BL70D,CC11R,CC11S,CC24,CC37,CC37Y,CC81,CG11,
CQ22,CQ37,CQ81,CT57,CT59,CT81,CX,NE22,NE37,NE79,NE81,SN11,SQ11,SQ70D.

99941   Zahn, T.P., Abate, F., Little, B.C., and Wender, P.H. Minimal brain dysfunction, stimulant drugs and autonomic nervous system activity. Archives
of General Psychiatry, March 1975, 32(3), 381-387. Topic Codes: BK04B,
BL25B,BL29B,BN04B,CV15B,DK48B,MG30,MG48B,PC07,TB09B,TB95B.

99945   Zajonc, R.B. Family configuration and intelligence. Science, April 16,
1976, 192, 227-235. Topic Codes: BI,BL06,BL67,BL70,BP07,NH74B,PM,SF,
SF26,SH74B,SI59,SJ05,SJ09,SJ22B,SN,SQ,SW,TA59D.

99949   Zajonc, R.B., and Bargh, J. Birth order, family size, and decline of SAT
scores. American Psychologist, July 1980, 35(7), 662-668. Topic Codes:
BL70,PE64,SC70,SJ07,SJ22,SQ,SW33,TA59D.

99953   Zajonc, R.B., and Markus, G.B. Birth order and intellectual development.
Psychological Reviews, 1975, 82(1), 74-88. Topic Codes: BL11,BP07,NA07I,
PG,PM,SF,SJ05,SJ07,SJ22,TB72.

99957   Zambelli, A.J. Auditory evoked potentials and selective attention in adolescents with a childhood diagnosis of minimal brain dysfunction [doctor-
al dissertation, State University of New York at Stony Brook, 1974]. Dissertation Abstracts International, August 1975, 36(2), 644B. Topic Codes:
BK11B,BL11,BL18B,DK48B,MG48B,NA07D,NA07I,PE10,PG,TB37B.

99961   Zambelli, A.J., Stamm, J.S., Maitinsky, S., and Loiselle, D.L. Auditory
evoked potentials and selective attention in formerly hyperactive adolescent boys. American Journal of Psychiatry, July 1977, 134(7), 742-747.
Topic Codes: BL18B,DK48B,DT13B,DT52B,MG,MG48B,MH07,NA07D,PI07,TA02,TA52,
TA59D,TB35B,TB37B.

99965   Zeitlin, S. Assessing coping behavior. American Journal of Orthopsychiatry, January 1980, 50(1), 139-144. Topic Codes: BL11,PE10,PG,TA80.

99967   Zendel, I.H., and Pihl, R.O. Torque and learning and behavior problems in
children. Journal of Consulting and Clinical Psychology, October 1980, 48
(5), 602-604. Topic Codes: BN44B,DT44,MG,MM,NA07D,P007,PP.

99968   Zentall, S.S. Behavioral comparisons of hyperactive and normally active children in natural settings. <u>Journal of Abnormal Child Psychology</u>, March 1980, 8(1), 93-109. Topic Codes: MG,MG30,NA07B,PE10,PE64,SC.

99969   Zigler, E., and Butterfield, E.C. Motivational aspects of changes in IQ test performance of culturally deprived nursery school children. <u>Child Development</u>, March 1968, 39(1), 1-13. Topic Codes: BL11,BL67,BL70,DT13, MH,NA07I,PG,PI,PM,SC59,SN,SQ,SW,TB78.

99973   Zimmerman, J., Rich, W.D., Keilitz, I., and Broder, P.K. Some observations on the link between learning disabilities and juvenile delinquency. Unpublished manuscript, National Center for State Courts, August 1978. Topic Codes: BL04D,BL70B,BL70D,CC37A,CC37H,CC37J,CC81,CE,CG11C,CG11CC, CG11T,CQ81,CT70,CT81,CV13,DT44D,MM11,NE81,PE64D,PP11,SC70D,SQ07,SQ11,TA70.

99977   Zinkus, P.W., and Gottlieb, M.I. Learning disabilities and juvenile delinquency. <u>Clinical Pediatrics</u>, October 1978, 17(10), 775-780. Topic Codes: BL48D,BN44D,CC37H,CC37J,CC37R,CC37W,CC371,CQ59,CV13DA,DT44D,DT48D, DT59D,MM11,MR11,MT48D,NE59,PE48D,PE64D,PO11,PP11,PR11,PS11,SC70D,TA03, TA59,TB09D,TB09K,TB93D,TB95D,TB98D.

99981   Ziskind, E., Syndulko, K., and Maltzman, I. Aversive conditioning in the sociopath. <u>Pavlovian Journal of Biological Science</u>, October-December 1978, 13(4), 199-205. Topic Codes: BL,DD00B,DT44B,ME,NL,PP,TA80,TB35BB.

99985   Ziskind, E., Syndulko, K., and Maan, I. Evidence for a neurologic disorder in the sociopath syndrome: Aversive conditioning and recidivism. In C. Shagass, S. Gershon, and A.J. Friedhoff (eds.), <u>Psychopathology and Brain Dysfunction</u>. New York: Raven Press, 1977. Topic Codes: BD07, BL25BB,BL29B,DT15,DT44BB,MG18B,ML15,MM07B,MP07,MS04,PE52B,PP07B,TB35BB.

99989   Zuckerman, M. The sensation seeking motive. <u>Progress in Experimental Personality Research</u>, 1974, 7, 79-148. Topic Codes: CC11U,CC24,CC371,MK, NL,PE30,TA80.

99993   Zurif, E.B., and Bryden, M.P. Familial handedness and left-right differences in auditory and visual perception. <u>Neuropsychologia</u>, 1969, 7, 179-187. Topic Codes: BN44,PO,TA80,TB81.

99997   Zussman, J.U. Relationship of demographic factors to parental discipline techniques. <u>Developmental Psychology</u>, November 1978, 14(6), 685-686. Topic Codes: BL70,PY,SI57,SI57P,SJ22,SQ,SU,SW.

APPENDIX: HIERARCHICAL LISTING

BL07BD	Crime
BL08	Blood Pressure
BL08B	Hyper/Hypotension
BL08BB	and Behavioral and Mental Disorders
BL08BD	and Crime
BL11	Child Growth and Development
BL11C	and Crime
BL18	Evoked Potentials
BL18B	and Behavioral and Mental Disorders
BL18D	and Crime
BL22	Fetal Growth and Development
BL25	Galvanic Skin Response
BL25B	and Behavioral and Mental Disorders
BL25BB	Antisocial Personality
BL25D	and Crime
BL27	Gestational Age
BL27K	Smallness for Gestational Age
BL27KL	and Later Outcome
BL29	Heart Rate
BL29B	and Behavioral and Mental Disorders
BL29D	and Crime
BL31	Infant Growth and Development
BL33	Infant, Newborn, Growth and Development
BL48	Motor Skills and Disorders
BL48B	and Behavioral and Mental Disorders, Other
BL48D	and Crime
BL52	Nervous System Growth and Development
BL52D	Central Nervous System Growth and Development
BL52DB	and Behavioral and Mental Disorders
BL52DD	and Crime
BL59	Pulse
BL59D	and Crime
BL67	Racial Differences
BL67B	and Behavioral and Mental Disorders
BL67BB	Antisocial Personality
BL67D	and Crime
BL70	Sex Differences
BL70B	and Behavioral and Mental Disorders
BL70BB	Antisocial Personality
BL70D	and Crime
BN	Physiological Factors, Nervous System
BN04	Arousal
BN04B	and Behavioral and Mental Disorders
BN04BB	Antisocial Personality
BN04D	and Crime
BN44	Laterality
BN44B	and Behavioral and Mental Disorders
BN44BB	Antisocial Personality
BN44D	and Crime
BN44H	and Intelligence
BN68	Sleep and Sleep Disorders
BN68B	and Crime
BN70	Speech and Speech Disorders
BN70D	and Crime
BP	Pregnancy and Birth Conditions
BP02	and Outcome
BP02B	Behavioral and Mental Disorders of Child
BP02D	Crime of Child
BP03	Alcohol Drinking during Pregnancy
BP04	Anesthesia and Drug Use during Pregnancy
BP07	Birth Intervals
BP07B	and Behavioral and Mental Disorders
BP07D	and Crime
BP22	Fetus
BP22F	Fetal Growth and Development
BP26	Gestational Age
BP26G	Smallness for Gestational Age
BP26GD	and Later Outcome

```
BP44              Labor and Delivery
BP46              Maternal Age at Pregnancy
BP47              Maternal Disease and Injury during Pregnancy
BP48              Maternal Psychological State during Pregnancy
BP52              Nutrition and Diet during Pregnancy
BP53              Obstetric History
BP57              Parity
BP59              Physical Characteristics of Gravida
BP61              Placenta
BP63              Prenatal Care
BP70              Smoking during Pregnancy
BP89              X-Ray Exposure during Pregnancy
C            Criminology and Criminological Factors
CC              Causes and Correlates of Crime by Offender Classes
CC11              Criminality
CC11A               and Age
CC11B               and Automatisms and Seizures
CC11C               and Behavioral and Mental Disorders
CC11D               and Biological Factors
CC11E               and Body Constitution
CC11F               and Brain Abnormalities
CC11G               and Childhood Factors
CC11H               and Drug Abuse and Alcohol Drinking
CC11I               and Educational Factors
CC11J               and Employment
CC11K               and Epilepsy
CC11L               and Family Factors
CC11M               and Genetic Factors
CC11N               and Intelligence
CC11O               and Neurological Factors
CC11P               and Personality
CC11Q               and Pre/Perinatal and Infanthood Factors
CC11R               and Race
CC11S               and Sex
CC11T               and Socioeconomic Status
CC11U               Specific Tests Listed in Article
CC24              Female Offenders
CC24B               and Behavioral and Mental Disorders
CC37              Juvenile Delinquency
CC37A               and Age
CC37B               and Behavioral and Mental Disorders
CC37BB                Antisocial Personality
CC37C               and Biochemical Factors
CC37D               and Blood Pressure
CC37E               and Body Constitution
CC37F               and Brain Abnormality, Disease, and Injury
CC37G               and Child/Infant Growth and Development
CC37H               and Cognitive, Language, and Learning Disorders
CC37I               and Drug and Alcohol Abuse
CC37J               and Educational Factors
CC37K               and Environment
CC37L               and Epilepsy
CC37M               and Family Factors
CC37N               and Genetic Factors
CC37O               and Head Injuries
CC37P               and Health, Disease, and Injury
CC37Q               and Intelligence
CC37R               and Laterality
CC37S               and Minimal Brain Dysfunction
CC37T               and Neurological Abnormality, Disease, and Injury
CC37U               and Nutrition and Diet
CC37V               and Outcome in Adulthood
CC37W               and Personality
CC37X               and Pre/Perinatal and Infanthood Factors
CC37Y               and Race
CC37Z               and Socioeconomic Status
CC371               Specific Tests Listed in Article
CC67              Recidivism
```

```
DF60BD                   Crime
DF67              Respiratory Distress Syndrome
DF67B                and Later Outcome
DF70              Smallness for Gestational Age
DF70B                and Later Outcome
DK         Nervous System Abnormality, Disease, and Injury
DK07             Brain Abnormality, Disease, and Injury
DK07B                and Behavioral and Mental Disorders
DK07BB                   Antisocial Personality
DK07D                and Crime
DK09             Central Nervous System Abnormality, Disease, and Injury
DK09B                and Behavioral and Mental Disorders
DK09D                and Crime
DK11             Cerebral Palsy
DK11B                and Behavioral and Mental Disorders
DK11D                and Crime
DK18             Epilepsy
DK18B                and Behavioral and Mental Disorders
DK18D                and Crime and Aggression
DK18S                Temporal Lobe Epilepsy
DK18SB                   and Behavioral and Mental Disorders
DK18SD                   and Crime
DK46             Mental Retardation
DK46B                and Behavioral and Mental Disorders, Other
DK46D                and Crime
DK48             Minimal Brain Dysfunction
DK48B                and Behavioral and Mental Disorders
DK48D                and Crime
DP         Pregnancy and Birth Complications
DP11             and Outcome
DP11B                Behavioral and Mental Disorders of Child
DP11D                Crime of Child
DP22             Fetal Diseases
DP22D                Fetal Alcohol Syndrome
DP22H                Fetal Distress
DP22P                Smallness for Gestational Age
DP44             Labor and Delivery Complications
DP46             Maternal Disease and Injury during Pregnancy
DP48             Mortality, Pre/Perinatal and Infant
DP58             Placental Complications
DP60             Pregnancy Toxemias
DP81             Vaginal Bleeding during Pregnancy
DT         Symptoms and Manifestations
DT02             Amnesia
DT02B                and Crime
DT04             Anoxia
DT04E                and Later Outcome
DT04EB                   Behavioral and Mental Disorders
DT04ED                   Crime
DT06             Aphasia
DT06B                and Crime
DT08             Apnea
DT08E                and Later Outcome
DT10             Automatism
DT10B                and Crime
DT13             Cognition and Cognition Disorders
DT13B                and Behavioral and Mental Disorders, Other
DT13D                and Crime
DT15             Dyslexia
DT15B                and Crime
DT30             Headaches
DT42             Language and Language Disorders
DT42B                and Behavioral and Mental Disorders, Other
DT42BB                   Antisocial Personality
DT42D                and Crime
DT44             Learning and Learning Disorders
DT44B                and Behavioral and Mental Disorders, Other
DT44BB                   Antisocial Personality
```

```
DT44D                    and Crime
DT46                 Memory and Memory Disorders
DT48                 Motor Skills and Disorders
DT48B                    and Behavioral and Mental Disorders, Other
DT48D                    and Crime
DT52                 Neurological Soft Signs
DT52B                    and Behavioral and Mental Disorders
DT52D                    and Crime
DT59                 Perception and Perceptual Disorders
DT59B                    and Behavioral and Mental Disorders, Other
DT59D                    and Crime
DT67                 Seizures and Convulsions
DT67B                    and Crime
DT69                 Sleep and Sleep Disorders
DT69B                    and Crime
DT71                 Speech and Speech Disorders
DT71D                    and Crime
M            Behavioral and Mental Disorders
MA               Accident Proneness
MA07                 and Behavioral and Mental Disorders, Other
MA11                 and Crime
MB               Affective Disorders
MB11                 and Crime
MC               Aggression
MC11                 and Crime
MD               Alcohol Drinking and Alcoholism
MD07                 and Behavioral and Mental Disorders, Other
MD07B                    Antisocial Personality
MD11                 and Crime
ME               Antisocial Behavior
ME07                 and Crime
MF               Behavior and Behavioral Disorders
MF11                 and Crime
MG               Child Behavioral and Mental Disorders
MG02                 and Outcome in Adulthood
MG02B                    Behavioral and Mental Disorders
MG02D                    Crime
MG04                 Autism, Infantile
MG04G                    and Later Outcome
MG04GB                       Behavioral and Mental Disorders
MG11                 Conduct Disorders
MG11B                    and Crime
MG18                 Enuresis
MG18B                    and Antisocial Personality
MG18D                    and Crime
MG21                 Fingersucking
MG30                 Hyperkinetic Syndrome
MG30B                    and Behavioral and Mental Disorders, Other
MG30BB                       Antisocial Personality
MG30D                    and Crime
MG48                 Minimal Brain Dysfunction
MG48B                    and Behavioral and Mental Disorders
MG48D                    and Crime
MH               Cognition and Cognition Disorders
MH07                 and Behavioral and Mental Disorders, Other
MH11                 and Crime
MI               Drug Abuse
MI04                 and Antisocial Personality
MI07                 and Crime
MK               Impulsive Behavior
MK11                 and Crime
ML               Language and Language Disorders
ML02                 and Behavioral and Mental Disorders, Other
ML02B                    Antisocial Personality
ML03                 and Crime
ML04                 Aphasia
ML04B                    and Crime
ML15                 Dyslexia
```

```
ML15B               and Crime
MM              Learning and Learning Disorders
MM07                and Behavioral and Mental Disorders, Other
MM07B                   Antisocial Personality
MM11                and Crime
MN              Memory and Memory Disorders
MN04                Amnesia
MN04B               and Crime
MO              Mental Retardation
MO07                and Behavioral and Mental Disorders, Other
MO11                and Crime
MP              Nail Biting
MP07                and Behavioral and Mental Disorders, Other
MP11                and Crime
MQ              Neurotic Disorders
MQ11                and Crime
MR              Perception and Perceptual Disorders
MR07                and Behavioral and Mental Disorders, Other
MR11                and Crime
MS              Personality Disorders
MS02                and Crime
MS04                Antisocial Personality
MS04B               and Crime
MT              Psychomotor Disorders
MT04                Automatism
MT04B               and Crime
MT48                Motor Skills and Disorders
MT48B                   and Behavioral and Mental Disorders, Other
MT48D                   and Crime
MU              Psychotic Disorders
MU11                and Crime
MU70                Schizophrenia
MU70B               and Crime
MV              Sexual Behavior and Disorders
MV07                and Behavioral and Mental Disorders, Other
MV11                and Crime
MW              Sleep and Sleep Disorders
MW11                and Crime
MX              Social Behavior and Social Behavior Disorders
MX07                and Behavioral and Mental Disorders, Other
MX11                and Crime
MY              Speech and Speech Disorders
MY11                and Crime
MZ              Suicide
N           Named Groups and Study Methods
NA          Age Groups
NA07            Child
NA07B               Child Behavior
NA07D               Child Behavioral and Mental Disorders
NA07DB                  and Outcome in Adulthood
NA07DD                      Behavioral and Mental Disorders
NA07DF                      Crime
NA07I               Child Growth and Development
NA07ID                  and Crime
NA31            Infant
NA31A               and Later Behavioral and Mental Disorders
NA31B               and Later Crime
NA31C               Infant Abnormality, Disease, and Injury
NA31D               Infant Behavior
NA31F               Infant Growth and Development
NA31R               Infant Neurological and Physical Examination
NA33            Infant, Newborn
NA33A               and Later Behavioral and Mental Disorders
NA33B               Infant, Newborn, Abnormality, Disease, and Injury
NA33D               Infant, Newborn, Behavior
NA33F               Infant, Newborn, Growth and Development
NA33I               Infant, Newborn, Neurological and Physical Examination
NA44            Longitudinal Studies
```

```
SL              Hospitalization
SL07              and Behavioral and Mental Disorders
SL11              and Crime
SM              Housing
SM07              and Behavioral and Mental Disorders
SM11              and Crime
SN              Racial Differences
SN07              and Behavioral and Mental Disorders
SN07B               Antisocial Personality
SN11              and Crime
SO              Religion
SO07              and Behavioral and Mental Disorders
SO11              and Crime
SQ              Sex Differences
SQ07              and Behavioral and Mental Disorders
SQ07B               Antisocial Personality
SQ11              and Crime
SQ70              Sex Roles
SQ70B               and Behavioral and Mental Disorders
SQ70D               and Crime
SR              Social Behavior and Social Behavior Disorders
SR01              and Behavioral and Mental Disorders, Other
SR02              and Crime
SR03              Aggression
SR03B               and Crime
SR04              Antisocial Behavior
SR04B               and Crime
SR69              Sexual Behavior and Disorders
SR69B               and Behavioral and Mental Disorders, Other
SR69D               and Crime
SS              Social Conditions
SS07              and Behavioral and Mental Disorders
SS09              and Crime
SU              Socialization
SU11              and Crime
SW              Socioeconomic Status
SW07              and Behavioral and Mental Disorders
SW07B               Antisocial Personality
SW11              and Crime
SW16              Education of Parent or Household Head
SW18              Employment of Parent or Household Head
SW33              Income of Parent or Household Head
SW56              Occupation of Parent or Household Head
SY              Weapons
SY11              and Crime and Aggression
T             Tests and Measures
TA              Kinds of Tests
TA02              and Behavioral and Mental Disorders
TA02B               Antisocial Personality
TA03              and Crime
TA04              Achievement Tests
TA52              Neurological and Physical Examinations
TA52K               Infant Neurological and Physical Examination
TA52M               Infant, Newborn, Neurological and Physical Examination
TA55              Neuropsychological Tests
TA57              Parents' Reports of Children's Behavior
TA59              Psychological Tests
TA59D               Cognition, Language, and Learning Abilities Tests
TA70              Self-Reports of Violence and Crime
TA74              Teachers' Reports of Children's Behavior
TA80              Other Tests
TB              Specific Tests and Test Groups
TB02              Apgar
TB05              Bayley Scales of Infant Development
TB09              Bender-Gestalt Test
TB09B               and Behavioral and Mental Disorders
TB09D               and Crime
TB09K               Koppitz Error Score
```

TB12	Benton Right-Left Discrimination Test
TB12B	and Crime
TB15	Beta Examination
TB15B	and Crime
TB19	Buss-Durkee Hostility Inventory (BDI)
TB19B	and Crime
TB21	California Achievement Test (CAT)
TB21B	and Behavioral and Mental Disorders
TB21D	and Crime
TB23	California Psychological Inventory (CPI)
TB23B	and Crime
TB25	Cattell Infant Scales
TB25B	and Behavioral and Mental Disorders
TB27	CPP Behavior Profile
TB33	Drawing Test
TB33B	and Crime
TB33G	Goodenough-Harris Scoring
TB33GD	and Crime
TB35	Electroencephalography
TB35B	and Behavioral and Mental Disorders
TB35BB	Antisocial Personality
TB35D	and Crime
TB37	Evoked Potentials
TB37B	and Behavioral and Mental Disorders
TB37D	and Crime
TB38	Eysenck Personality Inventory
TB38B	and Crime
TB40	Finger Tapping Test
TB40B	and Behavioral and Mental Disorders
TB40D	and Crime
TB42	Gesell Developmental Schedule
TB44	Graham-Ernhardt Block Sort Test
TB46	Halstead-Reitan Batteries
TB46B	and Crime
TB49	Hand Test
TB49B	and Behavioral and Mental Disorders
TB49D	and Crime
TB51	Holzman Inkblot Technique
TB51B	and Crime
TB53	Illinois Test Of Psycholinguistic Abilities (ITPA)
TB53B	and Crime
TB55	Iowa Test of Basic skills
TB57	Lincoln-Oseretsky Test of Motor Maturity
TB57B	and Behavioral and Mental Disorders
TB57D	and Crime
TB59	Maudsley Personality Inventory
TB59B	and Crime
TB61	Minnesota Multiphasic Personality Inventory (MMPI)
TB61B	and Crime
TB64	Offer Self-Image Questionnaire (OSIQ)
TB64B	and Crime
TB66	Porteus Maze Test
TB66B	and Behavioral and Mental Disorders
TB66D	and Crime
TB68	Primary Mental Abilities Test (PMA)
TB68B	and Crime
TB70	Quick Test
TB70B	and Crime
TB72	Raven's Progressive Matrices (RPM)
TB72B	and Crime
TB74	Rorschach Inkblot Technique
TB74B	and Crime
TB76	Scientific Research Associates' Non-Verbal Test (SRA-NV)
TB76B	and Crime
TB78	Stanford-Binet Intelligence Scales
TB78B	and Behavioral and Mental Disorders
TB78D	and Crime
TB81	Tachistoscopic Tests

INDEX

55400,61650,61750,68130,69760,71400,
81210,92200,93200,98500,98650,99210,
99255,99315.
Asphyxia
See:
 Anoxia
Autism, Infantile (MG04) 02300,05950,
 05970,20600,34700,36000,46560,58800,
 89000,94920,99010,99305.
 and Later Outcome (MG04G) 94990.
  Behavioral and Mental Disorders
   (MG04GB) 07450,20630,35360,
   88800,94940.
Automatism (DT10,MT04) 41100,59820,
 63400,66950,71500,87000,98840.
 and Crime (DT10B,MT04B) 21500,40700,
  44900,62400,75400,81700.
 See also:
  Epilepsy
Autonomic Nervous System (BK04) 11900,
 28200,31130,38660,40000,54000,54230,
 60000,69000,71730,79300,99350,99580.
 and Behavioral and Mental Disorders
  (BK04B) 09930,26260,26800,27480,
  38400,48500,50100,70000,70400,
  97950,99565,99580,99941.
  Antisocial Personality (BK04BB)
   06000,09700,43970,54300,66950,
   67300,69890,81950,84810,84820,
   99230,99350.
 and Crime (BK04D) 06000,19360,30600,
  32970,43970,47200,51970,52650,
  59800,64970,67600,67700,68160,
  69895,69900,70300,70450,70500,
  70700,75500,84820,85300,85400,
  91300,99335,99800,99925.
 See also:
  Arousal
  Galvanic Skin Response
  Heart Rate
  Pulse
Avoidance Learning
 See:
  Learning and Learning Disorders
  Socialization
Bayley Scales
 See under:
  Tests and Measures
Behavior and Behavioral Disorders (MF,
 PE) 00100,00910,00995,01000,01150,
 04560,07030,07050,07230,09870,09960,
 11750,19070,20630,21595,24450,27170,
 27250,28330,30670,32930,32980,35380,
 36380,37150,37970,38400,39850,40430,
 41050,48200,48250,50350,54230,54300,
 55150,56450,57850,59820,59860,62330,
 62550,63400,64400,64850,66060,67220,
 69000,69225,69500,70300,72690,73900,
 74030,75800,79215,79700,83960,84095,
 84870,85970,86950,87250,87960,87970,
 88900,91500,92080,92610,98730,98910,
 99040,99095,99110,99310,99695,99775,
 99808,99869,99929.
 and Crime (MF11,PE01) 02450,10130,
  17570,19360,27915,28550,28580,
  29250,30100,30230,32970,37150,
  40730,47100,47200,51970,55260,

56990,58450,59640,59690,59800,
 59890,61650,68400,69200,71720,
 74040,85960,98640,99360,99853,
 99929.
Behavior Modification and Mental
 Health Services (CV06) 00550,01200,
 04500,06000,12200,19060,22800,23000,
 25300,28550,28590,30200,33600,37100,
 37200,40730,42200,48690,53260,54310,
 55150,55990,56830,59890,61850,64030,
 68130,69270,69500,69730,70200,71710,
 72050,72800,74040,75400,77300,78400,
 80030,80040,81300,81930,84300,87850,
 87910,87960,89175,92400,92530,92610,
 98560,98641,98725,98980,99045,99110,
 99345,99365,99430,99460,99475,99550,
 99625,99685,99805,99873.
 Effects on Offenders, Antisocial
  Persons (CV06C) 04800,06800,08450,
  09850,11400,15150,16860,17150,
  17200,17570,21000,21500,22900,
  24000,26900,28580,28750,32970,
  43990,44410,46790,47100,47200,
  51700,51900,52000,52900,53090,
  54300,56860,59800,60400,63700,
  67400,68200,68400,68650,69290,
  71720,72860,75500,77305,80830,
  81200,82250,84100,84860,84890,
  87920,89700,94010,95300,95400,
  96350,96500,98637,98650,98830,
  98840,98945,98990,99105,99425,
  99680.
Behavioral and Mental Disorders (M)
 00100,00910,09870,59530,59690,59890,
 61650,64760,69270,89550,92360.
Bender Gestalt
 See under:
  Tests and Measures
Bilirubin Level (BD30B) 12000,12450,
 27900,34700,59400,74700,76400,98965.
 and Later Outcome (BD30BA) 10650,
  13100,46675,54730,77000,88430,
  91850.
 See also:
  Infant Abnormality, Disease, and
   Injury
  Infant Neurological and Physical
   Examination
  Infant, Newborn, Abnormality, Disease, and Injury
  Infant, Newborn, Neurological and
   Physical Examination
Biochemical Factors (BD) 04330,09200,
 10200,27170,27430,30670,31450,45300,
 50500,50600,54300,55205,56000,57950,
 59820,65430,65900,66680,69000,71500,
 73800,85970,86950,91600.
 and Behavioral and Mental Disorders
  (BD07) 01150,07230,08400,09350,
  16850,19350,21595,29400,42200,
  45330,46400,47200,50000,50100,
  56530,63420,67200,67220,71350,
  84950,85970,89500,93700,96700,
  99120,99230,99295,99560,99565,
  99841,99985.
 and Crime (BD11) 00300,11800,19360,
  21950,25920,42200,44220,47200,

65300,65400,65570,65600,66130,66160,
68700,78615,79215,79217,84000,99335,
99435,99780.
  and Behavioral and Mental Disorders
    (BE07) 07455,09350,47200,50100,
    61000,70000,79207,80890,84700,
    98910.
  and Crime (BE11) 07455,19200,23700,
    27915,31900,32970,33600,33800,
    34400,34750,36700,37600,41570,
    42400,44200,47200,49790,66460,
    67700,68300,71760,72960,75400,
    76900,76930,87100,87990,98680,
    99795.
Body Length
  See:
    Birth Length
    Body Constitution
    Infant Neurological and Physical
      Examination
    Infant, Newborn, Neurological and
      Physical Examination
Body Weight
  See:
    Birth Weight
    Body Constitution
    Infant Neurological and Physical
      Examination
    Infant, Newborn, Neurological and
      Physical Examination
Brain (BK11B) 00650,00700,00950,00995,
  03200,04015,04030,04040,04050,04075,
  04080,04090,04530,06000,06090,07230,
  07250,08400,08800,09370,09990,10130,
  10230,10300,10500,10600,12750,12800,
  13100,13150,13630,13650,14050,18200,
  19360,20580,21595,23800,26260,27150,
  28100,28450,28560,28590,29080,29250,
  30860,31530,31930,32050,32970,33600,
  34350,35350,35650,37600,38100,38130,
  38660,39850,40550,40600,41530,41970,
  42200,44419,46200,47100,47900,48050,
  48700,49800,50060,53260,53750,54000,
  54300,54730,55290,55450,56900,57730,
  57760,57767,58590,59620,59640,59680,
  59820,60700,61230,61800,62250,64030,
  64430,64550,64850,64900,64950,65430,
  65460,66600,66650,67190,68050,69000,
  69220,69230,71770,72150,72200,72300,
  73800,73900,74200,74660,75500,75700,
  75800,76790,78430,80000,84080,84300,
  84950,85100,85700,87700,87970,88000,
  89810,90350,90550,90800,90980,92340,
  92600,93670,93680,94050,94290,94680,
  94920,95400,96900,98675,98760,98765,
  98910,99110,99120,99325,99440,99448,
  99470,99485,99505,99555,99620,99655,
  99785,99957.
  See also:
    Central Nervous System
    Electroencephalography
    Evoked Potentials
    Laterality
    Limbic System
Brain Abnormality, Disease, and Injury
  (DK07) 00900,03100,04010,04080,
  07800,08700,08900,09990,12450,13624,

25600,28500,30860,31130,31530,31700,
31800,32050,32100,33250,35350,35600,
36300,38660,38670,40520,41050,41700,
43250,43300,43500,44419,45100,46010,
46675,49950,54000,54730,57730,57850,
59620,61150,61230,61520,63900,64950,
71500,73800,74250,75800,76400,77000,
77100,77318,78430,79270,81630,84080,
85100,86200,90400,90500,90800,91050,
92100,93680,94290,94680,95400,96900,
97700,98732,98760,98995,99025,99140,
99280,99448,99470,99485,99500,99535,
99785.
  and Behavioral and Mental Disorders
    (DK07B) 01400,07230,07500,07540,
    07570,08400,08750,09370,10130,
    10300,10500,10800,12200,13250,
    16500,16725,17600,17700,20580,
    20600,21595,22000,22600,28560,
    28590,29080,29250,31930,32100,
    35700,36000,38130,38400,39850,
    39900,40500,40700,41970,42200,
    43300,46400,47200,47800,47900,
    48700,48900,49800,50060,53400,
    53500,54900,56450,57000,57200,
    57790,57793,57800,58900,60700,
    61000,61350,63400,64030,64550,
    64850,66650,67200,69500,69800,
    70000,70400,72300,72500,72600,
    73900,76500,76790,79600,79700,
    79800,80900,84870,84880,85000,
    87000,87940,87970,88200,88460,
    89000,89100,89410,89600,89810,
    90600,92080,93670,93700,94920,
    94960,96700,97950,98720,98732,
    98840,98905,98910,99010,99020,
    99045,99075,99320,99400,99507,
    99550,99555,99610,99620,99625,
    99655,99790,99808,99849,99905,
    99917,99921.
    Antisocial Personality (DK07BB)
      08800,26260,34350,47000,67300,
      84500,94700.
  and Crime (DK07D) 00500,02300,03900,
    07455,08800,10130,10450,12200,
    14050,17100,19360,19500,24030,
    28550,28560,28590,29250,31930,
    32300,32970,33600,34400,38000,
    40220,40700,42200,43180,44417,
    44700,49190,51400,55450,56896,
    57790,59640,59800,63710,63850,
    66400,66500,66600,67700,67900,
    68300,70450,72880,72950,75400,
    75500,77500,81700,81900,82000,
    82100,83800,85450,85975,89810,
    90980,92600,92650,92680,97300,
    97400,97680,98150,98655,98785,
    99060,99265,99270,99590,99916,
    99917,99921,99925.
  See also:
    Epilepsy
    Mental Retardation
    Minimal Brain Dysfunction
Broken/Single-Parent Homes (SJ09)
  18300,19900,20200,30260,58400,60200,
  80350,92320,99335,99829,99945.
  and Behavioral and Mental Disorders

46500,46600,46676,46680,46760,47400,
47600,47900,48680,49350,49800,50200,
51300,51950,52050,52160,53000,53230,
53260,53400,53670,54100,54230,54400,
54500,55100,55200,55290,55340,55360,
55500,55600,55700,55800,55950,55970,
55980,56060,56100,56400,56830,56890,
56930,56960,57060,57100,57500,57775,
57785,57790,57950,58000,58300,58450,
58560,59000,59100,59660,59730,59760,
59860,60500,61000,61150,61230,61290,
61350,61500,61510,61900,62270,62330,
62460,63480,63830,64000,64400,64600,
64670,64690,64830,65200,65300,65400,
65600,65700,65750,65900,66200,66300,
66400,66760,68050,68100,68130,68250,
68700,68860,69000,69500,69730,71100,
71400,71705,71770,72060,73100,74660,
75300,76000,76300,76790,77328,77335,
78900,79217,79270,79400,79500,80050,
80160,82100,82400,82800,84000,84300,
84700,84800,84805,84895,85900,87130,
87860,88430,88800,88900,88940,89410,
91500,92000,92250,92670,92900,93400,
93680,93700,94050,94100,94290,94750,
94920,94940,94960,94980,94990,95000,
95100,95350,95400,96000,96600,96800,
97480,98625,98645,98660,98665,98675,
98685,98695,98700,98710,98732,98775,
98792,98798,98895,98900,98905,98910,
98915,98960,98965,98980,99125,99130,
99140,99325,99370,99395,99445,99460,
99485,99490,99520,99530,99535,99540,
99545,99550,99555,99595,99600,99605,
99610,99615,99620,99630,99635,99655,
99660,99665,99700,99705,99745,99750,
99755,99790,99808,99810,99865,99893,
99897,99913,99953,99957,99965,99969.
and Crime (BL11C,NA07ID,PG11) 02450,
  02800,03400,03600,06000,06350,
  10100,10130,10830,14740,15000,
  15150,15500,17100,21590,24400,
  27915,28700,30500,31105,31200,
  32600,35800,36700,36800,37150,
  40430,42400,46040,47200,52900,
  53100,55360,55985,59600,59640,
  62900,67300,67600,67700,68130,
  70600,70700,71730,81300,84100,
  86900,92000,92800,99013,99215.
  See also:
    Body Constitution
Child Psychiatry
  See:
    Behavior Modification and Mental
      Health Services
    Child Behavioral and Mental Disor-
      ders
Child Psychology
  See:
    Behavior Modification and Mental
      Health Services
    Child Behavior
    Child Behavioral and Mental Disor-
      ders
    Child Growth and Development
Child Rearing

See:
  Parent-Child Relations
  Socialization
Cognition and Cognition Disorders
  (DT13,MH,PI) 00200,00930,04620,
  06090,06350,06700,07465,07540,07570,
  08900,09200,09230,09250,09370,09960,
  09990,09995,10200,11000,13630,13800,
  14030,14250,16400,16870,17170,17500,
  20630,20700,21300,23300,27200,27920,
  29050,30830,31130,32100,33050,34140,
  35700,37600,38180,38400,38450,38660,
  39850,40520,40600,40800,43030,46100,
  46200,46250,46760,47700,47800,47900,
  48000,48400,48900,49800,52160,54100,
  54900,55500,55600,56200,56990,57767,
  58300,58400,58600,59660,60000,61300,
  62100,62200,63630,64400,64650,64850,
  64950,66760,68860,69000,69800,71100,
  72300,72400,75800,75900,78500,78650,
  79300,79400,81860,81930,84600,84895,
  85100,85680,87860,87895,88200,88430,
  88460,91500,92090,92250,93400,94400,
  94670,97480,97500,97600,97950,98600,
  98610,98695,98920,99140,99325,99485,
  99495,99550,99600,99869,99893,99969.
  and Behavioral and Mental Disorders,
    Other (DT13B,MH07,PI07) 01400,
    04080,04590,07540,07570,08730,
    09370,10500,10600,13400,14300,
    15600,19370,20580,20630,27250,
    28760,32930,34670,36000,38400,
    39850,56530,59700,61600,63400,
    77325,79207,81930,90200,93700,
    98775,99375,99380,99385,99550,
    99825,99961.
  and Crime (DT13D,MH11,PI11) 08730,
    15500,19360,26700,27000,27915,
    28760,31200,32970,41990,43800,
    44417,59800,62450,67700,79205,
    85930,88150,89700,91300,91400,
    92610,94640,97400,99645,99795.
  See also:
    Intelligence
    Language and Language Disorders
    Learning and Learning Disorders
    Memory and Memory Disorders
    Perception and Perceptual Disor-
      ders
Conduct Disorders (MG11) 00400,01150,
  01800,02450,04400,04560,04648,07500,
  08600,09500,13400,14100,15600,17150,
  17200,19070,20580,22110,22600,22800,
  22900,25200,25300,26400,26800,27000,
  28250,28900,30900,34140,34350,38000,
  38300,38450,38600,39700,40750,43750,
  44200,44420,44600,45400,51600,51900,
  52000,52500,58500,58700,60100,62550,
  63000,64200,64500,66900,67300,67600,
  69100,70600,70700,70900,72950,77220,
  77320,78600,79227,84200,84300,84470,
  85900,88800,89410,98625,98641,98643,
  98644,98660,98695,98880,99510,99660,
  99805.
  and Crime (MG11B) 01300,04500,07400,
    08100,15500,23500,27915,47200,

08450,08600,09850,11400,12790,
14050,16300,16850,16860,17570,
19360,19700,19800,19900,20000,
20200,20300,20500,20575,21000,
23700,24000,24500,24600,25500,
26100,26900,27100,27910,28550,
28580,29250,32970,33000,33600,
37970,40730,40750,41980,44200,
44600,44700,45400,45500,45600,
46780,46785,46795,46900,47000,
47100,47200,49000,50090,51500,
51700,52300,53110,53950,54310,
54340,55400,57550,59560,59800,
59890,60580,61650,61680,61750,
63660,63810,63850,65550,65950,
66100,66900,67030,67300,68450,
69290,70200,70450,70900,71000,
71720,72860,74150,75500,76840,
76860,76890,76900,76930,77302,
78200,79220,79260,80130,83930,
83990,84520,84580,84820,87830,
87940,91300,91400,91930,94640,
94700,95200,95300,95400,95800,
96500,97400,98150,98250,98650,
98705,98740,98745,98750,98755,
98843,98990,99005,99055,99100,
99105,99195,99205,99210,99220,
99225,99230,99240,99245,99250,
99255,99260,99315,99590,99680,
99695,99710,99770,99901,99917,
99921,99925,99929.
and Biological Factors (CC11D)
00100,02450,05430,09850,11700,
13200,19360,23700,24400,25920,
26400,27100,28560,29250,30230,
31100,32970,33600,34750,35380,
37600,38680,42380,44200,46790,
47200,50090,51500,53110,53240,
54340,55915,56530,56893,57400,
59600,59800,64060,64160,64970,
66130,66160,66460,66490,67600,
69850,70200,70450,71720,71760,
72830,75500,76900,79220,81830,
83930,84560,88440,90940,91300,
91400,91590,98150,98755,98830,
99055,99222,99725,99730,99795,
99841.
and Body Constitution (CC11E) 05430,
07455,12790,30400,32970,33600,
34750,37600,37970,44200,66460,
71760,72960,99695,99795.
and Brain Abnormalities (CC11F)
07455,10130,19360,19800,28550,
28590,29250,31930,32970,33600,
33700,47100,48050,55450,58150,
59800,63850,66600,70200,72880,
72900,75500,80020,82000,87940,
92600,93700,94700,98785,98820,
98825,99060,99265,99270,99590,
99770,99917,99921,99925.
and Childhood Factors (CC11G) 02450,
12790,16300,20200,21000,26100,
27250,30200,32970,33600,44700,
47100,47200,53240,55400,59890,
66030,66400,66900,75500,86500,
87100,93100,96500,98705,99260,
99929.
and Drug Abuse and Alcohol Drinking

(CC11H) 06000,10100,10670,10680,
11800,13190,16850,16860,19360,
19600,19800,20200,20510,21140,
25500,33600,43090,43100,43930,
45400,45500,45600,47100,47200,
51990,59890,66900,70450,75500,
83900,84520,84560,86600,92610,
94660,95200,95800,98150,98735,
99105,99180,99185,99190,99200,
99210,99230,99255,99265,99590,
99770,99901.
and Educational Factors (CC11I)
02450,13620,19360,27100,44200,
44300,45400,47000,47200,49000,
53240,66900,75500,87890,95200,
98745,98825,99185,99230,99255,
99590,99901,99929.
and Employment (CC11J) 44200,44700,
66900,92610,95200,99590,99901.
and Epilepsy (CC11K) 04280,19360,
44700,44800,44900,59800,64060,
64430,66600,70450,82020,92600,
99770.
and Family Factors (CC11L) 02450,
12790,19700,20100,20200,20300,
21000,24500,24600,31105,33600,
44200,44700,45400,45600,47100,
47200,52500,53110,53240,54740,
66030,66460,66900,69850,70200,
70260,70350,71000,75500,79000,
80750,83900,83960,83990,87300,
93100,95200,97200,97900,99185,
99200,99215.
and Genetic Factors (CC11M) 02450,
04090,04280,05430,07455,07460,
10670,10680,13200,18520,19360,
20510,23700,24400,24450,24500,
24600,27250,30230,31105,32970,
33600,36430,37600,44220,47200,
48050,51500,51930,53110,55915,
57400,59800,64115,66600,70200,
70260,70265,70450,71760,72860,
75500,76840,76860,76880,76890,
76900,76920,76930,79215,80890,
81830,83930,83960,83990,86450,
87300,90940,93660,94010,94675,
97200,98860,99055,99695,99925.
and Intelligence (CC11N) 02450,
12790,13200,19360,32970,33600,
37600,40300,44200,47200,49000,
51990,53240,59690,59800,59890,
60580,66030,66100,66160,70200,
70350,71760,75500,83930,87890,
90920,91400,95300,98150,98745,
98750,98820,98825,99055,99100,
99185,99220,99230,99245,99255,
99590,99645,99710,99795,99929.
and Neurological Factors (CC11O)
06000,07455,13620,19360,28590,
29250,33600,40700,44700,46900,
47000,47200,52650,59800,60580,
61680,65950,66600,69895,70200,
70350,78200,94000,95800,97400,
97900,99925.
and Personality (CC11P) 00400,02100,
02450,05690,06000,07600,08600,
12790,16850,16860,17570,19360,
19600,21000,26400,26900,28550,

66000,66800,66900,68600,69500,
70450,75500,83800,83900,84520,
86600,86900,87980,94660,98400,
98500,98650,98735,98745,99105,
99255,99590,99901.
Drug Utilization (CV15) 01150,06000,
28100,31800,41970,42900,44500,45300,
46100,54310,54900,59680,71500,88000,
94100,98600.
    and Behavioral and Mental Disorders
      (CV15B) 04010,04015,08400,12200,
      13190,13700,19350,22000,25200,
      27700,28560,29400,29560,37100,
      41100,41980,42380,42393,43900,
      43980,47100,47200,48500,50000,
      52770,53700,53750,57200,57800,
      58560,61350,64200,71500,72860,
      74030,77305,89800,90000,90100,
      90300,94920,95400,96700,97060,
      97800,97950,99085,99095,99120,
      99448,99515,99550,99560,99625,
      99685,99833,99857,99905,99913,
      99941.
    and Crime (CV15D) 09850,13190,22200,
      28560,42200,42380,42400,47100,
      47200,51900,53700,53750,54340,
      63700,66490,70450,72830,72860,
      73940,89900,94230,94260,97060,
      99060.
Drug Utilization in Pregnancy
    See:
      Anesthesia and Drug Use during
        Pregnancy
Dyslexia (DT15,ML15) 02300,04350,
    07400,07465,11450,17380,24100,39850,
    40500,44678,48900,49800,53670,53690,
    55290,56450,56800,56900,57000,63400,
    69500,74020,79390,81100,88500,88800,
    89100,90600,90700,91900,92500,93700,
    96800,96850,98720,98820,98905,99130,
    99140,99485,99790,99808,99933,99985.
    and Crime (DT15B,ML15B) 03250,03800,
      51500,63400,86050,99260.
Dysphasia
    See:
      Aphasia
Dyspnea
    See:
      Apnea
Education (SC) 04075,16870,21150,
    35900,36330,44300,47200,49800,55970,
    57775,61260,66030,68600,69470,71730,
    72630,76790,88300,88900,91500,93000,
    93800,99485,99968.
    See also:
      Preschool Programs
      School Behavior and Performance
      Socioeconomic Status
Educational Level (SC18) 00200,01600,
    01700,06230,09000,12300,26000,39400,
    40300,51600,54200,55000,58000,69200,
    69500,73200,86900,87900,91100,92690,
    97850,98820,98935,99450,99821.
    and Behavioral and Mental Disorders
      (SC18B) 42390,42700,57790,61150,
      61290,86700,99230,99448,99901.
    and Crime (SC18D) 04750,09500,19500,
      20200,27915,29800,39600,45400,

49000,61330,64700,66000,66800,
66900,71710,82060,84100,87980,
93300,95200,98825,99185,99255,
99590,99795.
EEG
    See:
      Electroencephalography
Electrodermal Response
    See:
      Galvanic Skin Response
Electroencephalography (TB35) 00700,
    00900,01100,07455,11200,30860,31400,
    31700,33800,35400,37000,38140,38400,
    40550,40600,44500,47900,49800,49900,
    70200,71500,76100,76790,76840,79270,
    84090,85100,87700,96850,96980,98732,
    99115.
    and Behavioral and Mental Disorders
      (TB35B) 01400,09370,09400,10130,
      13700,15400,16600,27700,28590,
      29250,29400,31530,36400,37100,
      37200,39850,41100,42200,43900,
      44500,48500,48700,53260,54900,
      57000,58900,61100,68300,71500,
      75270,75400,81660,81700,84080,
      86960,87000,90000,90100,90200,
      93700,94920,97950,98732,98840,
      99060,99285,99290,99515,99520,
      99565,99655,99720,99851,99905,
      99925,99961.
    Antisocial Personality (TB35BB)
      09700,33700,34400,36400,40750,
      42200,47000,47100,47200,47550,
      58150,72950,75400,76100,80060,
      94700,98840,99981,99985.
    and Crime (TB35D) 00500,09600,10130,
      28590,29250,33700,34400,40220,
      40750,42200,44900,47200,49600,
      58150,59640,62400,63100,63700,
      65950,66400,67300,68300,69850,
      69895,70450,70500,70600,70700,
      72880,72950,75400,76100,78200,
      80980,81700,85300,90980,93200,
      95430,95800,96525,97900,98820,
      99060,99175,99415,99770,99916,
      99917,99925.
Employment (SD) 24200,58530,64250,
    97850,99395.
    and Behavioral and Mental Disorders
      (SD07) 64250,71600.
    and Crime (SD11) 04075,44200,44700,
      57780,66800,66900,95200,98990,
      99170,99420,99475,99590,99901.
    See also:
      Socioeconomic Status
Enuresis (MG18) 00550,00900,04560,
    22100,25300,43900,47600,48690,59700,
    60900,61900,71400,71500,71700,79207,
    85650,85900,98700,99550.
    and Antisocial Personality (MG18B)
      49170,93700,99985.
    and Crime (MG18D) 05900,14740,17130,
      24100,30000,49170,55400,71900,
      93200,98845.
Environment (SF) 02000,02450,02800,
    04040,04620,08800,09200,09250,10200,
    12270,13190,14250,17500,19060,19355,
    21300,22300,23200,23400,24200,27500,

63000,63090,63850,70450,72950,
81700,94000,95800,99921,99925.
See also:
  Birth Injuries
  Brain Abnormality, Disease, and
    Injury
Headaches (DT30) 17130,17500,19500,
  19900,43900,62400,63400.
Health, Disease, and Injury (DD)
  00910,04560,05930,06260,21595,23700,
  28200,28590,29040,29070,29250,30670,
  34800,38660,47300,47500,47600,48200,
  49500,50400,50500,51950,57766,58000,
  58530,98685,98700,99065,99580,99595,
  99600,99610.
  and Behavioral and Mental Disorders
    (DD00) 00100,00910,01000,01150,
    04015,04080,04620,06090,07030,
    07230,09370,10100,10300,10650,
    12550,17100,19070,22360,22600,
    27170,27250,28560,28870,31930,
    38000,38900,39850,40770,42393,
    46675,49800,50000,51500,51970,
    53200,54400,56450,59530,59860,
    61150,62330,63400,66650,79390,
    81750,82900,87700,94990,98690,
    98910,98980,99050.
  Antisocial Personality (DD00B)
    09960,20000,24450,26260,32980,
    47200,56530,61900,81660,99690,
    99845,99981.
  and Crime (DD01) 13190,14750,15150,
    17100,17130,19900,21280,28550,
    28560,31930,32980,38000,40770,
    47200,51500,53950,54750,55260,
    62400,62800,62900,63000,63090,
    63810,66000,66400,67600,77318,
    80550,81750,91580,92650,93990,
    94000,98680,98725,98820,98825,
    98845,99170,99305,99695,99929.
  See also:
    Birth Injuries
    Infant Abnormality, Disease, and
      Injury
    Infant, Newborn, Abnormality, Dis-
      ease, and Injury
Health, Disease, and Injury in Pregnancy
  See:
    Maternal Disease and Injury during
      Pregnancy
Heart Rate (BL29) 04310,07470,17140,
  27600,28200,29070,38400,46300,55600,
  60000,69000,74200.
  and Behavioral and Mental Disorders
    (BL29B) 47200,48500,54920,70000,
    84810,84820,93700,97800,97950,
    98590,99941,99985.
  and Crime (BL29D) 30600,47200,52650,
    69890,84820,84830,98830,99335.
Hematocrit
  See:
    Hematologic Factors
Hematologic Factors (BD30) 07000,
  12000,12450,20630,27900,28560,34700,
  38100,39050,39100,39200,41970,46676,
  47500,47600,52200,56560,56893,59400,
  59620,66130,66160,66490,67220,75000,

76400,80950,89450,89500,93650,98965,
99305.
See also:
  Anemia
Hemoglobin
  See:
    Hematologic Factors
Heredity
  See:
    Genetic Factors
Homicide (CT57F) 06000,07900,09500,
  10660,11600,19500,22600,25500,27270,
  28050,30000,32950,34000,39600,42200,
  49200,49600,50300,51990,52800,55900,
  57270,57780,58150,60580,64730,71900,
  74040,78200,81200,82020,87100,87900,
  88600,88700,90980,91500,93200,95430,
  96500,96940,97000,97900,98500,98650,
  98740,98745,99180,99205,99232,99255,
  99410,99415,99420,99425,99770,99817,
  99921,99925.
  and Suicide (CT57FT) 34400,57270,
    63080,99240.
Hormones
  See:
    Biochemical Factors
    Sex Hormones
Hospitalization (CV30,SL) 09870,13100,
  22380,47300,47500,51950,54310,66300.
  and Behavioral and Mental Disorders
    (CV30B,SL07) 28870,40730,54310,
    54400,61000,77305,81200,84470,
    93990,98840,99448,99845,99893.
  and Crime (CV30D,SL11) 05900,14750,
    17130,28580,40730,54310,54750,
    59890,62460,62800,62900,63090,
    63850,69290,71720,77318,81200,
    84470,94000,94010,99240,99901.
Hostility
  See:
    Aggression
Housing (SM) 27430,98685,98700.
  and Crime (SM11) 48495,60800.
  See also:
    Crowding
    Location of Offense
Hyper/Hypotension (BL08B,DD28) 00600,
  13100,34800,45200,54920,56100,57500,
  59820,75230,99580.
  and Behavioral and Mental Disorders
    (BL08BB,DD28B) 47200,61000,67220,
    67600.
  and Crime (BL08BD,DD28D) 00600,
    09700,10190,17130,19360,26400,
    27915,47200,67600,97030.
Hyper/Hypotension in Pregnancy
  See:
    Maternal Disease and Injury during
      Pregnancy
    Pregnancy Toxemias
Hyperactivity
  See:
    Hyperkinetic Syndrome
    Minimal Brain Dysfunction
    Motor Skills and Disorders
Hyperbilirubinemia
  See:
    Bilirubin Level

Location of Offense (CN) 58200,99210.
Longitudinal Studies (NA44,NJ) 01000,
01900,04750,06350,09230,21400,21580,
25300,26400,26750,28800,38300,43600,
43700,46680,47200,52160,55500,57000,
57766,58000,58100,60600,60800,64230,
64250,65570,66800,66900,69200,69900,
70000,70200,70300,72690,72700,73100,
74010,77100,77200,78700,85300,85400,
86500,87500,88900,90700,98100,98875,
98910,98915,98950,99153,99445,99485,
99520,99560,99610,99821.
   from Birth to 4 Years (NA44B,NJ03)
   13050,21600,29050,29100,31600,
   35300,38500,44500,52050,53600,
   54400,64100,68050,87450,87600,
   93900,94100,95350,95770,96900,
   98685,99740,99750,99755,99760,
   99765,99881.
   from Birth to 7-11 Years (NA44D,
   NJ06) 07540,07570,08900,09900,
   15100,15300,15350,15900,17600,
   17800,17900,18000,18100,27400,
   27430,27800,27900,29200,29300,
   31500,35100,35200,35360,35400,
   39000,39350,42000,46530,46760,
   47500,47600,49300,49400,52600,
   55200,55800,58600,65300,65900,
   66200,66300,74660,74700,76200,
   76300,76400,76700,76800,80050,
   84000,85850,85900,96000,98965,
   99010,99530,99595,99600,99605,
   99700.
   from Birth to 11-17 Years (NA44F,
   NJ09) 06350,14600,27910,27915,
   42100,43030,51300,55100,55980,
   56100,65300,65400,69800,70400,
   70600,70700,71800,88440,98895,
   98900,98905.
   from Birth to over 18 Years (NA44H,
   NJ12) 06260,09995,28870,53000,
   54920,69850,99330,99335.
   from 8 Months to 7 Years (NA44K,
   NJ17) 27920,41900.
   from 4 to 7 Years (NA44N,NJ20)
   17400,27920,47700.
   from 4 to 11-18 Years (NA44P,NJ23)
   10100,26300.
   from 7 to 11-18 Years (NA44S,NJ27)
   14850,29700,40430,61500.
   from 7 to over 18 Years (NA44V,NJ30)
   37150,83560.
Maternal Absence/Deprivation (SI46)
15000,24700,31130,31750,32800,33700,
34600,37600,97850,99395,99893.
   and Behavioral and Mental Disorders
   of Child (SI46B) 09250,16500,
   24700,28250,61500,70000,98685,
   99160,99885.
   and Crime of Child (SI46D) 02200,
   14150,19700,19900,24600,27915,
   33300,68400,99215,99410.
Maternal Age
   See under:
   Mother
Maternal Age at Pregnancy (BP46)
05100,07000,09350,13100,18750,18760,
21580,23400,23800,24800,25900,27915,

32030,34200,35100,42000,44200,46675,
46760,55260,59500,63500,64100,65900,
66200,68800,70400,74800,75200,76950,
77000,80400,80500,84000,84865,86150,
91000,98795,98815,98965,99610,99740,
99810.
Maternal Disease and Injury during
   Pregnancy (BP47,DP46) 00900,05950,
   07000,07540,07570,08200,09350,13100,
   18750,18760,21580,23800,23900,27915,
   29300,31130,36300,36450,36600,38100,
   46675,48300,56400,56900,59400,65900,
   71750,72000,74200,74250,74700,74900,
   75000,75230,76790,76950,77000,84865,
   93550,93600,93650,94100,98685,98690,
   98700,98980,99740.
Maternal Psychological State during
   Pregnancy (BP48) 13100,16150,31130,
   76790,77000,98000,98685,98690,98700,
   99885,99889.
Memory and Memory Disorders (DT46,MN,
   PQ) 00930,10200,17100,29080,32050,
   39850,49800,51350,55600,56890,56900,
   59820,63400,64950,69000,72200,72400,
   72950,78500,81000,86000,88000,88200,
   91900,99308.
   See also:
   Amnesia
Mental Retardation (DK46,MO) 00910,
05000,07500,07540,07570,13050,13200,
20600,26260,29200,31130,35000,36330,
43980,44920,48250,52050,53000,53070,
57200,57790,63600,63900,65900,71500,
74400,76200,76300,76790,79800,82090,
83960,85100,85970,90500,94800,94850,
98690,98905,99020,99030,99130,99485,
99595,99600,99605,99610,99750,99785.
   and Behavioral and Mental Disorders,
   Other (DK46B,MO07) 00910,04080,
   07540,07570,17600,17700,17800,
   27300,36000,36380,42390,44380,
   47200,50100,50750,53980,56830,
   61100,67200,71600,76790,77305,
   79330,84060,89000,99877.
   and Crime (DK46D,MO11) 09500,22500,
   45700,46000,47200,48495,49600,
   53240,62270,66800,83930,84060,
   87915,92450,96920,98150,98650,
   99795.
Minimal Brain Dysfunction (DK48,MG48)
04800,06090,07455,07500,07700,07800,
08200,13700,16200,16800,19350,20580,
21580,22360,26600,27170,32050,35400,
36600,58100,64690,69830,76600,76790,
76800,77100,77330,81630,81660,85000,
85100,85680,87850,89320,90300,92380,
96980,97800,99030,99405,99440,99485,
99745,99833,99865,99909.
   and Behavioral and Mental Disorders
   (DK48B,MG48B) 02140,02150,04530,
   04560,06090,07230,08200,09370,
   10130,12200,16500,16600,19370,
   20580,22000,27170,27460,27700,
   29400,29700,36600,37100,39800,
   39850,40830,46400,47200,48500,
   50000,52770,53150,55930,57200,
   57792,59280,59700,59730,60600,
   61100,61290,61560,61580,64200,

24800,24900,26750,29300,34100,34700,
35400,43000,43900,45100,46600,46650,
46760,47500,49100,50600,52200,52600,
55200,55930,57778,59400,60700,61800,
63600,74600,79500,98915,99010.
and Outcome (BP02) 01000,04310,
04330,05950,07530,12000,12100,
13100,17140,18750,18760,18790,
19380,21580,21600,21800,23800,
24900,25900,26000,27930,28500,
29200,29300,31130,32030,34200,
35100,35200,36300,36450,37550,
38100,38900,39000,39100,39200,
42000,42100,42900,43000,45100,
46600,46650,46675,46760,47500,
49100,49300,49800,50600,52600,
53150,55200,56400,56900,57300,
57950,58000,59400,59500,60250,
61800,63500,63695,64100,66200,
71770,71800,74250,74450,75230,
76150,76790,76950,77200,84000,
84080,84095,84865,86150,91000,
93550,93650,94100,94200,95600,
95700,95750,95770,96000,96900,
98100,98685,98695,98700,98795,
98965,98980,99310,99525,99610,
99740,99785,99889.
Behavioral and Mental Disorders of
Child (BP02B) 02140,02150,04080,
05970,07540,07570,08400,09350,
12550,15000,17100,18780,27900,
29050,34100,34700,36600,37100,
38900,43900,44419,46400,53150,
55200,55930,58600,60250,60700,
61100,63600,63850,65900,69600,
69650,69700,70400,72600,74050,
76790,79600,79650,79700,79900,
85700,87200,92080,92360,93670,
98680,98690,99010,99310,99810,
99885,99889.
Crime of Child (BP02D) 15000,
15100,15150,16150,27915,40700,
54750,55260,62800,62900,63000,
63850,98680.
See also:
Alcohol Drinking during Pregnancy
Anesthesia and Drug Use during
Pregnancy
Birth Intervals
Fetus
Gestational Age
Labor and Delivery
Maternal Age at Pregnancy
Maternal Disease and Injury during
Pregnancy
Maternal Psychological State dur-
ing Pregnancy
Nutrition and Diet during Preg-
nancy
Obstetric History
Parity
Physical Characteristics of Grav-
ida
Placenta
Prenatal Care
Smoking during Pregnancy
X-ray Exposure during Pregnancy
Pregnancy Toxemias (DP60) 04100,05000,

07000,25900,26000,36600,37500,38100,
46675,56100,56450,58100,59400,71770,
72600,74800,76790,77000,79700,85850,
86200,98685,98690.
Prematurity (DF60) 12450,24800,34100,
38140,39100,39400,43000,59400,71300,
71750,76950,84300,84865,98795.
and Later Outcome (DF60B) 02140,
02150,12440,15000,15100,21600,
23800,28840,29300,31130,31400,
34200,35600,36300,37575,38140,
41100,46400,46675,46760,47600,
56450,56900,58100,63500,63600,
77000,79700,79800,84000,87500,
98685,98710,98980,99015,99020,
99030,99700,99740.
Behavioral and Mental Disorders
(DF60BB) 09350,10300,28330,
69600,69700,70000,91050,98820,
99030,99550,99610,99810.
Crime (DF60BD) 16150,98820.
Prenatal Care (BP63) 13100,21580,
23800,27915,46675,47200,71800,74250,
75230,76790,84300,99155.
Preschool Programs (SC59) 06230,24200,
26300,32800,54500,80030,80040,84100,
93400,99933,99969.
Primary Mental Abilities Tests
See under:
Tests and Measures
Prisoners and the Criminally Institutionalized (CQ59,CV13DA,NE59) 00970,
01150,03200,03400,05430,09850,10190,
11150,12790,13190,13200,13620,13624,
17570,24400,25950,28580,28590,28750,
29250,32970,34750,35380,35900,36200,
37600,41080,41980,42380,42396,43200,
44220,46785,46790,47100,47200,51970,
52650,53090,54310,54930,55260,57060,
57550,57765,59220,59560,59600,59640,
59690,59800,59890,62780,62800,63000,
63100,63660,63810,63950,65550,66100,
66460,66490,66950,67300,68300,68400,
69100,69270,69290,69895,70900,71000,
71720,71760,72880,76880,76920,77302,
79280,80830,81750,83960,83990,84100,
84820,85300,85400,85960,87100,87990,
88400,88440,89360,89450,90920,90980,
91350,91600,92088,92390,92610,92800,
93200,94230,94260,94640,94700,95200,
95300,95800,96100,96350,97030,97900,
98250,98637,98650,98740,98745,98750,
98830,98843,98890,99005,99055,99090,
99185,99205,99210,99215,99222,99225,
99230,99250,99435,99645,99837,99841,
99873,99901,99916,99977.
Problem Solving
See:
Adaptation, Psychological
Intelligence
Property Offenses (CT59) 02200,05600,
10100,10680,11600,16900,19300,19600,
20510,24000,25000,26100,27100,27915,
30300,30830,30900,31100,33700,38300,
38600,39700,40750,41000,41600,44200,
44600,44800,45400,45700,49000,49600,
51000,51100,51200,52300,58500,59690,
62400,64115,64700,66030,66900,67300,

03700,03800,04670,05600,10660,
11600,11700,11800,12790,13200,
16160,18300,19360,20000,20100,
21280,23700,24400,25000,25500,
27910,27915,31100,33500,33600,
34000,34400,34600,37600,38600,
40670,42393,43750,44600,45600,
45700,47200,50300,51100,51200,
57780,59220,60800,61200,62300,
64700,66700,67400,67600,67700,
67800,68300,69270,70260,70450,
71760,77240,77300,79280,85200,
86800,87940,92700,93900,94675,
95000,95500,95800,96300,96920,
97000,98300,98400,98500,98650,
98745,98930,98970,98975,98985,
99080,99142,99180,99205,99215,
99245,99275,99420,99425,99735,
99917,99937,99973.
See also:
  Female Offenders
  Female Sample
Sex Hormones (BD70) 08400,13150,25900,
  26000,35700,37600,46200,47900,49100,
  49800,50500,54000,54600,59300,61800,
  62000,62200,69000,71730,71770,71800,
  84095,84900,88100,93680,98960,99505.
  and Crime and Aggression (BD70B)
    10230,11800,12150,21950,25920,
    30230,30300,30400,31100,42200,
    42400,47200,51500,52400,55915,
    59600,59800,59820,66490,70200,
    71730,71760,72830,72970,73800,
    75400,78610,78615,79220,80800,
    84540,84560,84565,85300,95400,
    98655,98725,99695.
  and Intelligence (BD70K) 09995,
    14250,70200.
Sex Offenses (CT68) 06000,12150,12790,
  21000,27270,28050,28580,31930,37970,
  39700,42380,43180,44800,44900,45700,
  46060,48460,49600,52300,53950,66030,
  72830,72860,73960,79220,84560,84565,
  84580,87900,87940,92200,92700,94050,
  94640,94700,95800,98150,98400,98500,
  98705,98725,98745,99195,99200,99220,
  99230,99245,99255,99330,99335,99590,
  99710,99770,99873,99901,99921,99925.
Sex Roles (SQ70) 36200,37600,46200,
  47900,48600,50200,54200,65100,71730,
  94400,98695.
  and Behavioral and Mental Disorders
    (SQ70B) 44414.
  and Crime (SQ70D) 25000,34600,40670,
    41000,42800,66030,77240,92700,
    94600,98300,98400,98500,99695,
    99817,99937.
Sexual Behavior and Disorders (MV,
  PE66,SR69) 04560,05460,06000,10900,
  16400,20900,30670,31100,33600,37600,
  46200,53100,55700,61800,66030,71800,
  72970,79300,88000,99505.
  and Behavioral and Mental Disorders,
    Other (MV07,PE66B,SR69B) 04015,
    12790,28760,31930,35370,42380,
    53950,56830,58590,66800,66900,
    69500,83800,86900,98644,99365.
  and Crime (MV11,PE66D,SR69D) 02450,

09600,12790,19360,28580,30230,
31930,34750,40700,42380,42400,
44200,47800,49600,49800,53950,
55915,57400,71760,72830,79220,
81830,83900,93200,98725,99210,
99901.
Sibling Constellation
See:
  Birth Intervals
Siblings (NH70,SH70) 02450,04080,
  09995,42370,47200,76750,76790,77000,
  95750,98915,99735,99929.
  and Behavioral and Mental Disorders
    (NH70B,SH70B) 09960,64230,74050,
    80890,87130,89100,99000,99545,
    99849,99885.
  and Crime (NH70D,SH70D) 10890,32970,
    64115,70200,70265,76890,78100,
    83960,83990,86800,95500,99055,
    99735.
See also:
  Twins
Skin Conductance Level
See:
  Galvanic Skin Response
Sleep and Sleep Disorders (BN68,DT69,
  MW) 04080,04560,07250,12550,17150,
  22100,28500,37600,38400,44500,47200,
  48500,54400,59300,59700,64200,67300,
  71500,71700,85650,85900,98915.
  and Crime (BN68B,DT69B,MW11) 47200,
    98845.
Smallness for Gestational Age (BL27K,
  BP26G,DF70,DP22P) 21600,29040,29070,
  29100,31130,34200,35350,35400,38900,
  39000,46600,46676,50600,57950,59400,
  71300,72000,75000,75100,84865.
  and Later Outcome (BL27KL,BP26GD,
    DF70B) 07540,07570,09930,23800,
    27915,29070,31130,32030,34200,
    35350,46675,56900,57950,77000,
    79500,91850,98965,98980,99020,
    99700,99740.
Smoking during Pregnancy (BP70) 13100,
  14600,16150,18750,27915,31000,35100,
  37100,39100,39200,39400,39500,42000,
  42100,46675,46676,47300,47400,50400,
  50600,59400,63200,63695,71750,75000,
  75200,76790,76950,80400,80500,84000,
  84865,85975,98700.
Social Behavior and Social Behavior
  Disorders (MX,PE68,SR) 00800,02100,
  04530,04700,06600,07000,08150,09250,
  10450,10900,16710,20560,21150,28250,
  30670,32800,41050,53070,59820,61900,
  62360,64400,67000,73000,84805,85500,
  85650,85900,85960,92690,97480,98730,
  98792,98895,98905,99013,99080,99445,
  99450,99485,99510,99595,99893,99897.
  and Behavioral and Mental Disorders,
    Other (MX07,PE68B,SR01) 00100,
    00550,01000,01150,02450,04080,
    04560,05950,09995,12790,17150,
    19070,19370,20580,20630,27170,
    28550,28760,35360,37150,39850,
    40430,40730,46675,47200,49800,
    56830,62330,63400,74150,77220,
    77320,79207,83560,85625,85700,

68300,70300,71500,71600,72950,
74025,74660,76950,77000,79207,
79230,81750,83600,84000,84500,
84865,84880,85000,85680,86100,
88200,88500,89000,89150,90200,
90350,90550,90700,90980,92250,
92670,93700,94000,94700,97030,
97680,98830,98980,99010,99045,
99055,99345,99410,99425,99535,
99620,99650,99675,99720,99790,
99800,99809,99851,99881,99921,
99925,99961.

Neuropsychological Tests (TA55)
00650,00700,00930,03250,04020,
04080,06350,07455,07465,07540,
07570,09370,10300,10500,10600,
12730,12750,13620,13622,13624,
13650,14250,16725,18780,19370,
20580,20630,25600,27910,27915,
28450,28590,29600,32050,37550,
38130,38140,40600,40800,41940,
49800,53690,55290,56060,56890,
58590,59280,59640,59800,60000,
61150,61290,61295,62450,63080,
63400,64950,66650,66760,66950,
69225,69230,72300,72400,78430,
84600,84880,85100,85400,89550,
90700,94680,96980,97300,97400,
98625,98655,98820,98825,99050,
99308,99325,99485,99575,99645,
99917,99921,99925,99927.

Parents' Reports of Children's Behavior (TA57) 00550,06100,06230,
14250,15900,16000,16720,17150,
17600,18000,20600,21400,22100,
26600,27170,27500,28870,29700,
32100,33300,40830,41400,41500,
43700,43750,54960,55260,55360,
58700,60500,60800,60900,64200,
68650,69200,70000,71700,77320,
78100,85900,88500,89410,90200,
91050,92900,97950,98875,98915,
99050,99275,99445,99595,99625.

Psychological Tests (TA59) 01300,
02100,04015,04400,04640,04700,
06500,07030,09700,09900,10300,
10900,11800,12550,12790,13400,
14100,14250,14700,17170,17200,
17400,18780,18800,19380,20550,
20560,20600,20900,21580,22200,
24300,24450,25100,25200,25300,
25700,26400,26750,27000,28000,
28870,30260,30300,30830,32100,
32330,32700,32980,33000,33150,
33300,33500,35350,35800,37000,
37150,37550,40000,41600,43100,
43750,46760,46780,47700,48600,
48800,49200,50200,50300,52300,
52900,54930,55360,56990,57060,
57785,59100,59730,59760,59860,
60600,61150,61540,63660,63830,
64130,66000,66650,66760,66800,
66950,67220,68250,69100,69800,
70000,70300,70900,71000,71600,
72950,74040,76050,77400,77500,
79280,80830,82080,82900,84080,
84900,85200,85400,85650,90700,

91050,91300,91960,92040,92090,
92300,92630,92800,93400,93700,
94550,94690,94750,95400,95800,
98637,98655,98705,98730,98790,
98800,98830,98850,98865,99080,
99085,99300,99335,99365,99590,
99690,99790,99914,99925,99977.

Cognitive, Language, and Learning Abilities Tests (TA59D)
00995,01700,03100,04080,04650,
06030,06260,06300,06350,07465,
07540,07570,09370,09850,09995,
10200,11450,14300,14600,15370,
15700,18800,19370,21300,22000,
22300,25200,27000,27200,27915,
27920,28700,28750,28900,29050,
29200,32100,32970,33500,34140,
34700,37000,40300,40600,41100,
41600,43800,46000,46678,46760,
47200,47900,49000,49800,50800,
51300,52160,52780,52900,53100,
53240,54100,55260,55340,55600,
55800,56200,56600,56700,56800,
56900,56930,56960,58300,59100,
59800,60200,60580,61580,63900,
63950,64650,64950,66000,66030,
68400,68700,69000,69800,69850,
70300,74000,75800,76100,78100,
78430,78900,79207,81400,81500,
82040,82250,82900,84850,85000,
85100,85700,85930,87990,88150,
90700,91900,92250,93800,94300,
94400,96100,96800,96940,96980,
97700,97950,98150,98600,98625,
98745,98775,98890,98920,98980,
99055,99160,99165,99370,99390,
99410,99485,99590,99645,99650,
99675,99720,99795,99817,99945,
99949,99961.

Teachers' Reports of Children's
Behavior (TA74) 00990,01150,
03200,06230,15370,15900,16000,
16720,17400,20580,21400,22200,
26600,27480,27500,28250,29200,
29700,33300,33500,35000,40830,
41400,41500,43600,43700,43750,
44481,46350,47700,50800,55360,
58700,59260,59280,60100,61200,
61290,61350,62330,64200,66730,
68650,69800,70000,71700,72990,
73000,77320,78100,80160,84200,
88500,89340,89360,89410,90000,
90100,90200,92250,92900,97950,
98875,99050,99080,99335,99370,
99510,99540,99595,99625,99660,
99810,99865.

Other Tests (TA80) 00200,00600,
00990,00995,01000,04010,04050,
04080,04330,04560,04620,05930,
06350,07350,07465,07470,08800,
09350,09850,09910,09995,10190,
10300,10500,10600,10650,10800,
12750,13100,13150,13190,14250,
14500,17150,17170,18760,18780,
19355,19380,20550,20560,20580,
20630,21150,21550,21580,21590,
24200,24450,25300,25600,27170,

15400,15500,23500,27915,28050,
28400,43200,49700,52748,55900,
62300,63100,79200,83700,85600,
86100,87915,89200,98820,98825,
99710,99921.
Wide Range Achievement Test [WRAT]
(TB98) 04650,09400,27400,29300,
35100,35200,38200,46676,46678,
46680,49400,49450,61230,66200,
85100,96000,96850,98965,99465,
99535.
    and Behavioral and Mental Disor-
    ders (TB98B) 00200,09370,
    15370,22000,27900,29700,31950,
    50000,76790,77325,81100,85000,
    90200,90700,93700,96800,99720,
    99790.
    and Crime (TB98D) 00400,03250,
    03600,03800,09910,15500,26220,
    27915,28400,35900,37000,43200,
    44300,49000,51500,63950,66700,
    67900,74000,86100,92450,96940,
    99977.
See also:
    Electroencephalography
    Infant Neurological and Physical
        Examination
    Infant, Newborn, Neurological and
        Physical Examination
    Self-Reports of Violence and Crime
Theft
See:
    Property Offenses
Toxic Substances, Exposure to (DA)
00100,31130,46675,99600.
Twins (NH74,SH74) 02000,07200,09995,
17500,23200,23700,29200,38100,44500,
46600,47200,47600,54450,60200,73300,
74600,76750,77000,87700,97700,99595.
    and Behavioral and Mental Disorders
    (NH74B,SH74B) 01000,10700,10800,
    16100,16200,23700,27250,29400,
    30700,35700,36000,46400,49800,
    50100,69400,87300,87700,96700,
    99945.
        Antisocial Personality (NH74BB,
        SH74BB) 47200.
    and Crime (NH74D,SH74D) 18500,18520,
    20000,20100,20400,23700,31105,
    32970,34400,42200,47200,68300,
    69895,69900,70255,70450,75400,
    87300.
See also:
    Adoptees
    Environment
    Genetic Factors
Unemployment
See:
    Employment
Urban Crime
See:
    Crime in Urban Areas [under Geo-
        graphic Area]
Vaginal Bleeding during Pregnancy
(DP81) 07000,08200,09350,27915,
36600,46675,56400,56450,58100,59400,

72600,76950,77000,79700,84865,85850,
86150,86200,95700,98700,99010,99370,
99700.
Values
See:
    Culture
    Personality
    Socialization
Victims (CX,NE79) 07900,10890,11800,
19300,33600,34000,37900,40400,40900,
45900,51000,51100,51900,57780,64730,
65800,67500,93200,95400,96940,99180,
99195,99200,99205,99245,99841,99937.
Violence, Prediction and Assessment of
(CY) 03500,03600,03650,03700,21500,
27915,28580,32950,33600,33700,41080,
44417,44800,49000,51500,53230,54960,
55400,58500,59220,59690,63100,64730,
65460,65800,66000,68160,70800,70900,
71720,72800,72810,74000,77260,87980,
88400,92000,98650,98655,99360,99410,
99585,99817.
Violence Scales (CE81) 03200,03400,
03600,33600,47200,72800,99817.
Violent Offenders and Violence (CC81,
CQ81,CT81,NE81) 02300,03600,03700,
05050,05600,06000,09850,10230,10660,
12790,15000,15100,15110,15150,19360,
19700,21500,27915,27950,29250,32950,
33600,34000,40000,40220,40770,42200,
42396,44417,47100,47200,51500,52700,
53235,53700,54960,59220,59640,59800,
59890,64730,68160,68200,70200,70900,
71703,71720,72800,74040,77260,80020,
80600,82000,83800,85300,85400,85450,
86600,87980,89450,90980,91500,93680,
94230,94260,95200,95400,95430,96525,
97000,98725,98975,99235,99330,99335,
99340,99360,99410,99585,99590,99813,
99817,99937,99973.
    and Age (CC81A) 03500,27915,31100,
    32950,34000,39600,49000,59640,
    66000,80760,87940,99185,99585,
    99770,99813,99817.
    and Alcohol Drinking (CC81B) 04800,
    11800,12150,19360,19500,21140,
    25500,40400,52700,53700,59890,
    63710,66000,66495,72950,81700,
    83800,95430,99190,99222,99255,
    99770.
    and Automatisms and Seizures (CC81C)
    04800,19360,19500,19900,21500,
    44900,62450,63090,72880,72950.
    and Behavioral and Mental Disorders
    (CC81D) 00500,02100,04900,12790,
    13622,13624,15150,19500,19900,
    21000,21140,24030,25500,27950,
    28580,29250,30300,36530,40770,
    42200,43950,44600,49000,49005,
    49600,52300,52700,53235,53700,
    55400,55900,56600,57270,58500,
    59690,59800,59890,61210,61295,
    63090,63100,63700,63850,64500,
    65800,65950,66000,67300,68200,
    70900,71703,71720,72800,74000,
    74025,74040,77318,77600,78200,

About the Compilers

DEBORAH W. DENNO is a Research Associate and Lecturer in the Center for Studies in Criminology and Criminal Law in the Wharton School at the University of Pennsylvania.

RUTH M. SCHWARZ is a Program Analyst for the New Jersey Department of Corrections, Juvenile Detention and Monitoring Unit.

DATE DUE

NOV 3 0 1992	DHUW R NOV 30 REC'D		
SW MAR 1 5 1999	SW/R MAR 1 5 1999		
GAYLORD			PRINTED IN U.S.A.